Senior Law Handbook

2012 Edition

A Colorado Legal Information and
Reference Guide for Aging Adults

Sean C. Bell

Managing Editor

A joint project of the Elder Law and Trust and Estate Sections
of the Colorado Bar Association

CONTINUING LEGAL EDUCATION IN COLORADO, INC.

COLORADO BAR ASSOCIATION • DENVER BAR ASSOCIATION

2012

Senior Law Handbook
2012 Edition

ISBN: 978-1-930993-90-7

Published by:

CONTINUING LEGAL EDUCATION IN COLORADO, INC.
1900 Grant Street, Suite 300
Denver, Colorado 80203
Phone: (303) 860-0608

Website: www.cobar.org/slh

COLORADO BAR ASSOCIATION
1900 Grant Street, Suite 900
Denver, Colorado 80203
Phone: (303) 860-1115

Lisa Travis Fischer, J.D.
Acquisitions Editor/Manager
Colorado Bar Association CLE

Susan Hoyt
Legal Editor
Colorado Bar Association CLE

Cover photograph courtesy John Fielder © 2012, visit johnfielder.com.

Cover design by Trish Wilkinson

COLORADO BAR ASSOCIATION CLE
*CLE in Colorado, Inc. is the nonprofit educational arm of the
Colorado Bar Association and the Denver Bar Association*

The *Senior Law Handbook — 2012 Edition* and any attached or referenced pages have been written or compiled for general information purposes only. The information contained in the *Senior Law Handbook* is not intended to be, nor is it, legal advice. The *Senior Law Handbook* material does not intend to create, nor does it create, an attorney-client relationship. Legal advice of any nature should be sought from legal counsel.

How to Cite This Book

As the first full citation, you may cite this book as:
Senior Law Handbook, 2012 Ed. (Sean C. Bell, ed., CLE in Colo., Inc.).

After the first full citation, you may cite this book as:
Senior Law Handbook, supra n. ___, at ___.

Acknowledgment

Production of the *Senior Law Handbook*, 2012 Edition, required the editors to Shepardize® the citations used in the book. The research was made possible by a generous contribution from the Colorado Bar Association CLE's technology partner, LEXIS-NEXIS®.

Individual chapters of from this handbook are available for free download at www.seniorlawday.org. Information about the next Senior Law Day is available there as well.

Publisher's Note

The *Senior Law Handbook* is designed to provide aging adults and their caregivers and families with useful information on myriad subjects pertinent to their legal concerns. It is compiled due to the gracious donation of time and intellect by our volunteer authors. We would like to thank all of the authors for their generous contributions of time and their willingness to share their expertise with Colorado's older adults. We especially thank Sean Bell, our managing editor, for his continued dedication. We would also like to thank John Fielder, who donated the use of his beautiful photo that adorns the front cover of this edition.

Much of the information in the *Senior Law Handbook* is based on current laws and practices in Colorado, as well as policies and programs of the federal government. **The information provided in the *Senior Law Handbook* is not intended to replace the advice and services of an attorney.** We urge you to contact an elder law and/or probate attorney for advice relating to the particulars of your situation.

Individual chapters are available for free download at www.seniorlawday.org. Information about Senior Law Day can also be found at www.seniorlawday.org. Several counties in Colorado offer Senior Law Day on different days during the year, with a variety of programming and formats. If you have attended Senior Law Day, or you have comments or suggestions regarding the *Senior Law Handbook*, please visit www.seniorlawday.org to give us your feedback. We welcome all comments, and continuously strive to keep the *Senior Law Handbook* a helpful and informative resource for Colorado adults.

Lisa C. Travis Fischer, J.D.
Acquisitions Editor/Manager
Colorado Bar Association CLE

Susan Hoyt
Legal Editor
Colorado Bar Association CLE

Editor's Note

The *Senior Law Handbook* was produced this year by the Colorado Bar Association's Civic and Community Affairs Committee of the Elder Law Section and the Trust and Estate Section, and in conjunction with CLE in Colorado, Inc. Our mission with the *Senior Law Handbook* is to help older people better understand the laws that affect their daily lives. Today's society is complex, and we are hopeful that this *Handbook* provides some plain-language insights into society's relationship to older adults. That said, laws and programs change, and can apply differently to people depending on their individual circumstances. The *Senior Law Handbook* is only intended to be an initial information source. The lists of agencies and other resources at the end of each chapter, and throughout the book, can be used for more specific and up-to-date information.

Although the *Handbook* has been greatly expanded in recent years in an effort to provide important information, its chapters are necessarily brief, considering the variety of subjects covered, and the handbook is not intended to completely discuss any topic. Therefore, it cannot, and is not intended to, replace the advice and services of an attorney, any professional, or agency.

In addition to our gratitude to the authors for all their time and energy, the Civic and Community Affairs Committee would like to thank Catherine McHughs and Mel Reveles in the CBA Internet and Technology Department for their assistance in maintaining the internet presence of the *Senior Law Handbook*.

Most importantly, the Committee wishes to acknowledge the support by and contributions of CLE in Colorado, Inc., the nonprofit legal education branch of the CBA. Each spring, CLE's Publications Department produces this handbook that you are now holding. The Committee could not undertake this project without the support of CLE's Gary Abrams, Dawn McKnight, Lisa Travis Fischer, Mary Dilworth, and Monica Santillanes, or without the hands-on involvement of Susan Hoyt. We would most particularly like to thank Ms. Hoyt for her great production management, as well as for editing and proofing our authors' manuscripts.

Lastly, we would like to extend a special thanks to all of the wonderful CBA and CLE staff and their families, who so graciously donate their time to assist at Senior Law Day. It would not be possible without them.

Sean C. Bell, Esq.
Bell Law Firm, LLC
April 2012

Table of Contents

About the Managing Editor

Sean C. Bell, Esq.
Bell Law Firm, LLC
4450 Arapahoe Ave., Ste. 100
Boulder, CO 80303
(303) 415-2540
www.BellElderLaw.com
sbell@seanbelllaw.com

Sean Curran Bell is in private practice at Bell Law Firm, LLC. Mr. Bell represents clients and assists the courts in Adams, Boulder, Broomfield, Denver, Larimer, and Weld counties. The focus of his practice is elder law, estate planning, and probate, with a particular interest in guardianship and conservatorship cases. He is active in the Colorado Bar Association's Sections on Trust and Estate and Elder Law.

Mr. Bell is committed to ensuring that the public has good access to legal information. He is the managing editor of the *Senior Law Handbook*, a joint publication of the Colorado Bar Association and CLE in Colorado, and he is a member of the planning committee for Senior Law Day.

Mr. Bell also has a Master of Laws in Environmental Law and is keenly interested in putting his many years of environmental experience to work for our state, our country, and our world as we seek to address the myriad issues that face our peoples, our lands, and our waters. We must learn to properly cherish our elders and our world.

About the Authors

Jennifer M. Ballentine, M.A.
Life Quality Institute
501 S. Cherry St., Ste. 700
Denver, CO 80246
(303) 398-6317
www.lifequalityinstitute.com
jballentine@lifequalityinstitute.org

Chapter 27 — *Hospice and Palliative Care: Options for Care at the End of Life*

Jennifer Ballentine knows the end-of-life world from a number of perspectives: as advocate, educator, and ethicist, and also as a hospice volunteer, hospice family member, palliative care professional, and cancer survivor. Past Director of Programs for the Colorado Center for Hospice & Palliative Care and Executive Director of Namaste Comfort Fund, she currently serves as Executive Director of Life Quality Institute, Colorado's premier provider of palliative and end-of-life education.

She is co-chair of the Colorado Advance Directives Consortium and a member of the Denver Hospice Ethics Committee, the National Hospice & Palliative Care Organization Professional Education Committee, the National Hospice Work Group Research and Education Forum, and several taskforces for the Center to Improve Value in Health Care. She also serves on the Board of Directors for the Colorado Healthcare Ethics Forum. She holds a master's degree in End-of-Life Studies from Regis University, a certificate in Gerontology from the University of Colorado at Colorado Springs, and a B.A. from Oberlin College.

Michael Benidt
Sheryl Kay
Golden Compass, Inc.
13842 Legend Wy., Unit 102
Broomfield, CO 80023
(303) 517-3584
www.GoldenCompass.com
Michael@goldencompass.com
Sheryl@goldencompass.com

Chapter 33 — *Facebook: The Good, the Bad, and the Ugly*

Michael Benidt and Sheryl Kay both left other endeavors to start computer training companies, not because they were good at it, but because they weren't! They have developed into "the only speakers who treat technology with the disrespect it deserves." Their classes and seminars all show the underlying belief that technology should serve people, not the other way around. They have maintained a special commitment to teach older adults and have worked with such organizations as Kaiser-Permanente, Orlando Regional Healthcare, Memorial Hermann Hospital in Houston, Leading Age Colorado, and more. Their other national clients include Seattle Pacific University, the Florida Health Care Association (FHCA); the National Rural Electric Cooperative Association (NRECA), the Washington State Department of Commerce, and the U.S. Department of Health and Human Services. You can learn more about them and read their blog at www.golden compass.com.

Marianne Blackwell, Esq.
Director, Office of Gift Planning
University Advancement
Colorado State University
521 University Services Center
Ft. Collins, CO 80523-7115
(970) 491-7862
www.plannedgiving.colostate.edu
mblackwell@ua.colostate.edu

Chapter 16 — *Estate and Succession Planning for Farmers and Ranchers*
Chapter 18 — *Philanthropy and Planned Giving*

Marianne Blackwell is the Director of the Office of Gift Planning at Colorado State University. She received her B.A. in psychology from the University of Oklahoma in 1982 and her J.D. from the University of Oklahoma School of Law in 1985, and has practiced in the areas of bankruptcy, civil litigation, contracts, family law, wills, and probate. Marianne is a member of the American Bar Association and the Colorado Bar Association, and a former member of the Oklahoma Bar Association. She is also a member of the Trust and Estate Section of the Colorado Bar Association, the Larimer County Bar Association, the Partnership for Philanthropic Planning (formerly the National Committee on Planned Giving), the American Council on Gift Annuities, the Colorado Planned Giving Roundtable (Board Member), and the Council for Advancement and Support of Education.

Elizabeth A. Bryant, Esq.
Elizabeth A. Bryant PC
1866 Vine St., 2nd Fl.
Denver, CO 80206
http://eablaw.com
ebryant@eablaw.com

Chapter 19 — **Estate Planning for Nontraditional Families**

Elizabeth A. Bryant practices in the areas of estate planning, probate, small business formation, and real property. Ms. Bryant received her law degree from the University of Denver College of Law in 1990, where she was general and technical editor of the *Denver*

University Law Review. She is a member of the Colorado, Denver, Colorado Women's, and Colorado GLBT bar associations. She is a current appointee on the Colorado Supreme Court's Unauthorized Practice of Law Committee. She is a fellow in the American College of Trust and Estate Counsel and a member of the Women's Estate Planning Council. She is a frequent presenter on the topic of estate planning for non-traditional families. Ms. Bryant is active in the Trust and Estate Section of the Colorado Bar Association. She has also been active in civic endeavors and has served on the board of trustees of the Women's Foundation of Colorado and the Alexander Foundation. She was a founding director of the Denver metropolitan affiliate of the Susan G. Komen Breast Cancer Foundation.

Gregory B. Cairns, Esq.
Cairns & Associates, P.C.
3900 E. Mexico Ave., Ste. 700
Denver, CO 80210
(303) 481-6345
cairnslaw@aol.com

Chapter 10 — *Workers' Compensation and Seniors*

Mr. Cairns' practice focuses on workers' compensation defense and related employment law. Mr. Cairns attended the University of Wisconsin at Madison, where he received a B.A. with honors in psychology in 1975. He obtained his law degree from the University of Texas at Austin in 1982. Mr. Cairns has been licensed to practice law in Colorado since 1982.

Mr. Cairns has 29 years of experience as a defense attorney in matters relating to workers' compensation and employment law. He has published several articles in *The Colorado Lawyer* concerning employment issues and pre-judgment interest, and has been a frequent speaker concerning workers' compensation, pre-employment testing, the American with Disabilities Act of 1990, and the Family and Medical Leave Act of 1993. He is the founder and principal instructor for The Center for Workers' Compensation Training, a private occupational school.

Mr. Cairns, who hails from Wisconsin, is president of Cairns & Associates, P.C., in Denver, Colorado. He has argued three cases to the Colorado Court of Appeals and two cases to the Colorado Supreme Court. His groundbreaking article on prejudgment interest has been cited favorably two times by the Colorado Supreme Court. Mr. Cairns has served as president of Professionals in Workers' Compensation, and he won that organization's honors for "Outstanding Respondent Attorney" and "President's Award" for exceptional service. In 2003, he was named one of the "Outstanding Lawyers of America." In 2009, Mr. Cairns received the Lance Butler Award from the Colorado Bar Association, Workers' Compensation Section, for meritorious service in the practice of workers' compensation.

John J. Campbell, Esq.
Law Offices of John J. Campbell, P.C.
4155 E. Jewell Ave., Ste. 500
Denver, CO 80222
(303) 290-7497
www.jjcelderlaw.com
jcampbell@jjcelderlaw.com

Chapter 1 — *Social Security Benefits*
Chapter 3 — *Health Insurance Beyond Medicare*
Chapter 4 — *Medicaid*
Chapter 5 — *Government Programs and Financial Assistance*

John J. Campbell currently operates The Law Offices of John J. Campbell, P.C., a small boutique firm concentrating in the area of elder law. He is the owner and senior attorney. Mr. Campbell's practice concentrates in the areas of elder law, estate planning, probate law, guardianships and conservatorships, Social Security, SSDI, SSI, Medicare, Medicaid, Medicare set-aside trusts, and disability trusts, and he offers special consultations in settlement of personal injury and workers' compensation claims involving public benefits.

Mr. Campbell graduated with a B.S. in business administration (*magna cum laude*) from the University of Missouri at St. Louis in 1984, and received his J.D. from the University of Missouri at Columbia School of Law in 1986 in the top one-third of his class. He received the Ike Skelton Memorial Award for Trial Practice in 1986.

Mr. Campbell is certified as an Elder Law Attorney by the National Elder Law Foundation. He is a Medicare Set-Aside Consultant Certified (national certification obtained through the International Commission on Health Care Certification). Mr. Campbell is a member of the Colorado Bar Association (Trust and Estate Section and Elder Law Section), the Arapahoe County Bar Association, the Missouri Bar Association, the National Academy of Elder Law Attorneys, and the National Alliance of Medicare Set-Aside Professionals. Mr. Campbell was selected as a fellow of the Colorado Bar Foundation in 2006. He served as a co-chair of the Colorado Bar Association, Elder Law Section from 2006 to 2008 and serves on the Colorado Bar Association Board of Governors and its Executive Council for 2011-2012.

Shari D. Caton, Esq.
Poskus, Caton & Klein, P.C.
303 E. 17th Ave., Ste. 900
Denver, CO 80203
(303) 832-1600
www.poskuscatonklein.com
caton@poskuscatonklein.com

Chapter 23 — *Powers of Attorney*

Shari D. Caton is a founding member of the law firm Poskus, Caton & Klein, P.C. and frequent speaker on elder law issues. She graduated with honors from the University of New Mexico School of Law in 1998. Prior to law school, she graduated *summa cum laude* from North Carolina Wesleyan with a B.A. in justice and public policy and a minor in psychology. She practices in the areas of estate litigation, estate planning, disability planning, public benefits, probate, wills and trusts, and guardianships and conservatorships. She currently serves on the Executive Council of the Elder Law Section of the Colorado Bar Association and has authored chapters for CLE in Colorado's *Elder Law Handbook*. Ms. Caton continually strives to serve the public, and provides service to the community through the Alzheimer's Association, the Denver Probate Court *pro se* clinic, and the Diabetes Network. She is a current member of the National Academy of Elder Law Attorneys and the American, Colorado, New Mexico, and Douglas County bar associations.

Doni Dolfinger
CO 100017629/NMLS 266569
Reverse Mortgage Specialist
Universal Lending Corporation
6775 E. Evans Ave.
Denver, CO 80224
(303) 791-4786
http://ddolfinger.ulc.com
ddolfinger@ulc.com

Chapter 20 — *Reverse Mortgages*

Doni Dolfinger is a seasoned mortgage professional who has worked in real estate and mortgage banking since 1979. Doni closed the first FHA-insured reverse mortgage loan in Colorado in 1990. Working exclusively with reverse mortgages for 20 years, she has closed over 1,800 reverse mortgage loans. She is employed by Universal Lending Corporation, a locally owned and operated mortgage company, where she is a mortgage banker and a member of the National Reverse Mortgage Lenders Association, Colorado Mortgage Lenders Association, Better Business Bureau, National Association of Insurance and Financial Advisors, Northeast Coalition for Seniors, Affiliate Members of South Metro Denver Realtor Association, and Jefferson County Association of Realtors. Recognized as an expert in her field, she has been instrumental in educating realtors, financial planners, elder law attorneys, mortgage professionals, and seniors throughout Colorado.

Aaron R. Eisenach, CLTC, LTCP
Krieger & Associates. . . an ICB Company
1900 Wazee St., Ste. 1538
Denver, CO 80202
(303) 697-8988
aeisenach@kriegerltc.com

Chapter 7 — *Long-Term Care Insurance*

Aaron R. Eisenach is the Vice President, Western Region, of Individual Commercial Brokerage, Inc. (ICB). Mr. Eisenach oversees the Denver satellite branch of ICB, doing business locally as Krieger & Associates. . . an ICB Company. As a national wholesaler of LTC planning solutions, ICB represents leading LTC insurance companies and products, including traditional policies, Life/LTC and Annuity/LTC combination products, and solutions for employer groups. Prior to assuming his current position, he ranked in the top seven agents nationwide in sales for three years straight with one of the largest insurance carriers in the country. He is a member of the American Association for Long-Term Care Insurance (AALTCI), the National Association of Insurance and Financial Advisors (NAIFA), and the Metro Denver Association of Health Underwriters (MDAHU). He has earned the industry designations of LTCP (Long-Term Care Professional) and CLTC (Certified in Long-Term Care). He was recently elected as President of the LTC Forum of Colorado.

Aaron's passion for long-term care insurance began when his grandfather spent many years receiving care due to Alzheimer's disease. Aaron's father also lost a battle with Alzheimer's, but his long-term care insurance policy protected the family from many of the physical, emotional, and financial consequences associated with long-term care. A native of Colorado, Aaron graduated with honors from Colorado State University. He and his wife, Cheryl, enjoy raising their four children at their home outside of Brighton. Coaching Little League sports, helping his children with 4-H projects, and gardening are a few of the activities that take up his free time.

Aaron L. Evans, Esq.
Benson & Case, LLP
1660 S. Albion St., Ste. 1100
Denver, CO 80222
(303) 757-8300
www.bensoncase.com
evans@bensoncase.com

Chapter 28 — *What to Do When Someone Dies: Responsibilities of the Personal Representative and Trustee Under Probate*

Aaron Evans is a Senior Partner in the Denver law firm Benson & Case, LLP. He has gained expertise in the areas of probate and probate litigation, trusts and estates, estate planning, wills, elder law, guardianships, and conservatorships. Mr. Evans is a member of the Trust and Estate Section of the Colorado Bar Association (CBA), the Statutory Revisions

Committee, and the Denver Bar Association, and is the former chair for the CBA Rules and Forms Committee for 2008–2010.

Mr. Evans was admitted to practice in Colorado in 1996; he is also admitted to the U.S. District Court for the District of Colorado. He attended college at the State University of New York at Oswego, where he received his B.A. in 1993, and Gonzaga University, where he received his J.D. in 1996. Mr. Evans is active in the probate bar and elder law community. He volunteers time each month at the Denver Probate Court, as well as answering questions for the general public.

Lew Forester
Senior Solutions Director
The Senior Hub, Inc.
2360 W. 90th Ave.
Federal Heights, CO 80260
(303) 426-4408
www.seniorhub.org
lforester@seniorhub.org

Chapter 30 — *Programs, Services, and Resources for Older Adults*

Lew Forester has been Senior Solutions Director with The Senior Hub since 1997. Senior Solutions encompasses five distinct programs and services: care management, information and problem solving, minor home repair, emergency food bank, and free medical equipment lending. Older adults, along with their families and caregivers, are given extensive counseling and resources to address a wide variety of needs. Senior Solutions also oversees the content and annual production of the widely distributed *Senior Solutions Resource Guide.*

Mr. Forester has a bachelor's degree in English, with post-graduate study in social work and human services. He is creator and founding member of the Adams County Resource Specialists group and has served on the Adams County Community Adult Protection Team since 1999. He served for four years as a volunteer ombudsman with the Denver Regional Council of Governments (DRCOG). Mr. Forester also writes an advice column for seniors, "Ask Lew," which appears in the Senior Hub *Advisor*, distributed with the *Sentinel* newspapers.

Rebecca L. Franciscus, Esq.
Enforcement Division Staff Attorney
Denver Regional Office
U.S. Securities and Exchange Commission
1801 California St., Ste. 1500
Denver, CO 80202
(303) 844-1000
www.sec.gov

Chapter 17 — *Annuities*

Rebecca Franciscus joined the U.S. Securities and Exchange Commission in 2001 as an Enforcement Division Staff Attorney after several years in private practice in New York City. She first practiced in the Commission's New York Regional Office and joined the Denver Regional Office in 2002. The Commission's mission is to protect investors; maintain fair, orderly, and efficient markets; and facilitate capital formation.

Melody K. Fuller, Esq.
Melody K. Fuller, P.C.
1526 Spruce St.
Boulder, CO 80302
(303) 928-2348
melodyfuller@1526spruce.com

Chapter 14 — *Grandparent Custody and Visitation Issues*

Melody K. Fuller, Esq. is a solo practitioner in Boulder, where she practices family law. She was formerly a partner/shareholder at Cooper, Tanis, Fuller & Cohen, P.C. in Broomfield, where she practiced family law from 2002 to 2010. She received her J.D. from the University of Colorado School of Law in 1980 and has practiced law in Colorado since then. She was the managing attorney for Boulder County Legal Services from 1986 to 2001, representing and advising clients and assisting pro bono attorneys in a wide variety of civil cases. She is known for working with special populations and cases, such as low-income, disabled, GLBT, domestic violence, psychological parents, and grandparents.

Ms. Fuller is a former president of the Boulder County Bar Association and has served on the Colorado Bar Association Board of Governors since 2007. She is the current president of the Boulder County Bar Foundation and a vice-president of the Colorado Bar Association.

M. Carl Glatstein, Esq.
Glatstein & O'Brien LLP
2696 S. Colorado Blvd., Ste. 350
Denver, CO 80222
(303) 757-4342
www.denverprobatelaw.com
carl@denverprobatelaw.com

Chapter 25 — *Conservatorship of Adults*
Chapter 26 — *Guardianship of Adults*

Mr. Glatstein is a partner in the Denver law firm Glatstein & O'Brien LLP, practicing primarily in the field of elder law. He served as co-chair for the Colorado Bar Association (CBA) joint subcommittee on the Uniform Guardianship and Protective Proceedings Act (1997 to 2000), and chairs the Civic and Community Affairs Committee, which assists with the planning of Senior Law Day and the *Senior Law Handbook*. He is also a member of the CBA Elder Law Section (co-chair, 1994 to 1996, and council member) and the CBA Trust and Estate Section. He is a member of the National Academy of Elder Law Attorneys; the American College of Trust & Estate Counsel; the Denver Community Bioethics Committee (chair, 1999 to 2000); the Adams County Community Adult Protection Team; the Guardianship Alliance of Colorado; and the National Guardianship Association.

Mr. Glatstein has been an adjunct professor of elder law at the University of Denver Sturm College of Law since 2005. He co-authored *Colorado Guardianship and Conservatorship Law and Practice* (Bradford Publishing, 2006). He authored "Highlights of Colorado's New Guardianship and Conservatorship Law," published in the January 2000 issue of *The Colorado Lawyer*, and is the reviser for "Guardianships," Krendl, *Colorado Methods of Practice*, 4th and 5th eds. (West Group, 2003 to 2010). His materials have been used in training and resource manuals by state and county social services and law enforcement agencies, and in numerous continuing legal education programs. He is a frequent lecturer on elder law topics, including guardianships and conservatorships, Medicaid issues, and financial exploitation of the elderly.

Erica L. Johnson
Ambler & Keenan LLC
950 S. Cherry St., Ste. 1650
Denver, CO 80246
www.ambler-keenan.com
erica@ambler-keenan.com

Chapter 19 — Estate Planning for Nontraditional Families

Erica L. Johnson is an associate in the law firm of Ambler & Keenan, LLC. She received a B.S. in broadcasting management from Northern Arizona University in 1989. She was awarded a J.D. from the University of Denver College of Law. Erica's practice emphasizes estate planning, probate, trust administration, and second parent adoption. She is a member of the American Academy of Estate Planning Attorneys. She has been appointed by Mayor Hickenlooper to the Mayor's GLBT Commission for 2012-2013. Her other professional associations include membership in the Denver Bar Association, the Trust and Estate Section of the Colorado Bar Association, the Colorado Women's Bar Association, the Colorado Lesbian and Gay Bar Association, the Denver Gay and Lesbian Chamber of Commerce, the Society of Financial Service Professionals, and the Women's Estate Planning Council. She is a frequent speaker and author on the topic of estate planning for non-traditional families. Erica was awarded the Professional Woman of the Year award from the Denver Gay and Lesbian Chamber of Commerce in 2006. She is a Colorado native, born and raised in Littleton.

Thomas R. Kennedy, Esq.
Staff Attorney
Office of Regional Counsel
U.S. Department of Veterans Affairs
155 Van Gordon St.
Box 25126
Denver, CO 80225
(303) 914-5822
Thomas.Kennedy1@va.gov

Chapter 6 — *Veterans' Benefits*

Thomas R. Kennedy has been a staff attorney with the U.S. Department of Veterans Affairs since July 1989. Preceding his appointment to the VA, Mr. Kennedy was in private practice. He obtained his B.A. and Master's of Public Administration degrees from the University of Colorado. He obtained his J.D. from the University of Denver in 1982 and was admitted to the Colorado bar that same year. Mr. Kennedy has represented the VA in various fiduciary, probate, labor and employment, bankruptcy, debt recovery, release of information, legal-medical, and tort matters. Mr. Kennedy authored an article on veterans benefits for the October 2005 issue of *The Colorado Lawyer*, and teaches CLE classes on the VA's fiduciary program.

Michael Kirtland, Esq.
Kirtland & Seal, L.L.C.
90 S. Cascade, Ste. 480
Colorado Springs, CO 80901
(719) 448-0734
www.kirtlandseal.com
mak@kirtlandseal.com

Chapter 24 — *Medical Advance Directives*

Michael Kirtland is a partner in the Colorado Springs law firm Kirtland & Seal, L.L.C. His practice is concentrated in the areas of trusts and estates, estate planning, wills, probate and ancillary probate, elder law, guardianships and conservatorships, marital agreements, and taxation related to those areas. Mr. Kirtland was admitted to practice in Alabama in 1994 and in Colorado in 2004. He is also admitted to the U.S. District Courts for the Middle District of Alabama and the District of Colorado, the U.S. Courts of Appeals for the Tenth and Eleventh Circuits, the U.S. Tax Court, and the U.S. Supreme Court. He attended Coe College, where he received his B.A. in 1974, and the University of Colorado at Colorado Springs, where he received an M.P.A., *summa cum laude*, in 1981. He received his J.D., *magna cum laude*, from Faulkner University in 1993, and his LL.M. in Taxation from the University of Alabama in 1999.

Mr. Kirtland is a member of the El Paso County, Colorado, and American bar associations. He is a member of the El Paso County Bar Association Probate Section; the Colorado Bar Association Elder Law, Trust and Estate, and Alternative Dispute Resolution sections; and the American Bar Association Senior Lawyers Division, where he is a Council Member, and a member of the sections on Alternative Dispute Resolution and Real Property, Trust and Estate Law, of which he is past chair of the Elder Law Group. He is also an acquisitions editor for the Book Publishing Committee. Mr. Kirtland is a member of the Ethics Committee of the El Paso County Medical Society and a member of the Colorado Bar Association Ethics Committee. He is a member of the board of directors of the National Elder Law Foundation.

Mr. Kirtland serves as a member of the Judicial Performance Commission for the Fourth Judicial District of Colorado. He belongs to the Alabama State Bar (where he is a Registered Mediator), the American Inns of Court in Colorado Springs, the National Academy of Elder Law Attorneys, the National Elder Law Foundation, the Air Force Association, and the Military Officers Association of America. Mr. Kirtland is one of only ten Certified Elder Law Attorneys in Colorado.

Michele M. Lawonn, J.D., P.T.
Medical-Legal Advocates, LLC
P.O. Box 371073
Denver, CO 80237
(303) 751-7012
www.medicallegaladvocates.com
mlawonn@aol.com

Chapter 2 — *Medicare*
Chapter 3 — *Health Insurance Beyond Medicare*
Chapter 5 — *Government Programs and Financial Assistance*
Chapter 22 — *Hospital Discharge Planning: Advocating for*
Seniors' Medicare Rehabilitation Benefits
Chapter 31 — *Aging in Place: Maintaining Your Independence at Home*

Michele M. Lawonn is the principal of Medical-Legal Advocates, LLC, in Denver. Her elder law firm utilizes a multi-faceted approach for aging adults and their caretakers to facilitate the maintenance of aging adults' quality of life through the appropriate use of legal planning, rehabilitation utilization, the exploration and assessment of safe housing options, assessment of medical management issues, medical advocacy, and end-of-life advocacy. Her legal practice concentrates in the areas of elder law, Medicare, probate, guardianships and conservatorships, estate planning, end-of-life planning, wills and trusts, and mediation.

Ms. Lawonn obtained her J.D. from the University of Denver College of Law and was a member of the *University of Denver Law Review*. She received a B.S. (*cum laude*) in physical therapy from the University of North Dakota School of Medicine. Ms. Lawonn is a member of the Colorado Bar Association (CBA) Elder Law, Trust and Estate, and Alternative Dispute Resolution sections and a member of the Denver Bar Association. She is the former CBA Elder Law Section liaison to the Legislative Policy Committee, and a past member of the Elder Law Section Executive Council. She was appointed by Congresswoman Diana DeGette as an alternate delegate to the 2005 White House Conference on Aging.

Ms. Lawonn is licensed to practice law in Colorado and California, the U.S. District Court for the District of Colorado, and the Tenth Circuit Court of Appeals. She also is licensed to practice physical therapy in Colorado.

The Honorable John P. Leopold
JAMS
410 17th St., Ste. 1600
Denver, CO 80202
(303) 534-1254
www.jamsadr.com
jleopoldjams@gmail.com

Chapter 29 — *Family Discussions, Decisions, and Dispute Resolution*

The Honorable John P. Leopold has been an arbitrator, mediator, special master, and statutory judge with JAMS since his 2006 retirement as Chief Judge of the Eighteenth Judicial District in Colorado. A native New Yorker, Judge Leopold attained his B.A. in government from Colby College in Maine in 1968. He served in the U.S. Air Force from 1968 to 1972, then received his J.D. from the University of Denver Sturm College of Law in 1974. He was in private practice from 1974 to 1987, until his appointment to the district court bench in 1987 by Governor Roy Romer. He also served as Associate Municipal Court Judge in Littleton and Sheridan from 1985 to 1987.

Judge Leopold is a member of the Colorado, Arapahoe County, and Colorado Women's bar associations; the Thompson G. Marsh Inn, American Inns of Court; and is the immediate past chair of the Law Alumni Council of the University of Denver Sturm College of Law. He is a Fellow of the American Academy of Appointed Masters. In January 2012, he received the third Martin P. Miller Lifetime Achievement Award from the Arapahoe County Bar Association. In 1999, he received the Judicial Excellence Award from the American Board of Trial Advocates, the Colorado Judicial Branch Outstanding Judicial Officer Award in 2001, and the Colorado Community Corrections Board's lifetime membership in 2000. Judge Leopold also served as lead faculty for Advanced New Judge Orientation from 2000 to 2006, and is a frequent presenter and speaker at judicial and legal conferences in Colorado.

Barbara Martin-Worley
Director, Consumer Fraud Protection
Denver District Attorney's Office
201 W. Colfax Ave., Dept. 801
Denver, CO 80202
(720) 913-9036
www.denverda.org
bmw@denverda.org

Chapter 11 — *Arm Yourself with Consumer Protection Information*
Chapter 12 — *Protecting Yourself from Crime*

Barbara is a gerontologist who has worked in the field of aging for 30 years. She began her career as a grants coordinator for the District 10 Area Agency on Aging in Montrose, and served from 1981 to 1989 as the Executive Director of Senior Support

Services in Denver. For the past 20 years, Barbara was the Denver County Extension Director for Colorado State University. As an aging specialist, she has served on elder abuse steering committees initiated by Colorado Attorneys General Ken Salazar and John Suthers, and is a past member of the Denver Commission on Aging. She is presently the Director of Consumer Fraud Protection for the Denver District Attorney's Office. Barbara attained both graduate and undergraduate degrees in gerontology. She is a certified mediator and arbitrator and is a volunteer Victim Assistant with the Douglas County Sheriff's Office.

Elizabeth "Beth" Mitchell
Ambler & Keenan LLC
950 S. Cherry St., Ste. 1650
Denver, CO 80246
www.ambler-keenan.com
bmitchell@ambler-keenan.com

Chapter 19—Estate Planning for Nontraditional Families

Beth Mitchell is an attorney in the law firm of Ambler & Keenan, LLC. Beth devotes her practice to estate planning, Medicaid planning, elder law, Special Needs planning, and probate and trust administration. She is board certified as a Certified Elder Law Attorney (CELA) through the National Elder Law Foundation, and she is a Veterans Administration accredited attorney. She is a member of the American Academy of Estate Planning Attorneys, the National Academy of Elder Law Attorneys, the Denver Bar Association, and the Colorado Bar Association, where she is a member of the Elder Law Section.

Beth sincerely enjoys working with families to make sure that estate matters are handled correctly and efficiently, as well as helping seniors and the disabled qualify for Medicaid. She is a frequent speaker for professionals and the public on educational topics involving estate planning and elder law.

Beth received her B.A. in English and Speech Communications from Drake University in Des Moines, Iowa. She was awarded her J.D. from the University of Denver College of Law, where she was an editor for the *Preventive Law Reporter* and an active member of the University of Denver Student Law Office's Battered Women's Clemency Project.

In her spare time, Beth enjoys giving her time to the community as volunteer. She sits on the board of directors of the Alliance of Professional Women and the Dominican Sisters Home Health Agency, an organization providing free in-home health care to the sick and poor in Denver. She has also volunteered with hospice patients.

Beth is admitted to practice law in the State of Colorado, the United States District Court for the District of Colorado, and the Tenth Circuit Court of Appeals.

Prior to joining Ambler & Keenan, LLC, Beth's diverse background included working for the Colorado Bar Association, with the Iowa Coalition Against Domestic Violence as an AmeriCorps member, and interning with South Dakota Senator Tim Johnson on Capitol Hill. She is a South Dakota native who loves to travel and has enjoyed living in Iowa, New York, Washington, D.C., and Colorado.

Amy Nofziger, M.A.
Manager, Program Leader
AARP Foundation/AARP ElderWatch
303 E. 17th Ave., Ste. 210
Denver, CO 80203
(720) 947-5306
www.aarpelderwatch.org
anofziger@aarp.org

Chapter 11 — *Arm Yourself with Consumer Protection Information*

Amy has been with AARP Foundation's ElderWatch program since its inception in 2001. Prior to her current position as Manager, Program Leader, Amy was the Program Coordinator. Amy is responsible for overall program management and operations, including consumer outreach, volunteer management, design and technological coordination of database and website, grant management, and strategic partnerships. Amy actively participates with national consumer groups such as the National Association of Consumer Agency Administrators (NACAA) and the National Consumers League (NCL). Currently, Amy is the chair of the advisory board of the Colorado Coalition for Elder Rights and Abuse Protection (CCERAP). She has presented to close to 20,000 seniors and professionals on consumer fraud.

Amy has a degree in criminology/sociology from Ohio University, a certificate in gerontology from the University of Denver, and is a trained mediator. Amy is a graduate of Regis University with a Master of Arts degree, with specialization in Leadership. Amy was recognized by the *Denver Business Journal* as one of the 2011 Top Forty under 40 leaders. She actively participates in the Denver Chamber Foundation program, Leadership Denver.

Amy volunteers with many cancer awareness causes, including Project Valentine, and is on the Board of Directors for the Colorado Ovarian Cancer Alliance. She is a trainer for Survivors Teaching Students at the local medical school; this innovative program helps educate future doctors on the realities of cancer from the patient perspective.

Marcia G. O'Brien, Esq. (Retired)
Glatstein & O'Brien LLP
2696 S. Colorado Blvd., Ste. 350
Denver, CO 80222
(303) 757-4342
www.denverprobatelaw.com

Chapter 26 — *Guardianship of Adults*

Marcia G. O'Brien retired as a partner in the Denver law firm of Glatstein & O'Brien LLP, where she practiced in the areas of elder law, probate litigation, probate administration, and estate planning. Ms. O'Brien has spoken numerous times on a variety of topics related to her areas of practice, and she taught the course, "Basic Estate Planning for the Modest Estate," for the University of Denver College of Law, Institute of Advanced Legal Studies.

She received her A.B. degree (*cum laude*) from Occidental College and her J.D. from the University of Denver College of Law.

Heather M. Porreca
Area Agency on Aging
Denver Regional Council of Governments
1290 Broadway, Ste. 700
Denver, CO 80203
(303) 480-5629
www.drcog.org
hporreca@drcog.org

Chapter 21 — *Assisted Living and Nursing Home Issues*

Heather M. Porreca has been a long-term care ombudsman with the Denver Regional Council of Governments since 2006. As a long-term care ombudsman, she advocates for the residents in assisted living residences and assists in empowering and educating residents. In the past 10 years, Ms. Porreca has worked as a home and community based services (HCBS) case manager in both Denver and Jefferson counties. She also worked as a community relations specialist for Total Longterm Care. Ms. Porreca received her bachelor's degree in sociology from the University of Northern Colorado and a paralegal certificate from Denver Career College.

Jennifer Reeves
Area Agency on Aging
Denver Regional Council of Governments
1290 Broadway, Ste. 700
Denver, CO 80203
(303) 480-6788
www.drcog.org
jreeves@drcog.org

Chapter 21 — *Assisted Living and Nursing Home Issues*

Jennifer Reeves has been a long-term care ombudsman with the Denver Regional Council of Governments since 2008. As a long-term care ombudsman, she advocates for residents in nursing homes and assists in empowering and educating residents and long-term care consumers. Ms. Reeves' career in long-term care spans more than a decade, and includes working directly in both nursing homes and assisted living residences. Ms. Reeves was educated at the Metropolitan State College of Denver, and holds a Bachelor of Science in Health Care Management.

Zane Robertson
Active Minds
990 Krameria St.
Denver, CO 80220
(303) 320-7652
www.ActiveMinds.com
Zane@ActiveMinds.com

Chapter 32 — *Lifelong Learning and the Aging Brain*

Zane is the President and Co-Founder of Active Minds®, a Denver-based provider of educational seminars for seniors. He is a frequent speaker on lifelong learning and senior education. He is a past member of the Denver Commission on Aging. Over the past 20 years, Zane has founded four companies and led two others as president or chairman. He is a former officer in the Colorado chapter of the Young Presidents' Organization and has served on the boards of several organizations, including the Denver Coalition for Seniors. Zane holds a B.A. from Carleton College and an M.B.A. from Stanford University.

Jamie J. Roth, Esq.
Brown & Brown, P.C.
1250 E. Sherwood Dr.
Grand Junction, CO 81501
www.brownandbrownpc.com
jamie@brownandbrownpc.com

Chapter 8 — *Financial Difficulty for Seniors*

Jamie J. Roth, Esq. is an attorney with Brown & Brown, P.C., a law firm serving Colorado's Western Slope with offices in Grand Junction and Glenwood Springs. She graduated from the University of Colorado School of Law in 1997, and obtained her LL.M. in taxation from New York University in 2011. Her practice focuses in the areas of estate, tax, and long-term care planning, and probate, including contested litigation.

Clara Brown Shaffer, Esq.
Law Office of Brown & Brown, P.C.
1250 E. Sherwood Dr.
Grand Junction, CO 81501
(970) 243-8250
www.brownandbrownpc.com
clara@brownandbrownpc.com

Chapter 15 — *Estate Planning: Wills, Trusts, and Your Property*

Clara joined Brown & Brown, P.C. in December 2007. She graduated from the University of Puget Sound in 2003 with a Bachelor of Arts degree in anthropology, and received her Juris Doctorate degree from the University of San Francisco School of Law in 2006. She is a member of the Trust and Estate Section of the Colorado Bar Association, the Estate Planning (Orange Book) Forms Committee, the Statutory Revisions Committee, and the Mesa County Bar Association. Clara is a member of the National Academy of Elder Law Attorneys. Her practice focuses primarily on estate planning, estate administration, special needs planning, elder law, and long-term care planning.

William M. Sheets
Senior Director of Development
Office of Gift Planning
University Advancement
Colorado State University
521 University Services Center
601 S. Howes
Fort Collins, CO 80523-7115
(970) 491-4679
www.plannedgiving.colostate.edu
Bill.Sheets@Colostate.edu

Chapter 16 — *Estate and Succession Planning for Farmers and Ranchers*
Chapter 18 — *Philanthropy and Planned Giving*

William M. "Bill" Sheets is the Senior Director of Development for the Office of Gift Planning in the Division of Advancement at Colorado State University. Bill received his B.S. in agricultural sciences in 1974 and an M.S. in agricultural economics in 1977 from Purdue University. Bill has been involved in the creation of three companies, working as a real estate manager, real estate appraiser and broker, and consultant to private industry and city and state governments concerning resource management. Bill has held advancement positions with Purdue University, Winrock International, and the University of Kentucky prior to joining the Advancement and Strategic Initiatives staff at Colorado State University in 2005. He is president of the National Agricultural Alumni Development Association, an association of 46 land grant universities, 3 state universities, and 6 not-for-profit organizations associated with agriculture and natural resources.

Paul Dean Tayloe, Jr.
Chief, Support Services Division
Denver Regional Office
U.S. Department of Veterans Affairs
155 Van Gordon St.
Box 25126
Denver, CO 80225
(303) 914-5750
www.va.gov
paul.tayloe@va.gov

Chapter 6 — *Veterans' Benefits*

Paul Dean "Dean" Tayloe, Jr., is the Chief of the Support Services Division for the Denver VA Regional Office of the U.S. Department of Veterans Affairs. A native of Kentucky, Dean served in the United States Air Force from 1968 until 1972. Dean received his bachelor's degree from Eastern Kentucky University in 1973 and a master's of public administration degree in 1975. Dean started his career with the VA in 1974 as part of the Veterans

Representative on Campus program to help Vietnam veterans obtain their educational and other benefits. Since then, he has served in a variety of positions, including Educational Liaison Representative; Chief, Field Section; Assistant Veterans Services Officer; Public Affairs Officer; and Supervisor of the Fiduciary Program for the States of Colorado and Wyoming; and he has been the Chief of Support Services since June 2006. Dean has nearly 37 years of experience with the programs administered by the VA.

Andrew W. Volin, Esq.
Sherman & Howard L.L.C.
633 17th St., Ste. 3000
Denver, CO 80202
(303) 299-8268
www.shermanhoward.com
AVolin@shermanhoward.com

Chapter 9 — *Employment Discrimination*

Andy Volin has practiced over 20 years in the Labor and Employment Law Department of Sherman & Howard L.L.C. in its Denver office. He helps companies treat their workforce fairly, advising and defending employers and their management in disputes involving employment discrimination, wrongful discharge, and wage and hour law. In 2006–2008, Mr. Volin served as the management-side co-chair of the Labor and Employment Section of the Colorado Bar Association. He is a contributing author to CBA-CLE's *The Practitioner's Guide to Colorado Employment Law* and the *Senior Law Handbook*. Mr. Volin received both his B.A. and J.D. from the University of Virginia.

Kimberly R. Willoughby, Esq.
Willoughby & Eckelberry, LLC
303 E. 17th St., Ste. 910
Denver, CO 80203
(303) 839-1770
www.willoughbylaw.com
kim@willoughbylaw.com

Chapter 13 — *Family Relationships*

Kimberly R. Willoughby is founder of Willoughby & Eckelberry, LLC, a small firm limited to domestic relations practice, probate, and estate planning. Ms. Willoughby received her undergraduate degree in 1991, *magna cum laude,* from the University of Colorado at Boulder, and her J.D. from the University of Virginia in 1994. She was the articles editor for *The Journal of Law and Politics*. Ms. Willoughby is a fellow of the American Academy of Matrimonial Lawyers; has served on the Executive Council of the Colorado Bar Association (CBA) Family Law Section; is a member of the Trust and Estate Section of the CBA; and has served on the boards of the CBA, CLE, the Denver Bar Association, the Colorado Women's Bar Association, and the Thompson Marsh Inn of Court.

Paulette Wisch, CML
CO 100019009/NMLS 258672
Reverse Mortgage Manager
Universal Lending Corporation
6775 E. Evans Ave.
Denver, CO 80224
(303) 759-7354
www.ulcreverse.com
pwisch@ulc.com

Chapter 20 — *Reverse Mortgages*

Paulette Wisch has personally helped thousands of seniors achieve financial security and independence with a reverse mortgage. Paulette was instrumental in working with FHA to bring the reverse product to market in 1989, and ever since then she has been an advocate for the program and Colorado's seniors. A mortgage professional since 1972, she switched her specialization to reverse mortgages to run FHA's pilot program. Recognized as an expert in her field, Paulette has spent the last 23 years educating seniors and their adult children, and professionals in banking, finance, home health, and financial planning about the benefits of a reverse mortgage.

Rose Mary Zapor, M.A., J.D.
The Zapor Law Office, P.C.
7126 W. Alaska Dr., Ste. 112
Lakewood, CO 80226
(303) 881-6354
(303) 881-6354
www.zapormediation.com
zaporlaw01@yahoo.com

Chapter 29 — *Family Discussions, Decisions, and Dispute Resolution*

Rose Mary Zapor, M.A., J.D., is an attorney and mediator at The Zapor Law Office, P.C. Ms. Zapor's practice is limited to elder law, mediation, child and family investigation, and parenting coordinator/decision-maker determinations. Ms. Zapor helps families to make decisions and plan for life-changing events through estate planning and Medicaid planning in her elder law practice. She holds a certificate in family mediation from the Center for Dispute Resolution in Boulder, and a certificate in forensic interviewing from Columbus, Ohio. She is a member of Elder Answers, Mediate.com, and the National Association of Elder Law Attorneys.

Ms. Zapor holds several degrees, including a B.A. in communications and history and an M.A. in education. Ms. Zapor earned her J.D. from the University of Denver College of Law. Ms. Zapor has appeared on *Good Morning America*, Court TV, MSNBC, and *Larry King Live* and has been quoted in *The Washington Post*, *New York Times*, *Rocky Mountain News*, and *The Denver Post*.

Chapter 1

Social Security Benefits

John J. Campbell, Esq.
Law Offices of John J. Campbell, P.C.

SYNOPSIS

1-1.   Retirement Benefits

1-2.   Disability Benefits

1-3.   Supplemental Security Income Benefits

1-4.   Statewide Social Security Offices

1-1. Retirement Benefits

When you work and pay Social Security taxes, you earn Social Security credits. Most people earn the maximum of four credits per year.

The number of credits you need to get retirement benefits depends on your date of birth. If you were born in 1929 or later, you need 40 credits (10 years of work). People born before 1929 need fewer than 40 credits (39 credits if born in 1928; 38 credits if born in 1927; etc.).

If you stop working before you have enough credits to qualify for benefits, your credits will remain on your Social Security record. If you return to work later on, you can add more credits so that you qualify. No retirement benefits can be paid until you have the required number of credits.

If you are like most people, you will earn many more credits than you need to qualify for Social Security. These extra credits do not increase your Social Security benefit. However, the income you earn while working will increase your benefit, as you will learn in the next section.

Your benefit amount is based on your earnings averaged over most of your working career. Higher lifetime earnings result in higher benefits. If you have some years of no earnings or low earnings, your benefit amount may be lower than if you had worked steadily.

Your benefit amount also is affected by your age at the time you start receiving benefits. If you start your retirement benefits at age 62 (the earliest possible retirement age), your benefit will be lower than if you waited until a later age.

Social Security will give you a personalized benefit estimate at your request. Call their toll-free number, (800) 772-1213, to ask for a *Request for Earnings and Benefit Estimate Statement*. Within four to six weeks of completing and returning the form to Social Security, you will receive a statement of your earnings record and estimates of your Social Security benefits for early retirement, full retirement, and retirement at age 70. Social Security will also give you an estimate of the disability benefits you could receive if you become severely disabled before you are eligible for full retirement, as well as the amount of benefits payable to your spouse and other eligible family members due to your retirement, disability, or death.

Full Retirement Age

The usual retirement age for people retiring now is age 65. Social Security calls this "full retirement age," and the benefit amount that is payable is considered the full retirement benefit.

Because of longer life expectancies, the full retirement age will be increased in gradual steps until it reaches age 67. This change started in the year 2003 and affects people born in 1938 and later.

Age to Receive Full Social Security Benefits	
Year of Birth	*Full Retirement Age*
1937 or earlier	65
1938	65 and 2 months
1939	65 and 4 months
1940	65 and 6 months
1941	65 and 8 months
1942	65 and 10 months
1943-1954	66
1955	66 and 2 months
1956	66 and 4 months
1957	66 and 6 months
1958	66 and 8 months
1959	66 and 10 months
1960 or later	67

Early Retirement

You can start your Social Security benefits as early as age 62, but the benefit amount you receive will be less than your full retirement benefit.

If you take early retirement, your benefits will be permanently reduced based on the number of months you will receive checks before you reach full retirement age. If your full retirement age is 65, the reduction for starting your Social Security at age 62 is about 20 percent; at age 63, it is about 13-1/3 percent; and at age 64, it is about 6-2/3 percent.

If your full retirement age is older than 65 (that is, you were born after 1937), you still will be able to take your retirement benefits at age 62, but the reduction in your benefit amount will be greater than it is for people retiring now.

As a general rule, early retirement will give you about the same total Social Security benefits over your lifetime, but in smaller amounts to take into account the longer period you will receive them.

Some people stop working before they reach age 62. In that case, it is important to remember that during years with no earnings, you miss the opportunity to increase your benefit amount by replacing lower earnings years with higher earnings years.

Delayed Retirement

Not everyone retires at full retirement age. You may decide to continue working full time beyond that time. In that case, you can increase your Social Security benefit in two ways.

Each additional year you work adds another year of earnings to your Social Security record. Higher lifetime earnings may result in higher benefits when you retire.

In addition, your benefit will be increased by a certain percentage if you delay retirement. These increases will be added in automatically from the time you reach your full retirement age until you start taking your benefits, or you reach age 70. The percentage varies depending on your year of birth. See the chart below for the increase that will apply to you.

If you plan to start your retirement benefits after age 62, it is a good idea to contact Social Security in advance to see which month is best to claim benefits. In some cases, your choice of a retirement month could mean additional benefits for you and your family.

It may be to your advantage to have your Social Security benefits start in January, even if you do not plan to retire until later in the year. Depending on your earnings and your benefit amount, it may be possible for you to start collecting benefits even though you continue to work. Under current rules, many people can receive the most benefits possible with an application that is effective in January.

If you are not working, or your annual earnings are under the Social Security earnings limits, or you plan to start collecting your Social Security when you turn 62, you should apply for benefits three months before the date you want your benefits to start.

Increases for Delayed Retirement	
Year of Birth	*Yearly Rate of Increase*
1917-1924	3.0%
1925-1926	3.5%
1927-1928	4.0%
1929-1930	4.5%
1931-1932	5.0%
1933-1934	5.5%
1935-1936	6.0%
1937-1938	6.5%
1939-1940	7.0%
1941-1942	7.5%
1943 or later	8.0%

Important Point: If you decide to delay your retirement, **be sure to sign up for Medicare at age 65.** In some circumstances, medical insurance costs more if you delay applying for it. Other information about Medicare is in Chapter 2.

Retirement Benefits for Widow(er)s

Widow(er)s can begin receiving benefits at age 60 or age 50 if disabled. If you are receiving widows or widowers (including divorced widows or widowers) benefits, you can switch to your own retirement benefits as early as age 62, assuming you are eligible and your retirement rate is higher than your widow(er)'s rate. In many cases, a widow(er) can begin receiving one benefit at a reduced rate and then switch to the other benefit at an unreduced rate at full retirement age. The rules vary depending on the situation, so you should talk to a Social Security representative about the options available to you.

Family Benefits

If you are receiving retirement benefits, some members of your family also can receive benefits. Those who can include:

- Your wife or husband age 62 or older;
- Your wife or husband under age 62, if she or he is taking care of your child who is under age 16 or disabled;
- Your former wife or husband age 62 or older;
- Children up to age 18;
- Children age 18 to 19, if they are full-time students through grade 12; and
- Children over age 18, if they are disabled.

Spouse's Benefits

A spouse receives one-half of the retired worker's full benefit unless the spouse begins collecting benefits before age 65. In that case, the amount of the spouse's benefit is permanently reduced by a percentage based on the number of months before she or he reaches 65. However, if your spouse is taking care of a child who is under age 16 or disabled and receiving Social Security benefits, your spouse gets full benefits, regardless of age.

If you are eligible for both your own retirement benefits and for benefits as a spouse, Social Security always pays your own benefit first. If your benefit as a spouse is higher than your retirement benefit, you will receive a combination of benefits equaling the higher spouse benefit.

Maximum Family Benefits

If you have children eligible for Social Security, each will receive up to one-half of your full benefit. But there is a limit to the amount of money that can be paid to a family. If the total benefits due your spouse and children exceed this limit, their benefits will be reduced proportionately. Your benefit will not be affected.

Benefits For a Divorced Spouse

A divorced spouse can get benefits on a former husband's or wife's Social Security record if the marriage lasted at least 10 years. The divorced spouse must be 62 or older and unmarried. If the spouse has been divorced at least two years, he or she can get benefits, even if the worker is not retired. However, the worker must have enough credits to qualify for benefits and must be age 62 or older. The amount of benefits a divorced spouse gets has no effect on the amount of benefits a current spouse can get.

If You Work and Receive Social Security at the Same Time

You can continue to work and still receive retirement benefits. Your earnings in (or after) the month you reach your full retirement age will not affect your Social Security benefits. However, your benefits will be reduced if your earnings exceed certain limits for the months before you reach your full retirement age: age 65 for persons born before 1938 and gradually increasing to age 67 for persons born in 1960 or later.

If you are under full retirement age, $1 in benefits will be deducted for each $2 in earnings you have above the annual limit. In the year you reach your full retirement age, your benefits will be reduced $1 for every $3 you earn over a different annual limit until the month you reach full retirement age. Then you can work without any reduction in the amount of your monthly benefits, no matter how much you earn. These limits increase each year as average wages increase.

If other family members receive benefits on your Social Security record, the total family benefits will be affected by your earnings. This means Social Security will offset not only your benefits, but those payable to your family as well. If a family member works, however, the family member's earnings affect only his or her benefits.

Special Monthly Rule

A special rule applies to your earnings for one year, usually your first year of retirement. Under this rule, you can receive a full Social Security check for any month you are "retired," regardless of your yearly earnings. Your earnings must be under a monthly limit. If you are self-employed, the services you perform in your business are taken into consideration as well.

Your Benefits May Be Taxable

About 20 percent of people who get Social Security have to pay taxes on their benefits. This provision affects only people who have substantial income in addition to their Social Security.

At the end of each year, you will receive in the mail a *Social Security Benefit Statement* showing the amount of benefits you received. You can use this statement when you are completing your federal income tax return to find out if any of your benefits are subject to tax.

Pensions from Work Not Covered by Social Security

If you get a pension from work where you paid Social Security taxes, it will not affect your Social Security benefits. However, if you get a pension from work that was not covered by Social Security — for example, the federal civil service, some state or local government employment, or work in a foreign country — your Social Security benefit may be lowered or offset.

Leaving the United States

If you are a United States citizen, you can travel or live in most foreign countries without affecting your eligibility for Social Security benefits. However, there are a few countries — Cambodia, Cuba, North Korea, Vietnam, and many of the former Soviet republics (except Estonia, Latvia, Lithuania, and Russia) — where Social Security cannot send Social Security checks.

If you work outside the United States, different rules apply in determining if you can get your benefit checks.

Most people who are neither U.S. residents nor U.S. citizens will have 25.5 percent of their benefits withheld for federal income tax.

1-2. Disability Benefits

Social Security Disability Insurance Benefits (SSDIB), formerly known as Social Security Disability Income (SSDI), is a federal entitlement program in which eligibility does not depend upon financial need. SSDIB is an income benefit from Social Security available to blind or disabled persons under age 65 who have earned a sufficient number of qualifying quarters of work.

Disability is determined according to the criteria in § 1382c(a)(3) of the Social Security Act. To be considered "disabled," you must have a diagnosed medical condition (including mental illness) that is expected to last at least 12 months or to result in death. Further, you must be unable to engage in substantially gainful activity due to your medical condition. Generally, you are deemed to be engaging in substantially gainful activity if you are able to earn at least $1,010 per month ($1,690 if you are blind).

The number of work quarters needed to qualify for SSDIB benefits depends upon your age when you become disabled. If you are age 31 or older, you will need at least 20 qualifying quarters within the 10-year period immediately before your application for SSDIB. If you are under age 24, you will need only six qualifying quarters; if you are between the ages of 24 and 31, you will need enough qualifying quarters to account for having worked half of the time between age 21 and your age at the onset of your disability. There is a five-month waiting period from the date of the onset of disability before payment of SSDIB benefits begins.

SSDIB does not pay for medical care. However, after you have maintained SSDIB eligibility for at least 24 consecutive months, you will automatically become eligible for Medicare. If you are disabled with amyotrophic lateral sclerosis (ALS), you do not have to wait 24 months to become eligible for Medicare.

If you are an SSDIB recipient who wishes to return to the work force, you may earn in excess of $720 per month during a nine-month trial period without losing benefits. After that, you can continue to be eligible for SSDIB while working for an additional 36 months. If you are also entitled to Medicare benefits, those Medicare benefits can continue for up to 8-1/2 years after you return to work.

Children may also receive SSDIB benefits, but only from a disabled, retired, or deceased parent who was eligible for Social Security benefits. Sometimes benefits are also available to the spouse or divorced spouse of an insured disabled person.

SSDIB Offset

If you are a disabled worker under age 65 and you receive workers' compensation benefits for lost wages (indemnity), it is possible that your indemnity payments could cause your SSDIB benefits to be reduced if your combined SSDIB and workers' compensation indemnity benefits total more than 80 percent of your "average current earnings." Social Security will determine your average current earnings and the amount of your SSDIB offset, if any. This reduction stops when you reach age 65 and your disability benefits are replaced by Social Security retirement benefits.

1-3. Supplemental Security Income Benefits

Supplemental Security Income (SSI) is a financial needs-based public benefit program, which provides income to the elderly, blind, or disabled. SSI is federally funded and governed solely by federal law. SSI does not pay for medical care. However, in Colorado, if you are eligible for SSI, you will also be eligible to have medical benefits through the

Medicaid program. An individual applying for SSI must meet strict income and resource tests to qualify.

The monthly income limits for SSI are identical to the maximum federal SSI benefit: $698 for an individual and $1,048 for a married couple. Generally, any asset that is spent or disposed of by the individual in the same calendar month as it is received is considered "income." Income under SSI regulations consists of both earned and unearned income.

Earned income consists of your wages, as well as net earnings from self-employment. Unearned income consists of your income from other sources, including support and maintenance furnished in cash or in kind; payments from an annuity, workers' compensation, old-age pension, survivors and disability insurance, and unemployment benefits; payments occasioned by the death of another (which would include payments from an inheritance, life insurance policy, or wrongful death action); support and alimony payments; and earnings of and additions to a non-exempt trust of which you are a beneficiary.

Income (and resources) can also be "deemed" under SSI regulations. That is, if you are living at home with your ineligible spouse or child, you will be deemed to have access to a portion of the spouse's or child's income. Generally, an individual under age 18 living with his or her family will also be deemed to have access to a portion of his or her ineligible parents' incomes. However, for individuals who do not live in the same home as their families, the income of a spouse, child, or parent is not deemed available. For individuals who have resident alien status and are eligible for SSI, the income and resources of a sponsor are deemed to the individual, regardless of whether they live in the same household.

SSI exempts the first $20 per month of your unearned income, the first $65 of your earned income, and one-half of your monthly earned income over $65. In Colorado, you may also receive a state benefit in addition to the federal SSI benefit. These state payments are also exempt, as are certain other types of income. These income exemptions are often referred to as the "income disregards."

Generally, to qualify for SSI you must have nonexempt income below $698. Earned and unearned income from sources other than SSI, after deducting the income disregards, will offset your SSI benefit on a dollar-for-dollar basis. An offset for other income that reduces your SSI benefit to $0 will make you ineligible.

There are also restrictions on resources. Resources are assets consisting of cash or other liquid assets that (1) could be converted to cash and (2) are not spent or disposed of in the month received. Certain exempt resources, including your house, one car, your personal property, household goods, a burial space, or a pre-paid burial plan are not counted. Nonexempt resources are restricted to a total of no more than $2,000 for individuals and $3,000 for married couples.

Transfers Without Fair Consideration

Individuals often consider making gifts of their excess resources to reduce those resources to eligibility levels. To prevent the abuse of this strategy, federal laws impose penalty periods for certain transfers without fair consideration during the "look-back period" of 36 months preceding the filing of the SSI application. During a resulting penalty period, the individual may not qualify for SSI.

To calculate the penalty period for any transfers of resources, the total uncompensated value of all transfers made during the look-back period is divided by the maximum SSI benefit plus any corresponding state payment. Under Medicaid law, the penalty period is calculated by dividing the uncompensated value of the transfer by the average monthly cost of nursing home care for an individual in the state in which the individual lives. The maximum penalty period is 36 months.

While transfers of resources are generally penalized under SSI law, certain transfers of resources are exempt and will *not* incur a penalty period. These exempt transfers are essentially the same as those for Medicaid long-term care and Home and Community Based Services (HCBS) benefits.

1-4. Statewide Social Security Offices

Social Security Offices

General information: (800) 772-1213
For updates: www.ssa.gov

Alamosa Office 602 Del Sol Dr., Ste. 1-A Alamosa, CO 81101 (888) 475-0297	**Durango Office** 103 Sheppard Dr., Ste. 120 Durango, CO 81303 (888) 472-6115	**Lakewood Office** 13151 W. Alameda Pkwy. Lakewood, CO 80228 (800) 772-1213
Aurora Office 14280 E. Jewell Ave., Ste. 250 Aurora, CO 80012 (800) 772-1213	**Ft. Collins Office** 301 S. Howes St., 4th Floor Ft. Collins, CO 80521 (866) 336-7385	**Littleton Office** 8000 Southpark Ln. Littleton, CO 80120 (800) 772-1213
Boulder Office 4949 Pearl E. Cir., Ste. 101 Boulder, CO 80301 (800) 772-1213	**Glenwood Springs Office** 201 14th St., Rm. 101 Glenwood Springs, CO 81601 (866) 220-7898	**Montrose Office** 1805 Pavilion Dr. Montrose, CO 81401 (866) 758-1317
Cañon City Office 115 N. 10th St. Cañon City, CO 81212 (866) 272-5728	**Grand Junction Office** 825 N. Crest Dr. Grand Junction, CO 81506 (866) 931-7120	**Pueblo Office** 3769 Parker Blvd. Pueblo, CO 81008 (888) 737-1761
Colorado Springs Office 1049 N. Academy Blvd. Colorado Springs, CO 80909 (888) 880-0688	**Greeley Office** 5400 W. 11th St., Ste. A Greeley, CO 80634 (877) 405-9195	**Trinidad Office** 111 Waverly Ave. Trinidad, CO 81082 (866) 755-5009
Denver Office 1500 Champa St., 2nd Floor Denver, CO 80202 (800) 772-1213	**La Junta Office** 1314 E. 3rd St. La Junta, CO 81050 (888) 221-0429	

Chapter 2

Medicare

Michele M. Lawonn, J.D., P.T.
Medical-Legal Advocates, LLC

SYNOPSIS

2-1.   Medicare

2-2.   Medicare Benefits Covered

2-3.   Appeal Rights

2-4.   Resources

This chapter will clarify important information you need to know about Medicare. It also will answer your questions about eligibility requirements and enrollment processes. This chapter outlines the services that Medicare Part A, Part B, and Part C cover, and provides a brief discussion of the prescription drug program covered under Part D, which became effective in 2006. Medicare payment policies, payment methods, and appeal processes are explained, and the advantages and disadvantages of each are discussed.

2-1. Medicare

Medicare is a three-part federal health insurance program managed by the Social Security Administration. It helps pay hospital and medical costs for people who are 65 years or older, and for some people with disabilities who are under 65. Overall, Medicare is not a "means tested" program. This means that your eligibility for Medicare benefits (except for Medicare Part B) does not depend upon the amount of your income or your resources. The monthly premium structure changed in 2007 for Medicare Part B benefits, and in 2011 for Medicare Part D. These premiums are now determined by your income (means determination). Medicare Part D has an income-related monthly adjustment amount that is paid to Medicare.

Medicare Hospital Insurance is called Medicare Part A. It usually covers a medically necessary stay in the hospital. It also may cover skilled nursing care and rehabilitation in a nursing facility or health care in your home after you leave the hospital. It is very important to notice that Medicare Part A does *not* cover doctors' and ambulance services. Medicare Part B covers these services (see below).

Medicare Medical Insurance is called Medicare Part B. In order to get Part B coverage, you must choose it and pay a monthly premium. Medicare Part B reimburses at the rate of 80 percent of the reasonable charge for medically necessary covered services.

Medicare Part B covers doctors' services, ambulance and outpatient services, preventive services, and medical supplies. It also covers home health services prescribed by your physician even if you have not been hospitalized. It must be *medically necessary* based on such criteria as a change in your functional status — for example, due to a fall or injury.

The premium structure for Part B changed in 2007, and income is now considered. This is the income-related monthly adjustment amount. The monthly premium ranges from $99.90 to $319.70 (see chart, below). The monthly premium is significantly higher based on a lower income if a married beneficiary has an income greater than $85,000 and files a separate tax return, rather than a joint return.

The majority of Medicare Part B beneficiaries will have a premium increase of $3.50 in 2012, with approximately 27 percent of beneficiaries having a premium decrease of $15.50 because they were new enrollees; their incomes changed in 2011, affecting premium amounts; they do not have their Medicare Part B premiums withheld from their Social Security benefit payments; or they have their Medicare Part B premiums paid on their behalf by Medicaid.

The Social Security Administration (SSA) automatically determines your Medicare Part B premium, based on tax returns filed with the Internal Revenue Service, usually two years prior to the determination of the premium or on the most recent federal tax return provided. You will receive a notice from the SSA each fall outlining your next year's Medicare Part B premium and containing instructions on how to appeal the premium amount. If you have had a significant change in income (especially a decrease in income) due to such major life changing events as marriage, divorce, the death of your spouse, retirement, or loss of retirement income, you should provide the SSA with updated tax information and challenge the premium amount.

Medicare Part C is also called Medicare Advantage. It requires eligible participants to elect this coverage and assign their Medicare Part A and Part B benefits to a private company approved by Medicare. Technically, Medicare Advantage plans must cover the same medically necessary services and benefits that are covered under original Medicare Parts A and B. However, the criteria for determination of "medical necessity" and eligibility for services, such as for rehabilitation and therapy services, may differ. These plans also may provide additional benefits that are excluded under Medicare Parts A and B, such as a wellness program and vision and dental care.

You can either elect to have original Medicare Parts A and B or you can elect to enroll in a Part C plan (health maintenance organization (HMO), preferred provider organization (PPO), or private fee-for-service plan (PFFS)). Since January 1, 2011, if you are in a Medicare Advantage (Medicare Part C) plan and you want to change back to a Medicare fee-for-service plan, you can disenroll between January 1 and February 14 of each year.

Medicare Part D, which covers the prescription drug program, began in January 2006, and is intended to cover prescription drugs as a result of the Medicare Prescription Drug Improvement and Modernization Act of 2003. The annual open enrollment period for Medicare Part D is from November 15 to December 31. This is also the period in which you can change your plan enrollment.

MEDICARE PART B AND PART D PREMIUMS

Tax Return Income (Individual)	Joint Tax Return Income (Married Couples)	Tax Return Income (Married Filing Separately)	2012 Monthly Part B Premiums (each person)	2012 Monthly Part D Premiums (each person)
Up to $85,000	Up to $170,000	Up to $85,000	$99.90 (Standard premium)	Plan premium
$85,001 to $107,000	$170,001 to $214,000		$139.90 (Standard premium plus $40)	Plan premium plus $11.60
$107,001 to $160,000	$214,001 to $320,000		$199.80 (Standard premium plus $99.90)	Plan premium plus $29.90
$160,001 to $214,000	$320,001 to $428,000	$85,001 to $129,000	$259.70 (Standard premium plus $159.80)	Plan premium plus $48.10
Over $214,000	Over $428,000	Over $129,000	$319.70 (Standard premium plus $219.80)	Plan premium plus $66.40

Medicare Eligibility

You are eligible for Medicare if:

▶ You are age 65 or older and qualify for Social Security or Railroad Retirement benefits, even if you are not actually receiving them;

▶ You are a former federal employee who retired on or after 1983;

▶ You are disabled and have met the Social Security or Railroad Retirement disability requirements for 24 months or two years;

▶ You have end-stage kidney (renal) disease and have been treated with dialysis for three months (generally, you become eligible for Medicare benefits on the first day of the third month of dialysis treatment); or

▶ You have Lou Gehrig's disease (ALS). You become eligible for Medicare benefits as soon as you are determined to be eligible for Social Security Disability Income (SSDI) benefits, without the requirement of the 24-month waiting period.

If you are age 65 or older but not eligible under the above requirements, you may still choose to enroll in the Medicare program. You must live in the United States and have been a citizen or legal alien for at least five years. If you choose to enroll, you must pay monthly premiums that are generally higher than those charged to eligible beneficiaries. The 2012 Medicare Part A monthly premiums for voluntary enrollees are $451 per month if you have paid into Social Security for 29 or fewer quarters, and $248 per month if you have paid into Social Security for 30 to 39 quarters.

How to Enroll

People who elect and receive Social Security retirement benefits before they are 65 automatically will be enrolled in Medicare at age 65. People who have been receiving Social Security Disability benefits for 24 months also will automatically be enrolled in Medicare. These people will receive a Medicare card in the mail from the Social Security Administration three months before their 65th birthday (or on the 24th month of disability), along with a notice informing them of their Medicare Part A enrollment and that they automatically will be enrolled in Medicare Part B unless they refuse this coverage. If you are in one of these categories and do not receive your notice and card, contact the Social Security Administration.

If you have not chosen early retirement, you should apply for Medicare three or fewer months before your 65th birthday or up to three months after your birthday month, even if you plan to continue working. This is the initial enrollment period. As the age of eligibility for full Social Security benefits is increasing, many people may need to enroll in Medicare at age 65 without also registering for Social Security benefits. If you do not apply at this time, you may miss your opportunity to timely enroll in Medicare Parts A and B, as you can only sign up between January 1 and March 31 of each year, with coverage beginning on July 1. This is known as the general enrollment period.

Also, there is a 10 percent penalty added to the premium for each full 12-month period an individual is late in enrolling for Medicare Part B, unless you qualify for the "Special Enrollment Period" (you have group health plan insurance coverage based upon the current employment of you or a family member). So, it is very important that you enroll as soon as you are eligible, unless you are still covered by your own or your spouse's employee health plan. Then, you can enroll for Part B at any time or during the eight-month period beginning when the employment or group health plan coverage ends, whichever first occurs.

Your monthly Medicare Part B premiums are deducted from your Social Security check. If you are not yet receiving Social Security, you will be billed for these premiums.

2-2. Medicare Benefits Covered

Benefits Covered Under Part A

Hospital Services

Hospital services (considered reasonable and medically necessary by Medicare) are covered for a hospitalization in an acute care hospital, an inpatient rehabilitation facility (IRF), or a long-term acute care hospital (LTAC). These services can include:

▶ Semi-private room and board, including special care units;

▶ General nursing services;

▶ Inpatient prescription drugs;

▶ Supplies;

▶ Use of equipment normally furnished by the hospital;

▶ Operating and recovery room costs;

▶ Blood transfusions after the first three pints;

▶ Diagnostic, therapeutic, or rehabilitative services and items the hospital normally furnishes; and

▶ Inpatient mental health care in a psychiatric hospital (lifetime maximum benefit of 190 days).

Skilled Nursing Facility (SNF) Services

These include:

▶ Skilled nursing care;

▶ Semi-private room and board;

▶ Physical, occupational, and speech therapy;

▶ Medical social services;

▶ Inpatient prescription drugs; and

▶ Use of durable medical equipment such as wheelchairs, walkers, and special beds.

A skilled nursing facility also may furnish intermediate and custodial care, which is not a covered benefit. Medicare only pays if you receive skilled nursing or therapy services or both and pays only under specific circumstances.

Hospice Services

Hospice care is concerned with maintaining a person's quality of life as she or he approaches death. Hospice is appropriate for people with a terminal illness who have a life expectancy of six months or less if the disease process runs its normal course. Beneficiaries or their designees must sign a written hospice election form with the hospice organization of choice, choosing hospice care over regular Medicare Part A covered benefits for the terminal illness. This election can be cancelled at any time.

The Medicare Part A hospice benefit *does not* include payment for room and board at a skilled nursing facility or hospice facility. However, if the beneficiary also has Medicaid benefits, Medicaid generally will cover this cost of room and board. Hospice benefits include:

▶ Physician services;

▶ Skilled nursing care;

▶ Physical, occupational, and speech therapy for purposes of symptom control or to enable the beneficiary to maintain functional skills;

▶ Durable medical equipment (DME) such as hospital bed and wheelchair rental;

▶ Pain-relieving medication and all other medications (*Note:* Medicare Part D changes some of these reimbursements);

▶ Medical social services;

▶ Home health aide and homemaker services;

▶ Medical supplies and appliances;

▶ Spiritual, grief, and loss counseling; and

▶ Short-term inpatient care not for treatment of the terminal disease.

Benefits Covered by Part A and Part B

Home Health Care Services

Medicare benefits covered by Part A and Part B pay for home health care ordered by your physician and provided by a certified Medicare home health care agency. This benefit is limited to "reasonable" and "medically necessary" intermittent care. The beneficiary may choose any Medicare-certified home health care agency, and there is no cost to the beneficiary for these home health care services. Covered home health care services include:

▶ Skilled nursing care;

▶ Physical, occupational, and speech therapy;

▶ Limited services of a home health aide to assist the beneficiary with his or her activities of daily living (ADLs);

▶ Medical social services;

▶ Medical supplies; and

▶ Equipment provided by the agency.

Medicare Benefits Covered by Part B

After the yearly deductible of $140 is met, Part B covers 80 percent of the Medicare-approved amount of the following medically necessary services and items:

▶ One-time "Welcome to Medicare" physical exam;

▶ Annual "wellness" visit, including a health risk assessment to:

  ○ Establish and update beneficiary's medical history;

  ○ Create lists of current medical providers and medications;

  ○ Conduct routine measurements such as blood pressure, blood sugar, height, weight, and body mass index (BMI);

  ○ Assess cognitive status; and

  ○ Establish a 5 to 10 year schedule for preventive services and screenings.

▶ Physicians' services;

▶ Ambulance services;

▶ Home health services prescribed by a doctor if you have not been hospitalized or met the required three-day hospitalization to trigger Medicare Part A benefits;

▶ Outpatient physical, occupational, and speech therapy (the maximum yearly benefit for 2012, unless changed by Congress, is capped at $1,880 for physical and speech therapy skilled services combined and $1,880 for occupational therapy skilled services). Services received in an outpatient hospital department are exempt from the yearly benefit caps;

▶ Rental or purchase of durable medical equipment (DME) such as walkers, wheelchairs, and all-in-one commode chairs;

▶ Prosthetic and orthotic devices and medically necessary shoes such as for diabetics;

▶ Services in an emergency room, outpatient clinic, or ambulatory surgery center;

▶ Some hospital outpatient services and supplies (such as diagnostic x-ray tests, CT scans, MRIs, and radium and radioactive isotope therapy);

▶ Effective January 1, 2011, due to the Affordable Care Act (Health Care Reform of 2010), these preventive services and tests are provided free of charge to the beneficiary at specified intervals: vaccinations (flu, pneumonia, and hepatitis B shots); mammograms; Pap smears; HIV testing; and screening tests for abdominal aortic aneurysm, bone density, cardiovascular health, colorectal cancer, diabetes, and prostate cancer;

▶ Smoking cessation counseling, as ordered by your physician for up to two cessation attempts within a 12-month period, with each cessation attempt having up to four face-to-face visits. You must be diagnosed with a smoking-related illness or using medication that may be affected by tobacco to claim this benefit;

▶ Diabetes education and some supplies;

▶ Surgical dressings, splints, and casts;

▶ Limited chiropractic care;

▶ A percentage of the cost of oxygen and equipment;

▶ Kidney dialysis services and supplies;

▶ Kidney disease education services;

▶ Medical nutritional therapy services for diabetic and kidney disease patients (effective January 1, 2011, this is provided free of charge);

▶ Blood transfusions;

▶ Cardiac rehabilitation programs;

▶ Pulmonary rehabilitation programs; and

▶ Outpatient mental health care — you pay 20 to 45 percent of the Medicare-approved amount.

Services and Supplies NOT Covered by Medicare Parts A or B

Although Medicare has broad coverage, it does not pay for many services and supplies. These non-covered services include:

▶ Acupuncture;

▶ Custodial care in a skilled nursing facility or at home;

▶ Services not "reasonable" or "medically necessary" as defined by Medicare;

▶ Room and board costs for a person on hospice who resides at a skilled nursing facility or hospice facility (see the "Hospice Services" section, above);

▶ Services the patient has no legal duty to pay for;

▶ Services paid by a governmental agency;

▶ Personal comfort items;

▶ Routine check-ups other than the "Welcome to Medicare" one-time physical examination done within the first six months of enrolling in Part B;

▶ Homemaker services;

▶ Hearing aids/examinations (Medicare does cover some hearing tests);

▶ Eye glasses/routine eye examinations;

▶ Most chiropractic services;

▶ Cosmetic surgery;

▶ Dental care;

▶ Optional private hospital rooms;

▶ Orthopedic shoes; and

▶ Health care while traveling outside the United States.

Medicare Benefits Covered by Part C (Medicare Advantage)

If you are entitled to benefits under Medicare Part A and also are enrolled under Part B, you may choose to receive Medicare Part C from a Medicare Advantage plan. Medicare Part C plans must provide the services currently available under original Medicare Parts A and B, and usually include a prescription drug benefit. These plans may offer supplemental benefits, for which a separate premium may be charged. Part C provides beneficiaries with alternatives to original fee-for-service Medicare.

Medicare Advantage plans may include health maintenance organizations (HMOs), preferred provider organizations (PPOs), and private fee-for-service plans (PFFS). The plans available to a Colorado resident are dependent upon the county of residence.

Some Medicare beneficiaries choose to enroll in Medicare Advantage plans because the monthly premiums usually are lower and additional services are provided at lower costs to them. Before enrolling in a Medicare Advantage plan, investigate whether it will meet your particular health care and rehabilitation needs.

Medicare Payment Policies

As with private insurance policies, Medicare Parts A and B have deductibles that you must pay before Medicare pays anything. Part B has a monthly premium, which is deducted from your Social Security check. Medicare Parts A and B also have co-insurance payments that go into effect after certain Medicare payments are made. You then must share some of the costs with Medicare.

Part A

The Medicare Part A hospitalization benefit has a deductible of $1,156 (in 2012) for each "benefit period" or "spell of illness." Medicare measures your use of Part A hospital insurance with "benefit periods," which also are called "spells of illness." A benefit period is a period of consecutive days during which medical benefits for covered services, with certain maximum limitations, are available to you, the beneficiary. Your first benefit period begins the first day you enter a hospital after your insurance goes into effect.

A new benefit period of 90 days of hospitalization coverage (60 full benefit days and 30 co-insurance days) begins each time you are hospitalized, if it has been at least 60 consecutive days since your last discharge from a hospital or skilled nursing facility. Each benefit period is called a "spell of illness," and the number of benefit periods or spells of illness is unlimited. There is a deductible of $1,156 for each new benefit period or spell of illness. For example, if you have two hospitalizations, or spells of illness, in 2012, your total deductible amount would be $2,312.

Hospital Care

The Medicare Part A benefit allows you to receive up to 90 days of hospital care for each spell of illness. The following is what you must pay:

▶ For the first 60 consecutive days, Medicare requires you to pay only the deductible for the spell of illness, which in 2012 is $1,156. Medicare pays the remaining covered expenses.

▶ For the next 30 days (days 61 to 90), Medicare requires that you pay a co-payment or co-insurance charge for each day you are in the hospital. For 2012, this daily co-insurance rate is $289. Medicare pays the remaining covered expenses.

▶ Each beneficiary has a lifetime reserve of 60 days for days 91 to 150. This benefit is not renewable. Any number of the lifetime reserve days can be used for any spell of illness, up to the maximum the beneficiary has. So, after day 90, you may use some or all of your 60 lifetime reserve days. The 2012 co-insurance daily charge for each lifetime reserve day is $578. Medicare pays the remaining covered expenses for each day, up to a 60-day maximum. A beneficiary can elect not to use these lifetime reserve days.

Skilled Nursing Care

Medicare Part A hospitalization insurance benefits provide up to 100 days of inpatient extended care benefit coverage for skilled nursing and skilled therapy services. However, there is no absolute right to payment for all 100 days unless they are "reasonable" and "medically necessary."

Medicare Part A pays 100 percent of all costs for the first 20 days of covered skilled nursing care and skilled therapy services in a Medicare-certified facility after you are discharged from a hospital, following the required stay of at least three consecutive days, which does not include the day of discharge. Your care must begin within 30 days of the hospital discharge. There are a few exceptions to this 30-day admit rule.

Days 21 through 100 require a daily co-insurance rate of $144.50, and Medicare pays the remaining covered expenses. After 100 days, you are responsible for payment of the full amount and Medicare pays nothing. However, you may be eligible for Medicaid payment for long-term care and during the application process (see Chapter 4, "Medicaid"). The level of care requirements for skilled nursing facility coverage are very restrictive. Rarely do individuals receive the full 100 days of coverage.

Home Health Visits

Home care services must start within 14 days of your discharge from the inpatient hospital or skilled nursing facility. Medicare Parts A and B pay for the *full* approved cost of home health visits by a Medicare-certified home health agency following a treatment plan of care prepared by a nurse or a physical, occupational, or speech therapist and approved by your physician. Strict requirements limit the coverage of home health services. The person receiving services must be "confined to her or his home" or "home bound" in order to receive home health services. This means it would take considerable and taxing effort to leave home. The person may be able to leave home for doctor appointments, an occasional walk or drive, or other limited trips outside the home. Another requirement is that the services are needed only on an intermittent basis, rather than continually.

Home health care agencies *must* give the beneficiary a minimum of two days' notice of their intent to either cut back or terminate services. This notice must also explain the procedure for seeking review of the termination or cut back in services. If Medicare refuses to cover you for these types of services, you have a right to appeal this decision. You should appeal any discharge or termination of services decision with which you do not agree. You may want to ask an attorney or someone else knowledgeable about Medicare to help you through the appeal process.

Hospice Care

The usual deductibles and co-payments do not apply to hospice care. Unless your prescriptions are covered from some other source or Medicare Part D, you pay 5 percent of the cost for prescription drugs, up to $5 per outpatient prescription. You also pay 5 percent of the cost of respite care, up to a maximum equal to the yearly inpatient hospital deductible.

Part B

Medicare Part B payment rules for covered medical services:

▶ Services must be reasonable and medically necessary, as defined by Medicare; and

▶ Medicare pays 80 percent of the approved charge after you pay your yearly deductible of $140 in 2012, a decrease of $22 from the 2011 premium. You pay the remaining 20 percent, plus any difference between the doctor's charge and the approved charge.

The approved charge is the amount that Medicare considers to be the value of the services you received. It is not always the same as the amount that the provider bills you for the services.

Medicare Payment Methods

Under Medicare Part A, you do not have to send in any bills you receive from a participating hospital, skilled nursing facility, or home health agency. The health care provider will file the claim for you, and Medicare will pay its share directly to the provider. You will then receive a Medicare Summary Notice (MSN) explaining what Medicare paid. If you disagree with this payment, you have the right to appeal (see section 2-3, "Appeal Rights").

Payment is made two ways under Medicare Part B Medical Insurance:

1) **Assigned Claims.** Participating physicians and health care providers who accept assignment will bill Medicare directly. You are responsible only for 20 percent of the approved Medicare Part B charge and not for any additional amount above the approved charge. If the doctor is a participating physician who has agreed to take Medicare assignment, then he or she has agreed not to charge above the

Medicare approved rate, and also to accept the Medicare approved rate as payment in full. The simplest way to find out if the doctor is a participating physician who has agreed to take Medicare assignment is to ask in advance.

2) **Non-Assigned Claims.** With this method, the physician or health care provider sends in a completed claim form, but the payment from Medicare is paid directly to you. You are then responsible for paying the provider the full amount of the bill for the services provided to you. Under this method, a physician or health care provider may bill you for the full charges, even if it is more than the Medicare approved charge.

With non-assigned claims, you are responsible for payment of the difference between the Medicare approved charge and the actual charge. For example, if the bill was $100 and the Medicare approved charge was $90, you would be responsible for the difference of $10 ($100 minus $90), plus 20 percent of the approved charge (20 percent times $90 equals $18), for a total payment of $28. The doctor cannot charge more than 115 percent of the approved charge.

Under either payment system, as Medicare Part B pays a maximum of 80 percent of the approved charge, you must pay at least 20 percent of the approved charge plus any unpaid part of your $140 (for 2012) annual Medicare Part B deductible. You pay your share directly to the physician or health care provider.

The Medicare Prescription Drug Plan: Part D (Under Title 16 of the Social Security Act)

On January 1, 2006, the Medicare prescription drug plan began. Medicare has contracted with private companies to offer this drug coverage. Colorado currently has 28 stand-alone prescription drug plans (plans that only cover drugs) provided by private insurance companies and approved by Medicare. These plans have varying premiums, deductibles, and benefits. (For more information, go to www.dora.state.co.us/insurance/senior/senior.htm; click on "Medicare Supplements," then "Medicare Supplement Insurance: Medigap Options for Colorado Consumers.") There are 33 Medicare Advantage (HMO, PPO, PFFS) plans and other Medicare health plans that provide prescription drug coverage in conjunction with health care coverage. These companies offer a variety of options, with different covered prescriptions and different costs. Medicare prescription drug plans are voluntary. If you want to participate, you must choose a plan offering the coverage that best meets your needs and then enroll. In most cases, there is no automatic enrollment to get a Medicare prescription drug plan.

Medicare prescription drug plans vary, but in general, this is how they work. When you join, you will pay a monthly premium (cost varies from $20 to $246.20 for Colorado plans) in addition to any premiums for Medicare Part A and Part B. Medicare prescription drug plans can offer basic coverage or more generous coverage for higher premiums. Joining is your choice. However, just as described above for enrollment in Part B, if you do not join when you are first eligible, you may have to pay a higher premium if you choose to join later. You will have to pay this higher premium for as long as you have a Medicare prescription drug plan.

Enrollment

To enroll, you must be eligible for Medicare Part A or Part B. You can first enroll three months before you become eligible for Medicare and until three months after you become eligible for Medicare. This is called the "initial enrollment period." Enrolling is your choice. Contact a counselor at the Colorado Senior Health Insurance Assistance Program (SHIP; (888) 696-7213) to assist you with the selection and enrollment process.

You can also find up-to-date Medicare information and answers to your questions anytime on Medicare's official website, www.medicare.gov. Or, you can call (800) MEDICARE ((800) 633-4227; TTY (877) 486-2048). This toll-free help line is available 24 hours a day, seven days a week to answer your questions. *Note:* after your initial enrollment period, you can change your plan during the open enrollment period, which is from November 15 to December 31 each year. Your new Medicare prescription drug plan will begin January 1 of the following year.

Plan Costs to You

In 2012, the standard drug benefit plan includes your payment of an annual maximum deductible of $320 (the Colorado plans range from $0 to $320) prior to payment of any prescription drug costs. Also, effective January 1, 2012, higher income Medicare beneficiaries will have an income-related adjustment to their Medicare Part D premiums. This new income means adjustment is estimated to affect less than 5 percent of Medicare beneficiaries. Refer to the "Medicare Part B and Part D Premiums" rate chart in section 2-1 for premium amounts.

▶ If your yearly drug costs are $0 to $320 (or your deductible), you pay 100 percent of these costs.

▶ If your yearly drug costs are $320.01 to $2,930 in the initial coverage, you pay 25 percent of your yearly costs and your plan pays the other 75 percent (*e.g.*, you would pay $632.50 for $2,530 in prescriptions).

▶ If your yearly drug costs are $2,930.01 to $4,700, you pay 100 percent of your drug costs for the amount between $2,930.01 and $4,700. This is called the "donut hole," "coverage gap," or "coverage in the gap." However, effective January 1, 2011, the Affordable Care Act legislation (health care reform) works to decrease this coverage gap by providing a "Medicare Gap Discount Program." In 2012, it provides a 50 percent discount on name-brand formulary drugs, and a 14 percent discount on all generic formulary medications from manufacturers who have agreed to participate in this discount program.

▶ For catastrophic coverage, in 2012, when your total expense on formulary drugs reaches $4,700 (this is the total retail cost of all covered medications), you pay the higher of 5 percent of your drug costs or $2.60 per month for generic drugs and $6.50 per month for name-brand drugs for the rest of the calendar year, and your plan pays the rest.

Additional Low-Income Assistance

The 2012 monthly income figures for Low-Income Subsidy eligibility are not available as of this writing, as the 2012 federal poverty guidelines have not been released. The 2011 federal poverty guidelines are applicable by law until March 1, 2012, as are the following 2011 income figures. The maximum income eligibility figure is set at 150 percent of the federal poverty guideline for an individual. It is anticipated that the 2012 figures for income will be close to or the same as the 2011 figures, due to poor economic conditions. Look for any income figure changes on or after April 1, 2012.

If your monthly income is below $1,361 ($16,332 annual income) for a single person or $1,839 ($22,068 annual income) if you are married and living with your spouse, you may qualify for extra financial assistance through the Low-Income Prescription Drug Subsidy Program. Slightly higher income levels may apply if you provide half-support to other family members living with you, or if you work or reside in Alaska or Hawaii.

Effective January 1, 2012, if your resources (including your bank accounts, stocks, bonds, IRAs, mutual funds, life insurance policies with face values over $1,500, and real estate, but not counting your home, car, burial plots, or irrevocable burial plan contracts) are less than $13,410 (for a single person) or less than $26,120 (for a married couple), you may qualify for extra help paying for your Medicare prescription drug costs. You can apply for this Low-Income Subsidy through the SSA or your State Medical Assistance Office. If the SSA can determine your eligibility by its internal records, an application will be sent to you. For others, you must apply.

The amount of subsidy you get depends on your income and resources. You still must join a Medicare prescription drug plan for Medicare to pay for any of your drug costs.

If you qualify for the Low-Income Subsidy or "Extra Help" program, you will have continuous drug coverage and will pay only a small amount for your prescriptions. The SSA (at (800) 772-1213, TTY at (800) 325-0778, or www.ssa.gov) can provide more information on the Low-Income Subsidy for prescription drug costs and information on how to apply for it.

2-3. Appeal Rights

Medicare beneficiaries are required to receive written notice of termination of services, non-coverage, and cutbacks in coverage pursuant to Medicare Parts A and B. Original Medicare Parts A and B Fee-For-Service Plans have five levels of appeals of the denial of payment of services. (*See* www.cms.hhs.gov/OrgMedFFSAppeals; see also www.medicareadvocacy.org for numerous articles.) The notice should state the appeal procedure you need to follow.

Most appeals must be written, and must be filed within the number of days stated on the notice. It is recommended that all appeals and related correspondence be sent via certified mail, with a return receipt requested, so you have proof that you sent your appeal and it was done on time. Usually the appeal forms are included with the notices. Otherwise, the appeal forms can be obtained from the Medicare website at www.medicare. gov. *Note:* if you have a Medicare Advantage Plan (Medicare Part C), you need to read your

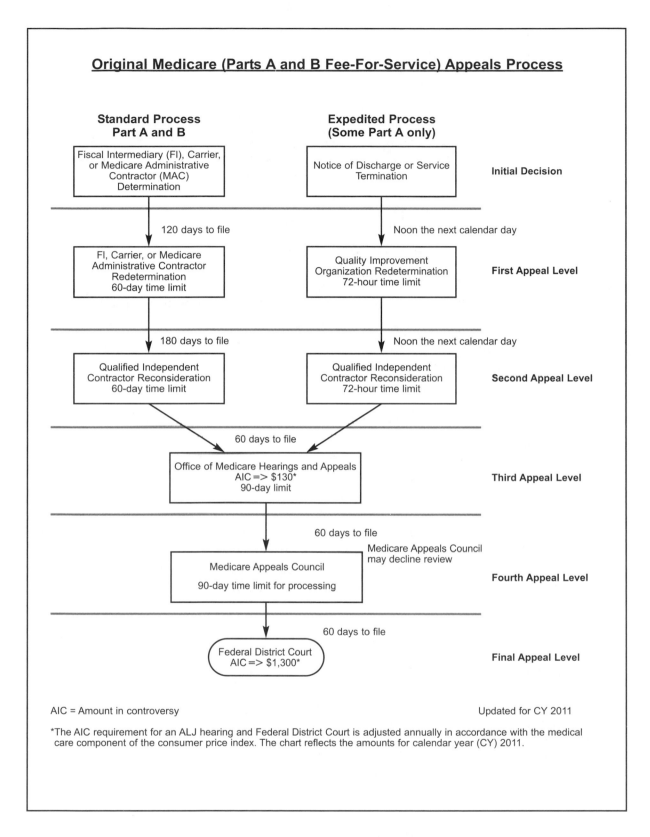

Original Medicare (Parts A and B Fee-For-Service) Appeals Process

Standard Process Part A and B	Expedited Process (Some Part A only)	
Fiscal Intermediary (FI), Carrier, or Medicare Administrative Contractor (MAC) Determination	Notice of Discharge or Service Termination	**Initial Decision**
120 days to file	*Noon the next calendar day*	
FI, Carrier, or Medicare Administrative Contractor Redetermination 60-day time limit	Quality Improvement Organization Redetermination 72-hour time limit	**First Appeal Level**
180 days to file	*Noon the next calendar day*	
Qualified Independent Contractor Reconsideration 60-day time limit	Qualified Independent Contractor Reconsideration 72-hour time limit	**Second Appeal Level**

60 days to file

Office of Medicare Hearings and Appeals
AIC => $130*
90-day limit

Third Appeal Level

60 days to file

Medicare Appeals Council may decline review

Medicare Appeals Council

90-day time limit for processing

Fourth Appeal Level

60 days to file

Federal District Court
AIC => $1,300*

Final Appeal Level

AIC = Amount in controversy

Updated for CY 2011

*The AIC requirement for an ALJ hearing and Federal District Court is adjusted annually in accordance with the medical care component of the consumer price index. The chart reflects the amounts for calendar year (CY) 2011.

Diagram available at www.cms.hhs.gov/OrgMedFFSAppeals, under "Downloads."

plan materials carefully to learn how to file an appeal and whether you have the right to an "expedited review" or fast appeal.

Parts A and B

Original Medicare Parts A and B plans send you a Medicare Summary Notice (MSN) every three months. This MSN lists all the services you have had and states whether Medicare paid for these services. It also states your appeal rights. If Medicare denies payment of your claim, you may ask for an informal review or redetermination of the decision from the Medicare contractor by:

1) Circling the items you disagree with on the MSN;

2) Writing an explanation on the MSN, which is signed and dated;

3) Including your telephone number;

4) Attaching any supporting documentation to the redetermination request;

5) Sending the MSN or a copy by certified mail, return receipt requested, to the Fiscal Intermediary (FI), Carrier, or Medicare Administrative Contractor (MAC) listed in the appeals section of the MSN; and

6) Keeping a copy of all documents you send.

You must ask for that review within 120 days of the date of the decision in the MSN. If you still disagree with Medicare's decision of redetermination, you have 180 days from the date you receive this second denial of payment to submit a written request for review and reconsideration to the Qualified Independent Contractor (QIC). This is the second level of appeal. If you disagree with the independent review, and the amount in dispute is $130 or more, you may ask for a formal hearing from the Office of Medicare Hearings and Appeals from an Administrative Law Judge (ALJ). This is the third level of appeal. You must do so within 60 days of Medicare's review decision. If you still disagree with the decision of the Office of Medicare Hearings and Appeals, you then can appeal within 60 days to the Medicare Appeals Council, which ultimately may decline a review. This is the fourth level of appeal.

Your fifth and final avenue of appeal is to the federal district court for judicial review if the amount in dispute is $1,300 or more for appeals filed in 2012. If both you and Medicare maximize the time limits allowed for sending an appeal and giving a redetermination, your final appeal to the federal district court can take almost 23 months. Considering the present caseload of Colorado federal district court judges, it probably will take in excess of a year for your appeal to be determined, unless your appeal can be expedited.

To appeal a denial of Medicare approval for a hospital admission, continued hospital stay, discharge, or termination of services, call the Colorado Foundation for Medical Care at (303) 695-3300, or (800) 727-7086 outside Denver.

If you feel your Medicare-covered services from a hospital, skilled nursing facility, home health care agency, comprehensive outpatient rehabilitation center, or hospice are ending too soon, you might have the right to a "fast" or "expedited" appeal with an independent reviewer to determine if your services should continue. You have by noon on the next calendar day after receiving the Notice of Discharge or Service Termination to appeal this decision for the Quality Improvement Organization Redetermination, which has 72 hours (3 days) to make its decision. Your second level of appeal is to the Qualified Independent Contractor and must be done within 72 hours of the first denial. It also has 72 hours to give its decision.

If you still have concerns with this decision, your third level of appeal is to file an appeal within 60 days to the Office of Medicare Hearings and Appeals. You then follow the procedure and timelines as stated for a regular appeal. The Colorado Senior Health Insurance Assistance Program (SHIP), (888) 696-7213, (303) 894-7944, or (800) 930-3745 (toll-free), can assist you with filing an appeal.

Supplemental Health Insurance (Medigap)

Since Medicare does not pay all your medical or long-term care expenses, private insurance companies sell insurance to supplement Medicare, which is known as "Medigap" coverage. Supplemental Health Insurance is especially important to have for covering your daily co-insurance charges and deductibles, such as for hospitalization in days 61 through 150, skilled nursing facility days 21 through 100, and Medicare Part B 20 percent beneficiary responsibility for charges. It is highly recommended coverage. See Chapter 3, "Health Insurance Beyond Medicare," for information on Medigap or supplemental coverage. There is a six month open enrollment period starting the first month you are 65 years old *and* enrolled in Medicare Part B.

Medicare Information Resources

If you need help or more information, an excellent Medicare resource is the non-profit organization, the Center for Medicare Advocacy, Inc. Its website is www.medicareadvocacy.org. It has a large library of excellent articles on a variety of Medicare topics.

You also can look at www.medicare.gov. This is Medicare's official consumer website, where you can find the most up-to-date Medicare information and answers to your questions anytime. You also can call (800) MEDICARE ((800) 633-4227; (877) 486-2048 for TTY users). This toll-free help-line is available 24 hours a day, 7 days a week, and has customer service representatives to answer your questions in either English or Spanish. These customer service representatives, however, may not be willing or able to answer any questions from currently non-eligible Medicare beneficiaries, such as family members of a beneficiary or educators.

The SSA sends free booklets providing detailed information on Medicare when you enroll. Also, the SSA provides periodic updates to information concerning Medicare Part A and Part B, as these programs are subject to change and review by Congress and the Centers for Medicare and Medicaid Services, formerly Health Care Financing Administration (HCFA).

The "Medicare & You 2012" handbook should have been mailed to each Medicare beneficiary between late October and late November 2011. You can also view it at www.medicare.gov (Click on "Resource Locator," then "Medicare & You Handbook," or call (800) MEDICARE ((800) 633-4227) to request a copy. TTY users should call (877) 486-2048.)

2-4. Resources

See section 5-6, "Resources," in Chapter 5, "Government Programs and Financial Assistance," for county department of social services offices. See Appendix B, "Legal Resources," for a list of legal aid services in various Colorado locations. See section 11-6, "Resources," in Chapter 11, "Arm Yourself with Consumer Protection Information," for a list of Area Agencies on Aging. For more information about Medicare and Medicaid, call your nearest senior center.

Medicare Information:

U.S. Department of Health and Human Services
Provides counseling and information on Medicare benefits, eligibility guidelines, etc.
200 Independence Ave., SW
Washington, D.C. 20201
(877) 696-6775
www.hhs.gov

The Center for Medicare Advocacy, Inc.
National nonprofit organization and excellent Medicare resource.
National office:
P.O. Box 350
Willimantic, CT 06226
(860) 456-7790
www.medicareadvocacy.org

Washington, D.C. office:
1025 Connecticut Ave. NW, Ste. 709
Washington, D.C. 20036
(202) 293-5760

Centers for Medicare and Medicaid Services
7500 Security Blvd.
Baltimore, MD 21244
www.cms.gov

Medicare Claims and Helpline
(800) 633-4227
(877) 486-2048 (TTY)
www.medicare.gov

Social Security Administration
(800) 722-1213
(800) 325-0778 (TTY)
www.ssa.gov

Tricare for Life
> (866) 773-0404
> (877) 363-1303 (pharmacy)
> www.tricare.mil/mybenefit

Health Insurance Counseling for Information:

Colorado Senior Health Insurance Assistance Program (SHIP)
Provides Medicare denial of services appeal filing assistance and answers questions about Medigap policies, long-term care insurance, Medicare rights and protection, and Medicare health plan choices.
> 1560 Broadway, Ste. 850
> Denver, CO 80202
> (888) 696-7213
> www.dora.state.co.us/insurance/senior/senior.htm

AARP — Colorado Chapter
Provides counseling and information on health insurance to AARP members.
> 303 E. 17th Ave., Ste. 510
> Denver, CO 80203
> (866) 554-5376 (Colorado)
> (888) 687-2277 (National)
> www.aarp.org/states/co

Colorado Division of Insurance
Provides information on Medicare benefits, Medigap, etc.
> 1560 Broadway, Ste. 850
> Denver, CO 80202
> (303) 894-7499
> (800) 930-3745
> www.dora.state.co.us/insurance

Colorado Foundation for Medical Care
> 23 Inverness Wy. E., Ste. 100
> Englewood, CO 80112-5708
> (303) 695-3300
> www.cfmc.org

Colorado Gerontological Society and Senior Answers and Services
Provides counseling regarding health insurance issues, Medicare, etc.
> 3006 E. Colfax Ave.
> Denver, CO 80206
> (303) 333-3482
> www.senioranswers.org

Chapter 3

Health Insurance Beyond Medicare

John J. Campbell, Esq.
Law Offices of John J. Campbell, P.C.

Michele M. Lawonn, J.D., P.T.
Medical-Legal Advocates, LLC

SYNOPSIS

3-1. Know Medicare Gaps

Though most retired Americans over age 65 are covered by Medicare, they need to know its benefits and shortcomings.

Here are some of the major gaps left by Parts A and B of Medicare coverage. You must pay for:

▶ The inpatient hospital deductible for each benefit period;

▶ Daily co-insurance for long inpatient hospital stays per benefit period;

▶ Inpatient psychiatric care beyond 190 lifetime days;

▶ Daily co-insurance for Medicare-certified skilled nursing beyond 20 days per benefit period;

▶ All nursing home care other than Medicare's maximum of 100 skilled days;

▶ Home health care that is not skilled;

▶ The annual deductible for outpatient services;

▶ Co-insurance of 20 percent on outpatient hospital, doctors', and suppliers' services;

▶ Amounts in excess of Medicare-approved charges (up to 115 percent);

▶ Medical expenses while traveling abroad;

▶ Nonprescription drugs;

▶ Routine care, such as annual physicals (in 2011, most preventive care is covered);

▶ Dental exams;

▶ Eyeglasses;

▶ Hearing aids;

▶ Equipment that is considered non-medical or custodial; and

▶ Physical, occupational, or speech therapy after a maintenance level is attained and skilled therapy services are no longer indicated.

3-2. Options for Supplemental Medicare

To fill these gaps, many retirees obtain additional insurance coverage. Options include:

▶ Purchasing Medicare supplemental (Medigap) insurance;

▶ Enrolling in a Medicare Advantage plan, such as a Health Maintenance Organization (HMO);

▶ Continuing coverage to complement Medicare under an employer's group retirement plan;

▶ Appling for federal or state assistance programs, if eligible. This includes Qualified Medicare Beneficiary (QMB), Specified Low-income Medicare Beneficiary (SLMB), Qualified Individual 1 (QI-1), as well as standard Medicaid programs;

▶ Using military or veterans' hospitals, TRICARE for Life, if eligible;

▶ Purchasing long-term care insurance to cover nursing home and home health care costs; or

▶ Paying expenses out-of-pocket.

Some of these options are considered in more detail in the material that follows. State assistance programs are covered in Chapter 4, "Medicaid," and federal programs are covered in Chapter 2, "Medicare."

3-3. Supplemental Insurance

Standardized Plans

Medigap, or Medicare supplemental insurance, is a specialized type of insurance that coordinates benefits with original Medicare. It specifically fills some of the gaps left by Medicare, such as deductible and co-insurance, and, in some cases, may add additional benefits.

In Colorado, approximately 35 companies market these plans. There are 20 Medicare Advantage (health maintenance organization (HMO), preferred provider organization (PPO), or private fee-for-service (PFFS) plans) or other Medicare health plans that provide prescription drug coverage with health coverage. Federal law mandates that each state adopt standardized Medigap benefit packages. Colorado permits the sale of 10 standardized plans that must be labeled Plan A, Plan B, Plan C, and so on, through Plan N (*see* Exhibit 3A of this chapter). Any company selling Medigap is required to offer Plan A. Other plans are marketed at the company's option. Policies purchased before the standardization (May 1993 in Colorado) are subject to standards in effect when purchased.

Effective January 1, 2006, new Medigap policies may no longer provide prescription drug coverage.

3-4. Protecting Customers

Colorado has regulations that govern Medigap policies, including:

▶ Each applicant must receive an outline of coverage.

▶ A free-look period of 30 days is provided, during which time the applicant may cancel the policy and receive a full refund.

▶ The maximum pre-existing medical condition waiting period is six months from the date the policy is in force.

▶ If the applicant is replacing a Medicare supplement policy, no waiting period by the replacement insurer is allowed if it has already been met.

▶ Medicare supplement policies must be guaranteed renewable for life. This means that companies cannot cancel or fail to renew a policy for any reason other than failure to pay premiums or misrepresentation.

▶ Agents are prohibited from selling duplicative insurance, using high-pressure tactics, and pressuring consumers to switch policies.

▶ A six-month open enrollment period exists when an individual first signs up for Medicare Part B (including disabled individuals under age 65), during which time Medigap coverage cannot be denied because of pre-existing conditions. Disabled individuals have a second open enrollment period when they turn age 65.

3-5. How to Compare Policies

Since all Medigap policies are standardized, comparing policies is fairly easy. When comparing policies, consider:

▶ **Cost.** Premiums differ among companies for the same benefits, so it is important to compare premiums. Most companies increase premiums at some defined anniversary as the policyholder ages. In addition, most companies raise premiums annually as their costs go up.

▶ **Financial stability of the company.** You can call rating companies such as Weiss Research Inc., Standard & Poor's, Moody's, Duff & Phelps, or A.M. Best Company to check the financial rating of a company, or check the resources at your public library or on the Internet.

▶ **Waiting period.** By law the maximum waiting period for pre-existing conditions is six months. Some companies have shorter waits; others have no wait. In some situations, when an individual has prior creditable coverage, a company may have to waive some or all of the waiting period.

▶ **Customer service.** Learn how efficiently claims are processed by asking friends who have filed claims with that company or ask your doctor's bookkeeper.

▶ **Health underwriting standards.** A company may refuse to issue a policy because of a pre-existing health condition, except during the open enrollment period (and in some other limited situations).

3-6. Medicare Advantage Plans

Starting in 2011, the annual open enrollment period is from October 15 through December 7 for Medicare beneficiaries to supplement Medicare through one of the Medicare Advantage plans. Unlike "original" Medicare, these plans require the beneficiary to assign his or her Medicare benefits to an insurance company, for example, a health maintenance organization (HMO), and agree to receive all Medicare benefits, gap-filling benefits, and any extras such as prescription drugs from a network of providers set by the insurer. Medicare Advantage plans generally do not provide the same level of skilled therapy rehabilitation services (physical, occupational, and speech therapy) as original Medicare fee-for-service plans.

Currently in Colorado, the Medicare Advantage plans available can be HMO plans, preferred provider organization (PPO) plans, or private fee-for-service (PFFS) plans. However, only HMO plans will be discussed in this chapter.

Health Maintenance Organizations

HMOs provide or arrange for health services for a set monthly fee. Most Medicare HMOs have contractual arrangements with the federal government under which the HMO agrees to provide Medicare and supplemental benefits in return for a fixed payment from the government for each enrollee. The enrollee continues to pay the Medicare Part B monthly premium, as well as a monthly premium to the HMO, if any.

Currently, most Medicare HMOs have a lock-in feature. That means if the patient goes to a non-HMO doctor or hospital, neither the HMO nor Medicare will pay the bills. A few HMOs omit this lock-in feature, which means if the patient receives services outside the HMO network, Medicare, not the HMO, will pay the balance left by Medicare.

To be eligible to enroll in an HMO, a Medicare beneficiary must meet the following requirements:

▶ Have Medicare Parts A and B, and live in an area served by the HMO.

▶ Not have end-stage kidney disease (ESRD).

To disenroll from an HMO and return to standard Medicare, the beneficiary must notify the HMO in writing at least one month in advance.

3-7. Employer Group Health Plans

Many retired individuals who have Medicare have additional health insurance coverage resulting from their own or their spouse's employment. These employer group health plans (EGHPs) are secondary to Medicare. That means that Medicare pays benefits first, and the EGHP pays what is not covered by Medicare. EGHPs are not strictly regulated by the states, as are Medigap policies. This means that EGHP benefits can differ from plan to plan and are not subject to minimum benefit requirements.

Since some plans are excellent, it may be prudent to keep the EGHP as a back-up to Medicare if the premium is low and the benefits are good, especially prescription drugs and dental care. However, some EGHPs pay few benefits because the complex coordination of benefit formulas are difficult to understand, and benefits change annually.

3-8. Long-Term Care Insurance

Long-term care is the most common catastrophic health expense. It can range from simple help with activities of daily living at home, such as bathing and dressing, to highly skilled nursing care. Though families continue to provide the majority of services to elderly relatives in the home, long-term care also is provided by nursing homes, senior centers, home health agencies, adult day care centers, and assisted living facilities. It is estimated that more than 25 percent of those people who live to age 65 eventually will need some kind of long-term care. Half will stay in a nursing home less than 90 days and the other half will stay at least several months.

Depending on location and quality, annual costs in a nursing home easily can exceed $60,000. Medicare pays only a small percentage of nursing home costs since it only covers short-term skilled care, usually following hospitalization. Medigap insurance and employer health insurance plans seldom pay anything toward nursing home care. Nationally, when their assets have been spent down to the qualifying level, almost half of nursing home residents eventually are covered by Medicaid (see Chapter 4, "Medicaid").

It is possible to buy insurance specifically for nursing home care. New federal tax laws give favorable treatment to those who purchase this type of insurance. Long-term care insurance pays the policyholder a specified amount for each day that he or she qualifies for benefits. Depending on the policy, it may make payments when the individual needs home care, lives in an assisted living facility, attends adult day care, or resides in a nursing facility.

Some of the variables to consider when shopping for long-term care insurance are:

▶ **Age.** The risk of being admitted to a nursing home increases rapidly after age 75. Some insurance companies will not offer long-term coverage to persons older than 80 or 82.

▶ **How benefits are paid.** Most long-term care insurance pays a fixed daily amount rather than a percentage of the costs. Daily benefits can range from $50 per day to $250 per day. Many policies pay actual costs up to the daily benefit selected by the policyholder, while other plans pay the full daily benefit selected.

▶ **Covered settings.** Companies generally offer coverage for home care, assisted living, and nursing home care. The best coverage covers all these living settings.

▶ **Benefit triggers.** Under some contracts, benefits are paid when care is medically necessary. Others pay when the policyholder loses the ability to perform certain activities of daily living: dressing (should include braces and artificial limbs), bathing, toileting, eating (should include taking medications), transferring (moving in and out of a chair), remaining continent, or when the person suffers cognitive impairment.

▶ **Length of coverage.** Purchasers select coverage for a specific period of time, perhaps only for two years or indefinitely. The insurance company pays the daily benefit for the number of years selected when the policyholder meets the requirements for services.

▶ **Elimination of "waiting" period.** (Also called a deductible period.) This refers to the number of days the individual must qualify for benefits before the insurance will begin to pay benefits. Most plans offer choices ranging from no wait to a one-year wait. The longer the wait, the lower the premium.

▶ **Health underwriting.** Most companies ask very detailed health questions before deciding to insure the applicant. They are especially sensitive to such risks as heart problems, leukemia, rheumatoid arthritis, Alzheimer's disease, Parkinson's disease, people already bedridden, and people with known mental or physical disorders. Companies would rather refuse business than assume a bad risk. Policies can be later canceled if patient information is found to be inaccurate or fraudulent.

▶ **Renewability of policies and premiums.** Long-term care policies issued in Colorado beginning July 1, 1990, must be guaranteed renewable. This means the company will not cancel or fail to renew the policy as long as the insured pays the premiums on time. Policies issued in Colorado prior to 1990 might not be guaranteed renewable. The premium is determined by the applicant's age at the time the policy is issued, and usually does not increase because the policyholder ages, although it may eventually be raised for everyone.

▶ **Inflation protection.** Consumers can purchase benefit increase options to protect against the rising costs of long-term care. This kind of protection increases premiums but is a very important benefit.

For more information, see Chapter 7, "Long-Term Care Insurance."

3-9. Resources

Colorado Division of Insurance
    1560 Broadway, Ste. 850
    Denver, CO 80202
    (303) 894-7499
    (800) 930-3745
    www.dora.state.co.us/insurance

Colorado Senior Health Insurance Assistance Program
    (888) 696-7213
    www.dora.state.co.us/insurance/senior/senior.htm

Exhibit 3A.
Benefits of the Twelve Standardized Medicare Supplemental (Medigap) Insurance Plans

MEDIGAP BENEFITS BY TYPE OF PLAN	A	B	C	D	F**	G	K	L	M	N
Part A Coinsurance days 61-90	X	X	X	X	X	X	X	X	X	X
Part A Coinsurance 60 lifetime reserve days	X	X	X	X	X	X	X	X	X	X
100% of Medicare covered expenses for additional 365 lifetime days	X	X	X	X	X	X	X	X	X	X
Part B Coinsurance	X	X	X	X	X	X	50%***	75%***	X	X
Reasonable cost of 3 pints of blood	X	X	X	X	X	X	50%***	75%***	X	X
Part A Inpatient Hospital Deductible		X	X	X	X	X	50%***	75%***	50%	X
Part A Skilled Nursing Facility Coinsurance			X	X	X	X	50%***	75%***	X	X
Part B Deductible			X		X					
Foreign Travel Emergency			X	X	X	X				
At-Home Recovery				X		X				
Part B Excess Charges					100%	X				
Preventive Care							X	X		
Prescription Drugs*										
Part A Hospice & Respite Care							50%***	75%***	X	X

* The prescription drug benefits may no longer be offered after December 31, 2005.

** Medigap F policies are also available with high deductible options.

*** 100% of all Part A & Part B Coinsurance after annual out of pocket ($4,660 for K; $2,330 for L).

Chapter 4

Medicaid

John J. Campbell, Esq.
Law Offices of John J. Campbell, P.C.

SYNOPSIS

The purpose of this chapter is to clarify important information you need to know about Medicaid. It will answer your questions about eligibility requirements and enrollment processes.

4-1. Medicaid

Medicaid is a federal-state medical assistance program for low-income recipients of public benefit programs. Medicaid provides more complete coverage than does Medicare, without significant payments from the beneficiaries. Only low-income persons with limited resources who are elderly, blind, disabled, or are low-income families can receive Medicaid.

Who Receives Medicaid?

Medicaid was created as an add-on health benefit to two welfare programs: Supplemental Security Income (SSI) and Aid to Families with Dependent Children (AFDC). AFDC was replaced by the Temporary Assistance for Needy Families (TANF) program. Recipients of either SSI or TANF, or those who would qualify for AFDC if it still existed, are eligible for Medicaid, as are Old Age Pension (OAP) recipients who are disabled or more than 64 years of age. People who would continue to receive those benefits except for earned income or cost of living increases often continue to receive Medicaid. Women with breast or cervical cancer may also qualify if they lack health insurance.

The eligibility rules for elderly or disabled people generally use the SSI income and resource rules. Total resources (bank accounts, property, etc.) may not exceed $2,000 for an individual, or $3,000 for a married couple. Some property does not count as a resource, like your residence, your car, some funeral items or plans, wedding jewelry, and life insurance with a cash value of $1,500 or less. For long-term care (see section 4-2, below), the income cap is three times the SSI payment standard for one, or $2,067 per month for 2012. For additional income and resource rules for couples, see "Spousal Protection" in section 4-2, below.

There are many additional eligibility rules, including citizenship requirements, special requirements for long-term care, and severe transfer restrictions (see "Estate Planning" in section 4-2, below).

What Services Are Covered?

In Colorado, Medicaid covers most necessary services, including hospital, nursing home, physician, prescriptions, medical supplies and equipment, skilled home care (nurse or Certified Nursing Assistant required), and assistance with transportation. In addition, non-skilled or personal in-home services are provided by Home and Community Based Services (HCBS) programs for specific groups such as the elderly and people with developmental disabilities, mental illnesses, AIDS, or other chronic disabilities.

While there is a co-payment for some services ($.50 to $10 or more in Colorado), Medicaid generally pays the entire charge approved by the Medicaid program. Additionally, most nursing home recipients must pay all but $50 per month of their income toward their care. Medicaid is the payor of last resort, so other insurance, including Medicare, must pay first.

How to Apply for Medicaid

Apply for Medicaid at your county Department of Social or Human Services. If you are receiving SSI, bring your SSI award letter. If you are eligible for SSI but are not receiving it, first go to your local Social Security office to apply for SSI. You can apply for OAP and Medicaid at the county Department of Social Services at the same time. Nursing home residents apply in the county in which the nursing home is located.

You will need to be able to verify income, resources, age, and disability, if any. You should bring the following documents with you:

▶ Proof of all income, including investment income, if any;

▶ Bank statements for all accounts;

▶ Copies of title or other proof of ownership of any real estate or other assets;

▶ Copies of life and health insurance policies;

▶ Proof of age, such as a birth certificate; and

▶ Medicare and Social Security cards.

While you may be asked to come back for another appointment with any documentation that is lacking, you have a right to sign the first page of the application when you first come in. This serves as your application date. If you cannot travel to the office, a responsible person can apply on your behalf.

Nursing home residents should tell the nursing home staff that they are applying for Medicaid. The law prohibits a nursing facility from requiring a third-party guarantee of payment.

4-2. Long-Term Care

Nursing home and Home and Community Based Services (HCBS) are available only when there is a medical need for nursing home-level care. HCBS may be available to help a recipient stay in his or her home, but only when the cost to the program is less than the cost of a nursing home. Twenty-four-hour care is not available in the home, since it would cost more than nursing home care. Because of the cost of long-term care, the income limit for eligibility is three times the SSI payment level (approximately $2,067), but see the "Estate Planning" subsection below for exceptions. There was a recent change to require proof of disability for long-term care.

Program of All Inclusive Care for the Elderly (PACE)

Another option available to frail elders is known as the Program of All Inclusive Care for the Elderly (PACE). This program provides comprehensive health care and supportive services for people 65 years and older. In Colorado, the PACE contract is currently managed by Total Long-Term Care (TLC) and is only available in the Denver metropolitan area and Colorado Springs. For more information, contact Total Long-Term Care at (720) 974-2411, or inquire about this program through your local county Department of Social Services.

Estate Planning

Even with the higher income cap, many people who have income too high to qualify for Medicaid long-term care are still unable to pay for nursing home care (since nursing homes charge more than $2,067 per month). In those cases, a trust — sometimes known as an "income trust" or "Miller trust" — may set aside enough income to make an individual eligible. Other forms of estate planning may preserve some assets. However, transfers to create eligibility can result in severe penalties, particularly if made within three years before applying for Medicaid (or five years, if the transfer took place on or after February 8, 2006, or if the transfer involved a trust). Because of the possible penalties, any financial planning should be done by an attorney with Medicaid expertise.

Spousal Protection

The "Spousal Protection rule" allows a spouse who remains at home to avoid poverty by keeping between $1,838.75 and $2,841 of the couple's monthly income, while the institutionalized spouse receives Medicaid. The community spouse generally may also keep his or her IRAs, pensions, other exempt property as described above under general Medicaid eligibility rules, and up to $113,640 in non-exempt resources. The spousal protection rules are indexed to the Consumer Price Index and change yearly.

Estate Recovery

Under a program known as the Colorado Estate Recovery Program, the state can recover Medicaid expenditures from the recipient's estate after he or she dies. The estate recovery program applies to people who were 55 years of age or older when they received such assistance, as well as to all institutionalized individuals. The program permits the state to file a claim against an individual Medicaid recipient's estate, including a lien on the home. After the person dies, the state can enforce the lien and recover the expenses paid by Medicaid from the proceeds of the sale of the property. No action is taken against the property while the Medicaid recipient is still living.

The home may be protected from recovery if a surviving spouse or dependent child is still living there. There are other exceptions to recovery. It is important to consult with an attorney knowledgeable about Medicaid eligibility concerning these provisions, since they are complex and subject to change.

4-3. New Medicaid Regulations Within the Deficit Reduction Act of 2005

On February 8, 2006, President Bush signed the Deficit Reduction Act (DRA) of 2005. This legislation contained several changes to the Medicaid regulations that will affect elderly individuals who apply for the program. Here are the major parts of the new rules.

Increases the Look-Back Period

Now, all transfers made on or after February 8, 2006, whether to individuals or to trusts, will be subject to a five-year look-back period rather than the prior three-year look-back period. This will make the application process more difficult and could result in more applicants being denied for lack of documentation, given that they will need to produce five years' worth of records instead of three years.

Postpones the Penalty Period Start Date

Under the old rules, if you made a transfer within the three years prior to a Medicaid application, you would incur a penalty period based on the amount of the gift. The penalty period would begin on the month that you made the transfer. The new law shifts the start of the period of ineligibility for a transfer of assets from the first day of the month of the transfer to the later of that date or "the date on which the individual is eligible for medical assistance under the State plan and would otherwise be receiving institutional level care." So, what does this mean? First, the penalty period does not begin until the individual moves to the nursing home or requires a level of care that is equal to nursing home care. Second, the penalty period does not begin until the person would be eligible for Medicaid, meaning until he or she has spent down to $2,000 (or a different asset limit in some states).

An example should help explain how this will work. Let's assume that a senior transfers $60,000 to her son on July 1, 2006, but keeps $100,000 in her name. Let's further assume that our senior falls and breaks her hip on July 1, 2007, and subsequently moves to a nursing home. The senior spends down her savings over the following year, leaving her eligible for Medicaid on July 1, 2008, but for the transfer penalty. Under the new law, because the penalty does not start until she is at a nursing home level of care and is down to the $2,000 asset limit (minus the normal exemptions such as the residence, a vehicle, personal property items, and a burial plot or plan), she would not be eligible until April 30, 2009. Unless the son can give back the $60,000 transfer, there will be no funds to pay for care unless a family member helps or the senior appeals and receives a waiver of the ineligibility period.

The Effective Date

The new transfer rules apply to all transfers occurring on or after the date of enactment of the DRA (February 8, 2006). Transfers made before February 8, 2006, will be judged under the old rule, where the penalty period begins in the month of the transfer.

Hardship Waivers

Each state will institute a process for seeking a hardship waiver where the application of the transfer penalty would result in deprivation of medical care that would endanger the applicant's health or life, or of "food, clothing, shelter, or other necessities of life." The process must include notice to applicants, a timely process for ruling on the application, and an appeal process.

The new law also permits the nursing home to apply on behalf of the individual for such a waiver upon receipt of consent from the resident or his or her personal representative. However, the waiver is only for hardship to the resident, not to the facility. If a facility cannot evict a nonpaying resident without providing alternative care and no alternative care exists, there is really no hardship to the resident, only the nursing home.

Annuities

The new rules require that the state be "named the remainder beneficiary in the first position for at least the total amount of medical assistance paid on behalf of the annuitant." The provision also provides that the state be the secondary beneficiary where a community spouse or minor or disabled child is the primary beneficiary.

The Valuable House Rule

Under the DRA, homes of nursing home residents in which the residents own more than $525,000 in equity shall be countable unless the nursing home resident's spouse, child under age 21, or blind or disabled child is living in the house. The effective date of this provision was January 1, 2006.

Deposits or Buy-Ins at Continuing Care Retirement Communities (CCRCs)

Any amount required for a deposit in a CCRC, or that is used for a buy-in at a CCRC, will now be counted as an asset. In the past, CCRCs would require, say, a $50,000 buy-in for residence but would provide for these funds to be held and returned to the person, or their beneficiaries, when the individual moved out or passed away. Under the new rule, these deposits will be seen as countable assets that will need to be recouped and spent down before Medicaid eligibility.

4-4. Medicaid Payment for Medicare Premiums, Deductibles, and Co-Payments

People whose income makes them ineligible for Medicaid may still qualify for one of three Medicaid programs that pay Medicare-related costs.

A Qualified Medicare Beneficiary (QMB) receives payment by Medicaid of all Medicare premiums, deductibles, and co-pays. The QMB income maximum is $928 for one person, and $1,246 for a couple.

Similarly, a Special Low-Income Medicare Beneficiary (SLMB) receives only payment of Medicare premiums. The SLMB income maximum is higher: $1,109 for one person or $1,491 for two.

Finally, a similar program called QI-1 can provide assistance with Medicaid premiums with income up to $1,246 for one person and $1,675 for two, but any assistance is subject to the availability of state funding.

Note that some earned income may be excluded for all three of these income caps, and that the income caps change annually as poverty figures are changed.

4-5. Resources

For more information about Medicare and Medicaid, call your nearest senior center.

See a list of county Departments of Social Services in section 5-6, "Resources."

Chapter 5

Government Programs and Financial Assistance

John J. Campbell, Esq.*
Law Offices of John J. Campbell, P.C.

Michele M. Lawonn, J.D., P.T.
Medical-Legal Advocates, LLC

SYNOPSIS

5-1. Old Age Pension

The Colorado Old Age Pension (OAP) program provides a minimum level of income to needy Colorado residents age 60 or older. To qualify, an applicant's countable income must be less than the OAP standard of need, which is $699. An applicant's resources must be below $2,000 for a single person, $3,000 for a couple.

The benefit calculation and resource rules are similar to those used in the SSI program.

Applications may be filed at the County Department of Human Services (see "Resources" in section 5-6, below). Documents to bring include:

▶ Proof of age (birth certificate);

▶ Proof of citizenship or resident alien status (birth certificate or naturalization certificate);

▶ Proof of Colorado residency (photo ID, mail);

▶ Proof of income and assets;

▶ Social Security or Supplemental Security Income (SSI) award letters or copies of checks;

▶ Bank statements; and

▶ Copies of life insurance policies.

5-2. Food Stamps

Seniors with limited income and resources may be eligible for food stamps. In general, people age 60 or older, living alone, must have countable income of less than $1,180 per month, and non-exempt resources of less than $2,000 to qualify. The limits are higher for couples and larger households. SSI and OAP recipients are automatically eligible for at least a minimal food stamp award.

The value of the food stamp award depends on the household income.

Household Income Limits			
Size	*Income per Month*	*Size*	*Income per Month*
1	$1,180	6	$3,249
2	$1,594	7	$3,663
3	$2,008	8	$4,077
4	$2,422	8+	Add for each: $414
5	$2,836		

Applications may be filed at the local county Department of Human Services offices. See "Resources" in section 5-6, below.

Colorado also recognizes categorical eligibility for food stamps where any member of the household is also eligible for Temporary Assistance for Needy Families (TANF), County Diversion Assistance, or State Diversion Assistance, and where all members of the household are eligible for SSI.

5-3. Energy Assistance Programs

The Governor's Energy Office (GEO) offers free energy efficiency upgrades and safety inspections for income-eligible households. The Energy $aving Partners (E$P) programs aim to lower energy bills, eliminate unsafe conditions, and improve the comfort of their recipients.

As energy costs continue to rise, investing in residential energy efficiency improvements becomes more attractive and more economically sensible. Unfortunately, limited discretionary income prevents many households from responding to price signals and incentives. At the same time, the burden of energy costs upon household income is the greatest for these consumers.

An average household consumes about 900 therms of gas and about 8,000 kilowatt hours (kWh) of electricity per year. Various factors affect the amount of energy that a household consumes, including the thermal efficiency of the home, the operating efficiency of the heating system, the number of occupants, the age of appliances, and consumption behaviors of the occupants. Recognizing the variability in needs, the GEO has designed a variety of energy efficiency services that are provided free of charge to eligible recipients.

There are many benefits to the home efficiency services provided by the GEO. Its programs are designed to assist income-qualified households, so reducing the recipient's energy costs is a top priority. In addition to reducing utility costs, its services offer a wide range of non-energy-related benefits. Because the GEO's services often include health and safety inspections, recipients can avoid hazardous conditions that could lead to fires or unsafe buildup of carbon monoxide. Recipients of these services will also benefit from a more comfortable living space as a result of increased climate control.

If you have received assistance from any of the following programs in the past 12 months, you are automatically eligible for the GEO's services: the Low-Income Energy Assistance Program (LEAP; described below), Temporary Assistance for Needy Families (TANF), Supplemental Security Income (SSI), OAP, or Aid to the Needy Disabled (AND). You also may qualify if you are on Medicaid. Apply for the GEO's services by calling (866) 432-8435 or contacting your local county department of social services. (See "Resources," section 5-6.)

An important energy assistance program is LEAP, which helps participants pay for winter home heating costs. To be eligible in the 2011-2012 season, your family household income needs to fall within 185 percent of the federal poverty level guidelines (see chart below), you must pay home heating costs to an energy provider or as part of your rent, and you must be a permanent and legal resident of the United States and Colorado. Applications will be accepted from November 1 through April 30.

LEAP Eligibility	
People in Household	*Gross Monthly Income Limits*
1	$1,361
2	$1,839
3	$2,316
4	$2,794
5	$3,271
6	$3,749
7	$4,226
8	$4,704
8+	Add for each: $478
(Figures current as of March 2012.)	

You can apply for LEAP at your local county Department of Human Services or by calling (866) HEAT-HELP (866-432-8435). You also can download a LEAP application online by going to www.cdhs.state.co.us. Click on "How do I?", then "get help with my utilities," then "How do I apply for energy assistance?" The application is available in English and Spanish.

5-4. Veterans' Benefits

Two programs provide benefits for disabled veterans.

Veterans with service-connected disabilities may be entitled to a compensation benefit regardless of their income or resources. The amount of the benefit depends on the level of disability. Veterans who are rated as being more than 30 percent disabled also are entitled to a benefit for their dependents.

Veterans with nonservice-connected disabilities also may be entitled to a pension benefit, but only if they are permanently and totally disabled and have limited income and assets.

When a veteran dies, the surviving spouse and minor children may be eligible for pension benefits if the survivors' incomes are below a certain level. If the death was due to a service-connected disability, the surviving spouse is eligible for benefits that are not income based.

Medical care is provided at Veterans Administration (VA) hospitals and clinics for all service-related medical conditions.

Hospital care at VA hospitals and nursing home care at VA nursing homes is available to veterans who have service-connected disabilities, who receive a VA pension, or who fall into other special categories, such as former prisoners of war. Hospital care may be provided, as space is available, to other veterans, if the veteran's income is below the eligibility limit.

The Veterans Administration may contribute to the cost of burial, headstone or marker, and a burial flag. The veteran may be eligible to be buried in a national cemetery.

To apply for VA benefits, write, call, or visit your local VA regional office. In Denver, it is at 155 Van Gordon St., Lakewood, CO 80228 or P.O. Box 25126, Denver, CO 80225. Telephone: (800) 827-1000. Or contact: Division of Veterans Affairs, 7465 E. 1st Ave., Ste. C, Denver, CO 80230, Telephone: (303) 343-1268.

Applicants for VA benefits are advised to seek the assistance of a veterans' advocate such as the Colorado Division of Veterans Affairs.

See Chapter 6, "Veterans' Benefits," for more information.

5-5. Telephone Assistance Program

The state Telephone Assistance Program provides for a discount on basic phone services for individuals receiving benefits from Old Age Pension, Aid to the Blind, SSI, and Aid to the Needy Disabled. Several telephone companies are currently participating, including Qwest and Comcast. Discounts range from $8 to $16 per month; there may also be a discount for installation of new phone service. For information on how to apply, call (800) 782-0721.

5-6. Resources

County Departments of Social Services

For updates, go to www.cdhs.state.co.us and click on "Services by County."

Adams County 7190 Colorado Blvd. Commerce City, CO 80022 (303) 287-8831	**Archuleta County** P.O. Box 240 (mail) 551 Hot Springs Blvd. (physical) Pagosa Springs, CO 81147 (970) 264-2182	**Boulder County** 3400 Broadway Boulder, CO 80304 (303) 441-1000
Alamosa County P.O. Box 1310 (mail) 8900 Independence Way, Bldg. C (physical) Alamosa, CO 81101 (719) 589-2581	**Baca County** 772 Colorado St. Springfield, CO 81073 (719) 523-4131	**Broomfield County** #6 Garden Center Broomfield, CO 80020 (720) 887-2200
Arapahoe County 14980 E. Alameda Dr. Aurora, CO 80012 (303) 636-1130	**Bent County** 215 2nd St. Las Animas, CO 81054 (719) 456-2620	**Chaffee County** P.O. Box 1007 (mail) 448 E. 1st St., Rm. 166 Salida, CO 81201 (719) 539-6627

Cheyenne County
P.O. Box 146 (mail)
51 South 1st (physical)
Cheyenne Wells, CO 80810
(719) 767-5629

Clear Creek County
P.O. Box 2000 (mail)
405 Argentine St.
Georgetown, CO 80444
(303) 679-2365

Conejos County
P.O. Box 68
Conejos, CO 81129
(719) 376-5455

Costilla County
P.O. Box 249 (mail)
123 Gasper St. (physical)
San Luis, CO 81152
(719) 672-4131

Crowley County
631 Main, Ste. 100
Ordway, CO 81063
(719) 267-3546

Custer County
P.O. Box 929 (mail)
205 S. 6th St. (physical)
Westcliffe, CO 81252
(719) 783-2371

Delta County
560 Dodge St.
Delta, CO 81416
(970) 874-2030

Denver County
1200 Federal Blvd.
Denver, CO 80204
(720) 944-3666

Dolores County
P.O. Box 485 (mail)
409 N. Main (physical)
Dove Creek, CO 81324
(970) 677-2250

Douglas County
4400 Castleton Ct.
Castle Rock, CO 80109
(303) 688-4825

Eagle County
P.O. Box 660 (mail)
551 Broadway (physical)
Eagle, CO 81631
(970) 328-8840

Elbert County
P.O. Box 544 (mail)
214 Comanche St. (physical)
Kiowa, CO 80107
(303) 621-3149

El Paso County
1675 Garden of the Gods Rd.
Colorado Springs, CO 80907
(719) 636-0000

Fremont County
172 Justice Center Rd.
Cañon City, CO 81212
(719) 275-2318

Garfield County
108 8th St., Ste. 300
Glenwood Springs, CO
81601
(970) 945-9191

Gilpin County
2960 Dory Hill Rd., Ste. 100
Black Hawk, CO 80422
(303) 582-5444

Grand County
P.O. Box 204 (mail)
620 Hemlock (physical)
Hot Sulphur Springs, CO
80451
(970) 725-3331

Gunnison County
225 N. Pine St., Ste. A
Gunnison, CO 81230
(970) 641-3244

Hinsdale County
311 N. Henson St.
Lake City, CO 81235
(970) 944-2225

Huerfano County
121 W. 6th St.
Walsenburg, CO 81089
(719) 738-2810

Jackson County
P.O. Box 338
350 McKinley St.
Walden, CO 80480
(970) 723-4750

Jefferson County
900 Jefferson County Pkwy.
Golden, CO 80401
(303) 271-1388

Kiowa County
P.O. Box 187 (mail)
1307 Maine St. (physical)
Eads, CO 81036
(719) 438-5541

Kit Carson County
252 S. 14th St.
Burlington, CO 80807
(719) 346-8732

Lake County
P.O. Box 884 (mail)
112 W. 5th St. (physical)
Leadville, CO 80461
(719) 486-2088

La Plata County
1060 E. 2nd Ave.
Durango, CO 81301
(970) 382-6150

Larimer County
1501 Blue Spruce Dr.
Ft. Collins, CO 80524
(970) 498-6300

Las Animas County
204 S. Chestnut St.
Trinidad, CO 81082
(719) 846-2276

Lincoln County
P.O. Box 37 (mail)
103 3rd Ave. (physical)
Hugo, CO 80821
(719) 743-2404

Logan County
P.O. Box 1746 (mail)
508 S. 10th Ave., Ste. 2
  (physical)
Sterling, CO 80751
(970) 522-2194

Mesa County
510 29-½ Rd.
Grand Junction, CO 81502
(970) 241-8480

Mineral County
P.O. Box 40 (mail)
1015 6th St. (physical)
Del Norte, CO 81132
(719) 657-3381, ext. 100

Moffat County
595 Breeze St.
Craig, CO 81625
(970) 824-8282

Montezuma County
109 W. Main, Rm. 203
Cortez, CO 81321
(970) 565-3769

Montrose County
1845 S. Townsend
Montrose, CO 81401
(970) 252-5000

Morgan County
P.O. Box 220 (mail)
800 E. Beaver Ave. (physical)
Ft. Morgan, CO 80701
(970) 542-3531

Otero County
P.O. Box 494 (mail)
Courthouse, 3rd & Colorado
  (physical)
La Junta, CO 81050
(719) 383-3100

Ouray County
P.O. Box 530 (mail)
177 Sherman St., Unit 104
  (physical)
Ridgeway, CO 81432
(970) 626-2299

Park County
59865 U.S. Hwy. 285
Bailey, CO 80421
(303) 816-5939

Phillips County
127 E. Denver, Ste. A
Holyoke, CO 80734
(970) 854-2280

Pitkin County
0405 Castle Creek Rd., Ste. 8
Aspen, CO 81611
(970) 920-5209

Prowers County
P.O. Box 1157 (mail)
1001 S. Main (physical)
Lamar, CO 81052
(719) 336-7486

Pueblo County
212 W. 12th St.
Pueblo, CO 81003
(719) 583-6160

Rio Blanco County
345 Market St.
Meeker, CO 81641
(970) 878-9640

Rio Grande County
P.O. Box 40 (mail)
1015 6th St. (physical)
Del Norte, CO 81132
(719) 657-3381, ext. 100

Routt County
P.O. Box 772790 (mail)
136 6th St. (physical)
Steamboat Springs, CO
  80477
(970) 879-1540

Saguache County
P.O. Box 215 (mail)
605 Christy Ave. (physical)
Saguache, CO 81149
(719) 655-2537

San Juan County
P.O. Box 376 (mail)
1557 Greene St. (physical)
Silverton, CO 81433
(970) 387-5326

San Miguel County
P.O. Box 96 (mail)
333 W. Colorado Ave.
   (physical)
Telluride, CO 81435
(970) 728-4411
 	
Sedgwick County
P.O. Box 27 (mail)
118 W. 3rd (physical)
Julesburg, CO 80737
(970) 474-3397, ext. 227
 	
Summit County
P.O. Box 869 (mail)
37 County Rd. 1005
   (physical)
Frisco, CO 80443
(970) 668-6198
	Teller County
	P.O. Box 9033 (mail)
	740 Hwy. 24 (physical)
	Woodland Park, CO 80866
	(719) 687-3335
	
	Washington County
	P.O. Box 395 (mail)
	126 W. 5th (physical)
	Akron, CO 80720
	(970) 345-2238
		Weld County
		P.O. Box A (mail)
		315 N. 11th Ave. (physical)
		Greeley, CO 80631
		(970) 352-1551
		
		Yuma County
		340 S. Birch St.
		Wray, CO 80758
		(970) 332-4877

Veterans Resources

For more information about veterans' benefits, see Chapter 6, "Veterans' Benefits."

Federal Veterans Administration

General Information Number: (800) 827-1000
TDD: (800) 829-4833
www.va.gov

Veterans Affairs Regional Office

155 Van Gordon
Lakewood, CO 80228
(800) 827-1000

State of Colorado Division of Veterans Affairs

This is the primary office for the State of Colorado Division of Veterans Affairs. It is separate from the United States Department, but provides advocacy and appeals assistance.

1355 S. Colorado Blvd.
Bldg. C, Ste. 113
Denver, CO 80220
(303) 343-1268
www.dmva.state.co.us

In General

Denver Veterans Center (for psychological counseling)
7465 E. 1st Ave., Unit C
Denver, CO 80230
(303) 326-0645

Disabled American Veterans State Office
1485 Holland St.
Lakewood, CO 80215
(303) 922-3631
www.davmembersportal.org/co/default.aspx

Colorado Legal Services Offices

The below offices help veterans with problems when dealing with government benefits and will intercede on their behalf.

www.coloradolegalservices.org

Alamosa (Alamosa, Conejos, Costilla, Mineral, Rio Grande, and Saguache counties)
Address: 603 Main St., Alamosa
Phone: (719) 589-4993

Boulder (Boulder County)
Address: 315 W. South Boulder Rd., Ste. 205, Louisville
Phone: (303) 449-7575

Colorado Springs (El Paso, Lincoln, and Teller counties; Chaffee, Custer, Fremont, and Park counties shared with other offices)
Address: 617 S. Nevada Ave., Colorado Springs
Phone: (719) 471-0380

Denver (Adams, Arapahoe, Broomfield, Denver, Douglas, Elbert, and Jefferson counties, as well as seniors in Clear Creek and Gilpin counties)
Address: 1905 Sherman St., Ste. 400, Denver
Phone: (303) 837-1313

Durango (Archuleta, Dolores, Hinsdale, La Plata, Montezuma, Ouray, San Juan, and San Miguel counties)
Address: 1474 Main Ave., Ste. 200, Durango
Phone: (888) 298-8483

Fort Collins (Larimer, Logan, Phillips, and Sedgwick counties)
Address: 211 W. Magnolia St., Fort Collins
Phone: (970) 493-2891

Frisco (Pitkin and Summit counties; Clear Creek and Gilpin seniors, call Denver office)
Address: 602 Galena St., Frisco
Phone: (800) 521-6968

Grand Junction (Delta, Garfield, Mesa, and Montrose counties)
Address: 200 N. 6th St., Ste. 203, Grand Junction
Phone: (970) 243-7817

Greeley (Morgan, Washington, Weld, and Yuma counties)
Address: 800 8th Ave., Ste. 202, Greeley
Phone: (970) 353-7554

Hayden (Grand, Jackson, Moffat, Rio Blanco, and Routt counties)
Address: 150 W. Jackson, Ste. 2A, Hayden
Phone: (800) 521-6968

La Junta (Baca, Bent, Cheyenne, Crowley, Huerfano, Kiowa, Kit Carson, Las Animas, Otero, and Prowers counties)
Address: 207-½ Colorado Ave., La Junta
Phone: (888) 805-5152

Leadville (Eagle and Lake counties)
Address: 505 Harrison Ave., Leadville
Phone: (800) 521-6968

Migrant Farmworker Division (all counties)
Address: 1905 Sherman St., Denver
Phone: (800) 864-4330

Pueblo (Pueblo county; Custer and Fremont counties shared with other offices)
Address: 1000 W. 6th St., Pueblo
Phone: (719) 545-6708

Salida (Chaffee, Custer, Fremont, and Park counties shared)
Address: 1604 H St., Ste. 201, Salida
Phone: (719) 539-4251

Governor's Advocate Corps

For help with issues and problems that arise when dealing with a department of the Colorado state government.

Citizen's Advocate Office
127 State Capitol
Denver, CO 80203
(303) 866-2885
www.colorado.gov/governor; click on "Offices of the Governor"

For Issues Regarding Medicaid

Department of Health Care Policy and Financing
State Social Services Building
1570 Grant St.
Denver, CO 80203-1818
(303) 866-3513
(800) 221-3943 (toll-free)
(800) 659-2656 (TDD)
24-hour Nurse Helpline for People on Medicaid: (800) 283-3221
www.chcpf.state.co.us

For Issues Regarding Public Assistance

Department of Human Services
www.cdhs.state.co.us, click on "How do I?"

For county departments of human services, look in the blue pages of your phone book under "County" or "City Government," or go to www.cdhs.state.co.us and click on "Services by County."

---

* Sean Mandel of the State of Colorado Governor's Energy Office (GEO) provided the overview of the GEO's programs for income-eligible energy assistance in section 5-3.

Exhibit 5A.
Original Medicare (Parts A and B Fee-for-Service)
Appeals Process

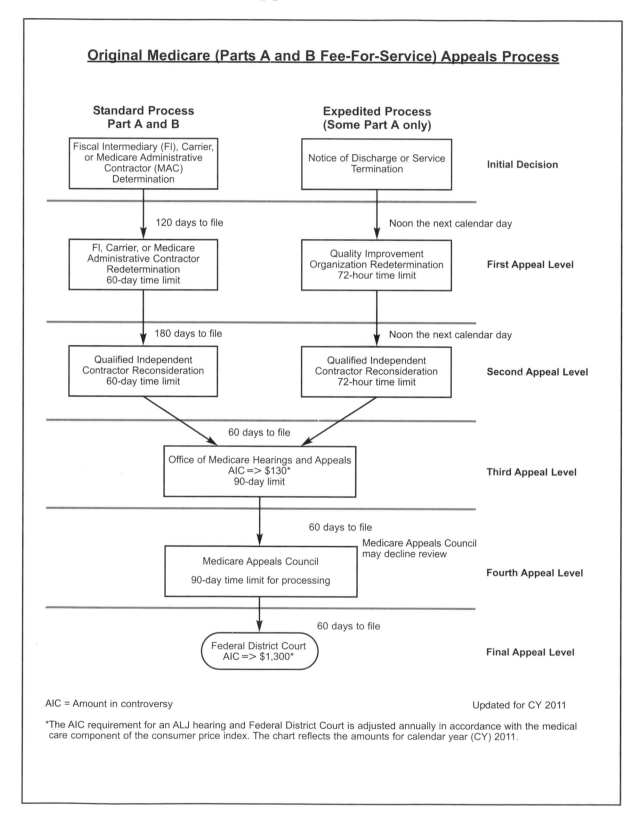

Original Medicare (Parts A and B Fee-For-Service) Appeals Process

Standard Process Part A and B	Expedited Process (Some Part A only)	
Fiscal Intermediary (FI), Carrier, or Medicare Administrative Contractor (MAC) Determination	Notice of Discharge or Service Termination	**Initial Decision**
120 days to file	*Noon the next calendar day*	
FI, Carrier, or Medicare Administrative Contractor Redetermination 60-day time limit	Quality Improvement Organization Redetermination 72-hour time limit	**First Appeal Level**
180 days to file	*Noon the next calendar day*	
Qualified Independent Contractor Reconsideration 60-day time limit	Qualified Independent Contractor Reconsideration 72-hour time limit	**Second Appeal Level**
60 days to file		
Office of Medicare Hearings and Appeals AIC => $130* 90-day limit		**Third Appeal Level**
60 days to file		
Medicare Appeals Council 90-day time limit for processing	Medicare Appeals Council may decline review	**Fourth Appeal Level**
60 days to file		
Federal District Court AIC => $1,300*		**Final Appeal Level**

AIC = Amount in controversy   Updated for CY 2011

*The AIC requirement for an ALJ hearing and Federal District Court is adjusted annually in accordance with the medical care component of the consumer price index. The chart reflects the amounts for calendar year (CY) 2011.

Chapter 6

Veterans' Benefits

Thomas R. Kennedy, Esq.
Office of Regional Counsel
U.S. Department of Veterans Affairs

Paul Dean Tayloe, Jr.
Denver Regional Office
U.S. Department of Veterans Affairs

SYNOPSIS

6-1.   Disability Compensation

6-2.   Pension Benefits

6-3.   Survivor Benefits

6-4.   Health Care Benefits

6-5.   Services and Aids for Blind Veterans

6-6.   Home Improvements

6-7.   Outpatient Dental Treatment

6-8.   Outpatient Pharmacy Services

6-9.   Nursing Home Care

6-10.   Domiciliary Care

6-11.   Medical Care for Dependents and Survivors

6-12.   Burial Benefits

6-13.   Resources

A variety of benefits provided by the U.S. Department of Veterans Affairs (VA) are available to eligible veterans and their families. This chapter focuses on benefits most likely to be of interest to older veterans and their families.

6-1. Disability Compensation

Disability compensation is a monetary benefit paid to veterans who are disabled by injury or disease incurred or aggravated during active military service. The service of the veteran must have been terminated through separation or discharge under conditions other than dishonorable. Disability compensation varies with the degree of disability and the number of dependents, and is paid monthly. The benefits are not subject to federal or state income tax. The payment of military retirement pay, disability severance pay, and separation incentive payments known as SSB (special separation benefits) and VSI (voluntary separation incentives) also affects the amount of VA compensation paid.

Former prisoners of war (POW) are eligible for disability compensation if they are rated at least 10 percent disabled from certain conditions presumed by federal law to be related to the POW experience. Former POWs who were imprisoned for at least 30 days are also eligible by federal law for certain presumptive conditions.

The Specially Adapted Housing Grant is available to severely disabled veterans or service members who are entitled to a home specially adapted for their needs due to loss of mobility. Under this entitlement, a temporary grant (TRA) may be available to veterans who are or will be temporarily residing in a home owned by a family member. Any veteran who is entitled to receive compensation for a service-connected disability for which he or she uses prosthetic or orthopedic appliances may receive an annual clothing allowance. The allowance also is available to any veteran whose service-connected skin condition requires prescribed medication that irreparably damages the veteran's outer garments.

Veterans whose service-connected disabilities are rated at 30 percent or more are entitled to additional allowances for dependents. The number of dependents and the degree of disability determines the additional amount.

A veteran who is determined by VA to be in need of the regular aid and attendance of another person, or a veteran who is permanently housebound, may be entitled to additional disability compensation or pension benefits. A veteran evaluated at 30 percent or more disabled is entitled to receive a special allowance for a spouse who is in need of the aid and attendance of another person.

6-2. Pension Benefits

Veterans with low incomes who are permanently and totally disabled, or are age 65 and older, may be eligible for monetary support if they have 90 days or more of active military service, at least one day of which was during a period of war. Generally, veterans who entered active duty on or after September 8, 1980, or officers who entered active duty on or after October 16, 1981, may have to meet a longer minimum period of active duty.

Requirements for eligibility to receive pension benefits include the discharge from active duty under conditions other than dishonorable. Permanent and total disability cannot be as a result of the veteran's own willful misconduct. Payments are made to qualified veterans to bring their total income, including other retirement or Social Security income, to a level set by Congress. Unreimbursed medical expenses may reduce countable income.

6-3. Survivor Benefits

Dependency and indemnity compensation (DIC) is a monthly tax-free benefit that may be available to a veteran's survivor. For survivors to be eligible, the deceased veteran must have died from (1) a disease or injury incurred or aggravated while on active duty or active duty for training; (2) an injury incurred or aggravated in the line of duty while on inactive duty training; or (3) a disability compensable by VA. Death cannot be the result of the veteran's willful misconduct. If a spouse remarries, eligibility for benefits ceases, but it may be restored if the marriage is terminated later by death, annulment, or divorce.

DIC also may be authorized for survivors of veterans who, at the time of death, were determined to be totally disabled as a result of military service, even though their service-connected disabilities did not cause their deaths. The veteran must have been discharged under conditions other than dishonorable. The survivor qualifies if (1) the veteran was continuously rated totally disabled for a period of 10 or more years immediately preceding death; (2) the veteran was so rated for a period of at least five years from the date of military discharge; or (3) the veteran was a former POW who died after September 30, 1999, and who was continuously rated totally disabled for a period of at least one year immediately preceding death. Payments are subject to offset by any amount received from judicial proceedings brought on account of the veteran's death.

6-4. Health Care Benefits

VA operates the nation's largest integrated health care system, with more than 1,400 sites of care, including hospitals, community clinics, nursing homes, domiciliaries, readjustment counseling centers, and various other facilities. For additional information on VA health care, visit www1.va.gov/health/index.asp.

Veterans will be assigned to the highest priority group for which they qualify. VA uses the priority group system to balance demand with available resources. Changes in VA's available resources may reduce the number of priority groups VA can enroll. If this occurs, VA will publicize the changes and notify affected enrollees. Veterans will be enrolled to the extent that Congressional appropriations allow. If appropriations are limited, enrollment will occur based on the following priorities:

Priority Group 1: Veterans with service-connected disabilities rated 50 percent or more and veterans determined by VA to be unemployable due to service-connected conditions.

Priority Group 2: Veterans with service-connected disabilities rated 30 or 40 percent.

Priority Group 3: Veterans with service-connected disabilities rated 10 and 20 percent, veterans who are former POWs or were awarded a Purple Heart, veterans awarded special eligibility for disabilities incurred in treatment or participation in a VA vocational rehabilitation program, and veterans whose discharge was for a disability incurred or aggravated in the line of duty.

Priority Group 4: Veterans receiving aid and attendance or house benefits and veterans determined by VA to be catastrophically disabled. Some veterans in this group may be responsible for co-payments.

Priority Group 5: Veterans receiving VA pension benefits or eligible for Medicaid programs, and nonservice-connected veterans and noncompensable, zero percent, service-connected veterans whose annual income and net worth are below the established VA means test thresholds.

Priority Group 6: Veterans of the Mexican border period or World War I; veterans seeking care solely for certain conditions associated with exposure to radiation, for any illness associated with combat service in a war after the Gulf War or during a period of hostility after November 11, 1998, for any illness associated with participation in tests conducted by the Defense Department as part of Project 112/Project SHAD; and veterans with zero percent service-connected disabilities who are receiving disability compensation benefits.

Priority Group 7: Nonservice-connected veterans and noncompensable, zero percent, service-connected veterans with income above VA's national means test threshold and below VA's geographic means test threshold, or with income below both the VA national threshold and the VA geographically based threshold, but whose net worth exceeds VA's ceiling (currently $80,000) who agree to pay co-payments.

Priority Group 8: All other nonservice-connected veterans and noncompensable, zero percent, service-connected veterans who agree to pay co-payments. (*Note*: Effective January 17, 2003, VA no longer enrolls new veterans in Priority Group 8.)

Veterans enrolling in Priority Group 5 based on their inability to defray the cost of care must provide information on their annual household income and net worth so VA may determine whether they are below the annually adjusted "means test" financial threshold. Veterans completing a financial assessment must report their annual gross household income plus net worth, which includes Social Security, U.S. Civil Service retirement, U.S. Railroad retirement, military retirement, unemployment insurance, any other retirement income, total wages from all employers, interest and dividends, workers' compensation, black lung benefits, and any other gross income for the calendar year prior to application for care. Also considered are assets such as the market value of property that is not the primary residence, stocks, bonds, notes, individual retirement accounts, bank deposits, savings accounts, and cash. VA also is required to compare veterans' financial assessment information with a geographically based income threshold. If the veteran's income is below the threshold where the veteran lives, he or she is eligible for an 80 percent reduction in the inpatient co-payment rates.

Nonservice-connected veterans and noncompensable, zero percent, service-connected veterans whose income is above the national "means test" threshold must agree to pay appropriate co-payments for care. If they do not agree to make co-payments, they are ineligible for VA care. Veterans whose income is determined to be above the means test threshold and below VA's geographically based income threshold are responsible for paying 20 percent of the Medicare deductible for the first 90 days of inpatient hospital care during any 365-day period.

With certain exceptions, a veteran must agree to pay co-payments for extended care. A veteran's application for extended care services (VAF 10-10EC) requires financial information used to determine the monthly co-payment amount, based on each veteran's financial situation.

Prosthetic and Sensory Aid Services

VA will furnish needed prosthetic appliances, equipment, and devices, such as artificial limbs, orthopedic braces and shoes, wheelchairs, crutches and canes, and other durable medical equipment and supplies to veterans receiving VA care for any condition. VA will provide hearing aids and eyeglasses to veterans who receive increased pension based on the need for regular aid and attendance or being permanently housebound, receive compensation for a service-connected disability, or are former POWs. Otherwise, hearing aids and eyeglasses will be provided only in special circumstances, and not for normally occurring hearing or vision loss.

6-5. Services and Aids for Blind Veterans

Blind veterans may be eligible for services at a VA medical center or for admission to a VA blind rehabilitation center. Services are available at all VA medical facilities through the Visual Impairment Services coordinator. In addition, blind veterans enrolled in the VA health care system may receive VA aids for the blind, including:

1) A total health and benefits review;

2) Adjustment to blindness training;

3) Home improvements and structural alterations to homes;

4) Specially adapted housing and adaptations;

5) Automobile grants;

6) Low-vision aids and training in their use;

7) Electronic and mechanical aids for the blind, including adaptive computers and computer-assisted devices such as reading machines and electronic travel aids;

8) Guide dogs, including the expense of training the veteran to use the dog; and

9) Talking books, tapes, and Braille literature.

6-6. Home Improvements

VA provides funding for eligible veterans to make home improvements necessary for the continuation of treatment or for disability access to the home and essential lavatory and sanitary facilities provided.

6-7. Outpatient Dental Treatment

Outpatient dental treatment provided by VA includes examinations and the full spectrum of diagnostic, surgical, restorative, and preventive procedures. Veterans eligible to receive dental care include:

1) Veterans having service-connected and compensable dental disabilities or conditions;

2) Former POWs;

3) Veterans with service-connected, noncompensable dental conditions as a result of combat wounds or service injuries;

4) Veterans with nonservice-connected dental conditions determined by VA to be aggravating a service-connected medical problem;

5) Veterans having service-connected conditions rated as permanently and totally disabling or rated 100 percent by reason of individual unemployability;

6) Veterans participating in a vocational rehabilitation program under Chapter 31 of Title 38 in the U.S. Code;

7) Certain enrolled homeless veterans participating in specific health care programs;

8) Veterans with nonservice-connected dental conditions for which treatment was begun while the veteran was an inpatient in a VA facility when it is necessary to complete such treatment on an outpatient basis; and

9) Veterans requiring treatment for dental conditions clinically determined to be complicating a medical condition currently under treatment.

Recently discharged veterans who served on active duty 90 days or more and who apply for VA dental care within 180 days of separation from active duty may receive a one-time treatment for dental conditions if the veteran's certificate of discharge does not indicate that the veteran received necessary dental care within a 90-day period prior to discharge or release.

6-8. Outpatient Pharmacy Services

Outpatient pharmacy services are provided free of charge to:

1) Veterans with a service-connected disability of 50 percent or more;

2) Veterans receiving medication for treatment of service-connected conditions;

3) Veterans whose annual income does not exceed the maximum VA annual rate of the VA pension;

4) Veterans receiving medication for conditions related to exposure to ionizing radiation;

5) Veterans receiving medication for conditions related to combat service in a war after the Gulf War or against a hostile force in a period of hostilities beginning after November 11, 1998;

6) Veterans receiving medication for conditions related to participation in Department of Defense tests conducted as part of Project 112/Project SHAD;

7) Veterans receiving medication for conditions related to sexual trauma experienced while serving on active duty;

8) Certain veterans receiving medication for treatment of cancer of the head or neck;

9) Veterans receiving medication as part of a VA-approved research project; and

10) Former POWs.

Other veterans will be charged a co-payment for each 30-day or less supply of medication.

To eliminate a financial hardship for veterans who require an unusually large amount of medications, there is a maximum co-payment amount that veterans enrolled in Priority Groups 2 through 6 pay in any single year. The medication co-payment applies to prescription and over-the-counter medications, such as aspirin, cough syrup, or vitamins, dispensed by a VA pharmacy.

Medication co-payments are not charged for medications injected during the course of treatment or for medical supplies, such as syringes or alcohol wipes. In the event over-the-counter drugs are ordered, the veteran can choose to purchase them at a local pharmacy.

6-9. Nursing Home Care

VA provides nursing home services through three national programs: VA owned and operated nursing homes, state veterans homes owned and operated by the state, and contract community nursing homes. Each program has its own admission and eligibility criteria. VA owned and operated homes typically admit residents requiring short-term skilled care, or who have a 70 percent or more service-connected disability, or who require nursing home care because of a service-connected disability. The state veterans home program is a cooperative venture between VA and states whereby VA provides funds to help build the home and pays a portion of the costs for veterans eligible for VA health care. States, however, set eligibility criteria for admission. The contract nursing home program is designed to meet the long-term, nursing home care needs of veterans who may not be eligible and/or qualify for placement in a VA or state veterans home or if there is no VA or state home available.

To be placed in a nursing home, veterans generally must be medically stable, have a condition that requires inpatient nursing home care, and be assessed by an appropriate medical provider to be in need of institutional nursing home care. They also must meet the eligibility requirements for the home to which they are applying. For VA nursing homes, they may have to pay a co-payment depending on their financial status. VA social workers can help interpret eligibility and co-payment requirements.

In addition to nursing home care, VA offers other extended care services either directly or by contracting with community agencies, including adult day care, respite care, geriatric evaluation and management, hospice and palliative care, and home-based primary care. These services may require co-payment.

6-10. Domiciliary Care

Domiciliary care provides rehabilitative and long-term health maintenance care for veterans who require minimal medical care but do not need the skilled nursing services provided in nursing homes. VA may provide domiciliary care to veterans whose annual income does not exceed the maximum annual rate of VA pension or to veterans the Secretary of Veterans Affairs determines have no adequate means of support. The co-payments for extended care services apply to domiciliary care.

6-11. Medical Care for Dependents and Survivors

CHAMPVA, the Civilian Health and Medical Program of the Department of Veterans Affairs, provides reimbursement for most medical expenses: inpatient, outpatient, mental health, prescription medication, skilled nursing care, and durable medical equipment. To be eligible for CHAMPVA, an individual cannot be eligible for TRICARE (the medical program for civilian dependents, provided by the Department of Defense) and must be one of the following: (1) the spouse or child of a veteran who VA has rated permanently and totally disabled for a service-connected disability; (2) the surviving spouse or child of a veteran who died from a VA-rated service-connected disability, or who, at the time of death, was rated permanently and totally disabled; or (3) the surviving spouse or child of a military member who died in the line of duty, not due to misconduct. However, in most cases, these family members are eligible for TRICARE, not CHAMPVA.

A surviving spouse under age 55 who remarries loses CHAMPVA eligibility on midnight of the date of remarriage. However, eligibility may be re-established if the remarriage is terminated by death, divorce, or annulment, effective the first day of the month after the termination of the remarriage or December 1, 1999, whichever date is later. A CHAMPVA-eligible surviving spouse who is 55 or older does not lose eligibility upon remarriage. Individuals who have Medicare entitlement may also have CHAMPVA eligibility secondary to Medicare. Eligibility limitations apply.

6-12. Burial Benefits

Veterans discharged from active duty under conditions other than dishonorable and service members who die while on active duty, as well as spouses and dependent children of veterans and active duty service members, may be eligible for VA burial and memorial benefits. The veteran does not have to predecease a spouse or dependent child for them to be eligible for benefits.

With certain exceptions, active duty service beginning after September 7, 1980, as an enlisted person, and after October 16, 1981, as an officer, must be for a minimum of 24 consecutive months or the full period of active duty (as in the case of reservists or National Guard members called to active duty for a limited duration). Eligibility is not established by active duty for training in the reserves or National Guard.

Reservists and National Guard members, as well as their spouses and dependent children, are eligible if they were entitled to retirement pay at the time of death, or would have been if they were over age 60.

Burial in a VA national cemetery is available for eligible veterans and their spouses and dependents at no cost to the family, and includes the gravesite, grave liner, opening and closing of the grave, a headstone or marker, and perpetual care as part of a national shrine. For veterans, benefits also include a burial flag (with a case, for active duty veterans) and military funeral honors. Family members and other loved ones of deceased veterans may request Presidential Memorial Certificates.

VA operates 124 national cemeteries, of which 84 are open for new interments and 20 accept only cremated remains. Burial options are limited to those available at a specific cemetery but may include an in-ground casket, or interment of cremated remains in a columbarium, in the ground, or in a scatter garden. Surviving spouses of veterans who died on or after January 1, 2000, do not lose eligibility for burial in a national cemetery if they remarry. Burial of dependent children is limited to unmarried children under 21 years of age, or under 23 years of age if a full-time student at an approved educational institution. Unmarried adult children who become physically or mentally disabled and incapable of self-support before age 21, or age 23 if a full-time student, also are eligible for burial.

6-13. Resources

Phone Numbers

Education: (888) 442-4551

Headstones and markers: (800) 697-6947

Health care: (877) 222-8387

Life insurance: (800) 669-8477

Special health issues: (800) 749-8387

TTD: (800) 829-4833

VA benefits: (800) 827-1000

Websites

Burial and memorial benefits: www.cem.va.gov

Department of Defense: www.defense.gov

Education benefits: www.gibill.va.gov

Federal jobs: www.usajobs.gov

Health care eligibility: www.va.gov/healthbenefits

Home loan guaranty : www.homeloans.va.gov

Life insurance: www.insurance.va.gov/miscellaneous/index.htm

Mental health: www.mentalhealth.va.gov

Records: www.archives.gov/st-louis/military-personnel

Returning veterans: www.oefoif.va.gov

Veterans employment and training: www.dol.gov/vets

Veterans preference: www.fedshirevets.gov

Vocational rehabilitation and employment: www.vetsuccess.gov

VA benefit payment rates: www.vba.va.gov/bln/21/Rates

VA facilities: www2.va.gov/directory/guide/home.asp

VA forms: www.va.gov/vaforms

VA website: www.va.gov

Written Materials

Federal Benefits for Veterans and Dependents (2011 edition):
U.S. Department of Veterans Affairs
Office of Public Affairs
810 Vermont Ave. N.W.
Washington, D.C. 20420
www.va.gov/opa/publications/benefits_book.asp

Chapter 7

Long-Term Care Insurance

Aaron R. Eisenach, CLTC, LTCP
Krieger & Associates. . . an ICB Company

SYNOPSIS

The financial, emotional, and physical consequences of an extended care event to one's retirement plan, estate, and family members can be devastating. Many people choose not to confront the issue of long-term care planning until a chronic, debilitating illness or accident has already occurred, resulting in limited, and sometimes undesirable, choices.

As longevity continues to increase, more and more Americans will need long-term care at some point in life. Those who wish to preserve independence, afford high-quality care, and protect assets would be wise to plan ahead. For those who are still healthy and can afford the premiums, long-term care insurance may be the appropriate risk management tool.

7-1. Defining Long-Term Care

To define long-term care (LTC), let us begin by explaining what LTC is not. Long-term care is not acute care, which is medical care intended to cure or treat an individual with a critical illness or injury. Acute care aims to restore the patient's health to the previous level of functioning. Typically, acute care is provided in a hospital, perhaps an intensive care unit, by skilled medical professionals. Acute care is financed primarily by private health insurance, or Medicare for those 65 years of age and older.

Long-term care is also not subacute care, which is less intensive than acute care. Subacute care is usually provided in a regular hospital inpatient unit, lasts for a limited period of time, and is intended to restore the patient's health. Subacute care may be provided instead of or after acute care. Like acute care, skilled medical professionals provide subacute care, and it is covered by health insurance or Medicare.

Long-term care is chronic care — care provided over an extended period of time without expectation of a cure. LTC services include medical and non-medical care, providing for the health or personal needs of the care recipient. Often times, LTC does not require skilled medical professionals, as many people begin by receiving care at home provided by family, friends, or neighbors. Loved ones acting as caregivers deliver custodial care, which may include assistance with household chores; providing transportation; shopping; managing finances; helping with bathing, dressing, eating, or using the restroom; or supervising one with dementia. When home care is not an option, LTC may be provided in formal (paid) settings such as adult day care centers, assisted living facilities, skilled nursing facilities, or hospice facilities. Because a medical professional is usually not required for supervising one with dementia, or bathing, dressing, or feeding a loved one, long-term care is not generally covered by health insurance or Medicare. The primary sources of funding for long-term care are private funds, Medicaid, and long-term care insurance.

7-2. Who Needs Long-Term Care

The need for care can strike at any age and may last a few weeks or months, or for a number of years. According to the National Clearing House for Long-Term Care Information (www.longtermcare.gov), in 2008, 21 million people had a condition that caused them to need help with their health and personal care. Half of them were over 65 years old. About 70 percent of those over 65 will need some form of long-term care services at some point; more than 40 percent of those over 65 will spend time in a nursing home. By 2020, approximately 12 million people will need LTC services. Unfortunately for the young, the need for LTC can occur at any age: nearly 40 percent of people receiving long-term care services today are 18 to 64 years of age.

The following information was taken from *Long-Term Care Planning for Colorado Consumers*, published January 2006 by the Senior Health Insurance Assistance Program and Colorado Division of Insurance:

> [Sixty] percent of people who turn age 65 will need long-term care as they grow older and one in five who reach age 65 will spend more than two years in a nursing home. As our population ages the need for long-term care will increase, particularly for women. 22 percent of men and 41 percent of women can expect to have a nursing home stay longer than three months. At age 65, 14 percent of men and 31 percent of women are likely to have a nursing home stay longer than one year. Women are at most risk of a very long stay — 13 percent reportedly may have stays exceeding 5 years.

Note that the statistics above focus on care provided in nursing homes. Fortunately for those who have purchased LTC insurance policies, 49 percent of new LTC insurance claims in 2010 began as home care, 24 percent in assisted living facilities, and only 27 percent in nursing homes, as reported by the *American Association for Long-Term Care Insurance 2011 Sourcebook*.

The graph on the following page was published when the oldest baby boomer was 57, as indicated by the dashed line. Today, the leading edge boomers are turning 68. The message remains the same: a tidal wave of aging Americans are becoming more and more prone to needing long-term care.

7-3. Risk Factors

For some, an unhealthy lifestyle, such as a poor diet, smoking, lack of exercise, or obesity, increases the chance of needing long-term care. For others, good health may lead to longevity, and longevity generally increases the likelihood of receiving care. It is common knowledge that women on average outlive men. To wit, more than 70 percent of nursing

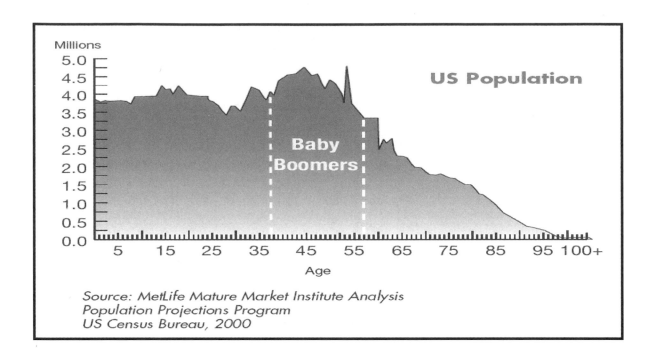

Millions

US Population

Baby Boomers

Age

Source: MetLife Mature Market Institute Analysis
Population Projections Program
US Census Bureau, 2000

home residents are female (National Nursing Home Survey, 2004). According to the Rocky Mountain MS Center, Colorado has always been thought to have an extremely high incidence of multiple sclerosis, a disease in which 80 percent of patients develop the condition between ages 16 and 45 (www.mscenter.org/content/view/145/180).

People living alone are more likely to need formal long-term care services from a paid provider. Some hereditary conditions may increase a person's risk of needing care. Finally, physically active adults may be more prone to an accident while skiing, cycling, or performing other activities.

7-4. Where Long-Term Care Is Received

Most people who need long-term care will be cared for at home; family and friends are the sole caregivers for 70 percent of the elderly (www.medicare.gov/longtermcare/static/home.asp). Home care agencies can provide additional assistance with part- or full-time homemakers, home health aides, and nurses.

Other community-based services include adult day care centers, assisted living facilities, and continuing care retirement communities (also known as life care communities). Respite care, which gives the primary caregiver a break from caregiving responsibilities, may be provided at home or in a facility. Skilled nursing facilities, often referred to as nursing homes, provide 24-hour care. Hospice care can be received in a nursing home, at home, or in a stand-alone hospice facility.

7-5. Cost of Long-Term Care

The following data was reported in the 2009 Genworth Financial Cost of Care Survey:

Nursing Home Daily Rates					
	Minimum Daily Rate	Maximum Daily Rate	Median Daily Rate	Median Annual Rate	5-Year Annual Growth*
Semi-Private Room					
Colorado Springs	$180	$204	$191	$69,733	6%
Denver	$145	$217	$197	$71,905	6%
Fort Collins	$178	$217	$194	$70,883	5%
Private Room					
Colorado Springs	$190	$381	$215	$78,475	7%
Denver	$185	$325	$234	$85,410	5%
Fort Collins	$198	$242	$220	$80,287	2%

Assisted Living Facility Monthly Rates (Private One Bedroom)					
	Minimum Daily Rate	Maximum Daily Rate	Median Daily Rate	Median Annual Rate	5-Year Annual Growth*
Colorado Springs	$2,400	$4,433	$3,178	$38,130	7%
Denver	$1,800	$4,459	$3,200	$38,400	7%
Fort Collins	$2,100	$3,470	$2,506	$30,075	11%

Home Care				
	Minimum Hourly Rate	Maximum Hourly Rate	Median Hourly Rate	5-Year Annual Growth*
Home Health Aide Services Hourly Rates (non-Medicare certified)				
Colorado Springs	$19	$26	$21	-1%
Denver	$14	$23	$21	3%
Fort Collins	$18	$25	$20	n/a
Home Health Aide Services Hourly Rates (Medicare certified)				
Colorado Springs	$18	$54	$24	-7%
Denver	$20	$90	$36	8%
Fort Collins	$24	$28	$25	0%
Homemaker Services Hourly Rates (non-Medicare certified)				
Colorado Springs	$17	$22	$19	4%
Denver	$14	$21	$20	2%
Fort Collins	$18	$25	$19	n/a

* Represents the compound annual growth rate based on Genworth Cost of Care survey data from 2005–2009

Adult Day Health Care Daily Rates			
	Minimum Daily Rate	Maximum Daily Rate	Median Daily Rate
Colorado Springs	$55	$59	$59
Denver	$44	$70	$61
Fort Collins	$70	$52	$50

The second component in the financial cost of LTC is the length of time care is needed. According to the *2008 Sourcebook for Long-Term Care Insurance Information*, published by the American Association for Long-Term Care Insurance, the average length of stay in a nursing home is 2.6 years for females and 2.3 years for males. The average stay for a female assisted living resident is 28.2 months, while men average 24 months. Scant reliable data exists to report an average length of need for home care, as much of this form of care is provided by family and friends. The financial costs can be enormous should one need care for a few years at home, then for two years in assisted living, and finally two years in a nursing home, not to mention the physical and emotional toll to the family.

7-6. Paying for Long-Term Care

Many Americans erroneously believe that Medicare will pay for long-term care services. According to www.medicare.gov, "Generally, Medicare does not pay for long-term care." Essentially, Medicare provides for rehabilitation by skilled providers. Most people who need LTC need personal or custodial care — that is, help with bathing, dressing, eating, etc., or supervisory care due to dementia. While it is true that Medicare can provide limited home health care and up to 100 days of nursing home care, it may prove costly to rely on Medicare to pay for any services. According to the 2011 Edition of the "Medicare and Medicaid Statistical Supplement" from the Centers for Medicare and Medicaid Services, the average number of days covered by Medicare in 2010 was 27. Private or employer-based health insurance works much the same. The Department of Veterans Affairs (VA) may provide LTC for service-related disabilities or for certain eligible veterans. However, the availability of services and the location of participating facilities for veterans may be an issue.

Medicaid is the state/federal assistance program that will pay the LTC costs for needy persons. To be eligible, one must have very limited income and assets. Often times, financial eligibility is met by spending down non-exempt assets on long-term care, depleting one's estate, and preventing the passing of an inheritance to loved ones. Married couples may also see retirement plans and other assets depleted while paying for the care of one spouse, leaving little for the healthy, surviving spouse. Medicaid pays for nearly half of all LTC costs in the United States.

Most people pay privately for LTC until their funds are depleted. One solution is long-term care insurance.

7-7. Reasons People Purchase Long-Term Care Insurance

As Rosalyn Carter once said, "There are only four types of people: those who have been caregivers, those who are caregivers, those who receive care, and those who will be caregivers in the future!" People who execute long-term care planning have often times been through a care event with a loved one and wish to protect themselves and their family from the devastating consequences of long-term care.

For many, long-term care planning includes two basic goals:

1) Should I someday need care, keep me at home for as long as possible, without severely impacting the lives of my loved ones around me.

2) Preserve the retirement plan and life savings so they can provide for the continuing lifestyle and obligations of my spouse or partner, and preserve the inheritance for those to whom I wish to leave a legacy.

For families, if extended care is needed for a loved one, the monthly income stream allocated for meeting obligations and maintaining lifestyle will be disrupted and reallocated. LTC insurance provides a stream of funds to pay for care and ensures that the loved one is safe and receiving quality care. This allows the spouse/partner and family to supervise the caregivers instead of being the caregivers. For those without a spouse and/or children, LTC insurance helps allay the fear of running out of money by paying for healthcare needs.

7-8. Traditional Long-Term Care Insurance

Most modern LTC insurance policies offered today are comprehensive, paying for home care, adult day care, assisted living facilities, nursing home care, hospice care, and respite care from a single pool of funds (also known as the lifetime maximum benefit). In the past, many policies allowed for two pools of funds: one benefit account for care in a facility, and a second pool for care at home. This form of LTC insurance, still available from some insurance companies, may be less flexible than the comprehensive form: if the policyowner exhausted his or her home care benefit account, no further benefits were payable until the policyowner received care in a facility.

The vast majority of policies offered today include two standardized ways to trigger the benefits of the policy. One trigger starts the benefits should the policyowner need substantial supervision due to a cognitive impairment, such as Alzheimer's, dementia, or senility. The other trigger is satisfied once the policyowner has a certification from a qualified health care practitioner that he or she requires stand-by or hands-on assistance with two or more out of six activities of daily living (ADLs). The six ADLs are bathing, dressing, eating, toileting, transferring, or continence. The certification includes an expectation that the care need will last at least 90 days. The satisfaction of only one benefit trigger is required. Provided the policyowner triggers his or her benefits, a plan of care is written by a licensed health care practitioner, ensuring appropriate levels of care and care settings.

There are three forms of traditional LTC insurance: reimbursement, cash, and indemnity. The most common form of LTC insurance, reimbursement policies, require that the claimant provides receipts for long-term care services covered by the policy. The insurance company then reimburses the claimant for actual expenses up to the daily or monthly maximum benefit of the policy at the time of claim. This is known as the "expense incurred method." Reimbursement policies typically require that the care services be provided by someone other than a spouse or family member. Some policies allow for home care to be from unlicensed providers, including friends and neighbors. One advantage of reimbursement plans is that any unused daily or monthly benefit remains in the benefit account for future use.

Cash plans are the most expensive form of LTC insurance, but are also the most flexible. Cash plans follow the "disability method": the full daily or monthly benefit is paid to the policyowner regardless of who is providing the care, and regardless of whether care was received that day or month. No proof of covered services is required. No doubt, future technology will deliver LTC in ways we may not even fathom today (*e.g.*, robots, sensors, monitors, etc.) — a cash policy can be used to pay for these futuristic methods. Drawbacks of cash plans include premium levels that may be double that of reimbursement plans, benefits that may exhaust faster than reimbursement plans, and concern that the benefits paid out to a power of attorney or family member of the policyowner are actually used for his or her care needs.

Like reimbursement policies, indemnity plans require proof of covered services from a qualified provider other than a family member or spouse. Unlike reimbursement plans, indemnity policies pay the full daily benefit (also known as a *per diem*) regardless of the actual cost of care. To illustrate, assume an indemnity policy has a daily benefit of $200. If the policyowner receives an hour of home care from an agency, the full $200 is paid to the policyowner, regardless of the cost of the hour of care. If the actual cost of the hour of home care was, say, $60, the policyowner pays the agency for the hour of care and has $140 left over to be used for any other purpose. Like cash plans, indemnity plans are not as common as reimbursement policies, and the benefits may be paid out faster than with a reimbursement policy. The premiums for indemnity policies are not substantially higher than the premiums for reimbursement policies.

7-9. Policy Building Blocks

Traditional LTC insurance policies include four building blocks: benefit amount, benefit period, inflation protection, and an elimination period.

The benefit amount is how much per day, per week, or per month the policy pays for care. A monthly benefit is the most flexible form of benefit amount, as one's benefit does not have a daily maximum benefit, but rather a monthly maximum benefit. For most comprehensive policies, the benefit amount is the same for all types of care (*e.g.*, nursing home, assisted living, and home care benefit). Some policies allow for the home care benefit to be a percentage below or above the nursing home benefit.

The benefit period may be thought of as the minimum length of time the benefits last before the policy is exhausted. Choices may include one to six years, 10 years, or an unlimited or lifetime benefit period. Assume a client has purchased a five-year benefit period and a $200 daily benefit. The resulting lifetime maximum benefit is $365,000 (1,825 days multiplied by $200). If it is a reimbursement policy, the benefits would last at least five years. If the actual cost of care is less than $200 per day, the policyowner is reimbursed the lesser amount, and future benefits remain in the lifetime maximum benefit for future use. In this example, the benefits stretch beyond the five-year benefit period.

All companies in Colorado must offer inflation protection. Three of the most common offers are described here, although more choices exist. The 5 percent automatic compound inflation rider increases the benefit amount 5 percent each year of the previous year's amount. The 3 percent automatic compound works much the same, except the increases equal 3 percent each year. The 5 percent automatic simple inflation calculates 5 percent of the original benefit amount, then adds that same amount each anniversary date of the policy. The following table illustrates the future value of the benefit amount and lifetime maximum benefit over time using each of the three choices.

Year	5% Automatic Compound		3% Automatic Compound		5% Automatic Simple	
	Daily Benefit	Max Benefit	Daily Benefit	Max Benefit	Daily Benefit	Max Benefit
1	$200	$365,000	$200	$365,000	$200	$365,000
10	$310	$566,235	$261	$476,242	$290	$529,250
20	$505	$922,337	$351	$640,030	$390	$711,750
30	$823	$1,502,389	$471	$860,146	$490	$894,250
40	$1,341	$2,447,234	$633	$1,155,965	$590	$1,076,750

The elimination period is the number of days the policyowner receives long-term care before benefits begin. The elimination period might also be thought of as a waiting period or a deductible: the longer the elimination period, the lower the premium. Common choices include 30, 60, 90, 180, or 365 days. Most policies require that the claimant actually receive formal care from a covered provider on a given day in order for that day to count towards the elimination period. Available as a built-in feature in some policies or as a rider in others, a calendar day elimination period does not require that one receives care for that day to count. Instead, every day the insured is otherwise benefit eligible counts towards the elimination period, even if formal care services are not required or received. Today, most policies include a cumulative for life crediting method: if the policyowner meets a day of elimination period, he or she will never need to meet that day of elimination period again, even if a second care event occurs in the future.

One popular rider available from leading insurance carriers is called the waiver of home care elimination period rider. Assume a policyowner includes a 90-day elimination period and includes the aforementioned rider. The elimination period for care in a facility is 90 days, while the elimination period for home care is zero days. Typically, the number of days home care is received counts towards the elimination period in the facility. Therefore, should the policyowner need care for 90 or more days, there would be no elimination period to meet for home care or for facility care.

The most common elimination period choice is 90 days, as consumers feel secure that they can afford to pay for the first 90 days of long-term care. However, if the policy-owner needs care in 20 or 30 years from the time of purchase, the cost of care may be several times more than the cost of care today. Consumers should carefully consider how much of their income and assets they wish to expose to this risk.

7-10. Other Popular Features and Riders

Couples may shop for a policy offering shared benefits, which allows two people to share policies. The availability of this option, along with higher premiums, has made the unlimited or lifetime benefit period less popular. Should both partners purchase a five-year benefit period, together they share a 10-year benefit period. One person could use all or a portion of the entire benefit account. One person might pass away without needing any benefits, leaving the remainder to the survivor. Some carriers stipulate that one spouse cannot completely exhaust policies.

A survivorship benefit allows the surviving spouse or partner to stop paying premiums upon the death of the first partner, provided the policy had been in force initially for 10 years without a claim.

Restoration of benefits allows for monies paid by the policy to be put back into the lifetime maximum benefit if the claimant recovers fully and no longer requires care for at least 180 consecutive days.

Most policies include a waiver-of-premium provision: premiums are waived as long as the policyowner is receiving benefits. Some older policies waive premiums only if the claimant is in a nursing home, or if the claimant has received benefits from the policy for at least 90 days.

Also included in most policies today is a care coordination or care advisory service, which assists with the development and coordination of the plan of care. Care coordination may help identify appropriate services and reputable providers of such services and help make arrangement for the services to begin.

All LTC insurance policies marketed must offer a nonforfeiture benefit rider, also known as the shortened benefit period. Should a policyowner with this rider surrender the policy after owning it for at least three years, the premiums paid into the policy will be available to pay for care some day in the future. Note that this is not a return-of-premium benefit, although return of premium at death is an optional rider on many policies.

7-11. Premiums

The premium one ultimately pays for an LTC insurance policy depends greatly on the choices concerning the four building blocks and optional riders described above. Other factors influencing the premium include:

▶ Age.

▶ Couples discount — married couples or those with a committed partner may save 30 to 40 percent on premiums if both apply and are approved. Many insurance carriers offer a 10 to 15 percent discount if only one spouse or partner applies or is approved.

▶ Health — most carriers offer a standard health rate as well as a 10 to 15 percent discount for excellent health.

Many Americans who purchased LTC insurance in the 1970s, '80s, and '90s have experienced premium increases. Such increases have been caused by underpricing of past policies, prolonged low interest rates that limit the return on invested reserves, high persistency (low lapse rates) of in-force policies, and higher-than-expected claims. All LTC insurance policies are guaranteed renewable for life, meaning the policyowner is the only one who can cancel the policy. Furthermore, the insurance company cannot unilaterally change any provision of the contract while it remains in force. In other words, the carrier cannot harm the policyowner with a contractual change. The carrier can, however, add language to make the policy better or more valuable to the policyowner. The only detrimental change allowed by the carrier is to increase the premiums for an identified class of insureds. Any rate increase for a class of insureds must be approved by the state division of insurance. Upon receiving a rate increase, policyowners may elect to keep the policy as-is and pay the higher premium, reduce the benefits and the corresponding premium to a more affordable level, or surrender the policy. Modern policies include a Contingent Nonforfeiture benefit. If premiums increase to a certain level, based on a table of increase percentages, the built-in Contingent Nonforfeiture benefit may be exercised. If such action is taken, the policy is converted to paid-up status, and, if the insured needs long-term care in the future, the past premiums remain on account with the insurance company to pay for care services.

Today, LTC insurance policies cost several times more than policies offered 10 to 20 years ago. While premium increases are never welcomed, consumers tend to hold on to policies purchased in the past, realizing that the premiums are a fraction of what a new policy would cost. Naturally, if one's health has changed for the worse, it may be impossible to replace the coverage.

One way to insulate against future rate increases is by purchasing a limited pay rider, such as a 10-year pay rider. With a 10-year pay rider, the policyowner pays the premium for 10 years, after which time the premium is paid-up for life. It follows that the policyowner cannot be required to pay more premiums after year 10, even if others with the same policy series have an increase. For those under 56, a more affordable option is a paid-up at age 65 rider. Although rare, carriers may offer a single-pay premium, which is guaranteed never to have a premium increase.

7-12. Combination Long-Term Care Insurance Policies

Insurance carriers have heard the concern of many older adults who have one very important objection to traditional LTC insurance: *If I never need this policy, do I get my money back?* Unless a return of premium at death rider was purchased, the answer is "no." Indeed, most reasonable people would much rather pay the LTC insurance premiums and never need long-term care, rather than require care services for a period of years. Still, consumers in their 60s, 70s, and even 80s may find it more palatable to fund a long-term care plan with a combination LTC insurance policy, also known as a hybrid, linked, or asset-based plan.

A life/LTC insurance combination (LTCi) policy allows the insured to fund a life insurance policy with a single premium payment, which may be returned to the consumer upon cancellation of the policy. Premiums can also be paid with an annual premium payment, or for a limited time such as a 10-year pay. Should the policyowner pass away without needing care, an income tax-free death benefit is paid to the beneficiaries of the life insurance. Should the policyowner need LTC before passing, the amount that would have been the death benefit is paid out in the form of LTC benefits over two, three, or four years. If the death benefit is exhausted, a continuation of benefits rider, acting much like a traditional LTC insurance policy, will continue to pay benefits for a specified period of time (*e.g.*, two, three, or four years, or unlimited).

A second form of hybrid policies is an annuity/LTC insurance combination policy. This type of annuity is funded with a single premium or a rollover from another non-qualified annuity. The value of the annuity grows tax-deferred, and can be used to pay for long-term care over a specified or selected number of years. Should the policyowner use all of the funds in the annuity to pay for LTC, a continuation of benefits rider is activated, extending the LTC benefit for another specified period of time. If the policyowner passes away without needing care, the annuity value transfers to the beneficiaries. This form of LTC insurance involves self-funding, as the initial benefits are taken from the policyowner's annuity account. This fact allows the insurance carrier to be somewhat more lenient in underwriting the health of the applicant.

The Pension Protection Act of 2006 (PPA) encourages the purchase of combination policies through certain tax incentives. In an annuity that is not an annuity/LTCi combination policy, should a withdrawal be made from the annuity to pay for care, the withdrawal is taxed as income until all of the growth in the annuity has been withdrawn. Due to the PPA, funds withdrawn from the annuity/LTCi policy to pay for qualified LTC services are received income tax-free after January 1, 2010. In addition, the charges against the cash value of a life/LTCi combination policy to pay for the accelerated death benefit and continuation of benefits rider are no longer considered to be taxable withdrawals. It is also now possible to perform an income-free, partial exchange or rollover from a non-qualified annuity to qualified long-term care insurance.

7-13. Partnership Plans

In the early 1990s, four states — California, Connecticut, Indiana, and New York — were part of a pilot project to promote the purchase of long-term care insurance. Known as the Original Partnership States, the program successfully encouraged consumers to take private responsibility for their LTC needs, and continues to do so to this day.

The Deficit Reduction Act of 2005 (DRA) was signed into law in 2006. Among other things, this federal law changed the look-back period for asset transfers from three years to five years and capped home equity at $525,000 for Medicaid eligibility. The DRA also enabled all remaining states beyond the original four to offer Partnership Plans. Beginning January 1, 2008, a traditional LTC insurance policy sold in Colorado may qualify as a Partnership Plan, which allows for special treatment of one's assets if LTC is needed some day. The stated goals of the Partnership program are (1) to assist the citizens of Colorado in planning for their future LTC needs through quality LTC insurance, (2) without depleting the consumer's resources and assets paying for care.

A Partnership Policy allows the policyowner to protect a dollar in non-exempt assets from Medicaid spend-down for every dollar the Partnership LTC insurance policy has paid out in benefits. This is known as dollar-for-dollar asset protection. Taking liberties to simplify the Medicaid qualification rules, an unmarried Colorado resident seeking to qualify for Medicaid to pay for long-term care can have a house, a car, and $2,000. His or her income must also meet strict qualification limits. Let us assume that our citizen also has $300,000 in non-exempt assets. Should our citizen suddenly suffer a stroke or other debilitating change in health, he or she must spend-down the $300,000 in assets before being eligible for Medicaid.

Now let us assume that our citizen purchased a Partnership LTC insurance policy. For every dollar the policy pays for qualified LTC expenses, Medicaid will disregard a dollar of his or her $300,000 in non-exempt resources when applying for Medicaid. If the policy paid $300,000 or more in benefits, all of the non-exempt resources may be disregarded. If the Partnership Policy paid out $200,000, and at the time of applying for Medicaid the remaining non-exempt assets were down to $200,000, our citizen could apply for Medicaid and disregard the $200,000 in assets. In addition, the disregarded assets are exempt from the estate recovery process at the Medicaid recipient's death.

To qualify as a Partnership Policy in Colorado, the policy must:

▶ Be approved by the Division of Insurance;

▶ Be a tax-qualified policy;

▶ Provide coverage to a person who was a resident of Colorado when coverage became effective;

▶ Have an effective date on or after January 1, 2008; and

▶ Meet certain inflation rider requirements based on age.

Partnership Policies do not cost more than non-Partnership Policies. Assuming the insurance carrier's policy has been approved by the state, the policy is automatically Partnership as long as the policyowner purchased inflation protection equal to or exceeding the minimum levels mandated by Colorado:

Less than age 61	5% automatic compound
	Consumer Price Index (CPI) automatic compound
Ages 61 to 75	3% automatic compound
	5% simple
	Consumer Price Index (CPI) automatic compound
	5% automatic compound until benefits double
76 and above	No inflation is required

States like Colorado that have begun to market Partnership Plans under authority of the Deficit Reduction Act of 2005 are known as DRA Partnership States. Should a Colorado resident move to another DRA Partnership State, the asset disregard from Medicaid spend-down follows the policyowner to the other state. This recognition of another state's Partnership program is referred to as reciprocity. Colorado and the other DRA Partnership states reserve the right to opt out of reciprocity in the future, although the author knows of no state that has opted out as of this writing.

Colorado's State Plan Amendment (SPA), which is Colorado's agreement with the federal government as to how the state will spend Medicaid dollars, was approved by the federal government with an effective date of October 1, 2006. Policies sold in Colorado prior to October 1, 2006, cannot be granted Partnership status. This fact does not mean that non-Partnership Policies written in the past are of lesser value. In fact, policies written more than a few years ago are, in most cases, already much lower in premium than policies being marketed today.

An insurance carrier has the discretion to allow a Colorado policyowner to exchange a non-Partnership Policy for a Partnership Policy if the effective date of the coverage was after October 1, 2006, and before January 1, 2008, assuming the policyowner included one of the age-based inflation riders listed above. Many carriers have chosen to only allow policies written on or after January 1, 2008, to be Partnership eligible. Contact your insurance agent and/or insurance company to find out the status of your coverage.

To date, the author knows of no life/LTCi or annuity/LTCi combination policy that qualifies as a Partnership Plan.

7-14. When Should One Purchase Long-Term Care Insurance?

The best time to purchase any form of insurance is before it is needed, as it is usually too late to obtain coverage once an insurable claim event occurs or becomes likely. LTC insurance is no different. The average age of people purchasing LTC insurance has been dropping steadily for years. Once a product sought after by retirees, LTC insurance is being considered a must-have by an increasing number of baby boomers. According to the *American Association for Long-Term Care Insurance 2011 Sourcebook*, 56 percent of purchasers in 2010 were between the ages of 55 and 65; 20.9 percent of buyers were 45 to 54; but only 19.3 percent were over 65.

Factors impacting the premiums go beyond age. Insurance carriers often sell a policy series for several years before introducing a new generation of coverage, often times pricing the new plan significantly higher than the premiums enjoyed by those who started earlier. A 50-year old considering a daily benefit today of $200 with the 5 percent automatic compound inflation rider would have to buy a $255 daily benefit at age 55 or $326 per day at age 60 in order to match the growth due to the automatic inflation adjustment inside the policy. Insurance companies frequently offer 10 to 15 percent discounts for those in excellent health, and a 30 to 40 percent discount for couples both applying and approved. Should the applicant lose one or both of these discounts in the future by waiting, the premiums will be significantly higher.

More important than paying lower premiums by starting young, those waiting until older ages to apply are risking their ability to qualify for coverage with their good health. In 2010, 24 percent of those ages 60 to 69 were declined coverage due to health; 45 percent of those 70 to 79 were declined; and 71 percent of applicants 80 and older were turned down. *American Association for Long-Term Care Insurance 2011 Sourcebook.*

7-15. Is Long-Term Care Insurance Right for Me?

To answer this question, begin with two basic questions:

1) Can I pass the health underwriting required by the insurance company to qualify for a policy?

2) Can I afford the premiums for a policy that meets my needs and expectations?

If the answer to one of these questions is "no," then LTC insurance may not be available or appropriate. If the answer to both questions is "yes," continue to become educated about this important topic. Talk with an insurance agent with expertise in LTC insurance. You may wish to work with an insurance broker who can help you consider more than one insurance carrier. The agent or broker may help you consider ways to pay the premiums, design a policy to fit your budget, compare and contrast the different types of LTC insurance, and more.

7-16. Tax-Qualified Versus Non-Tax-Qualified Policies

The Health Insurance Portability and Accountability Act of 1996 (HIPAA) created federally "tax-qualified" LTC insurance policies. Tax-qualified (TQ) policies offer certain income tax advantages over non-tax-qualified (NTQ) policies, as well as contractual differences as described in the table below.

Policies purchased prior to January 1, 1997, were grandfathered into TQ status unless material changes to the coverage were made to the policy after January 1, 1997. People purchasing LTC insurance on or after this date have been able to choose between TQ and NTQ, although less than 2 percent of LTC insurance policies purchased in 2007 were NTQ, according to the American Association for Long-Term Care Insurance *2008 LTCi Sourcebook*. The author suspects that the percentage of NTQ policies sold in 2010 is even less, as very few insurance companies offer NTQ.

The following table was taken from *A Shopper's Guide to Long-Term Care Insurance*, 2009 ed. (National Association of Insurance Commissioners):

Federally tax-qualified policies	Federally non-tax-qualified policies
1. Premiums can be included with other annual uncompensated medical expenses for deductions from your income in excess of 7.5 percent of adjusted gross income up to a maximum amount, adjusted for inflation.	1. You may or may not be able to deduct any part of your annual premiums. Congress and the U.S. Department of the Treasury have not clarified this area of the law.
2. Benefits that you receive and use to pay for long-term care services generally will not be counted as income. For policies that pay benefits using the expense incurred method, benefits that you receive in excess of the costs of long term care services may be taxable. For policies that pay benefits using the indemnity or disability methods, all benefit payments up to the federally approved *per diem* (daily) rate are tax-free, even if they exceed your expenses.	2. Benefits that you receive may or may not count as income. Congress and the U.S. Department of the Treasury have not clarified this area of the law.
3. To trigger the benefits under your policy, federal law requires you to be unable to do two activities of daily living without substantial assistance.	3. Policies can offer a different combination of benefit triggers. Benefit triggers are not restricted to two activities of daily living.
4. "Medical necessity" cannot be used as a trigger for benefits.	4. "Medical necessity" and/or other measures of disability can be offered as benefit triggers.
5. Chronic illness or disability must be expected to last for at least 90 days.	5. Policies don't have to require that the disability be expected to last for at least 90 days.
6. For cognitive impairment to be covered, a person must require "substantial supervision."	6. Policies don't have to require "substantial supervision" to trigger benefits for cognitive impairments.

7-17. Tax Incentives

The following is a summary of tax rules from the American Association for Long-Term Care Insurance (AALTCI). Neither the AALTCI nor the author provides tax advice. Consult a tax consultant or legal advisor for tax advice.

Rules for Individuals: Individual taxpayers who itemize their tax deductions can treat premiums paid for tax-qualified LTCi for themselves, their spouses, and any tax dependents as a personal medical expense based on the yearly maximum deductible limit (see chart, below).

Rules for Self-Employed: Self-employed individuals can deduct tax-qualified LTCi premiums as a trade or business expense similar to health and accident insurance. A tax-deduction (*sic*) is allowed for the self-employed individual, for his or her spouse, and other tax dependents. The yearly deductible maximum for each covered individual is the age-based limit (see chart.)

Rules for C-Corporations: C-Corporations benefit from complete deductibility of tax-qualified LTCi insurance (*sic*) protection as a business expense similar to traditional health and accident insurance.

Attained Age in 2011	Limitation of Premiums
Age 40 or less	$350
Age 41 to 50	$660
Age 51 to 60	$1,310
Age 61 to 70	$3,500
Age 71 and above	$4,370

I.R.C. § 213(d)(10).

Colorado: Credit for taxpayer and taxpayer's spouse in an amount equal to 25 percent of total premiums paid during the tax year, up to $150 for each policy. Available to taxpayers with federal taxable income under $50,000 or two individuals filing a joint return with taxable income under $100,000 if credit is claimed for two policies.

Finally, daily benefits received from a cash or indemnity policy are income tax-free, up to $310 per day in 2012. Benefits received above $310 are taxable as income unless used for qualified medical expenses. I.R.C. § 7702B(d)(4).

7-18. Choosing the Right Carrier

Know that there is no such thing as "the best company" or "the best policy," as different people have different needs. Clearly, the lowest premium does not necessarily mean the best value. Choose a carrier with high financial ratings from A.M. Best, Moody's, Standard & Poor's, and others. Look for a carrier that has written LTC insurance for more than just a few years. Consider whether your needs are best met by a reimbursement, indemnity, or cash plan, or a combination LTCi policy.

Insurance carriers differ on underwriting requirements for various medical conditions. One company might approve coverage on an individual with a health concern while another might refuse to insure an applicant for the same condition.

7-19. Health Care Reform and the CLASS Act

Author's Note: At this time, it appears that the CLASS Act will not be implemented, having been repealed in the U.S. House of Representatives on February 1, 2012. This action followed Health and Human Services Secretary Kathleen Sebelius' letter to Congress dated October 14, 2011, stating that she could not implement the Act and was suspending the program. Because it has not been repealed by the U.S. Senate, the information below is still included in this edition.

A new, government-run LTC insurance option for employees was established by the United States Congress under Section 8002 of the Patient Protection and Affordable Care Act of 2010 (also known as Health Care Reform). Known as the CLASS Act, the Community Living Assistance Services and Support (CLASS) program creates a voluntary national insurance plan for long-term support and services. One of the most attractive features is guaranteed coverage with no medical underwriting to all enrollees who pay the monthly premium and meet the work and age requirements.

Much is unknown about the specifics of the CLASS Act, as the federal government has until October 2012 to publish the final rules. Adding to the uncertainty is the efforts of some in our nation's capital to reform or repeal the CLASS Act. Assuming CLASS survives as-is and is made available to citizens after October 2012, here are the details:

▶ Eligibility: To enroll, individuals must be 18 years of age or older and receiving at least the minimum wages or income that are subject to Social Security taxes (currently estimated to be $1,120 per year).

▶ Enrollment: Assuming Health and Human Services meets the October 2012 deadline to publish final rules, the earliest employees could enroll would likely be 2013.

▶ Waiting period: Once enrolled, participants must wait for five years before benefits are available.

▶ Enrollment: Employers decide whether or not to offer CLASS to employees. If offering the program, employees are automatically enrolled unless they opt out. Premiums are paid through payroll deduction. If an employer opts out, an alternative enrollment process, to be defined by the U.S. Department of Health and Human Services (HHS), will be available.

▶ Qualifying for benefits:

　○ Enrollees must have paid premiums for at least five years and must have earned a minimum level of income for at least three of those five years.

　○ Like private long-term care insurance, CLASS is likely to have benefit triggers tied to the inability to perform two or more activities of daily living or have a comparable cognitive impairment that is expected to last 90 days or longer.

▶ Benefits: The benefit payment to CLASS enrollees is an average cash benefit of at least $50 per day, depending on the level of impairment. This cash benefit can be used for nearly any purpose, including non-medical services and paying a family member for help. Benefit payments, which increase over time at a rate based on the Consumer Price Index, continue indefinitely until the enrollee no longer meets the eligibility requirements.

▶ Cost: The monthly premiums for CLASS have yet to be determined by HHS. Estimates from the Congressional Budget Office and the U.S. Centers for Medicare and Medicaid Services state that the average monthly premium may be between $123 and $240.

CLASS Program – An Overview (Genworth Financial 2010).

7-20. Resources

A Shopper's Guide to Long-Term Care Insurance
Published by the National Association of Insurance Commissioners and available from an insurance carrier or agent, or online at www.naic.org or www.insureuonline.org/course_seniors.htm

Colorado's website dedicated to Partnership Plans
www.coloradoltcpartnership.org

National Clearinghouse for Long-Term Care Information
www.longtermcare.gov

The Centers for Medicare and Medicaid Services
www.cms.gov

Colorado Division of Insurance
(303) 894-7499
www.dora.state.co.us/insurance/senior/ltc.htm

Colorado Senior Health Insurance Assistance Program (SHIP)
(888) 696-7213
www.dora.state.co.us/insurance/senior/senior.htm

Colorado Division of Aging and Adult Services
(303) 866-2800

Veterans' benefits
www.va.gov

Chapter 8

Financial Difficulty for Seniors

Jamie J. Roth, Esq.
Brown & Brown, P.C.

SYNOPSIS

8-1. Financial Difficulty for Seniors

Seniors may be particularly vulnerable to the economic difficulties facing many Americans today. This chapter is intended to provide resources to tackle some of the common issues confronting seniors.

8-2. Credit Card and Consumer Debt

Chapter 11, "Arm Yourself with Consumer Protection Information," has a very helpful discussion about credit repair, debt collectors, and debt collection in court. Credit card rates and even outstanding balances can often be negotiated down by calling the credit card company.

Am I Obligated to Pay the Debts of My Spouse After His or Her Death?

The obligation of a surviving spouse to pay for the debts of a decedent has become an issue as retirement accounts and home equity have dwindled in our current economic situation. When someone dies in Colorado, any property that person owns that is subject to a secured debt (such as a car loan or a mortgage) is subject to collection by the secured creditor unless regular payments are made on the loan. Some assets are exempt from collection.

Some of the exemptions include a homestead exemption for up to $90,000 of home equity; an exempt property allowance of up to $30,000 worth of property; a family allowance of $30,000; life insurance proceeds paid to a beneficiary; and assets held in or paid from a pension, retirement plan, IRA, or other similar account. The remaining assets of a decedent's estate are generally available to unsecured creditors.

A surviving spouse or other family member who is acting as a personal representative for an estate must be very careful to properly pay estate debts. It is highly recommended that anyone thinking about serving as a personal representative consult with an attorney before making any distributions from an estate. If a personal representative distributes estate assets to beneficiaries before all creditors are paid, those beneficiaries and/or the personal representative could be liable to creditors up to the amount improperly distributed. See Chapter 28, "What to Do When Someone Dies: Responsibilities of the Personal Representative and Trustee Under Probate," for more information.

If a husband and wife have both signed a debt obligation, they are generally both responsible for repayment, even if one of them dies. Some creditors claim that surviving spouses are responsible for certain debts incurred individually by their deceased spouse if the debt is a "family expense." This is an unclear area in Colorado law. Different states have different rules regarding debt between spouses. Family members who are not spouses, such as children, parents, grandparents, brothers, sisters, or other family members, have no obligation to pay the decedent's debt unless they co-signed on the debt obligation.

Debt collectors may contact parents, friends and neighbors, or anyone believed to be handling the estate. The *Wall Street Journal* ran an article on December 3, 2011 regarding debt collection firms specializing in estate debts who have applied pressure to family members to pay credit card debts or medical bills that surviving family members had no legal obligation to pay. Any person contacted by a debt collector has certain protections under federal and Colorado law regarding debt collection. This is discussed in detail in Chapter 11, "Arm Yourself with Consumer Protection Information."

8-3. Taxes

Refund Anticipation Loans

A lot of businesses offer to loan you money until you get your tax refund from the IRS. Be careful about using these services. It is easy to electronically file your tax returns, and plenty of free help is available if you need it (see section 8-5, "Resources"). You can have the IRS deposit your refund directly into your bank account, which often takes only eight to fifteen days, and all of your refund goes right to you. If you borrow money in anticipation of your refund, the lender gets part of your tax refund — sometimes a big chunk.

Tax Problems

Low-Income taxpayers with a tax controversy can contact two clinics in Colorado:

1) San Luis Land Rights Council, Inc.: (866) 607-8462, (719)-672-1002, or www.landrightscouncil.org/contact.htm

2) University of Denver: (303) 871-6239 or www.piton.org/LowIncomeTaxpayerHelp

Property Taxes

Colorado law provides for a senior property tax exemption for seniors 65 years or older who live in Colorado and have owned their Colorado homes for at least ten years. When this exemption is in effect, qualifying seniors get a 50 percent break on their property tax bill, up to $100,000. Unfortunately, this program's funding has been suspended since 2009, but it may be restored in 2013 if approved by the Colorado legislature.

Colorado offers a Property Tax/Rent/Heat Rebate Program for low-income seniors aged 65 years or older and disabled persons. Qualified applicants can receive a rebate of up to $600 of property tax and $192 of heating expenses. Applications are available at every county assessor's office, through the Colorado Division of Property Taxation at (303) 777-1277, or online at www.colorado.gov/cs/Satellite/Revenue/REVX/1216116072809. Free assistance in completing the application is available.

The Colorado Senior Property Tax Deferral Program is a program for homeowners aged 65 years or older where the state makes tax payments directly to the county to pay the property tax due. These payments are loans, and the state will file a lien against the property, but no payment is due on the loan until the home is sold or the senior no longer qualifies for the program. The state charges interest at a market rate for the loan. Seniors can use this program for multiple years. To qualify, the home must be owned and occupied by the senior, and the property cannot generate rental income. The mortgage lender must agree that the state's lien will come first, before the mortgage.

8-4. Bankruptcy

Theory Behind Bankruptcy

Bankruptcy allows a person in debt to file financial information with the court showing the need for bankruptcy, and to receive a "discharge" or relief from certain types of debt. In *Local Loan Co v. Hunt*, the U.S. Supreme Court explained the purpose of bankruptcy is to give "the honest but unfortunate debtor . . . a new opportunity in life and a clear field for future effort, unhampered by the pressure and discouragement of preexisting debt." Bankruptcy carries significant disadvantages and has limitations. It should be considered only when other debt management options have failed. Bankruptcy has adverse effects on your credit rating for at least ten years, and may prevent you from receiving any type of loan or credit for some time after you file.

Types of Bankruptcy

An individual can file under one of four different "chapters" of the bankruptcy code. Each has different criteria for filing and some differences in the type of relief offered.

Chapter 7

This is known as a "liquidating" bankruptcy. The debtor will describe to the court all of its assets and debts. Certain types of assets are exempt from creditors. This varies from state to state. In Colorado, exempt assets may include real estate or mobile homes with a value of up to $90,000 if the homeowner is over 60 years of age; disability insurance payments; life insurance proceeds; state pensions; ERISA-qualified benefits; veterans' benefits; retirement accounts, up to certain limits; public benefits; vehicles worth up to $10,000 if the owner/debtor is over age 60; home furnishings worth up to $3,000; some earnings up to certain limits; tools of trade up to $20,000; and certain agricultural assets, including livestock and equipment, with a value of up to $50,000. Any nonexempt assets will be sold, and the proceeds will be used to pay creditors according to their statutory priority for repayment. If there are no nonexempt assets, the creditors receive nothing. A debtor will be presumed to be filing an abusive petition if his or her income is more than $6,000 per month, unless the debtor's nonpriority unsecured debt is sufficiently large.

Chapter 13

This is known as a "wage earner's" bankruptcy. This allows individuals with regular income to put in place a court-approved plan to pay all or part of their debts over 3 to 5 years. This type of bankruptcy allows a debtor to keep his or her property as long as the debtor complies with the repayment plan.

Chapter 12

This is similar to Chapter 13, but is specifically for debtors who are family farmers or fisherman.

Chapter 11

This is known as "reorganization." This type of bankruptcy is rarely filed by an individual, but is commonly filed by businesses. It allows a commercial enterprise to continue operation of a business and repay creditors through a court-approved plan.

Consultation with a bankruptcy attorney will help you decide if bankruptcy will help you, and what type of bankruptcy is best for your situation.

Filing for Bankruptcy

A debtor must pay a filing fee, and, along with the petition, must file a schedule listing all assets and liabilities, a schedule listing all income and expenses, a statement of financial affairs, a schedule of all contracts and leases, copies of tax returns, a list of all creditors, a list of all property, disclosure of all income, a list of all monthly living expenses, and a certification of attendance at credit counseling. Depending upon the type of bankruptcy filed, the debtor may also be required to file a statement of all interest in qualified educational funds and/or a repayment plan.

What Happens Once I File?

Filing for bankruptcy will result in an automatic stay where creditors must halt all efforts to collect debts. This stay can be lifted if a creditor requests relief from the court, or if the debtor is found to be delaying or otherwise abusing the bankruptcy process.

A creditor's meeting will be scheduled at the bankruptcy courthouse. The debtor must attend and answer under oath all of the creditors' questions regarding financial circumstances, a repayment plan, and related information.

The court will appoint a bankruptcy trustee, who is an impartial third party who can investigate or liquidate assets. The trustee has "avoiding powers" that allow the trustee to reverse payments the debtor made to favored creditors within 90 days of filing for bankruptcy (called "preferential payments"). The trustee can also take other actions to protect the integrity of the bankruptcy proceeding. The trustee can recommend that the court approve a repayment plan, or that the court dismiss a bankruptcy petition for fraud or other non-compliance.

If all of the requirements of the particular type of bankruptcy are followed by the debtor, certain types of debt will be discharged, meaning that the debtor does not have to pay them and the creditor cannot pursue the debtor.

Debts that Cannot be Discharged

Certain types of debts cannot be discharged in bankruptcy. The type of debt that is dischargable depends on the type of bankruptcy. Under § 523(a) of the bankruptcy code, debts that cannot be discharged include certain tax claims, child support, alimony, debts arising from willful or malicious injury caused by the debtor, governmental fines or penalties, student loans, overpayments by government programs, personal injury judgments resulting from the debtor driving under the influence, debts owed to retirement plans, secured debts, and debts to homeowner associations.

8-5. Resources

Resources Regarding Debts, Lending, and Collection Practices

Colorado Attorney General Consumer Resource Guides
Consumer resource guides available on many topics, including credit and lending.
www.coloradoattorneygeneral.gov/initiatives/consumer_resource_guide

AARP
AARP publishes several bulletins, including "6 Steps to a Realistic Debt Repayment Plan,"
"4 Little-Known Secrets About Credit Card Companies," and "Credit Card Negotiation 101."
www.aarp.org/money/credit-loans-debt/

Colorado Legal Services

Colorado Legal Services offers legal assistance to low income Coloradoans, and has legal information for the public, including information specific to consumer debt.

    1905 Sherman St., Ste. 400
    Denver, CO 80203
    (303) 837-1321
    www.coloradolegalservices.org

Consumer rights packet available for download at
    www.coloradolegalservices.org/documents/44291110_Debtor%20packet_(statewide).pdf?stateabbrev=/CO/

Wall Street Journal

Article referenced in section 8-2:
    "For the Families of Some Debtors, Death Offers No Respite."
    Wall Street Journal (Dec. 3, 2011), *available at*
    http://online.wsj.com/article/SB10001424052970204224604577030043890121710.html

Tax Resources

AARP Foundation Tax-Aide

AARP Foundation Tax-Aide offers services for people who pay low to moderate income taxes, with special attention for those 60 years or older. Service sites throughout Colorado.
    www.aarp.org/applications/VMISLocator/searchTaxAideLocations.action

Denver Asset Building Coalition

Free tax preparation services for Colorado residents with low to moderate income.
    2980 Curtis St.
    Denver, CO 80205
    (303) 388-7030
    www.denverabc.org

The Piton Foundation

The Piton Foundation offers free income tax return preparation for low income taxpayers, including assistance with earned income tax credits and applications for the Property Tax/Rent/Heat Rebate Program.
    370 17th St., Ste. 5300
    Denver, CO 80202
    (303) 825-6246
    www.piton.org/taxhelpcolorado

Colorado Legal Services

Colorado Legal Services offers legal assistance to low income Coloradoans, and has legal information for the public, including information specific to income and property taxes.

> 1905 Sherman St., Ste. 400
> Denver, CO 80203
> (303) 837-1321
> www.coloradolegalservices.org

Other Tax Resources:

- IRS forms and publications can be found at: www.irs.gov/formspubs/index.html
- Colorado forms and tax information can be found at: www.colorado.gov/revenue/tax
- A website providing links to a number of tax related topics is: http://taxtopics.net/
- Public libraries often provide print or online access to tax forms and tax information.

Bankruptcy Resources

AARP

AARP has a web page devoted to money issues, including credit, loans, and debt. There are several useful articles available, including "Avoiding Bankruptcy," at:

> www.aarp.org/money/credit-loans-debt/info-12-2008/pond_avoiding_bankruptcy.html

Colorado Legal Services

Colorado Legal Services offers legal assistance to low income Coloradoans, and has legal information for the public, including information specific to bankruptcy.

> 1905 Sherman St., Ste. 400
> Denver, CO 80203
> (303) 837-1321
> www.coloradolegalservices.org

United States Courts

"Bankruptcy Basics" guides and videos are published by the administrative office of the United States Courts.

> www.uscourts.gov/FederalCourts/Bankruptcy/BankruptcyBasics.aspx

Denver Bar Association

The Denver Bar Association offers a free bankruptcy clinic twice a month. Details can be found here:

> www.denbar.org/index.cfm/ID/111/dba/Legal-Clinics/#bankruptcy

Chapter 9

Employment Discrimination

Andrew W. Volin, Esq.*
Sherman & Howard L.L.C.

SYNOPSIS

9-1.   Age

9-2.   Race, Color, Religion, Sex, and National Origin

9-3.   Disability

9-4.   Before Filing a Charge of Discrimination

9-5.   Filing a Charge of Discrimination

9-6.   Resources

There are several types of discrimination that are illegal in the United States, such as discrimination based upon a person's age, race, color, religion, sex, national origin, and disability. These types of discrimination may occur in several venues, such as employment, housing, and other public accommodations. Both federal and state laws prohibit discrimination.

The federal Age Discrimination in Employment Act (ADEA) makes it illegal for an employer to discriminate against employees because of their age.

Another federal law, Title VII of the Civil Rights Act of 1964, as amended, protects individuals from discrimination because of their race, color, religion, sex, and national origin in the areas of voting, public accommodations, public facilities, public education, federally assisted programs, and employment.

Federal law also makes it illegal to discriminate against people with disabilities. Under the federal Americans with Disabilities Act, it is illegal to discriminate against people with disabilities in employment, public accommodations, and government services.

In addition to these federal laws, Colorado has a state law known as the Anti-Discrimination Act. Like the federal laws noted above, this state law prohibits discrimination against individuals in employment based on their disability, race, creed, color, sex, religion, age, national origin, or ancestry. Like the federal laws, it also prohibits discrimination in the areas of public accommodations and housing. However, in addition, Colorado law also prohibits discrimination on the basis of sexual orientation and being married to another employee, neither of which are currently covered by federal law.

The federal laws generally apply only to employers with at least 15 employees (the ADEA requires 20). However, Colorado law generally applies to any employers with at least two or more employees (the prohibition on marital status discrimination only applies to employers with more than 25 employees).

Employers are prohibited from discriminating in a variety of employment issues, such as job advertisements; hiring; pay and benefits, which affect compensation; promotion; demotion; and termination.

Employment discrimination includes adverse actions directly motivated by discriminatory intent, as well as adverse actions that may not be caused by a discriminatory intent but nevertheless have an adverse impact on employees in a protected group.

9-1. Age

The federal Age Discrimination in Employment Act (ADEA) makes it illegal for an employer to discriminate against a qualified employee because of his or her age. Employees who are 40 years or older are protected from discrimination based on their age. Employers are prohibited from treating qualified workers, 40 years or older, less favorably than other employees because of the older worker's age. Employers covered by this statute include those who employ 20 or more employees.

The Colorado statute prohibiting age discrimination contains an exception permitting employers to compel retirement for workers between the ages of 65 and 70 who have held executive or policy-making positions and have access to immediate retirement benefits of at least a certain amount. The ADEA does not have this upper-age exception. Employers covered by the Colorado statute include those who employ two or more employees.

These statutes were enacted to protect older workers from stereotypes, including beliefs that older workers are slow, unable to adapt to change, unable to learn current technology or procedures, or that they should retire at a certain age.

The Older Workers Benefit Protection Act (OWBPA) is an amendment to the ADEA limiting the manner in which an employee 40 years or older may waive his or her protections under the ADEA. Under the OWBPA, an individual may not waive any right or claim under the ADEA unless the waiver is understood and voluntary. Any release executed by an employee is not considered valid unless the following minimum guidelines of the OWBPA are met:

▶ The waiver is part of an understandable written agreement that specifically refers to rights under the ADEA;

▶ The individual does not waive rights that may arise after the date the waiver is executed;

▶ The waiver must be accompanied by consideration (*i.e.*, money) in addition to severance or other benefits that the employee is already entitled to receive;

▶ The waiver must advise the individual in writing to consult with an attorney before executing the waiver;

▶ The employee must be granted a period of at least 21 days within which to consider the agreement; and

▶ The waiver also must state that the offer remains revocable for at least seven days after the date of signature.

If the waiver is requested as part of an exit incentive, group layoff, or other program offered to a class of employees, then these requirements are altered somewhat. Rather than having 21 days to consider the terms, 45 days must be given. Also, the employer must provide information about how eligibility for the program was determined and the job titles and ages for those selected or eligible, as well as for those not selected or eligible.

9-2. Race, Color, Religion, Sex, and National Origin

Title VII of the Civil Rights Act of 1964, as amended by the Civil Rights Act of 1991 (Title VII), prohibits employment discrimination and/or harassment based on race, color, religion, sex, and national origin. Employers covered by this statute include those who employ 15 or more employees.

Employers covered by the Colorado statute, which prohibits this type of discrimination, include those who employ two or more employees. Colorado also prohibits discrimination based on sexual orientation, and, for employers with more than 25 employees, generally prohibits discriminating against a person because their spouse or fiancé is an employee.

9-3. Disability

Employment Protections for People with Disabilities

Title I of the Americans with Disabilities Act (ADA) offers protection from employment discrimination based on disability for qualified people with disabilities. The law covers employers with 15 or more workers.

Another federal law, Section 504 of the Rehabilitation Act, states that no qualified individual with a disability will be "excluded from the participation in, be denied the benefits of, or be subject to discrimination under any program or activity receiving federal financial assistance." This includes employment.

The Colorado Anti-Discrimination Act protects employees with disabilities from discrimination regardless of the number of workers employed.

Definition of Disability and Qualified Individual With a Disability

Under the civil rights protections listed above, the term "disability" means, with respect to an individual:

▶ A physical or mental impairment that substantially limits one or more of the major life activities of such individual;

▶ A record of such an impairment; or

▶ Being regarded as a having such an impairment.

In order to be considered a "qualified individual with a disability," a worker must be able to perform the essential functions of his or her job, with or without a reasonable accommodation. Essential functions are the necessary duties and activities of the job position.

Reasonable Accommodations

A "reasonable accommodation" is any change in the work environment or the way things are usually done that enables a person with a disability to perform the essential functions of the job. An accommodation is considered reasonable if it is feasible and meets the needs of the person with a disability.

An employer must make a reasonable accommodation to an employee with a known disability, unless the employer can show that the accommodation would cause an undue financial burden or hardship on the operations of its business, or that providing the accommodation would pose a direct threat to the health or safety of the employee or others.

Reasonable accommodations may be needed:

▶ During the application/interview process;

▶ To perform the essential functions of the job; or

▶ For the enjoyment of equal terms, conditions, and privileges of employment.

When an employee requests an accommodation, the employer can request medical documentation of the claimed disability and the need for the accommodation. Any medical information provided to the employer is to be treated as confidential and kept in a record separate from the employee personnel file.

An employee need not provide all of his or her medical files. The employee need only submit medical information relevant to the claimed disability and potential accommodation.

Requests for reasonable accommodations may include, but are not limited to:

▶ Changes in physical accessibility of the location or work site;

▶ Job restructuring;

▶ Modified work schedule;

▶ Acquisition or modification of work equipment;

▶ Modification of training materials or examinations;

▶ Modifications of policies;

▶ Altering how an essential function of the job is performed; or

▶ Reassignment to a vacant position.

Creating a reasonable accommodation is an individualized process and will vary from situation to situation, based on a person's limitations, the job, and the employer's business. Keep in mind that a reasonable accommodation is to be provided to enable the employee to perform the essential functions of the job.

An employee's request for a reasonable accommodation may, but need not, be written. The employer and employee should engage in a productive and interactive exchange to determine a reasonable accommodation appropriate to the needs of the employee. If a specific accommodation is requested, the employer should consider the specified request, but may provide an effective alternative.

9-4. Before Filing a Charge of Discrimination

If you suspect you have been the subject of employment discrimination covered by these federal or state laws, you have the right to file a complaint, known as a charge, with the Equal Employment Opportunity Commission (EEOC), or the Colorado Civil Rights Division (CCRD). Before doing so, you should consider whether there are routes to open lines of communication within your employment setting:

▶ Are you represented by a union that can advocate for your rights?

▶ Does your company employ an EEO or ADA coordinator or someone who monitors compliance with discrimination laws? (You might be able to find this information through your human resources department.)

▶ Are you a federal or state employee who may be required to enter into an internal process before filing a charge with the EEOC or CCRD?

▶ Is there an internal grievance procedure, an administrator with decision-making powers, or a board where your issues will be heard and addressed?

▶ Is there an opportunity to negotiate or mediate with your employer?

▶ Be aware of deadlines for filing charges, listed on the next page.

▶ Develop a plan to address employment discrimination.

9-5. Filing a Charge of Discrimination

Where to file a charge of employment discrimination:

Colorado Civil Rights Division (CCRD)
1560 Broadway, Ste. 1050
Denver, CO 80202
(303) 894-2997 or toll-free (800) 262-4845
TTY through Relay Colorado (711 plus regular phone number)

There are satellite offices in Pueblo and Grand Junction, but all intakes must be initiated by contacting the Denver office. The CCRD has jurisdiction over businesses regardless of the number of employees. The CCRD may offer either group or individual intakes about a complaint.

Equal Employment Opportunity Commission (EEOC)
303 E. 17th Ave., Ste. 410
Denver, CO 80203
(800) 669-4000
(800) 669-6820 (TTY)

The EEOC has jurisdiction for businesses with 15 or more employees.

Timelines for Filing to Protect Your Legal Rights

CCRD — six months from the date of employment discrimination.

EEOC — 300 days from the date of employment discrimination.

To protect your legal rights, you must contact the EEOC or CCRD within these timelines.

Federal, state, and/or union employees may have mandatory prerequisites to the deadlines listed above. Deadlines may be within a few days. Requirements may include filing with an internal EEO officer. Additionally, other employment claims may have different filing requirements and deadlines.

You generally must file a sworn written statement in order to file a charge with the EEOC or CCRD. Also, before a private lawsuit may be filed in court, you must exhaust administrative remedies with the agency. Prior to filing such a suit, you must receive a right-to-sue letter from the EEOC or CCRD (see "Filing a Charge," below).

Filing a Charge

As the charging party, you should be prepared to provide the who, what, when, where, and how concerning your complaint:

▶ Your name, address, and telephone number.

▶ Employer's name, address, telephone number, and number of employees, if known.

▶ A description and timeline of events, with any available documentation, to support your claim of discrimination.

▶ The names, addresses, and phone numbers of anyone who could support your claim of employment discrimination (witnesses).

▶ Documentation of your disability, if applicable.

When you file a charge of discrimination with the EEOC or CCRD, you will be assigned a charge number. An investigator will have primary responsibility for handling your complaint. The employer that you filed a charge against will have the opportunity to respond to your statements alleging discrimination.

You may be offered the chance to mediate with your employer. This step is voluntary.

You may be requested to submit additional information related to your charge.

After the claim has been investigated, the EEOC or CCRD will determine if there is "cause" to your complaint that may initiate further agency action.

If the EEOC or CCRD finds that there is "cause," it may require conciliation efforts, choose to pursue a lawsuit on your behalf, or provide you with a right-to-sue letter.

Even if the EEOC or CCRD does not find that there is "cause," you will still be provided with a right-to-sue letter that enables you to file a lawsuit asserting discrimination in a federal or state court. You will lose your right to sue if you do not file the complaint in court within 90 days from the date of the letter, with additional time for mailing.

9-6. Resources

If you believe that a federal program has discriminated against you, file a complaint with the federal agency that funds the program. Your U.S. senator or representative's office can tell you which federal agency to contact.

If you believe that your employer has discriminated against you, file a complaint with the Equal Employment Opportunity Commission (EEOC) or the Colorado Civil Rights Division (CCRD). (See discussion in section 9-5.)

CCRD
(303) 894-2997
(800) 262-4845 (toll-free, bilingual Spanish/English)
www.dora.state.co.us/civil-rights/

Colorado Department of Labor and Employment
Unemployment Benefits
(303) 318-9000
(800) 388-5515
www.coworkforce.com/UIB/

EEOC

Headquarters:
U.S. Equal Employment Opportunity Commission
131 M St., NE
Washington, D.C. 20507

(800) 669-4000
(202) 663-4900
(800) 669-6820 (TTY)
info@eeoc.gov
www.eeoc.gov

To be automatically connected with the nearest EEOC field office, call:
(800) 669-4000
(800) 669-6820 (TTY)

Denver Field Office:

303 E. 17th Ave., Ste. 410
Denver, CO 80203
(800) 669-4000
(800) 669-6820 (TTY)

Fair Housing Laws

www.civilrights.org/fairhousing/laws

Social Security Administration

(800) 772-1213
(800) 325-0778 (TTY)
www.ssa.gov

United States Department of Justice

950 Pennsylvania Ave., NW
Washington, D.C. 20530-0001
(202) 353-1555 or (202) 514-2000
AskDOJ@usdoj.gov
www.usdoj.gov

---

* This chapter was originally reviewed by Valerie L. Corzine, Esq., Legal Center for People with Disabilities and Older People.

Chapter 10

Workers' Compensation and Seniors

Gregory B. Cairns, Esq.
Cairns & Associates, P.C.

SYNOPSIS

10-1.   Workers' Compensation

10-2.   Benefits Available

10-3.   Filing a Workers' Compensation Claim

10-4.   Basic Forms

10-5.   Special Workers' Compensation Issues Pertaining to Seniors

10-6.   Resources

10-1. Workers' Compensation

Workers' compensation is a state insurance program designed to compensate workers who are injured on the job. The Colorado State legislature determines eligibility for benefits as well as amounts and duration of benefits.

Every employer in the State of Colorado is required to buy workers' compensation coverage for its employees, or qualify under the state's strict standards to be self-insured. The Colorado Workers' Compensation program is administered by a state agency, the Colorado Department of Labor and Employment, Division of Workers' Compensation. To learn more about the Colorado workers' compensation system, call the Division of Workers' Compensation customer service unit at (303) 318-8700, or visit their website at www. coworkforce.com/dwc. You will find the Division of Workers' Compensation website to be very informative and user friendly.

Employees who qualify for workers' compensation benefits cannot sue their employers in a federal or state district court using personal injury, negligence, or other "common law" theories of liability. This is because workers' compensation is considered an "exclusive remedy" for injury claims. An employee who is injured on the job, however, is not prohibited from suing his or her employer for violation of a federal anti-discrimination law such as the Americans with Disabilities Act or Title VII (discrimination based on race, age, gender, national origin, religion, etc.), or for sexual harassment, violation of the Family and Medical Leave Act, the Older Workers Benefits Protection Act, or the Age Discrimination in Employment Act.

The Colorado workers' compensation system is not easily understood by laypersons since it is governed by statutes, rules, and case law that are ever-changing and complicated. If you have questions about the workers' compensation system, call customer service at the Division of Workers' Compensation, or retain a attorney who specializes in workers' compensation.

10-2. Benefits Available

There are eight types of benefits available under the Colorado workers' compensation system:

Medical Benefits

An injured worker is entitled to all medical benefits that are reasonably necessary to cure or alleviate the effects of the industrial accident. Those benefits can include hospitalization costs, prescriptions, x-rays, surgery, physical therapy, medical transportation costs, prosthetic devices, bandages, and much more. Medical providers can only charge a certain amount for medical services and equipment, which is paid by the insurance company or self-insured employer. The injured worker does not make any co-payment. Medical benefits are available as long as necessary, sometimes even for life.

Temporary Total Disability

If a worker cannot work at his or her regular job at all, the worker is entitled to a wage replacement benefit known as temporary total disability (TTD). TTD is paid at the rate of 2/3 of the worker's average weekly wage, up to a state maximum amount. The state maximum amount for TTD from July 1, 2011, through June 30, 2012, is $828.03. These benefits are usually paid every two weeks. TTD lasts until the worker is at maximum medical improvement, released to regular employment, returns to work at full wage, misses a rescheduled doctor's appointment, or fails to return to an offer of modified duty.

Temporary Partial Disability

Temporary partial disability (TPD) benefits are paid when a worker returns to work earning less than his or her regular wage. In such a case, the worker is paid TPD by the following formula:

Average weekly wage at time of injury - average weekly wage after return to work x 2/3 = TPD rate.

For example, a worker who earns $600 per week at the time of injury who returns to work half-time earning $300 per week would receive $200 per week in temporary partial disability benefits ($600 **minus** $300 x 2/3 = $200).

Bodily Disfigurement

Bodily disfigurement is paid in addition to other benefits when a worker is left with a scar, amputation, or other bodily disfigurement. Beginning July 1, 2011, a worker may receive up to $4,396 for certain bodily disfigurements, and up to $8,792 for more serious bodily disfigurements. The maximum amount available for bodily disfigurement increases each year. Bodily disfigurement can be admitted by the insurance company or self-insured employer, or an injured worker may submit photographs to an administrative law judge (ALJ) for evaluation. Alternatively, the injured worker may appear live before an ALJ at a disfigurement hearing.

Permanent Partial Disability

The purpose of permanent partial disability (PPD) benefits is to compensate the injured worker for anticipated wage loss due to the effects of an industrial injury. Injured workers are compensated for their permanent partial disability based on a formula that varies depending on whether the injury is to a specific body part or to the "whole person." The formula for injuries to specific body parts (knees, eyes, wrists) does not take into consideration the age or average weekly wage of the injured employee. An injury to the "whole person" (for example, back, neck, or hernia) does take into consideration age and average weekly wage. Since the formulas for calculating permanent partial disability are not easily understood, an injured worker should consult with the Division of Workers' Compensation or an experienced attorney to determine whether an insurance company has properly calculated his or her PPD.

Permanent Total Disability

If an injured worker is unable to earn any wages for the same or any other employer, he or she can collect permanent total disability (PTD) benefits. PTD benefits are potentially payable until the death of the injured worker. Such benefits are paid at the rate of 2/3 of the worker's average weekly wage, without a cost of living increase. If a worker is entitled to permanent total disability benefits, he or she may ask for a lump-sum payment of those benefits up to $60,000. After the lump sum is paid, the remaining benefits due will be paid at a lower rate (amortized). The standard for proving entitlement to permanent total disability is difficult. An injured worker who turns down an offer of employment or vocational rehabilitation may not qualify for permanent total disability benefits. If an insurer can demonstrate that the worker has returned to work earning $4,000 or more, permanent total disability benefits may end.

Vocational Rehabilitation

Vocational rehabilitation is not a mandatory benefit in the Colorado workers' compensation system. Insurers do offer vocational rehabilitation services on occasion, however, in order to avoid a determination of permanent total disability.

Death Benefits

Death benefits are paid to the dependents of a deceased worker. Benefits are payable at a rate that is 2/3 of the average weekly wage of the deceased worker, up to a state maximum. Dependent spouses are eligible for death benefits for life or, upon remarriage, for two years beyond the date of remarriage. Minor children are eligible for dependent benefits until the age of 18 or, upon enrollment in an accredited institution of higher learning, until they are 21 years of age. If there are multiple dependents, all dependents share one amount. Death benefits are reduced by 50 percent of Social Security benefits received by the dependent.

10-3. Filing a Workers' Compensation Claim

There are three basic types of workers' compensation claims: **traumatic injury**, **occupational disease**, and **mental impairment**. A **traumatic injury** is an accidental injury that occurs at a specific time and place. An **occupational disease** is an injury due to the conditions at work that, over time, cause injury or disease. An example of an occupational disease is a carpal tunnel condition caused by repetitive motion at work. The third type of injury is **mental impairment**, which is an accidental injury that does not necessarily involve a physical injury that is due to an event or conditions at employment and that would cause symptoms of distress in a similarly situated employee. A mental impairment claim must be supported by evidence from a physician, it must result in either lost time from work or medical attention, and it must be primarily caused by some event or conditions at work. A mental impairment claim cannot be caused in full or in part by conditions of employment that are common to all fields of employment such as termination, promotion, suspension, or other disciplinary action at work.

If a worker feels that he or she has been injured because of work, the worker should notify the employer of the claim *in writing* within four working days. Alternatively, the employee may file a claim with the Division of Workers' Compensation by completing a form known as the "Worker's Claim for Compensation." This form, which can be found online at www.coworkforce.com/dwc, is easily understood and can be completed by a lay person. If you need assistance in completing the Claim for Compensation, consult with a representative from the Division of Workers' Compensation or retain an attorney to file one for you. There are no filing fees associated with filing a claim for workers' compensation or any subsequent document.

Once the employer is notified of the work-related injury, the employer must offer the worker a choice of at least two medical providers (two physicians, two clinics, or a physician and a clinic), unless the worker lives in a rural area. Failure to offer at least two treating providers within a short time after notice of the injury will result in the worker's right to choose his or her own provider.

Once the worker selects a medical provider, there are two ways to accomplish a change of treating physician. If the worker has not reached maximum medical improvement and no more than 90 days have passed after the date of injury, the worker may request a change of physician to one of the other medical providers offered at the time of injury. This request will automatically be granted. At any time, an injured worker may submit a written request for a change of treating physician to the insurance carrier. If the carrier does not respond within 20 days of the written request, the request will automatically be granted.

Once a claim is filed, the Division of Workers' Compensation notifies the worker's employer and the insurance company about the claim. The employer and its insurance company (known as "respondents"), then file a response to the Claim for Compensation indicating whether they will accept or deny your claim. If the respondents accept your claim, they file a "General Admission of Liability." If they deny your claim, they file a "Notice of Contest." If respondents deny the claim, a claimant may file an "Application for Hearing." Once an Application for Hearing is filed, the respondents will file a "Response to Application for Hearing" that indicates their position on issues the injured worker has endorsed, and endorsing their own defenses and offsets as appropriate. The Response to Application for Hearing will tell the injured worker a great deal about what the respondents think about the worker's claim.

Once a claim is filed, the parties may gather information from each other about the facts and theories known to them. This is called "discovery," and is usually conducted through questionnaires known as "Interrogatories and Requests for Production of Documents." Sometimes the parties will agree to take a deposition of an important witness, such as an employer representative or a doctor.

At any time after the Application for Hearing is filed, the parties may proceed to a prehearing conference to discuss procedural issues, or a settlement conference to try to resolve some or all of the issues in the case. Prehearings and settlement conferences are conducted by special judges known as Prehearing Administrative Law Judges. These judges have the power to make rulings concerning disputes about producing information, or when a hearing can commence. They also can help the parties settle the issues in dispute.

If the parties cannot resolve the issues on their own, they will proceed to a hearing before an Administrative Law Judge, known as a "merits judge." The merits judge, who is a specialist in workers' compensation claims, will decide all issues pertaining to the workers' compensation claim.

If a party disagrees with the decision of an Administrative Law Judge, it may appeal the order to an appellate body known as the Industrial Claim Appeals Office. A further level of appeal is the Colorado Court of Appeals. The ultimate appellate body for workers' compensation cases is the Colorado Supreme Court. Very few workers' compensation cases, however, are reviewed by the court of appeals or the supreme court.

10-4. Basic Forms

Most of the following forms can be found in the "Forms" section of the Division of Workers' Compensation website at www.coworkforce.com/dwc.

▶ **Workers' Claim for Compensation**
This is a form that a claimant completes to give information concerning his or her claim. This form could suffice as the employee's notice of injury that the employee is required to submit within four working days after an accidental traumatic injury, or 30 days from the "first distinct manifestation" of an occupational disease.

▶ **Notice of Contest**
This is a form completed by the insurance company or third-party administrator on behalf of the employer by which the respondents deny a claim.

▶ **Employer's First Report of Injury**
For certain injuries, an employer is required to file an Employer's First Report of Injury with its carrier within 10 days. The carrier or third-party administrator, in turn, will, as appropriate, file the Employer's First Report of Injury with the Division of Workers' Compensation to advise the Division and the injured worker about the claim.

▶ **General Admission of Liability**
Respondents admit for benefits on a form known as the General Admission of Liability. An injured worker does not need to respond to this notice, but he or she should review it carefully to make sure the respondents have admitted to all benefits that are appropriate.

▶ **Application for Hearing**
This is the form that either party can file if the party wants a hearing on an issue before an Administrative Law Judge. (Available from the Office of Administrative Courts, www.colorado.gov/dpa/oac.)

▶ **Response to Application for Hearing**
This form, usually filed by respondents, is used to advise the other side about their position pertaining to the issues endorsed on the Application for Hearing and to state any affirmative defenses or offsets they may have.

▶ **Order**
An order is the written decision of an Administrative Law Judge or any appellate body such as the Industrial Claim Appeals Office, the Colorado Court of Appeals, or the Colorado Supreme Court, or even the director of the Division of Workers' Compensation. If a party is dissatisfied with an order, he or she may appeal it within 20 days from the date on the certificate of mailing of that order.

▶ **Final Admission of Liability**
When respondents seek to close out most or all issues in the case, they file a Final Admission of Liability. Injured workers should review the Final Admission very carefully, because they have only 30 days from the date on the certificate of mailing to object to the Final Admission of Liability. If they fail to object in writing within 30 days, their case will be closed with respect to the issues concerned.

▶ **Objection to Final Admission of Liability**
This is the form that must be filed by the injured worker within 30 days from the date on the certificate of mailing of the Final Admission of Liability or else the claim will be closed as to the issues noted in the Final Admission of Liability.

▶ **Notice and Proposal to Select an Independent Medical Examiner**
Either the claimant or respondents can advise the other side that they wish to have an independent physician review a determination of the treating physician with respect to maximum medical improvement or permanent impairment, or other medical issues as well. The "Notice and Proposal," as it is called in shorthand, must be filed within 30 days from the treating physician's determination of maximum medical improvement and permanent impairment or 30 days from the mailing date of the Final Admission of Liability.

▶ **Application for Division Independent Medical Examination (DIME)**
This form, which is used to apply for a DIME, will indicate whether a DIME physician has been negotiated, whether the Division of Workers' Compensation needs to give the parties a panel from which they can select a DIME physician, and what issues the parties want the DIME physician to address.

If the parties cannot negotiate a doctor before the DIME, the Division of Workers' Compensation will provide three names randomly selected from a computer program. The requesting party will strike one of those names and the nonrequesting party will strike another. The remaining physician will conduct the DIME.

▶ **Request for Lump Sum Payment**
An injured worker can ask for a lump sum of up to $10,000 of permanent disability benefits simply by writing the insurance carrier or a third-party administrator for a self-insured employer. If the worker wants the remainder of his or her award, up to $60,000, paid in a lump sum, he or she must complete this form.

▶ **Final Payment Notice**
When a carrier has made the last payment on a case, it must file a Final Payment Notice with the Division of Workers' Compensation to advise the Division of its intention to close the file. Carriers are not required to send a copy of this final payment notice to the injured worker, so the savvy worker will write the carrier asking for this courtesy.

10-5. Special Workers' Compensation Issues Pertaining to Seniors

▶ **Permanent Partial Disability**

If an injured worker's injury is to a specific part of the body (for example, eye, knee, or wrist), the amount of benefits received is calculated with a formula that has nothing to do with the person's age. If the injured worker, however, suffers a "whole person injury" to the neck, back, spine, head, or internal organs, the worker's benefits are calculated with a formula that does reflect their age. By means of a number known as the "age factor," a carrier determines a person's disability. In Colorado, older workers have lower "age factors" than younger people, and therefore they usually receive less in permanent partial disability benefits when they have a whole person injury.

▶ **Permanent Total Disability**

As described above in section 10-2, "Benefits Available," an injured worker who can prove that he or she cannot earn any wages from the same or any other employer can qualify for permanent total disability benefits. These benefits, which are measured by 2/3 of the worker's average weekly wage at the time of injury, are usually payable for life. The older a worker is at the time of injury, the higher the probability of qualifying for permanent total disability benefits.

▶ **Apportionment for "Old Age"**

The only means of reducing workers' compensation benefits because of old age is use of the age factor (see above) in calculating permanent partial disability benefits. No other benefit may be reduced or paid differently for seniors. Apportionment may be available, however, when the effects of older age create a nonindustrial impairment that can be measured and subtracted out from the industrial impairment. Apportionment is a very complicated area of workers' compensation law, so injured workers should consult with the Division of Workers' Compensation or an attorney when they feel that respondents have unfairly apportioned out benefits in their case.

▶ **"Responsible for Separation from Employment"**

In some cases, an injured worker may not receive temporary total disability benefits if an Administrative Law Judge determines that he or she is "responsible for separation from employment." If an employee violates an employer's rule, does not show up for work, or voluntarily leaves employment for reasons unrelated to the injury, the carrier may refuse to pay temporary disability benefits. If the reason for separation is due to the injury, however, the carrier must pay full benefits. If seniors are scheduled to retire before or even after their injury, the carrier may take the position that they are "responsible for separation from employment," so the prudent worker is honest with the employer about the real reasons that he or she is unable to return to work.

▶ **Pre-Employment Testing**

Because some older workers bring a history of prior injuries and reduced physical capacity, many employers are administering physical fitness tests between conditional job offers and job placement. Such tests are legal under the Americans with Disabilities Act (ADA) if properly conducted. A job applicant, regardless of age, is required to be honest about his or her physical condition at all stages of the application process. Willfully misleading an employer about an applicant's ability to perform the essential functions of the job may result in a 50 percent reduction of nonmedical benefits if the worker is subsequently injured.

▶ **Fitness for Duty Testing**

Both the Americans with Disabilities Act and the Family and Medical Leave Act allow fitness for duty testing of certain employees within certain narrow guidelines. Like other employees, senior workers may be requested to demonstrate that they are "fit for duty" by completing medical questionnaires and physical examinations. Current employees have greater rights under the Americans with Disabilities Act, the Older Workers Benefit Protection Act, and the Age Discrimination in Employment Act, so an employer must be careful in disciplining, demoting, or terminating a senior worker based on the results of a fitness for duty examination. The prudent employer will follow a clearly understood process for evaluation of accommodations for a senior employee who has difficulties successfully completing a fitness for duty examination.

10-6. Resources

For additional information about the Colorado workers' compensation system, see:

▶ Division of Workers' Compensation website: www.coworkforce.com/dwc.

▶ *Workers' Compensation Guide for Employees*, published by the Division of Workers' Compensation. Available online at the Division of Worker's Compensation website (www.coworkforce.com/dwc) or in hard copy by calling the Customer Service Unit at the Division of Workers' Compensation: (303) 318-8700 or toll-free at (888) 390-7936.

▶ American Medical Association's *Guides to the Evaluation of Permanent Impairment*, 3rd ed. (rev. 2000).

Chapter 11

Arm Yourself with Consumer Protection Information

Amy Nofziger, M.A.*
AARP ElderWatch

Barbara Martin-Worley, M.A.*
Denver District Attorney's Office

SYNOPSIS

11-1. Recognize — Refuse — Report

Financial exploitation cannot be completely prevented, but we want to empower you as consumers and to educate you on how to Recognize, Refuse, and Report frauds in Colorado. It is the goal of this chapter to help you (1) learn the red flags of fraud; (2) recognize when someone is trying to victimize you; (3) learn when to say "no" and close the door or hang up the phone; (4) know how to report fraud to the appropriate agencies; and most importantly, (5) empower yourself. We value educating seniors because we know that education is the most important thing in preventing consumer fraud.

11-2. Identity Theft

Identity Theft

Identity theft is the fastest growing category of crime. Criminals, using a variety of methods, steal personal information from victims, including bank account, credit card, and Social Security numbers; driver's licenses; bank cards; telephone calling cards; and other key pieces of individuals' financial identities. Criminals use this information to impersonate victims, spending as much money as they can in as short a period of time as possible. Victims, faced with a damaged financial reputation and bad credit reports, spend months or even years trying to regain their financial health.

To protect against identity theft:

▶ Carry important documents in a close-fitting pouch instead of a purse that can be easily snatched or a wallet in your back pocket.

▶ Don't leave your purse unattended for even a moment in a grocery cart, restaurant chair, or other public areas.

▶ Do not carry extra credit cards, your checkbook, birth certificate, or passport in your wallet or purse. Carry your Medicare card only when you are obtaining health services.

▶ Protect your Social Security number (SSN). Don't carry your Social Security card with you.

▶ Don't have your SSN printed on your driver's license or checks.

▶ Don't give any part of your SSN or credit card number over the phone, unless you have initiated the call. One ploy criminals use is to call and pose as your bank or business and ask to "confirm" your SSN or other data.

▶ Shred pre-approved credit card offers and any papers that have your personal information using a cross-cut or confetti shredder.

▶ Never put your account number on an envelope or postcard.

▶ Keep a record of your credit card numbers, expiration dates, and customer service phone numbers.

▶ Do not pay bills by leaving the envelope, with a check enclosed, in your mailbox for carrier pickup; instead, drop off bills at the post office or pay your bills online.

▶ Have new boxes of checks sent to your bank or credit union rather than having them mailed to your home. Boxes of new checks are often stolen from mailboxes.

▶ Tell your credit card issuers to stop their marketing programs, including credit card convenience checks.

▶ "Opt out" of credit card solicitations by calling (888) 5-OPTOUT (567-8688). One contact will cover all three credit reporting agencies.

▶ Open credit card billing statements promptly and compare them with your receipts. Immediately report all discrepancies in writing. Under the federal Fair Credit Billing Act (FCBA), the card issuer must investigate billing errors if you report them within 60 days of the date your card issuer mailed you the statement.

▶ If you report the loss of your credit card before the card is used, the card issuer cannot hold you responsible for any unauthorized charges. If a criminal uses your card before you report it missing, your maximum liability will be $50.

▶ Request a free copy of your credit report once a year from the three major credit reporting companies: (877) 322-8228 or online at www.annualcreditreport.com.

▶ Do not allow anyone to come into your home to use the phone or get a drink of water, as he or she might be setting you up for a robbery.

If you think your identity has been stolen:

▶ Immediately file a report with the police, U.S. Postal Inspection Service, or the district attorney. You will need a copy of the police report or affidavit as proof that you were a crime victim.

▶ Contact the fraud departments of any one of the three major credit reporting companies and ask them to put a fraud alert on your account: Equifax (800) 525-6285; Experian (888) 397-3742; TransUnion (800) 680-7289.

▶ Send a copy of the report or affidavit to your creditors and the credit reporting companies. Under Colorado law, once they receive your report or affidavit, they cannot put negative information in your credit file. Close any accounts that you think have been taken over or opened fraudulently. Get new cards with new account numbers. If you notice any irregularities on a bank statement, immediately notify your bank. You may need to cancel checking and savings accounts and open new ones.

▶ Call your utilities, especially cell phone service providers. Tell them someone may try to get new service using your identification.

▶ Review the information available online at the Colorado Attorney General's website at www.coloradoattorneygeneral.gov or call (800) 222-4444 and ask for an Identity Theft Repair Kit.

Credit Repair

Newspapers, magazines, and the Internet are filled with ads offering to erase negative information in your credit file. The scam artists who run these ads can't deliver. Only time, a diligent effort, and a debt repayment plan can improve your credit.

Your only choice is to help yourself re-build a better credit record. Start by contacting your creditors when you realize that you are unable to make payments. If you need help working out a payment plan and a budget, contact the Money Management International at www.moneymanagement.org. Their services are free.

Credit Reporting Companies

Equifax
To order a credit report by:
Phone, (800) 685-1111
Internet, www.equifax.com
Mail, P.O. Box 740241
 Atlanta, GA 30374

Experian
To order a credit report by:
Phone, (888) EXPERIAN (397-3742)
Internet, www.experian.com

TransUnion
To order a credit report by:
Phone, (800) 888-4213
Internet, www.transunion.com
Mail, 2 Baldwin Pl.
 P.O. Box 1000
 Chester, PA 19022

Debt Collectors

If you cannot make your credit payments, the seller, loan company, or bank may give your debt to a lawyer or collection agency. These debt collectors can use any legal means to collect money you owe.

The federal Fair Debt Collection Practices Act and the Colorado Fair Debt Collection Practices Act control debt collectors' activities. They cannot do the following:

▶ Continue calling or writing after you tell them, in writing, that you do not want to be contacted;

▶ Call your friends or neighbors;

▶ Contact you or your boss at work if the collection agency knows your boss prohibits these types of calls;

▶ Call you before 8 a.m. or after 9 p.m., or use harassment or scare tactics;

▶ Threaten to file criminal charges against you, take your property, or garnish your wages without first filing a lawsuit to give you a chance to defend yourself (*Note*: A lawyer acting as a debt collector cannot threaten criminal prosecution); or

▶ Threaten you with any physical harm.

Debt Collection in Court

If you owe money to a creditor, he or she usually has the right to demand that you make payment in full.

If you miss a payment, pay less than the agreed amount, are late on a payment, or do something else that violates a written contract regarding the payments, the seller or creditor may have the right to demand payment of the full balance you owe on the debt. In this case, the creditor also may have the right to repossess the item you are making payments on.

If a loan company, bank, collection agency, or creditor decides to sue you, you must first be served with a summons to appear in court and a complaint that states why you are being sued. If you do not appear or respond, the other party may obtain a "default judgment" against you. This means the court can enter a judgment against you even though you are not present to defend yourself. A judgment is a court decision that you owe money. The judgment holder must follow legal procedures to try to collect on the judgment. The judgment holder may put a lien on your property, garnish your wages or bank account, or take personal property. However, the judgment holder cannot take certain property protected by law. This property is known as exempt property. Examples of exempt property include:

▶ Social Security, other government benefits, and pensions, which are exempt even when placed in a bank account;

▶ Household goods with a market value of up to $1,500 per person. Market value is the cost a willing buyer would pay for a product "as is";

▶ An automobile with a market value of up to $1,000 per person;

▶ Clothing with a market value of up to $750 per person;

▶ All prescribed health aids;

▶ All net wages if you earn less than a certain amount each week. If you earn more than a certain amount, a creditor cannot garnish more than 25 percent of your total net wages; and

▶ The first $30,000 of equity in your house.

A creditor may try to take your property even though it is exempt. If this happens, you must file a claim of exemption with the court. The creditor or the court should mail the proper forms to you. This form will list your exempt property and stop the creditor from taking it. It doesn't cost anything to file the claim of exemption, but you must act very quickly to protect your property.

11-3. Consumer Fraud

Quit Claim Deeds

Quit claim deed fraud is another type of financial crime on the rise. A quit claim deed is a term used in property law to describe a document that allows one person to transfer any interest in a piece of property to another person. An example of a circumstance where a quit claim deed may be used legitimately is when one spouse (grantor) is disclaiming any interest in property that the other spouse (grantee) owns.

However, fraudulent transfers of property occur when a person convinces or coerces another into signing a quit claim deed that transfers ownership of property yet not transferring the debt. Never sign a quit claim deed without getting the advice of an attorney. Once you have signed over property, it can be difficult or impossible to reverse.

Predatory Lending

Predatory lending schemes are also on the rise. Predatory lending is the name given to an assortment of loans that take advantage of persons who borrow money. Predatory lenders target older homeowners by offering attractive-sounding loan offers that drain the value from their property. Some warning signs that you are a target for a predatory loan:

▶ You've fallen behind in your mortgage payments or you are already in foreclosure.

▶ You're getting phone calls and visits from companies offering to help you pay off your debts.

▶ A friend, advisor, or relative asks you to sign some forms without letting you read them.

To prevent predatory lending:

▶ Beware of companies who contact you in person or by fliers offering a foreclosure relief service.

▶ Don't sign any forms or papers without reading and understanding what you're signing. If you're uneasy or feeling pressured, get advice from a lawyer or other advisor.

If you're having trouble paying your mortgage, contact your bank or mortgage company and discuss potential payment plans.

Hearing Aid Purchases

Unfortunately, scams involving hearing aid devices are prevalent. Some cautionary advice:

▶ Have an audiologist test your hearing before you decide to buy a hearing aid or replace an old one.

▶ Do not believe ads offering an effective hearing aid at a bargain price. You may get just what you pay for.

▶ Shop around and compare prices — for the fitting, adjusting, and servicing, as well as comparable aids.

By law, you may cancel an agreement to purchase a hearing aid within 30 days after receiving the hearing aid. You must return the hearing aid, and you are entitled to a full refund (except anything you may have paid for individualized ear molds). The law has other restrictions on the practices of hearing aid dealers. Talk to an attorney or the Better Business Bureau/Attorney General Consumer Line.

Pre-Paid Funeral Plans

Be cautious when investigating a pre-paid funeral agreement. These contracts engage a specific funeral home (or cemetery) to deliver specific services at a set price upon a person's death. While it is a good idea to plan ahead so your family knows your wishes, some pre-paid plans are risky.

▶ Read the policy carefully and understand all of its terms before you invest in the plan.

▶ Know what happens if your wishes or circumstances change.

▶ Only work with reputable companies that have been in business for over five years.

Health Insurance

▶ Do not purchase coverage you do not need or coverage that duplicates what you already have.

▶ Before buying or changing coverage, discuss your plans with someone you trust.

▶ The Colorado Division of Insurance operates a special counseling program for Medicare recipients and their families who need assistance in understanding Medicare benefits and coverage gaps, medical bills, and other insurance options, including long-term care insurance. For more information, call the Colorado Senior Health Insurance Assistance Program, (888) 696-7213.

Con Games

There are many con and street games that take advantage of people's trust and sometimes greed. To protect yourself from con games, simply *do not* respond to *any* stranger who approaches you on the street, at your door, or over the telephone.

In the **Pigeon-Drop Scheme**, the person running the scam will tell you that you have the chance to obtain money or valuable property. However, before you can get your "prize," you must first give the person your own money to be held as "collateral" to prove that you are trustworthy. Typically, you do not see either the person or your money again. If you are approached for what appears to be a pigeon-drop, immediately report it to the police.

In the **Bank Examiner Fraud**, someone poses as an official of the victim's bank. Using the ploy that the bank suspects a teller is stealing funds from the person's account, the bank "official" requests that the victim go to the bank and withdraw a large sum of money, usually $3,000 to $5,000, to give the cash to a "law enforcement" official who will be in the bank parking lot. According to the story, law enforcement will then mark the bills, which will enable them to catch the teller in the act of stealing from the victim's account. Remember that legitimate financial institutions never use their customers to investigate internal fraud. If you receive such a call, report it immediately to the police and your bank.

In the **Latin Lotto Con**, a Spanish-speaking person approaches the victim outside a store. An accomplice, posing as a stranger, happens by and offers to translate. The Spanish speaker claims to have a winning lottery ticket, but can't turn it in for fear of being deported as an undocumented alien. The con artist offers to split the winnings if the stranger and victim will turn in the ticket. To show trust, the translator says he and the victim will have to withdraw money from their bank accounts. Once the victim hands over the money, the con artist and accomplice give the victim the slip.

Another scam is the **Neighbor Assistance Con**. Going door to door, this con artist convinces victims that a neighbor has an emergency and needs money. Or a child may need an operation. Or a son needs to get to a dying mother. The stories can be very emotional and creative, but the con intends to take your money.

Sweepstakes Scams

Consumers are often enticed with a valuable prize or award to buy merchandise or services or to contribute to bogus charities. It isn't free if you have to pay a fee. If you have to buy a product like vitamins or light bulbs, pay a fee, or make a donation before you claim your award or receive your prize, you haven't won anything.

Sweepstakes companies prey on consumers' sense of greed and luck that they've won something for nothing. But sweepstakes companies are not in the business of giving away millions of dollars — they're in the business of making money.

Under Colorado's Sweepstakes and Contests Law, promoters are prohibited from engaging in any of the following:

▶ Falsely representing that you have won a prize;

▶ Falsely representing an item as a "prize" if it is given to all promotion recipients;

▶ Falsely representing that you have been specially selected or that you are in a select group of potential winners;

▶ Making false, deceptive, or misleading statements about your odds of winning or what you need to do to become eligible to win;

▶ Falsely representing that your envelope has been delivered by express or first-class mail;

▶ Displaying urgent messages on envelopes unless there is truly a limited time period for a sweepstakes entry and the true deadline is disclosed adjacent to the urgent message;

▶ Representing that sweepstakes entries accompanied by an order for products will be treated differently than entries without an order; and

▶ Creating a false impression of the solicitation's source, authorization, or approval.

The law requires a promoter to prominently disclose:

▶ A "No Purchase Necessary" message;

▶ The fact that the recipient has not yet won anything;

▶ The value of the prize;

▶ The odds of winning;

▶ The name of the promoter;

▶ The true deadline for entering the sweepstakes; and

▶ The official rules of the sweepstakes.

Law enforcement personnel recommend that you don't play sweepstakes, but if you do, remember:

▶ Don't pay to win. Buying products such as magazines doesn't increase your chances of winning a sweepstakes. You never have to pay to play when the contest is legitimate.

▶ No purchase is necessary to win. Prizes are free. If you have to pay before you can receive your prize, it's a purchase. It's against the law to require you to buy something to win a prize or participate in a sweepstakes or prize promotion.

▶ Be cautious of charities that use sweepstakes promotions. More of your donation is going to the promotion than to any charitable purpose.

▶ Keep your credit card and bank information to yourself. Never give your credit card number, bank account information, or Social Security number to anyone you don't know, especially if the reason is to verify your eligibility or to "deposit" winnings to your account.

▶ Lottery sweepstakes from foreign countries such as Canada and Australia are illegal. No foreign lotteries may be conducted in the United States.

▶ Participating in sweepstakes promotions is the best way for you to get on every junk mail list in the country. Selling your name to other direct mail marketers is a huge part of sweepstakes companies' business.

Telemarketing Scams

Coloradans lose millions of dollars a year to illegal telemarketers. A phone caller asks you to send money, and in return, you are promised that you will receive a much larger sum of money due to some unique opportunity. These callers are not salespeople just doing their job — they're criminals who will say anything to get your money. Do the following if you receive such a phone call:

▶ Be wary of a friendly voice or demeanor and someone who says they are a friend or relative but doesn't sound familiar.

▶ Never send money based on a promise given over the telephone from a stranger.

▶ If you suspect a scam, contact the police, your local District Attorney's Office, or the Better Business Bureau/Attorney General's Consumer Line at (800) 222-4444.

▶ For Canadian telemarketers, call Phone Busters at (888) 495-8501.

▶ It's hard to hang up on people, especially when the caller sounds so polite and friendly. But you wouldn't let a nice-looking stranger in your house or accept a ride from one, so handle telephone calls from strangers the same way.

Colorado No-Call Law

Under the Colorado Telemarketing No-Call Law:

▶ Residential telephone customers can place their telephone numbers on a no-call list free of charge. (The law does not apply to business telephone customers.)

▶ You can sign up for the no-call list by calling (800) 309-7041 or registering online at www.coloradonocall.com.

▶ Commercial telemarketers may not call or send faxes to you at your home if you have placed your telephone number(s) on the no-call list, unless the telemarketer has an "established business relationship" with you.

▶ Calls by charities, political groups, and other non-commercial organizations are not subject to the Colorado No-Call Law.

▶ You have the right under the federal Telemarketing Sales Rules to tell companies with whom you have established business relationships to put you on their "Do Not Call" lists.

▶ Report offending telemarketers to the Attorney General or district attorney's office. You can also use the Colorado Consumer Protection Act to sue in Small Claims Court if you are on the no-call list and get unwanted calls or fax transmissions from telemarketers.

▶ You can also add your home or cell phone numbers to the national Do Not Call list at www.donotcall.gov or by calling (888) 382-1222.

Federal Telemarketing Sales Rules

▶ Telemarketers can only call you between 8 a.m. and 9 p.m.

▶ Telemarketers must tell you it's a sales call, the name of the seller, and what they are selling before they make their pitch. If it's a prize promotion, they must tell you that no purchase or payment is necessary to enter or win.

▶ It's illegal for telemarketers to misrepresent any information; any facts about their goods or services; earnings potential, profitability, risk, or liquidity of an investment; or the nature of a prize in a prize promotion.

▶ Before you pay, telemarketers must tell you the total cost of the goods and any restrictions on getting or using them, or that a sale is final or non-refundable. In a prize promotion, they must tell you the odds of winning, that no purchase is necessary to win, and any restrictions or conditions of receiving the prize.

▶ It's illegal for a telemarketer to withdraw money from your checking account without your express, verifiable authorization.

▶ Telemarketers cannot lie to get you to pay, no matter how you pay.

Home Repairs and Improvement

▶ Choose the persons you hire to do repairs and improvements on your home very carefully. Don't do business with anyone who comes to your door offering a bargain because he says he has materials left over from another job.

▶ Ask for references from previous customers and examples of the contractor's past work.

▶ On larger projects, get at least three written bids, and don't always choose the lowest bidder. Contact the Better Business Bureau for a report on any contractor you're considering.

▶ Never pay money in advance or make a final payment until you are satisfied with the work.

▶ Get the contractor's full name, address, phone number, and vehicle license plate number.

▶ Ask the contractor to show you proof that he is bonded, carries liability insurance, and covers his workers with workers' compensation insurance.

▶ Before deciding to hire someone to do your home repairs, get a detailed written estimate.

▶ It is important to agree upon a fee *before* work begins.

▶ Always get a written contract that specifies everything that was in the estimate, including all charges and costs, specific materials to be used, and the start and completion dates. You and the contractor both must sign the contract to make it binding. It is always a good idea to review the contents of this contract with your attorney before you sign.

▶ Make the financing of your job separate from the contracting for the work. Compare loans as carefully as you compare estimates from workers. Watch out for contractors that want to steer you to a particular lender, and never give the contractor a mortgage on your home.

▶ If you sign a loan for home repairs that involves a mortgage, you can cancel the loan within three business days from the day you signed the contract.

▶ The contractor may be entitled to what is known as a mechanics' lien. The law grants this special lien on your property for work performed there and not paid for. A mechanics' lien can also result in a forced sale of your home. Don't make a final payment to a home improvement contractor unless you've received a "lien waiver," which is a document showing that the contractor has paid his subcontractors and suppliers. These parties can place a mechanics' lien against your property as well if they aren't paid by the general contractor.

11-4. Other Types of Financial Fraud

Auto Repairs

These are your rights under the Colorado Motor Vehicle Repair Act:

▶ An auto repair facility must give a written estimate that includes the total cost, completion date, a statement of your right to have parts returned (except exchanged or warranty parts), and a statement on storage fees. You waive the right to an estimate if you sign a waiver, the vehicle is towed to the facility, or the vehicle is left before or after business hours. A customer must receive an estimate on any charge over $100.

▶ If you have not been given a written estimate, the facility must call to get oral consent before the repairs can be done. The facility must record on the invoice or work order the date and time of the call, your name, the name of the employee making the call, and your phone number.

▶ The facility must give a written estimate that includes the cost of disassembly and reassembly and the costs of parts needed to replace those lost in disassembly. The facility must obtain oral consent before the repairs are completed. If more work causes an increase in the bill, the facility must obtain your consent before doing the work. The oral consent must be recorded as described above.

▶ All parts and labor charges must be written clearly on the final bill. If the facility has not gotten approval, the final bill cannot be more than 10 percent or $25 over the estimate, whichever is less.

▶ A facility may charge storage fees at the facility's discretion if the vehicle is not picked up within three business days of completion notification. Storage fees should be conspicuously printed on a separate authorization provided to the customer.

Charitable Organizations

The Colorado Charitable Solicitations Act controls the activities of the persons who place the calls or mail the letters and the organizations they represent. Here are some of your rights:

▶ You have the right to ask if the solicitor is registered with the Secretary of State.

▶ If you make a donation in response to a telephone solicitation, the solicitor is required to give you a written confirmation of the expected donation. The confirmation should contain:

- The name, address, and telephone number of the solicitor's organization;

- A disclosure that the donation is not tax deductible, if applicable;

- A disclosure that the solicitor is a paid employee of a for-profit professional fundraiser;

- The name, address, and phone number of the office from which the solicitation occurred; and

- The name, address, and phone number of the charity associated with the solicitation.

You may cancel your donation if the solicitor has failed to provide any of the above information. You have three days after you get the written confirmation to cancel. The solicitor must refund your donation within 10 business days of your cancellation.

To ensure your charitable dollars are wisely spent:

▶ Make an annual charitable giving budget and list — and stick to it! Give once to those charities on your list, and disregard all other solicitations.

▶ Remember that many organizations intentionally use names that are similar to the names of well-known charities.

▶ Get proof that your deduction will be tax deductible, such as a letter from the U.S. Department of the Treasury stating that the organization qualifies under § 501(c)(3) of the Internal Revenue Code.

▶ Find out how much of your donation will go to the charity for programs and services and how much will be spent on fundraising. Contact the Better Business Bureau's charity watchdog service at www.give.org or http://denver.bbb.org, or call (800) 222-4444 for a report.

Contracts

Every word in a contract is important. Before signing any contract, read it in its entirety. If you do not understand any part of the document, ask for clarification and/or consult an attorney. Do not do business with anyone who refuses to give you a copy of the complete contract before you sign it.

If you and the other party come to an agreement about something that is not written in the document, you must put that agreement in writing. To make sure there are no misunderstandings, document all additions or deletions from the original document and all parties should initial or sign next to each change.

Most contracts are binding as soon as you and the other party sign. However, contracts from door-to-door sales and any contract that calls for placing a lien on your house can usually be cancelled within three days. Consumers have one day to cancel a contract that was solicited over the telephone.

Put all notices of cancellation in writing. It is recommended to send cancellation notices by certified or registered mail so you have documentation showing when you sent the notice, as well as receipt of the notice by the company. Also, never sign a contract with blank spaces that can be filled in later.

Do not sign a contract that takes away your legal rights unless you understand and agree to the consequences of such action. Keep copies of all contracts, receipts, payment records, and letters you send about the product or service.

Before you sign any type of sales or services contract, ask yourself these questions:

▶ Do I really want what I am paying for?

▶ Do I understand the contract I am about to sign?

▶ Do I know the total price, including interest and other charges, I will have to pay?

▶ Do I know how many payments I will have to make?

▶ Can I get the same thing somewhere else for a better price?

▶ Am I getting any guarantees on the product or for the services I am paying for? (*Note:* Get all guarantees in writing.)

▶ Can I make the payments the contract requires?

Always remember that it will cost you far less to have an attorney review the contract before you sign than it will to have an attorney represent you in court because you made a deal that was unfair to you.

11-5. Prevention Tools

Security Freeze

If you don't anticipate opening any new credit accounts in the near future, you may want to consider placing a security freeze on your credit report. You have the option of requesting any consumer reporting agency (credit bureau) to place a security freeze on your credit report. A freeze means your file can't be shared with potential creditors. You must request separate security freezes for each of the three credit reporting agencies, *in writing via certified mail.* Please see Exhibit 11A at the end of this chapter for a sample letter you may use to request a security freeze.

Equifax Security Freeze
P.O. Box 105788
Atlanta, GA 30348
www.equifax.com; click on "Customer Service," then "Security Freeze."

Experian Security Freeze
www.experian.com/consumer/security_freeze.html

TransUnion Security Freeze
P.O. Box 6790
Fullerton, CA 92834-6790
www.transunion.com; click on "Credit Disputes, Alerts & Freezes, " then "Credit Freeze."

Consumer reporting agencies must place a security freeze on your credit report within five business days after receiving your written request and must send you written confirmation of the security freeze within ten business days. They will provide you with a unique personal identification number or password for you to use in providing later authorization for the release of information from your credit report.

If you want potential creditors to be able to access information on your credit report, you must request that the freeze be temporarily lifted and provide the following information:

▶ Proper identification;

▶ The unique personal identification number and password provided by the consumer reporting agency; and

▶ The proper information regarding the third party who is to receive the credit report or the time period that the report shall be available.

The consumer reporting agency must remove a security freeze within three business days of receiving a request. The initial security freeze is free of charge; however, the temporary or permanent removal of the freeze, as well as the reinitiating of a freeze, will cost up to, but no more than, $12 per action.

Colorado Consent to Release Information Statute

In 2000, the Colorado legislature passed C.R.S. § 26-3.1-206, whereby anyone over 60 or any "at-risk" adult may request and voluntarily sign an "Informed Consent Form" to be placed in their customer file. This voluntary action by the customer grants permission to the customer's financial institution to release information about any *future* suspicious account activity to appropriate agencies for the limited purpose of investigating known or suspected financial exploitation.

What to do next:

▶ Request an Informed Consent Form from your financial institution. If your bank or credit union is unfamiliar with this form, Exhibit 11B is an example of a form that *may* be accepted by your bank or credit union.

▶ Fill out the form, sign it, and instruct your financial institution to place it in your customer file for future use, should the need arise.

11-6. Resources

The following are excellent resources for information on your rights as a consumer or to report complaints:

For issues related to fraud:

24-Hour Identity Theft Hotline
Colorado Bureau of Investigation
ID Theft/Fraud Investigation Unit
690 Kipling St.
Denver, CO 80215
(855) 443-3489
(303) 239-4211
http://cloi.state.co.us/inv/ID_Theft/Index_IDTheft.html

Colorado Consumer Line
AARP ElderWatch, Better Business Bureau, Attorney General's Office
(800) 222-4444 (toll-free)
(303) 222-4444 (metro Denver)
www.aarpelderwatch.org
www.bbb.org
www.coloradoattorneygeneral.gov

Attorney General's Office Consumer Protection Section
For questions about credit and debt issues
(303) 866-4916

Denver District Attorney's Fraud Hotline
(720) 913-9179
(720) 913-9182 (TDD, for the hearing impaired)
www.denverda.org

Boulder District Attorney's Office
Consumer Protection: (303) 441-3700
www.bouldercounty.org/da

Adams County District Attorney's Office
Consumer Fraud: (303) 659-7720
www.adamsbroomfieldda.org

Arapahoe County District Attorney's Office
Consumer Fraud: (720) 874-8500
www.co.arapahoe.co.us/Departments/DA/DistrictAttorney.asp

Jefferson County District Attorney's Office
Consumer Fraud: (303) 271-6980
http://jeffco.us/da/index.htm

For Medicare insurance issues:

Colorado Senior Health Insurance Assistance Program
(888) 696-7213
www.dora.state.co.us/insurance/senior/senior.htm

To report financial and other abuse of the elderly:

Denver Department of Human Services, Adult Protection
(720) 944-2994

Colorado Department of Human Services, Adult Protective Services
(303) 866-2800

Colorado Coalition for Elder Rights and Adult Protection, Elder Rights Hotline
(800) 773-1366

For financial planning:

National Board of Certified Financial Planners
(888) CFP-MARK ((888) 237-6275)

Colorado Division of Securities
(303) 894-2320

To request a free copy of your credit report once a year from the three major credit reporting companies:

(877) 322-8228
www.annualcreditreport.com

Credit reporting agencies:

Equifax
(800) 685-1111
www.equifax.com

TransUnion
(800) 888-4213
www.transunion.com

Experian
(888) 397-3742
www.experian.com

For home repairs and improvements:

Denver Building Inspection Service
(720) 865-2982
www.denvergov.org/develpmentservices

To "opt out" of credit card solicitations:

(888) 5-OPTOUT (567-8688)
www.optoutprescreen.com

No-call lists:

In Colorado: (800) 309-7041 or www.coloradonocall.com
Nationally: (888) 382-1222 or www.donotcall.gov

For the Federal Communications Commission's information regarding digital television:

(888) 225-5322
(888) 835-5322 (TTY)
www.dtv.gov

Area Agencies on Aging:

Logan, Morgan, Phillips, Sedgwick, Washington, and Yuma counties:

Northeastern Colorado Association of Local Governments
Northeastern Region
231 Main St., Ste. 211
Fort Morgan, CO 80701
(970) 867-9409

Larimer County:

Larimer County Office on Aging
Northeastern Region
Larimer County Human Services
1501 Blue Spruce Dr.
Fort Collins, CO 80524
(970) 498-6807

Weld County:
> Weld County Area Agency on Aging
> Northeastern Region
> P.O. Box 1805
> 1551 N. 17th Ave.
> Greeley, CO 80632
> (970) 353-3800

Adams, Arapahoe, Broomfield, Clear Creek, Denver, Douglas, Gilpin, and Jefferson counties:
> Denver Regional Council of Governments
> Northeastern Region
> 1290 Broadway, Ste. 700
> Denver, CO 80203
> (303) 455-1000

Boulder County:
> Boulder County Aging Services Division
> Northeastern Region
> P.O. Box 471
> 3482 N. Broadway
> Boulder, CO 80306
> (303) 441-3570

Park, El Paso, and Teller counties:
> Pikes Peak Area Agency on Aging
> Southern Region
> 15 S. 7th St.
> Colorado Springs, CO 80905
> (719) 471-2096

Cheyenne, Elbert, Kit Carson, and Lincoln counties:
> East Central Council of Governments
> Northeastern Region
> P.O. Box 28
> 128 Colorado Ave.
> Stratton, CO 80836
> (719) 348-5562

Baca, Bent, Crowley, Kiowa, Otero, and Prowers counties:
> Lower Arkansas Valley Area Agency on Aging
> Southern Region
> 13 W. 3rd St., Rm. 110
> P.O. Box 494
> La Junta, CO 81050
> (719) 383-3166

Pueblo County:
Pueblo Area Agency on Aging
Southern Region
2631 E. 4th St.
Pueblo, CO 81001
(719) 583-6110

Alamosa, Conejos, Costilla, Mineral, Rio Grande, and Saguache counties:
South-Central Colorado Seniors, Inc.
Southern Region
1116 3rd St.
P.O. Box 639
Alamosa, CO 81101
(719) 589-4511

Archuleta, Dolores, La Plata, Montezuma, and San Juan counties:
San Juan Basin Area Agency on Aging
Western Region
701 Camino Del Rio, Ste. 312
Durango, CO 81301
(970) 259-1967

Delta, Gunnison, Hinsdale, Montrose, Ouray, and San Miguel counties:
Region 10 Area Agency on Aging
Western Region
Drawer 849
300 N. Cascade Ave.
Montrose, CO 81402
(970) 249-2436

Garfield, Mesa, Moffat, Rio Blanco, and Routt counties:
Associated Governments of Northwest Colorado
Western Region
P.O. Box 20000-5035
510 29½ Rd.
Grand Junction, CO 81502
(970) 248-2717

Eagle, Grand, Jackson, Pitkin, and Summit counties:
Northwest Colorado Council of Governments
Alpine Area Agency on Aging
Western Region
P.O. Box 2308
249 Warren Ave.
Silverthorne, CO 80498
(970) 468-0295

Chaffee, Custer, Fremont, and Lake counties:
Upper Arkansas AAA
Southern Region
139 E. 3rd St.
Salida, CO 81201-2612
(719) 539-3341

Huerfano and Las Animas counties:
Huerfano/Las Animas Area Council of Governments
South Central Council of Governments AAA
Southern Region
300 Bonaventure Ave.
Trinidad, CO 81082
(719) 845-1133

Legal Assistance Developer for the Elderly

The Legal Center for People with Disabilities and Older People
455 Sherman St., Ste. 130
Denver, CO 80203
(303) 722-0300
(303) 722-3619 (TTD)
www.thelegalcenter.org

Colorado Crime Victims Compensation Programs

First Judicial District
District Attorney's Building
500 Jefferson County Pkwy.
Golden, CO 80401
(303) 271-6846

Second Judicial District
201 W. Colfax, Dept. 801
Denver, CO 80202
(720) 913-9253

Third Judicial District
200 E. 1st St., Ste. 302
Trinidad, CO 81082
(719) 846-9224

Fourth Judicial District
105 E. Vermijo, Ste. 111
Colorado Springs, CO 80903
(719) 520-6915

Fifth Judicial District
P.O. Box 2000
Georgetown, CO 80444
(303) 679-2453

Sixth Judicial District
1060 Main Ave.
P.O. Drawer 3455
Durango, CO 81302
(970) 247-8850

Seventh Judicial District
1200 N. Grand Ave., Ste. D
Montrose, CO 81401
(970) 252-4266

Eighth Judicial District
201 La Porte, Ste. 200
Fort Collins, CO 80521
(970) 498-7200

Ninth Judicial District
109 8th St., Ste. 308
Glenwood Springs, CO 81601
(970) 945-8635

Tenth Judicial District
701 Court St.
Pueblo, CO 81003
(719) 583-6092

Eleventh Judicial District
136 Justice Center Rd., Rm. 203
Cañon City, CO 81212
(719) 269-0170

Twelfth Judicial District
426 San Juan Ave.
Alamosa, CO 81101
(719) 589-3691

Thirteenth Judicial District
400 Warner St.
Fort Morgan, CO 80701
(970) 542-3420

Fourteenth Judicial District
221 W. Victory Wy., Ste. 302
Craig, CO 81625
(970) 824-9143

Fifteenth Judicial District
110 E. Oak St.
Lamar, CO 81052
(719) 336-7446

Sixteenth Judicial District
323 Santa Fe, Ste. 201
La Junta, CO 81050-0928
(719) 384-8786

Seventeenth Judicial District
1100 Judicial Center Dr., Ste. 100
Brighton, CO 80601
(303) 835-5614

Eighteenth Judicial District
6450 S. Revere Pkwy.
Centennial, CO 80111
(720) 874-8607

Nineteenth Judicial District
P.O. Box 1167
Greeley, CO 80632
(970) 356-4010, ext. 4748

Twentieth Judicial District
Boulder County Courts Bldg.
1035 Kimbark St.
Longmont, CO 80501
(303) 682-6801

Twenty-First Judicial District
P.O. Box 20000-5031
Grand Junction, CO 81502
(970) 244-1643

Twenty-Second Judicial District
103 N. Chestnut St.
Cortez, CO 81321
(970) 564-2755

Elder Abuse:

Call 911 or your local police department.

Adult Protection

Call your county Department of Social Services. You may find a list of contact information for these offices at www.cdhs.state.co.us; click on "Services by County."

Colorado Coalition for Elder Rights and Adult Protection

(800) 773-1366

AARP ElderWatch
Through the Colorado Consumer Line: (800) 222-4444, option 2, for referrals and assistance information.
Metro Denver: (303) 222-4444

Denver District Attorney's Office
(720) 913-9000
www.denverda.org

Boulder District Attorney's Office
(303) 441-3700
www.bouldercounty.org/da

Adams/Broomfield counties District Attorney's Office
(303) 659-7720
www.adamsbroomfieldda.org

Arapahoe/Douglas counties District Attorney's Office
(720) 874-8500
www.co.arapahoe.co.us/Departments/DA/DistrictAttorney.asp

Jefferson/Gilpin counties District Attorney's Office
(303) 271-6800
http://jeffco.us/da/index.htm

---

*Based on a chapter originally written by Lisa Curtis, Office of the District Attorney, Second Judicial District, and later updated by Janice L. Friddle, AARP ElderWatch; Sally B. Hume, Esq., AARP Financial Security; and Robin Fudge Finegan, M.A., M.N.M., FEMA Region VIII.

Exhibit 11A.
Sample Letter for Credit Freeze Request

[Date]

Dear [Agency Name]:

Please place a security freeze on my credit file.

My name is _____.
(one name only, spouse must fill out separate request)

My former name was (if applies) _____.

My current address is _____.

My address has changed in the past five years. My former address
was _____.

My Social Security number is _____.

My date of birth is _____.

I have included photocopies of a government issued identity card AND proof
of residence such as a utility bill or phone bill.

Yours Truly,

Signature_____

Send by Certified Mail Only

Exhibit 11B.
Sample of Consent to Release Information Form

The information released under this form shall be provided to county Departments of Social Services or law enforcement agency personnel to investigate known or suspected financial exploitation of my accounts pursuant to C.R.S. § 26-3.1-206. The information obtained may also be furnished to the Denver District Attorney. The information obtained under this consent may only be used by those agencies in accordance with their official capacities and functions.

With this understanding, I, _____,
(Account Holder Name/Social Security number)

currently living at _____,
(Address)

hereby consent to the release of all information and records concerning my account(s) at the identified financial institution to Law Enforcement and/or Social Services Investigators.

Name of Financial Institution and Address (if available):

_____

_____

_____

_____ (initial) Please release any records requested.

_____ (initial) This consent shall remain in effect until I revoke it by submitting a written revocation to the financial institution.

Account Holder Signature _____

Print Name _____

Date of Birth _____

Date _____

Chapter 12

Protecting Yourself from Crime

Barbara Martin-Worley, M.A.*
Denver District Attorney's Office

SYNOPSIS

12-1. Protection from Street Crime

▶ Walk with confidence and remain aware of your surroundings.

▶ Do not walk alone on dark, deserted streets.

▶ Park in well-lit areas as close as possible to the door of a business.

▶ Ask a store clerk to walk you to your car.

▶ Lock your car doors at all times.

▶ Look under, around, and inside your car before getting in it.

▶ Keep your wallet or purse where pickpockets cannot reach it. A close-fitting pouch is more secure than a purse.

▶ Hold your purse firmly and do not leave it unattended on a counter, grocery cart, or car seat.

▶ Men should keep wallets in a front pants pocket or inside a suit coat pocket.

▶ Separate your cash, checks, and credit cards in your purse or pocket to reduce a loss if a pickpocket tries to take your wallet.

▶ Only carry the cards you know you will need that day, and never carry your Social Security card.

▶ Carry a driver's license and other important papers in a small wallet kept in your pocket.

▶ Never carry a large sum of money.

▶ Never write your PIN number on your ATM or Electronic Banking Transfer cards.

▶ Avoid ATM machines in deserted areas. Instead, use ATMs in stores or bank lobbies.

▶ Keep a list of your credit cards somewhere other than your wallet to make it easier to report a loss. Report any loss immediately.

▶ If you are going out alone at night, let someone know your plans. When out alone, keep a whistle or personal body alarm handy and hold your keys in your hand while walking.

▶ Avoid waiting at deserted bus stops. Walk to the next bus stop where others may be waiting. Also, consider taking a taxi and ask the driver to wait until you are inside at home.

▶ If you are riding the bus, be aware of anyone who might be staring at you. Tell the bus driver if you are concerned for your safety. You can prevent trouble by anticipating it.

▶ If someone grabs your purse, do not put yourself at risk by resisting. If you try to resist, you may be injured. Other options are to sit down to avoid being knocked down, make noise, whistle, or call for help. In any case, tell the police as soon as possible.

▶ Always remember — your life and well-being are more important than your belongings.

Victims' compensation programs help victims of violent crimes. For more information or an application form, contact your local district attorney's office.

12-2. Protection at Home

▶ When planning to be away from home, never hide a door key under the doormat, behind the shutter, or in a mailbox. These are the first places a burglar looks. A neighbor or family member can keep an extra key for you.

▶ Turn on some inside lights when you are away. Use timers to vary the lights you leave on. A dark home is an invitation to burglars.

▶ Keep outside lights near doors and large windows turned on. Strong outside lighting helps prevent burglaries.

▶ When you plan to be away from home a long time, tell the police. Ask a friend or family member to check your home each day, turn on different lights, pick up mail and newspapers, mow the grass, and set out trash on regular trash pick-up days.

▶ Lock your doors and windows whether you are at home or away, and remember to keep your screen or storm door locked.

▶ When at home, keep your shades pulled at night and whenever you are undressing. Be cautious as to who knows you are alone.

▶ When someone knocks at your door, first check to see who it is and do not open your door to a stranger. Ask for identification and references before you let anyone into your house. If the person shows you a business card, call the company for proof before you let the stranger into your home. Also, call the police or fire department if anyone claiming to be an officer is at your door.

▶ Use deadbolt locks that require a key inside and outside (but keep your key in the inside of the door in case of a fire).

▶ Consider replacing the glass in your door with Plexiglas or Lexan or covering it with a decorative iron grill.

▶ Keep all doors and windows in good repair.

▶ Inside locks should secure all windows, except emergency exits. Place a broomstick or pole in the track of sliding doors or windows so they cannot be forced open by a burglar.

▶ Trim shrubs and bushes hiding doors and windows because they make excellent cover for burglars.

▶ Do not keep large amounts of money in your house. Burglars look in your bedroom first for valuables, so put valuables somewhere else in the house or in a safe deposit box.

▶ Do not list your first name or address in the telephone book or on your mailbox.

▶ Call your local police department for a home security and personal safety review of your home.

▶ Call your local fire department for help designing a fire safety plan.

▶ Mark your valuables with an identification number or name. This makes it difficult for a burglar to sell your valuables and easier for the police to return them to you. Your local police department can refer you to an engraving service. Sometimes libraries will have engraving tools to loan. Photograph jewelry and artwork and keep copies of these in a safe deposit box or with your insurance agent.

12-3. Protection from Abuse

You do not have to accept threats or abuse from anyone, including your family. If someone close to you has threatened you with violence or abused you in any way, the Colorado Domestic Abuse law can help protect you. Under this law, you can get an **injunction**, which is an order to stop the abuser from contacting you or coming to your home or place of work.

Under this law the abuser must be:

▶ A current or former relative;

▶ Someone who lived or lives with you; or

▶ Someone you are or have been intimately involved with.

A temporary or permanent **restraining order** to prevent domestic abuse may include:

▶ Stopping an abuser from threatening, molesting, injuring, or contacting you; and

▶ Keeping the abuser from your home if you can show that you could be physically or emotionally harmed.

Even if someone does not fit the definition of an abuser under the Colorado Domestic Abuse law (such as a stranger or home health worker), you can still get a restraining order against him or her. Under this rule, the county court can give you a temporary or permanent restraining order if anyone has:

▶ Attacked, beaten, or molested you;

▶ Threatened your life; or

▶ Threatened to do serious bodily harm to you.

There is a special type of restraining order available to older persons. People 60 or older who have been emotionaliy abused can get a restraining order to prevent further emotional abuse. The abused person or any other person can ask for the restraining order.

With a temporary or permanent restraining order to prevent emotional abuse you can stop someone from:

▶ Verbal threats or assaults;

▶ Verbal harassment;

▶ The inappropriate use or threat of inappropriate use of medications;

▶ The inappropriate use of physical or chemical restraints;

▶ The misuse of a power of attorney that results in unreasonable confinement or restriction of your liberty if you are 60 or older; and/or

▶ The misuse of a guardianship or conservatorship that results in unreasonable confinement or restriction of your liberty if you are 60 or older.

You can get the necessary forms and instructions for all three types of restraining orders at the county court in the county where the abuser lives. The filing fee and sheriff's fee for service can be waived if you cannot afford to pay it. You can contact victims' assistance agencies to accompany you and assist you with the paperwork.

Victims' assistance programs and some legal services programs can help you prepare the forms you need. They also can refer you to safe shelters and other services.

You will want to file a copy of your restraining order with your local police department.

If your abuser disobeys the court order, call your local police or sheriff immediately for help. If you do not feel satisfied with their response, talk to the supervisor or captain of the district police station.

If you wish, you may cancel the order later by going back into court. However, consider this decision carefully and discuss your options with someone you trust.

12-4. Injunctions

A temporary or permanent restraining order to prevent domestic abuse may include:

▶ Restraining a party from threatening, molesting, injuring, or contacting any other party or the minor children of either of the parties;

▶ Excluding a party from the family home or the home of another party upon showing that physical or emotional harm would otherwise result; and/or

▶ Awarding temporary care and control of minor children of either party for up to 120 days.

You can get the necessary forms and instructions for this type of restraining order at county, district, and authorized municipal courts. You must go to the county where the abuser lives. The filing fee and sheriff's fee for service can be waived if you cannot afford to pay it. You can contact victims' assistance agencies to accompany you to court and assist you with the paperwork.

12-5. Protection from Emotional Abuse

If someone who does not fit the definition of an abuser under the Colorado Domestic Abuse law (such as a stranger or home health worker) threatens you or abuses you, you can use an injunction to get a restraining order against them.

Under this rule, the county court can give you a temporary and/or permanent restraining order if someone has:

▶ Attacked, beaten, or molested you;

▶ Threatened your life; or

▶ Threatened to do serious bodily harm to you.

You can get the necessary forms and instructions for this type of restraining order at the county court in the county where the abuser lives. The filing fee and sheriff's fee for service can be waived if you cannot afford to pay it. You can contact victims' assistance agencies to accompany you and assist you with the paperwork.

There is a special type of restraining order available to older persons. People 60 or older who have been emotionally abused can get a restraining order to prevent further emotional abuse. The abused person or any other person can ask for the restraining order.

A temporary and/or permanent restraining order to prevent emotional abuse may include restraining a party from acts that:

▶ Constitute verbal threats or assaults;

▶ Constitute verbal harassment;

▶ Result in the inappropriate use or threat of inappropriate use of medications;

▶ Result in the inappropriate use of physical or chemical restraints;

▶ Result in the misuse of a power or authority granted to a person through a power of attorney that results in the unreasonable confinement or restriction of the liberty of a person 60 years of age or older; and/or

▶ Result in the misuse of a power or authority granted to a person by a court in a guardianship or conservatorship proceeding that results in the unreasonable confinement or restriction of the liberty of a person 60 years of age or older.

12-6. Resources

Colorado Area Agencies on Aging Fund Title III Legal Programs provide free legal assistance to persons age 60 or older. For a referral to the program nearest you, call your local Area Agency on Aging or the State Legal Assistance Developer.

Area Agencies on Aging:

Logan, Morgan, Phillips, Sedgwick, Washington, and Yuma counties:
Northeastern Colorado Association of Local Governments
Northeastern Region
231 Main St., Ste. 211
Fort Morgan, CO 80701
(970) 867-9409

Larimer County:
Larimer County Office on Aging
Northeastern Region
Larimer County Human Services
1501 Blue Spruce Dr.
Fort Collins, CO 80524
(970) 498-6807

Weld County:
Weld County Area Agency on Aging
Northeastern Region
P.O. Box 1805
1551 N. 17th Ave.
Greeley, CO 80632
(970) 353-3800

Adams, Arapahoe, Broomfield, Clear Creek, Denver, Douglas, Gilpin, and Jefferson counties:
Denver Regional Council of Governments
Northeastern Region
1290 Broadway, Ste. 700
Denver, CO 80203
(303) 455-1000

Boulder County:
Boulder County Aging Services Division
Northeastern Region
P.O. Box 471
3482 N. Broadway
Boulder, CO 80306
(303) 441-3570

Park, El Paso, and Teller counties:
Pikes Peak Area Agency on Aging
Southern Region
15 S. 7th St.
Colorado Springs, CO 80905
(719) 471-2096

Cheyenne, Elbert, Kit Carson, and Lincoln counties:
East Central Council of Governments
Northeastern Region
P.O. Box 28
128 Colorado Ave.
Stratton, CO 80836
(719) 348-5562

Baca, Bent, Crowley, Kiowa, Otero, and Prowers counties:
Lower Arkansas Valley Area Agency on Aging
Southern Region
P.O. Box 494
13 W. 3rd St., Room 110
La Junta, CO 81050
(719) 383-3166

Pueblo County:
Pueblo Area Agency on Aging
Southern Region
2631 E. 4th St.
Pueblo, CO 81001
(719) 583-6110

Alamosa, Conejos, Costilla, Mineral, Rio Grande, and Saguache counties:
South-Central Colorado Seniors, Inc.
Southern Region
P.O. Box 639
1116 3rd St.
Alamosa, CO 81101
(719) 589-4511

Archuleta, Dolores, La Plata, Montezuma, and San Juan counties:
San Juan Basin Area Agency on Aging
Western Region
701 Camino Del Rio, Ste. 312
Durango, CO 81301
(970) 259-1967

Delta, Gunnison, Hinsdale, Montrose, Ouray, and San Miguel counties:
Region 10 Area Agency on Aging
Western Region
Drawer 849
300 N. Cascade Ave.
Montrose, CO 81402
(970) 249-2436

Garfield, Mesa, Moffat, Rio Blanco, and Routt counties:
Associated Governments of Northwest Colorado
Western Region
P.O. Box 20000-5035
510 29½ Rd.
Grand Junction, CO 81502
(970) 248-2717

Eagle, Grand, Jackson, Pitkin, and Summit counties:
Northwest Colorado Council of Governments
Alpine Area Agency on Aging
Western Region
P.O. Box 2308
249 Warren Ave.
Silverthorne, CO 80498
(970) 468-0295

Chaffee, Custer, Fremont, and Lake counties:
Upper Arkansas AAA
Southern Region
139 E. 3rd St.
Salida, CO 81201-2612
(719) 539-3341

Huerfano and Las Animas counties:
Huerfano/Las Animas Area Council of Governments
South Central Council of Governments AAA
Southern Region
300 Bonaventure Ave.
Trinidad, CO 81082
(719) 845-1133

Legal Assistance Developer for the Elderly

The Legal Center for People with Disabilities and Older People
455 Sherman St., Ste. 130
Denver, CO 80203
(303) 722-0300
(303) 722-3619 (TTY)
www.thelegalcenter.org

Colorado Crime Victims Compensation Programs

First Judicial District
District Attorney's Building
500 Jefferson County Pkwy.
Golden, CO 80401
(303) 271-6846

Second Judicial District
201 W. Colfax, Dept. 801
Denver, CO 80202
(720) 913-9253

Third Judicial District
200 E. 1st St., Ste. 302
Trinidad, CO 81082
(719) 846-9224

Fourth Judicial District
105 E. Vermijo, Ste. 111
Colorado Springs, CO 80903
(719) 520-6915

Fifth Judicial District
P.O. Box 2000
Georgetown, CO 80444
(303) 679-2453

Sixth Judicial District
1060 Main Ave.
P.O. Drawer 3455
Durango, CO 81302
(970) 247-8850

Seventh Judicial District
1200 N. Grand Ave., Ste. D
Montrose, CO 81401
(970) 252-4266

Eighth Judicial District
201 La Porte, Ste. 200
Fort Collins, CO 80521
(970) 498-7200

2012 Senior Law Handbook

Ninth Judicial District
109 8th St., Ste. 308
Glenwood Springs, CO 81601
(970) 945-8635

Tenth Judicial District
701 Court St.
Pueblo, CO 81003
(719) 583-6092

Eleventh Judicial District
136 Justice Center Rd., Rm. 203
Cañon City, CO 81212
(719) 269-0170

Twelfth Judicial District
426 San Juan Ave.
Alamosa, CO 81101
(719) 589-3691

Thirteenth Judicial District
400 Warner St.
Fort Morgan, CO 80701
(970) 542-3420

Fourteenth Judicial District
221 W. Victory Wy., Ste. 302
Craig, CO 81625
(970) 824-9143

Fifteenth Judicial District
110 E. Oak St.
Lamar, CO 81052
(719) 336-7446

Sixteenth Judicial District
323 Santa Fe, Ste. 201
La Junta, CO 81050-0928
(719) 384-8786

Seventeenth Judicial District
1000 Judicial Center Dr., Ste. 100
Brighton, CO 80601
(303) 835-5614

Eighteenth Judicial District
6450 S. Revere Pkwy.
Centennial, CO 80111
(720) 874-8607

Nineteenth Judicial District
P.O. Box 1167
Greeley, CO 80632
(970) 356-4010, ext. 4748

Twentieth Judicial District
1035 Kimbark St.
Longmont, CO 80501
(303) 682-6801

Twenty-First Judicial District
P.O. Box 20000-5031
Grand Junction, CO 81502
(970) 244-1643

Twenty-Second Judicial District
103 N. Chestnut St.
Cortez, CO 81321
(970) 564-2755

Elder Abuse:

Call 911 or your local police department.

Adult Protection

Call your county Department of Social Services. You may find a list of contact information for these offices at www.cdhs.state.co.us, click on "Services by County" for a list of offices.

Colorado Coalition for Elder Rights and Adult Protection

(800) 773-1366

www.ccerap.org

AARP ElderWatch

Through the Colorado Consumer Line: (800) 222-4444, option 2, for referrals and assistance information.

Metro Denver: (303) 222-4444

www.aarpelderwatch.org

Denver District Attorney's Office

(720) 913-9000

www.denverda.org

Boulder District Attorney's Office

(303) 441-3700

www.bouldercounty.org/da

Adams/Broomfield counties District Attorney's Office

(303) 659-7720

www.adamsbroomfieldda.org

Arapahoe/Douglas counties District Attorney's Office

(720) 874-8500

www.co.arapahoe.co.us/Departments/DA/DistrictAttorney.asp

Jefferson/Gilpin counties District Attorney's Office

(303) 271-6800

http://jeffco.us/da/index.htm

---

* Based on a chapter originally written by Lisa Curtis, Office of the District Attorney, Second Judicial District, and updated by Robin Fudge Finegan, M.A., M.N.M., FEMA Region VIII.

Chapter 13

Family Relationships

Kimberly R. Willoughby, Esq.
Willoughby & Eckelberry, LLC

SYNOPSIS

Family relationships are always changing, whether it be because of marriage, divorce, death, or birth. Grandparents often are affected by these changes. This chapter discusses issues that grandparents often must deal with, such as the right to visit grandchildren, and taking custody of or becoming a guardian to grandchildren. See also Chapter 14, "Grandparent Custody and Visitation Issues."

Marriage, divorce, change of name, and prenuptial agreements are issues affecting all ages. This chapter will familiarize you with the requirements for a divorce and issues to consider if you decide to remarry. You also will find out how to decide, before marriage, what rights you want to retain over certain property if divorce or death occurs.

Finally, this chapter discusses family violence and how Colorado laws can help you with protection orders.

13-1. Grandparents' Visitation Rights

If you have a dispute with your adult children or one of your children gets a divorce, you could be denied contact with your grandchildren. You have a remedy in court if a parent does not let you visit your grandchildren in the following situations:

▶ When the grandchild's parents are going through a divorce or legal separation;

▶ When the legal custody of the grandchild has been given to a party other than the parent, or the child has been placed outside of and does not reside in the home of the parent (but this does not cover a child who has been placed for adoption or whose adoption has been legally finalized);

▶ When the grandchild's parent, who is the child of the grandparent, has died;

▶ When the grandchild has lived with the grandparent for six months within the last six months; or

▶ When the grandparent has been appointed the legal guardian of the grandchild.

Grandparents have no recourse if the child and his or her parents are an intact family; they can seek a court order allowing grandparent visitation if, and only if, one of the above situations is present. If this basic criterion is met, the grandparent must file a motion and accompanying affidavit for grandparent visitation with the district court for the district in which there has been or is a child custody case. The motion and affidavit must set forth the facts supporting the requested order — that is, facts showing why it is in the child's best interest to spend time with the grandparent. Notice must be given to the party (or parties) who has legal custody of the grandchild. The court may make an order, with or without a hearing, granting (or denying) visitation rights whenever such an order would be in the best interest of the grandchild.

In order to determine that spending time with the child is in the child's best interest, some courts will order you to meet with a trained mediator and the child's parents or custodian to try to reach an agreement before the court listens to your case.

If the court gives you visitation rights, your rights continue even if the parents divorce or legally separate, or if one or both of the parents die. Your rights can end if the parents lose their rights over the child or if your grandchild is adopted. However, if your grandchild is adopted by his or her natural parent's new spouse (that is, a stepparent), you are entitled to seek grandparenting time so long as the child still remains with and in the legal custody of his or her natural parent. Ask a lawyer for advice about seeking visitation.

A motion for grandparent visitation cannot be filed more than once every two years unless there is a showing of good cause.

If the grandchild's custodial parent does not comply with court-ordered visitation, the law provides various remedies. Under the grandparent visitation law, you may file a motion asking the court to enforce such visitation. If you prove that the grandchild's custodian has not complied with the visitation order, the court has some tools to remedy the situation and can:

▶ Impose additional terms and conditions consistent with the court's previous order;

▶ Modify the previous order;

▶ Require the violator to post bond or security to ensure future compliance;

▶ Require that missed visitations be made up;

▶ Hold the violator in contempt of court and impose a jail sentence or bond; or

▶ Award the person denied visitation his or her attorney fees.

Grandparents' rights vary by state. All states now have laws enabling grandparents to petition for visitation rights with their grandchildren, but there are great variations from state to state. Therefore, you will need to research grandparents' rights under the law of another state if your grandchildren live in another state and are subject to that state's laws.

13-2. Custody of Grandchildren

Sometimes grandparents may have to care for grandchildren permanently or temporarily. Seniors caring for grandchildren for a brief time should get written permission from at least one parent to authorize emergency medical care for the child. A simple signed and dated note will work. If a grandchild will be with the grandparent for more than a brief time, the grandparent should have authority to protect the child, especially if the parents will be difficult to reach. There is a general provision in Colorado law governing people with disabilities that allows the child's parents to delegate "any of his powers regarding care, custody and property" of the child. This includes, but is not limited to, the power to make health care decisions and may be effective for up to 12 months. However, the grandparent cannot consent to the marriage or adoption of the grandchild. Legal stationery stores, some legal aid offices, law firms, and some senior centers have forms for this purpose. The form is generally titled "Parent's or Guardian's Delegation of Powers by Power of Attorney."

If you expect to care for your grandchild for an extended time, you may want legal guardianship of the child. A legal guardianship gives you ultimate authority over the child's care and well-being. You may apply to a district court to become your grandchild's guardian. If the parents do not agree to the guardianship, you must show the court why the child needs a guardian. Once you are appointed as a guardian, only the court may terminate the appointment.

With or without a guardianship, you may qualify for Temporary Aid to Needy Families (TANF) and Medicaid coverage for a grandchild in your care. In unusual circumstances, grandparents may seek full legal custody of a grandchild. To win such a case, you must show that it is in the child's best interest to transfer custody to you.

To be able to request custody of your grandchild, your grandchild must no longer be in the custody of either of his or her natural parents, or you must have had physical custody of your grandchild for six months continuously. If you had physical custody of your grandchild for six months, then you must have filed a petition for custody within six months of the termination of such physical custody. The court also can order the child's parents to pay child support and your legal fees.

13-3. Divorce

Divorce has become more common in recent years. In Colorado, you do not have to prove that a failed marriage is anyone's fault. A "no-fault" divorce will be granted based on your inability to get along with each other. You merely state that the marriage is "irretrievably broken."

A divorce decree restores your status to that of a single person. Also, it divides marital property and debts and provides for maintenance (also called alimony or spousal support) when appropriate. For couples with minor children, divorce settles custody, which is now called allocation of parental responsibility; visitation (also called parenting time); and child support issues. In Colorado, child support ends at age 19, and there is no provision for college in orders entered after July 1, 1997. Either spouse may receive temporary or permanent maintenance/spousal support, if he or she cannot support himself or herself through employment or assets. After need is established, the law considers the length and standard of living of the marriage and each person's job skills, income, resources, age, and health in deciding whether and how much maintenance (spousal support) to award.

You can get a divorce in Colorado if you or your spouse have been living in Colorado for at least 90 days prior to filing for divorce. This is true if you have been living in Colorado for at least 90 days before filing and your spouse has not.

The same laws and requirements apply to an action when filing for a legal separation. A legal separation decides all the issues a divorce decides, except that it does not free you to remarry. No less than six months after the decree of legal separation, there is an absolute right for either party to convert the legal separation to a divorce, upon filing of a written motion.

If you move to Colorado and leave your spouse behind in another state, a Colorado court may not be able to decide property, child custody, and support issues, even if the court has jurisdiction to grant a divorce. A family law attorney can help you determine in which state you should file your case.

If you cannot agree on care and support for minor children or the division of property or debts, these matters will be decided by the court. There is no legal requirement that you have a lawyer, but you may decide to hire or consult with one. One lawyer cannot ethically or practically protect the interests of both spouses.

Colorado is not a community property state; the law requires an equitable division of marital property. As a result, you have to decide three things: what is marital property, what is it worth, and what is a fair division. In Colorado, the court usually assumes that each party contributed to the marriage and the property of the parties and that an equal division of marital property is fair. Property each spouse had at the time of the marriage is generally separate property (not marital property subject to division). Thus, in all cases where property exists, but especially in short marriages, the court will consider the separate property each spouse had at the time of the marriage and still has at the time of the divorce, but will not divide separate assets. If one spouse has more separate property than the other, the court might not divide marital property equally.

You may have more property than you realize. Property isn't limited to your home, cars, and household items. Property also includes limited partnerships, business interests, investments, the cash value of life insurance, and pensions and retirement benefits that will pay in the future. In the absence of a marital or prenuptial agreement, all property acquired during the marriage is subject to division regardless of the name on the title. If part of a pension was earned during the marriage, that part is property the court can divide. If your divorce involves a pension, you should get legal advice.

13-4. Getting Your Divorce Without a Lawyer

If you and your spouse can reach an agreement on all issues, or wish to proceed without attorneys, you may do your own divorce without a lawyer representing you or your spouse. Some legal aid offices or other low-cost legal services offices can help you complete the necessary forms. For example, Denver District Court has an "Information and Referral Office," which sells packets of forms with lengthy instructions, and has a paralegal and volunteer attorneys to assist with the paperwork. Remember that any agreements not included in your court papers cannot be enforced later. You can also obtain instructions and forms online at www.courts.state.co.us.

If neither you nor your spouse can afford to pay the filing fee necessary to obtain a divorce, you may request a waiver of fees called "*In Forma Pauperis*." This allows you to file the documents free of charge, but only if you can prove to the court that you are in fact indigent and unable to pay the fee. The forms are available at the court clerk's office, or you may be able to get them from your local legal services or legal aid office.

13-5. Use of Former Name

You may use whatever name you wish. When you marry, you may keep your own name or use your spouse's name. You also can resume using your own name after you have started using your spouse's name. When you divorce, any former name may be restored. You may request the change of name as part of your divorce proceeding, and the court will grant it so long as you are not trying to defraud anyone by the name change.

13-6. Anticipating Marriage

Often, people marrying later in life have property or children from earlier marriages. A marital agreement (also known as a prenuptial agreement) allows the couple to decide, in advance, what rights each of them will retain over certain property if a divorce or death occurs. A verbal marital agreement is not enforceable. In order to be valid, a marital agreement must be in writing and signed by both parties, and the couple must first make a complete disclosure of their respective financial circumstances to each other. The couple can revoke or change the agreement later only by a signed written agreement. Retirement benefits only may be waived by a current spouse. People who want such an agreement should ask their own separate lawyers well before the wedding. If there is a divorce, dispute over a will, or other action where the property rights are an issue, a valid marital agreement will govern the matter.

Marital agreements also may be made between spouses who have been married for any period of time, so long as no action for dissolution of marriage or for legal separation has been filed or contemplated.

13-7. Marriage and Public Benefits

When a person who receives public benefits marries, his or her benefits can change or stop, depending on the person's age and which benefits he or she is receiving, as well as other factors. This section will outline some effects that marriage can have on some specific public benefit programs.

Social Security

Many people receive Social Security retirement benefits as the spouse of a qualified worker. That is because an individual who does not have a sufficient work history to receive Social Security benefits may be entitled to benefits on the work record of the spouse who does. In order to receive benefits as a spouse, the recipient must have a valid marriage to the qualified worker, through either a traditional marriage or by common law marriage. The spouse of a retired or deceased worker is eligible for benefits. Under certain circumstances, a divorced spouse is also eligible.

In general, to receive benefits as a widow or former spouse, a person must be unmarried. Remarrying may cause benefits to stop, under certain circumstances. Contact your local Social Security office for information.

Disability

When a worker becomes disabled, his or her spouse may be eligible for benefits under certain circumstances. While the spouse of a disabled worker is entitled to benefits in these situations, there are no equivalent benefits for the disabled spouse of the worker because the spouse is disabled.

Under certain circumstances, these benefits also are available to a divorced spouse of a disabled worker. In order to receive benefits, a divorced spouse of a disabled worker must not be married at the time of applying for benefits, and remarriage will cut off benefits.

While a disabled spouse is not entitled to benefits, a disabled surviving spouse or divorced spouse may be. Contact your attorney or local Social Security office for more information.

Supplemental Security Income (SSI)

With Supplemental Security Income (SSI), the effect of marriage is more complicated. Marriage can cause SSI benefits to decrease or even to end. For more information regarding these and other Social Security questions, you can consult Social Security online at www.ssa.gov or speak to an attorney.

Old Age Pension

Chapter 5, "Government Programs and Financial Assistance," explains the eligibility requirements for the Colorado Old Age Pension (OAP). Each spouse receives benefits as an individual, so for a couple the combined benefit would not decrease as with SSI payments. If both spouses receive SSI and OAP, their combined SSI income will go down, as explained above, but their total income will remain the same. If one of the spouses is eligible for OAP and the other is not, the income of the ineligible spouse will count as available ("deemed") to the eligible spouse. This is a serious problem because it can cause that spouse to lose Medicaid, which is an important benefit. Even if that individual had income from another source, and received only a small amount of OAP, loss of the Medicaid benefit may be crucial.

Medicaid for Long-Term Care

See Chapter 4, "Medicaid," for an explanation of benefits for spouses of a Medicaid long-term care recipient. Getting married does not affect the benefits of the long-term care recipient.

13-8. Protection from Family Violence

If a family or household member has threatened you with violence or abused you verbally or physically, you may request a protection order to prevent domestic abuse. Under the law, you can get an order keeping the abuser from threatening or injuring you, contacting you, or coming to your home, school, or workplace. The court can order the abuser to leave the family home if you both live there, and can issue orders for temporary custody if you have minor children. To qualify for this type of protection order, you must convince the court that there is imminent danger to the life or health of one or more people.

There also is a law that provides additional protection from emotional abuse for people 60 years of age or older, by allowing the court to issue an order protecting the person from the following kinds of abuse:

▶ Repeated acts of verbal threats or assaults;

▶ Repeated acts of verbal harassment;

▶ Repeated acts of inappropriate use or threat of inappropriate use of medications, physical restraints, or chemical restraints; or

▶ Repeated acts of the misuse of power or authority by a person through a Power of Attorney or in a guardianship or conservatorship proceeding, which results in a person being unreasonably confined, or his or her liberty being unreasonably restricted.

These protection orders are free. You can get the necessary forms and instructions from the court clerk at your county courthouse. If your abuser disobeys the court order and comes to your home or office, or threatens you, you can get immediate help from the police. These orders are valid either temporarily or permanently.

The Victim Assistance Program in your county district attorney's office can help you prepare the forms. It also can refer you to safe shelters and other services.

13-9. Common Law Marriage

In Colorado, there are three factors that must be present to establish a common law marriage. First, you must live together. There is no minimum amount of time — it can be for as little as one night. Second, you must hold yourselves out to be married — that is, you must tell other people you are married or represent to other people that you are married by owning property in joint tenancy or filing joint tax returns or health insurance forms, etc. Third, you must have an agreement that you are married. Without holding yourselves out as being married and the intent to be married, you are not common law married, regardless of how long you have lived together and whether you have children together.

Common law marriage is real marriage. Common law spouses have all the same rights and responsibilities as ceremonially married people.

Be aware that there is no such thing as common law divorce. Once you are married, whether by ceremony or by common law, you can terminate the marriage only by divorce. If you do not get a divorce after a common law marriage, all future marriages will be void, and your common law spouse will have all the benefits of a spouse, including the right to take a portion of your estate against your will and to receive various survivor benefits from the government or even from your retirement plan.

13-10. Resources

See general resource lists of Chapters 5, 11, and 15 for legal services offices, legal aid offices, and more.

Aging and Adult Services

Colorado Department of Human Services
1575 Sherman St., 10th Floor
Denver, CO 80203
(303) 866-2800
www.cdhs.state.co.us/aas

Jewish Family Service
3201 S. Tamarac Dr.
Denver, CO 80231
(303) 597-5000
http://jewishfamilyservice.org

Douglas County Adult & Senior Outreach Services
4400 Castleton Ct.
Castle Rock, CO 80109
(303) 668-4825
http://douglas.co.us/humanservices/Senior_Services.html

Elder Care Network of Larimer County
P.O. Box 272687
Fort Collins, CO 80527-2687
(970) 495-3442
www.eldercarenet.org

Chapter 14

Grandparent Custody and Visitation Issues

Melody K. Fuller, Esq.*
Melody K. Fuller, P.C.

SYNOPSIS

This chapter discusses issues that may arise involving grandparents and their grandchildren, specifically the rights to visit with grandchildren after family changes have occurred and the considerations involved when grandparents actually care for and raise their grandchildren, either temporarily or permanently.

14-1. Grandparent Visitation Issues

Courts traditionally do not interfere with relationships between parents and children — or between grandparents and grandchildren — when the family of origin is intact and where the children's safety or welfare is not in danger. However, when adult children divorce or where litigation takes place between parents who have never married, grandparents have the right, under Colorado law, to obtain court orders protecting their rights to visit with their grandchildren. The grandparent visitation statute allows courts to issue these orders in child custody cases that already have been filed with the courts. These cases involve:

1) Decrees of invalidity (annulment) of the parents' marriage, or decrees of dissolution of marriage or legal separation, and cases where courts have entered orders allocating parental responsibility between parents who have never married;

2) Cases where parental responsibilities for children have been given to someone other than the child's parents or the child has been placed outside of the home of a parent (except when a child has been placed for adoption or the adoption is final); and

3) Cases where a parent, who is the child of the grandparent, has died.

Where issues concerning a child's welfare have never been brought before a court — where families are intact and no court has been involved in the parent-child relationship — Colorado law does not permit grandparents to sue those parents for visitation. This is because in an intact family — where courts are not involved in children's issues — the decisions of parents for and about their children are private matters; the rights of parents to raise their children in intact families and to make decisions in what they believe to be their children's best interests are constitutionally protected.

In cases where a court has become involved in a child's life, however, grandparents may intervene — or may file independent legal actions — seeking court orders requiring parents to permit visitation and contact with their grandchildren. In order to obtain such an order in cases where this is legally possible, the grandparent must file a motion for grandparent visitation. This written request must be supported with a sworn affidavit reciting the facts supporting the grandparent's claim and must specifically state why this visitation is in the best interests of the grandchild. Each birth parent or other custodian of the child must receive a copy of both documents. Any parent or custodian can file a response and opposing affidavits. If no one asks for a hearing, then the court reviews the affidavits and the motions and can order visitation only if it determines that such is in the best interests of the child. If either side asks for a hearing, the court must hold one. The court then decides what visitation, if any, is in the best interests of the child and enters the appropriate order.

The court, in these cases, is required to make its decisions in the best interests of the child. The Colorado Supreme Court has said that the trial courts are required to give the parent's decisions concerning grandparent visitation special weight and significance. The trial court cannot simply substitute its own opinion for the decisions of the parent; the parent's determination is given preference and is presumed to have been made in the child's best interests. The grandparent's proof must overcome this presumption; the grandparent must establish by clear and convincing evidence that the visitation he or she seeks is in the best interests of the child. A grandparent can prove this by establishing, for example, that the parent denying visitation is unfit to make that decision. He or she might prove that the parent's decision is affirmatively wrong and that it is, in fact, psychologically harmful to the child. The grandparent can prove that visitation with the child — contrary to the parent's belief — is affirmatively in the child's best interests, but this has to be shown by clear and convincing evidence.

There is an important limitation on the court's power, even if it decides to order grandparent visitation; it cannot order a parent not to move outside of Colorado in order to preserve a previously adopted visitation schedule. The previous order concerning grandparent visitation would have to be modified, in the child's best interests, to accommodate the move.

Sometimes, after a divorce, one parent might remarry and the new stepparent may actually adopt the grandchild. This type of an adoption does not take away the biological grandparents' right to visitation with their grandchildren. However, if parental rights are terminated in a dependency and neglect proceeding and if the grandchildren are adopted by an entirely new family, the grandparents' rights to visitation with the adopted child will be severed.

If the grandparent visitation order is violated by the custodian of the child, the grandparent can ask the court to enforce the order. The grandparent seeking enforcement of the order must file a verified motion describing when and how the custodian violated the order. The court has to determine if the violation really occurred and it must also decide whether there is likely to be substantial and continuing noncompliance with the order. The court can then (1) deny the motion, if the allegations in the motion are not adequate; (2) schedule a hearing and give notice of the date and time of the hearing to both sides; or (3) order the parties to mediation — and if it fails, the court can schedule a hearing. If the court decides the custodian or the parent violated the order, it can impose additional terms and conditions, modify the order to meet the child's best interests, require the custodian or the parent to post a bond or security to ensure future compliance with the court's order, or require makeup visitation. In addition, the court could hold the violator in contempt of court and impose a fine or jail sentence. The court also has the power to make the violator of the order repay the grandparent for his or her costs and attorney fees.

A motion for grandparent visitation can only be made once every two years, unless the court finds good cause.

14-2. Custody of Grandchildren

More and more frequently, it seems, grandchildren actually live with their grandparents — rather than with either one of their birth parents — and grandparents raise these children to adulthood. Over 35,000 Colorado grandparents are responsible for the care of their grandchildren, who live with them. This creates a special set of concerns.

If the parent(s) and the grandparents agree to such an arrangement on a temporary basis, the parent needs to make sure that the grandparents have the power to make medical decisions for the children, take them in or out of school, or make any other decisions in their best interests that birth parents ordinarily make. This can be accomplished through a power of attorney where the mother or father or both actually assign their parental rights and responsibilities to the grandparents. These are formal legal documents and should be prepared by a lawyer and verified (signed in front of a notary public) by the parents and the grandparents. These assignments are only temporary and they generally only last for 12 months. Such a power of attorney can be used, for example, if a child needs medical treatment and the grandparent needs to prove that he or she has the authority to consent to the treatment or assume financial responsibility for it. The grandparent cannot use this power to consent to the adoption or marriage of the grandchild.

If more permanent arrangements for custody are contemplated, a grandparent may want to seek legal guardianship for a grandchild. This could also be important if a child has income or the right to money (such as a personal injury settlement) that, for one reason or another, cannot or should not be controlled by the parent. A grandparent can file a request with the district court to be appointed a legal guardian or conservator for a grandchild. A parent must be notified of this request; if the parent objects, the grandparent must be prepared to convince a judge, at a hearing, that this request is appropriate.

It may become necessary for a grandparent to seek legal decision-making and parental responsibilities for a grandchild. This used to be called "custody"; it is now called the "allocation of parental responsibilities." In Colorado, this is possible — even over the birth parent's objections — under certain circumstances. To have such a request considered by the court, a grandparent must be able to prove that the child is not presently in the physical care of one of his or her parents or that the grandparent had the physical care of the child for a period of six months or more and that no more than six months has passed since the child left the grandparent's physical care.

Whether a grandparent or other non-parent has had a child in his or her "physical care" depends upon the nature, duration, and frequency of the contact between the grandparent and the grandchild as well as the parent(s) and child. The grandparent's physical care need not be uninterrupted or exclusive of the parent's care. The court should consider the amount of time a child has spent in the actual physical possession of the grandparent and the psychological bonds grandparents or other non-parents develop with children who have been in their physical care and control for a significant period of time.

The case must be filed in the county where the child permanently lives or where the child is located. Notice of the petition for allocation of parental responsibilities must be provided to the birth parents, to any legal guardians, and to any custodian or another person who has been allocated parental responsibilities previously. These individuals must be given an opportunity to respond, in writing, or appear in court and be heard.

The court is required to make the decision as to allocation of parental responsibilities in the best interests of the child. The factors that the court is required to consider include:

1) The wishes of the parents;

2) The wishes of the child if he or she is mature enough to express a reasoned preference;

3) The relationship of the child, parents, grandparents, family members, and any other people who affect the child's best interests;

4) The child's adjustment to home, school, and community;

5) The mental and physical health of all parties involved;

6) The adults' respective abilities to encourage the sharing of love and contact between the child and the other parties;

7) The past pattern of the parents' and grandparents' involvement with the child;

8) Credible evidence of a history of child abuse or neglect on the part of the parents or grandparents; and

9) The abilities of the adults to put the child's needs and best interests ahead of their own.

It may be possible to have a child and family evaluator appointed by the court to make an investigation into these issues and make a report recommending an outcome that would be in the child's best interests. The court has the power to order the adults involved to cooperate with the evaluation. The evaluator has access to medical, mental health, education, and other reports concerning the child, although the child's consent has to be obtained before these records are released to the evaluator if the child is more than 15 years old.

In the end, it is the court's responsibility — and the child's right — to have decisions concerning the permanent allocation of parental responsibility be made in the child's best interests.

Child support, Social Security benefits, and public assistance may be available to grandparents with the allocation of parental responsibilities (APR) orders. Child support may be ordered for the benefit of a grandparent with APR. The amount of support ordered will be according to Colorado statutory guidelines based on the parent's (or parents') income. Assistance in establishing and collecting support is available for a small application fee through the state agency for each county, known as the Child Support Enforcement Unit (CSEU).

The Social Security Administration may pay benefits to grandchildren if benefits are not payable on the work record of a parent. If a child is not receiving benefits from a parent when the grandparent retires, becomes disabled, or dies, the grandchild may then be able to qualify for benefits if certain conditions are met. Generally, the biological parents of the child must be deceased or disabled, or the grandchild must be legally adopted by the grandparent. In addition, the grandchild must have begun living with the grandparent before age 18 and received at least one-half of his or her support from the grandparent for the year before the month the grandparent became entitled to retirement or disability insurance benefits, or died. Also, the natural parent(s) of the child must not be making regular contributions to the child's support.

Means-tested public assistance programs, such as Medicaid and food stamps, may be accessed through the county departments of human services. Grandparents should contact their county for information and assistance.

14-3. Resources

Administration on Aging
A federal agency offering resources for grandparents raising grandchildren: www.aoa.gov

AARP Grandparent Information Center
Provides a wide variety of resources for grandparents: www.aarp.org/families/grandparents

Colorado Legal Services
Provides legal advice and assistance for qualifying grandparents who are raising grandchildren: www.coloradolegalservices.org

The Foundation for Grandparenting
Has innovative ideas for grandparents as parents and a large selection of books. Also involved in education, research, programming, and networking around grandparenting: www.grandparenting.org

Grandparents as Parents
Helps individuals network with other grandparents: www.grandparentsasparents.org

Grandparents Resource Center
Works with grandparents and family members to facilitate harmony and foster intergenerational relationships, providing broader security for children in the family: http://grc4usa.org

The Grandparent Rights Organization
A grandparenting rights advocacy group: www.grandparentsrights.org

National Center on Grandparents Raising Grandchildren
Has a mission to improve the quality of life for intergenerational kinship care families via education, advocacy, and the promotion of sound legislation: http://chhs.gsu.edu/nationalcenter

Social Security Benefits for Grandchildren
Provides advice on Social Security benefits: www.ssa.gov/kids/parent5.htm

* The author would like to thank Magistrate Betty Strobel, Weld County Combined Courts, for her work on the chapter in 2008, and also Paul J. Kyed, Esq., for his review of the chapter for the 2009 Edition.

Exhibit 14A.
Instructions to File for Grandparent Visitation

INSTRUCTIONS TO FILE FOR GRANDPARENT VISITATION

> **These standard instructions are for informational purposes only and do not constitute legal advice about your case. If you choose to represent yourself, you are bound by the same rules and procedures as an attorney.**

GENERAL INFORMATION

◆ This information provides a guide to the forms necessary to file for grandparent visitation.

◆ A maternal or paternal grandparent of a child **may seek a court order** granting grandparent reasonable visitation rights when there is or has been judicial intervention into the marriage of the child's parents, a judicial placement of the child(ren) outside their family, or the death of the grandparent's child. This applies to the following cases:

1. A Domestic Relations **(DR)** Case that involves a Dissolution of Marriage, Legal Separation, Allocation of Parental Responsibilities or Invalidity of Marriage/Annulment.

2. A Juvenile **(JV)** case that involves Allocation of Parental Responsibilities or determination of Paternity.

3. Where the child's parent who is the child of the grandparent seeking visitation has died and a Probate **(PR)** guardianship case is pending or closed..

4. Where the child's parent, who is the child of the grandparent who is seeking visitation has died and a Probate **(PR)** decedent estate case is pending or closed. In this situation, the Pleading Affidavit must be filed in a new Juvenile (JV) action.

5. If the child is involved in a Juvenile **(JV)** case that involves Dependency and Neglect and the child has been placed outside of and does not reside in the home of the child's parent, the grandparents can seek visitation.

◆ A maternal or paternal grandparent of a child **cannot seek a court order** granting grandparent reasonable visitation rights under the following circumstances, since they do not have standing to request visitation:

1. If parental rights of the child have been terminated.

2. If the child has been placed for adoption or the adoption has been legally finalized.

3. If the parents of the child have not participated in a Domestic Relations, Juvenile or Probate case as identified in numbers 1 – 5 above.

◆ If the maternal or paternal grandparent(s) are eligible to file, they can file a Motion to Intervene pursuant to Rule 24 of the Colorado Rules of Civil Procedure or a Pleading Affidavit to request grandparent visitation in a new Juvenile **(JV)** action in cases where the child's parent, who is the child of the grandparent seeking visitation, has died, see number 4 above.

◆ The Motion to Intervene for Grandparent Visitation must be filed in the county where the child resides.

☒ If the **original DR, JV or PR** case is in a different county, you will need to file a Motion to Intervene along with a Motion for Change of Venue in the county where the original case is. Once the Court issues an Order for Change of Venue, you can file the Order along with the Pleading Affidavit for Grandparent Visitation in the county where the child resides.

◆ The Pleading Affidavit for Grandparent Visitation must be filed in the county where the child resides.

◆ If Colorado does not have the original case, you may need to file in the originating court. This is the court that has child custody jurisdiction. If this situation applies to you consult an attorney to assist with the filing of the documents.

◆ No grandparent may file a Pleading Affidavit seeking an order granting visitation rights more than once every two years, without court approval.

◆ If there are matters or issues that you and the other parties cannot resolve, mediation or other forms of alternative dispute resolution may be an option. For more information, call the State Office of Dispute Resolution at (303) 837-3672 or check with your local Court to obtain information on local mediators.

◆ Review the statute on this subject matter, see §19-1-117, C.R.S.

◆ If you have a disability and need a reasonable accommodation to access the courts, please contact your local ADA Coordinator. Contact information can be obtained from the following website:

http://www.courts.state.co.us/Administration/HR/ADA/Coordinator_List.cfm

COMMON TERMS

☒ Petitioner:		The person identified in the original Petition filed with the Court.
☒ Co-Petitioner:		The person identified in the original Petition filed with the Court.
☒ Respondent:		The person identified in the original Petition filed with the Court.
☒ Intervenor:		A person who voluntarily interposes in an action or other proceeding with the approval of the court.
☒ Stipulation:		A written agreement prepared by the parties.
☒ Parental Responsibilities:		This term includes both parenting time and decision-making responsibilities regarding the children. (The term "Custody" is no longer used.)
☒ Hearing Date:		The date that the parties must appear in Court.
☒ Mediation:		A confidential process whereby a trained neutral third party assists disputing parties to reach their own solution.
☒ Alternative Dispute Resolution:		A process that allows parties to resolve their dispute without litigating the matter in Court.
☒ May:		In legal terms, "may" is defined as "optional" or "can".
☒ Shall:		In legal terms, "shall" is defined as "required".

If you do not understand this information, please contact an attorney. You may also contact the Family Court Facilitator at your local courthouse, if one is available in your Judicial District.

FEES

The filing fees identified below are based on if you file a Motion to Intervene or an independent action by filing a Petition.

☒ The filing fee for an Intervenor is $ 181.00 in a Domestic Relations (DR) case or a Juvenile Paternity or Allocation of Parental Responsibilities (JV) case. No filing fee is required in a Probate (PR) or Juvenile Dependency and Neglect (JV) case.

☒ The filing fee for a Petitioner is $ 182.00.The Pleading Affidavit is filed in a Juvenile case.

If you are unable to pay the filing fee, you must complete the Motion to File without Payment and Supporting Financial Affidavit (JDF 205) and submit it to the Court. Once you submit the completed JDF 205 form and a blank Order (JDF 206), the Court will decide whether you need to pay the filing fee. Some Courts require mediation and may require these fees to be paid upon the filing of the case.

JDF 1700   R3-12   INSTRUCTIONS TO FILE FOR GRANDPARENT VISITATION   Page 2 of 5

Other fees that a party to the case may encounter are as follows:
- ❑ Certification Fee $13.00
- ❑ Copies of Documents (Documents on File) $.75 per page or $1.50 if double sided
- ❑ Copies of Documents (Documents not on File) $.25 per page or $.50 if double sided

FORMS

To access a form online go to **www.courts.state.co.us** and **click on the "Forms" tab.** The packet/forms are available in PDF and WORD by selecting **Domestic/Family – Modify Case – Grandparent Visitation**. You may complete a form online or you may print it and type or print legibly in black ink.

The forms and process identified below, only apply if you have elected to file as an Intervenor. If you file as a Petitioner, you may wish to consult with an attorney.

- ❑ JDF 1704 Motion to Intervene
- ❑ JDF 1705 Order to Intervene
- ❑ JDF 1701 Pleading Affidavit for Grandparent Visitation
- ❑ JDF 1702 Order re: Pleading Affidavit for Grandparent Visitation

STEPS TO FILING

Step 1: Complete Initial Forms.

Selecting these instructions indicates that you plan to intervene in a case. You must identify the parties as the Petitioner or Co-Petitioner/Respondent depending on their "title/role" in the original case. You will need to identify yourself as the "Grandparent(s) Intervenor(s)". The caption area needs to be completed on all forms filed. **Keep a copy of each form for your own records and make a copy to provide to the other party.**

❑District Court ❑Juvenile Court _____ County, Colorado Court Address:	
In re: ❑The Marriage of: ❑Parental Responsibilities concerning: Petitioner: and Co-Petitioner/Respondent: and concerning: Grandparent(s) Intervenor(s)	▲ COURT USE ONLY ▲
Attorney or Party Without Attorney (Name and Address): Phone Number: E-mail: FAX Number: Atty. Reg.#:	Case Number: Division Courtroom
Name of Form	

❑ **Motion to Intervene (JDF 1704):**

The purpose of this Motion, filed in pursuant to Rule 24 of the Colorado Rules of Civil Procedure, is for the parties to state why they wish to intervene in the case. Approval of the Motion allows the Court to add the parties to the case.

❑ Please complete all sections of this form.

❑ **Order to Intervene (JDF 1705):**

❑ Complete the caption only on this form.

❑ The Magistrate or Judge will complete the rest of the Order and give you and the other party a signed copy.

❑ **Pleading Affidavit for Grandparent Visitation (JDF 1701):**

The purpose of this Pleading Affidavit is for the parties to state the visitation being requested. It is important to provide details, for example, including times, days or dates, means of transporting the children and any other details specific to address your visitation.

❑ Please complete all sections of this form.

❑ You must provide a copy of the Pleading Affidavit for Grandparent Visitation to the party who has legal custody of the child or the party with parental responsibilities as determined by the Court.

❑ Complete the Certificate of Service portion. The purpose of the Certificate of Service is to notify the Court when and how you provided copies of the Motion to all parties in the case. This is very important, because the Court must have knowledge that all parties involved are aware of the Motion prior to any Court action being taken.

❑ **Order Re: Pleading Affidavit for Grandparent Visitation (JDF 1702):**

❑ Complete the caption only on this form.

❑ Provide the Court with the appropriate number of copies you would like.

❑ If you want any of the copies to be certified, you will need to provide the Court with $20.00 per certified copy.

❑ The Magistrate or Judge will complete the rest of the Order and give you and the other party a signed copy.

Step 2: You are Ready to File your Documents with the Court.

❑ Pay the Intervenor filing fee of $181.00, if applicable.

❑ The Motion to Intervene will be filed in the existing (JV, PR – Guardianship action, DR) case.

❑ If you filing a Motion to Intervene and there is an existing Paternity or Dependency and Neglect case, a new (JV) case will be established, since such cases are confidential and considered a non-public case.

❑ Provide the Court with all the documents identified in **Step 1**.

❑ Provide the Court with a self-addressed stamped envelope to receive a copy of the Order to Intervene, unless they are a mandatory e-file Court.

Step 3:   Provide All Documents Filed with the Court to the Other Part(ies).
- ❑ You must provide a copy of all documents filed with the Court to the part(ies) who have legal custody of the child or to the part(ies) with parental responsibilities as determined by the Court.

- ❑ Complete the Certificate of Service portion on both forms. The purpose of the Certificate of Service is to notify the Court when and how you provided copies of the Motion and Pleading Affidavit to all parties in the case. This is very important, because the Court must have knowledge that all parties involved are aware of the Motion to Intervene and the Pleading Affidavit regarding grandparent visitation prior to any Court action being taken.

Step 4:   Court Review of Motion to Intervene.
A hearing is not required. If you believe a hearing is necessary, please check with the Court to determine what their procedures are for the setting of a hearing. The Judge or Magistrate will review the Motion to Intervene and enter an Order as appropriate.

Step 5:   File Pleading Affidavit and Order.
The Pleading Affidavit and Order re: Pleading Affidavit for Grandparent Visitation must be filed in the county where the child resides.
- ❑ If the original DR, JV or PR case is in a different county, you will need to file a Motion for Change of Venue (JDF 1323) and an Order for Change of Venue (JDF 1324) in the county where the original case is. Once the Court issues an Order for Change of Venue (JDF 1324), you can file the Order along with the Pleading Affidavit for Grandparent Visitation in the county where the child resides.
- ❑ You will receive a signed copy of the Order Re: Pleading Affidavit for Grandparent Visitation.

Step 6:   Court Review of Pleading Affidavit for Grandparent Visitation.
A hearing shall be held if either party requests a hearing or if the Court determines that a hearing is in the best interests of the child. If you believe a hearing is necessary, please check with the Court to determine what their procedures are for the setting of a hearing.

- ❑ The Judge or Magistrate will review the Pleading Affidavit for Grandparent Visitation and enter an Order as appropriate.

If your visitation has been ordered and it is not being granted by the custodian, you have certain rights of enforcement, pursuant to §19-1-117.5, C.R.S.

Exhibit 14B.
Verified Pleading Affidavit for Grandparent Visitation

❑District Court ❑Juvenile Court _____ County, Colorado Court Address: _____ In re: ❑The Marriage of: ❑Parental Responsibilities concerning: _____ Petitioner: and Co-Petitioner/Respondent: and concerning: Grandparent(s) Intervenor(s):	
Attorney or Party Without Attorney (Name and Address):	▲ COURT USE ONLY ▲ Case Number:
Phone Number: E-mail: FAX Number: Atty. Reg. #:	Division Courtroom

VERIFIED PLEADING AFFIDAVIT FOR GRANDPARENT VISITATION PURSUANT TO §19-1-117, C.R.S. AND RULE 24 OF THE CIVIL RULES OF CIVIL PROCEDURE

> **Note to Responding Party:** If you disagree with this Pleading Affidavit, the Colorado Civil Rules of Procedure allow you to file a written response with the Court which must be filed within 21 days of the date this Pleading Affidavit was served on you or mailed to you.

The intervenor(s), the ❑maternal ❑paternal grandparent(s) of the minor child(ren), states the following for the purpose of establishing visitation between the grandparent(s) and the child(ren), pursuant to §19-1-117, C.R.S.

1. A Pleading Affidavit seeking an Order for grandparent visitation ❑has ❑has not been filed in the last two years. If one has been filed, please identify the date filed _____. If a Pleading Affidavit has been filed in the last two years, state reasons for good cause in section 8.

2. **Information about Intervenor (1):**   Check if in Military ❑

   Full Legal Name: _____ Date of Birth: _____

   Current Mailing Address: _____

   City: _____ State: _____ Zip Code: _____ Home Phone #: _____

   Email Address: _____ Cell Phone #: _____

   Intervenor has the following relationship with the minor child(ren):
   ❑child(ren)'s grandmother, **or** ❑child(ren)'s grandfather

JDF 1701 R1-12 PLEADING AFFIDAVIT FOR GRANDPARENT VISITATION PURSUANT TO §19-1-117, C.R.S. Page 1 of 4

3. **Information about Intervenor (2):**   Check if in Military ❏

   Full Legal Name: _____ Date of Birth: _____

   Current Mailing Address: _____

   City: _____ State: _____ Zip Code: _____ Home Phone #: _____

   Email Address: _____ Cell Phone #: _____

   Intervenor has the following relationship with the minor child(ren):
        ❏child(ren)'s grandmother, **or** ❏child(ren)'s grandfather

4. **Information about the Mother:**   ❏Petitioner ❏Respondent/Co-Petitioner   Check if in Military ❏

   Full Legal Name: _____

   Current Mailing Address: _____

   City: _____ State: _____ Zip Code: _____ Home Phone #: _____

   Email Address: _____ Cell Phone #: _____

5. **Information about the Father:**   ❏Petitioner ❏Respondent/Co-Petitioner   Check if in Military ❏

   Full Legal Name: _____

   Current Mailing Address: _____

   City: _____ State: _____ Zip Code: _____ Home Phone #: _____

6. **The minor child(ren) is/are:**

Full Name of Child	Present Address	Sex	Date of Birth

7. The parental rights of the parents of the minor child(ren) have been terminated.   ❏**Yes** ❏**No**
   If **Yes**, please furnish the case number: _____

8. Visitation with the grandparent(s) is in the child(ren)'s best interest for the following reasons:

   _____

   _____

   _____

   _____

   _____

   _____

   _____

   _____

9. The grandparent(s) wish(es) to have visitation with the minor child(ren) at the following times and under the following conditions:

_____

_____

_____

_____

_____

_____

_____

_____

_____

10. Transportation of the child(ren) will be as follows:

_____

_____

_____

_____

11. Have any Temporary or Permanent Protection/Restraining Orders or any Criminal Mandatory Protection/Restraining Orders (MRO) or Emergency Protection Orders been issued against the grandparent(s) or any of the parties within two years prior to the filing of this Petition?

☐**No**   ☐**Yes**   If your answer was **Yes**, complete the following:

The Protection/Restraining Order was ☐Temporary ☐Permanent ☐MRO and issued against

_____ in a ☐Municipal Court ☐County Court ☐District Court in the

County of _____, State of _____, in case number _____ on

_____ (date).

What was the subject matter of the Protection/Restraining Order or Emergency Protection Order?

_____

_____

_____

I/We respectfully request that this Court enter an Order for visitation between the intervenor(s)/grandparent(s) and the minor child(ren) as set forth in this Pleading Affidavit and any other orders necessary to effectuate the best interests of the child(ren).

VERIFICATION AND ACKNOWLEDGEMENT

I swear/affirm under oath that I have read the foregoing Pleading Affidavit and that the statements set forth therein are true and correct to the best of my knowledge.

_____   _____
Signature of Grandmother   Date   Signature of Grandfather   Date

_____   _____
Attorney Signature, if any   Attorney Signature, if any

Subscribed and affirmed, or sworn to before me   Subscribed and affirmed, or sworn to before me
by _____   by _____
in the County of _____,   in the County of _____,
State of _____, this _____   State of _____, this _____
day of _____, 20 _____.   day of _____, 20 _____.

My Commission Expires: _____   My Commission Expires: _____

_____   _____
Notary Public/Clerk   Notary Public/Clerk

CERTIFICATE OF SERVICE

I certify that on _____ (date) a true and accurate copy of this **Pleading Affidavit** was served on the other party by:

❑Hand Delivery, ❑E-filed, ❑❑Faxed to this number _____, **or**
❑by placing it in the United States mail, postage pre-paid, and addressed to the following:

To:

_____

_____

_____

_____

_____

_____

_____

_____

_____
(Your signature)

JDF 1701 R1-12 PLEADING AFFIDAVIT FOR GRANDPARENT VISITATION PURSUANT TO §19-1-117, C.R.S. Page 4 of 4

Exhibit 14C.
Order Re: Pleading Affidavit for Grandparent Visitation

☐District Court ☐Denver Juvenile Court
_____County, Colorado
Court Address:

_____

In re:
☐The Marriage of:
☐Parental Responsibilities concerning:

_____

Petitioner:

and

Co-Petitioner/Respondent:

and concerning:

Grandparent(s) Intervenor(s):

▲ **COURT USE ONLY** ▲
_____
Case Number:

Division   Courtroom

ORDER RE: PLEADING AFFIDAVIT FOR GRANDPARENT VISITATION

This matter comes before the Court on a Verified Pleading Affidavit for Grandparent Visitation filed on _____ (date) and/or hearing on _____ (date).

The Court has examined the records and evidence presented and has heard the testimony and statements of the parties and makes the following Findings and Orders:

1. Visitation ☐is ☐is not in the best interests of the child(ren).

2. Visitation is denied for the following reasons:

   _____
   _____
   _____

3. Visitation is granted and is as follows:

   _____
   _____
   _____
   _____

Date: _____

_____
☐Judge ☐Magistrate

CERTIFICATE OF MAILING

I certify that on _____ (date), I mailed, faxed, e-filed, or hand-delivered a copy of this Order to the following:
☐   Petitioner/Attorney
☐   Co-Petitioner/Respondent/Attorney
☐   Grandparent(s)/Attorney

_____
Clerk

JDF 1702 R1/11 ORDER FOR GRANDPARENT VISITATION

Exhibit 14D.
Motion to Intervene

☐District Court ☐Denver Juvenile Court
_____ County, Colorado
Court Address:

_____

In re:
☐The Marriage of:
☐Parental Responsibilities concerning:
_____

Petitioner:
and
Co-Petitioner/Respondent:

▲ COURT USE ONLY ▲

Attorney or Party Without Attorney (Name and Address):

Case Number:

Phone Number: E-mail:
FAX Number: Atty. Reg.#:

Division   Courtroom

MOTION TO INTERVENE

1. **I/We are filing this Motion to intervene in this action.**

2. **Information about Intervenor (1):**   Check if in Military ☐

    Full Legal Name: _____   Date of Birth: _____

    Current Mailing Address: _____

    City: _____ State: _____ Zip Code: _____ Home Phone #: _____

    Email Address: _____Cell Phone #: _____

    Intervenor has the following relationship with the minor child(ren):
        ☐child(ren)'s grandmother, ☐child(ren)'s grandfather ☐other: _____

3. **Information about Intervenor (2):**   Check if in Military ☐

    Full Legal Name: _____   Date of Birth: _____

    Current Mailing Address: _____

    City: _____ State: _____ Zip Code: _____ Home Phone #: _____

    Email Address: _____Cell Phone #: _____

    Intervenor has the following relationship with the minor child(ren):
        ☐child(ren)'s grandmother, ☐child(ren)'s grandfather ☐other: _____

I/We are requesting to intervene in this action for the following reasons:

_____

_____

_____

_____

_____

_____

JDF 1704   2/09   MOTION TO INTERVENE   Page 1 of 2

VERIFICATION

I/We have read the foregoing Motion and verify that the facts set forth in this document are true as far as I know or am informed.

_____   _____
Intervenor (1) Signature   Date   Intervenor (2) Signature   Date

_____   _____
Intervenor (1)'s Attorney Signature, if any   Intervenor (2)'s Attorney Signature, if any

CERTIFICATE OF SERVICE

I certify that on _____ (date) the original was filed with the Court; and a true and accurate copy of the *MOTION TO INTERVENE* was served on the other party by:
❏Hand Delivery, ❏E-filed, ❏Faxed to this number _____, **or** ❏by placing it in the United States mail, postage pre-paid, and addressed to the following:

To: _____   _____

    _____   _____

    _____   _____

    _____   _____

    _____
    (Your signature)

Exhibit 14E.
Order to Intervene

☐District Court ☐Denver Juvenile Court
_____County, Colorado
Court Address:

In re:
☐The Marriage of:
☐Parental Responsibilities concerning:

Petitioner:
and
Co-Petitioner/Respondent:

▲ **COURT USE ONLY** ▲

Case Number:

Division   Courtroom

ORDER TO INTERVENE

This matter comes before the Court on a Motion to Intervene filed on _____ (date) and/or hearing on _____ (date).

The Court, having reviewed the Motion to Intervene finds the following:

☐ The Order is **Granted** and the Intervenor(s) will be entered into the case as identified in the Motion.

☐ The Order is **Denied f**or the following reasons:

_____
_____
_____

Date: _____

_____
☐Judge ☐Magistrate

CERTIFICATE OF MAILING

I certify that on _____ (date), I mailed, faxed, e-filed, or hand-delivered a copy of this Order to the following:

☐ Petitioner/Attorney
☐ Co-Petitioner/Respondent/Attorney
☐ Grandparent(s)/Attorney

_____
Clerk

JDF 1705 2/09 ORDER TO INTERVENE

Exhibit 14F.
Delegation of Power by Parent or Guardian

DELEGATION OF POWER BY PARENT OR GUARDIAN
PURSUANT TO §15-14-105, C.R.S.

I, _____ (full name), parent or guardian of the minor child(ren) or incapacitated person(s) named below:

Full Name of Child or Incapacitated Person	Date of Birth	Relationship

I hereby authorize and appoint _____ (name of person), as Attorney in Fact for me with full authority to act in my place as follows:

1. To perform any and all acts necessary for the day-to-day care, custody, education, recreation, and property of the above-named minor child or incapacitated person, consistent with the provision of §15-14-105, C.R.S.

2. To authorize any and all medical and dental care for the health and well being of the minor child(ren) or incapacitated person(s). This care includes, but is not limited to medical and dental exams and tests, x-rays, surgeries, anesthesia, and hospital care.

This Special Power of Attorney does not give the Attorney in Fact the power to consent to the marriage or adoption of the child or incapacitated person.

This Special Power of Attorney shall be effective until _____ unless revoked earlier by the parent or guardian in writing. In any case, the authority granted herein shall not be valid for more than 12 months from the date of this document.

Date: _____   _____
                                    Parent/Guardian Signature

_____

Subscribed and affirmed, or sworn to before me in the County of _____,
State of _____, this _____ day of _____, 20 _____.

My Commission Expires: _____   _____
                                               Notary Public/Clerk

JDF 751 3/08 DELEGATION OF POWER BY PARENT OR GUARDIAN PURSUANT TO §15-14-105, C.R.S.

Chapter 15

Estate Planning: Wills, Trusts, and Your Property

Clara Brown Shaffer, Esq.
Law Office of Brown & Brown, P.C.

SYNOPSIS

Estate planning is a process designed to help people ensure their assets are distributed upon their death in accordance with their wishes. In some circumstances, when an individual has a taxable estate, complex planning is used to minimize the amount of estate tax due upon the person's death. Estate planning also allows clients to name people to act on their behalf in financial and medical situations when the client is unable to do so, and allows a client to name a guardian and/or conservator for a minor or disabled child.

Many options are available to you when planning how to pass on your estate. To plan the distribution of your assets, you must decide what to give away, when to give it, who will receive it, and when they will receive it. You also may want to consider some methods that are less expensive and others that will reduce any estate taxes.

This chapter addresses important estate planning issues, such as making a will, distribution of assets when there is no will, the probate process, bank account options, trusts, life insurance, and estate taxes.

Wills, trusts, and documents of ownership that transfer assets can be very complex. This chapter explains the basics of each of these choices, and some of the advantages and disadvantages they present. With this information, you will be able to seek further legal advice about the choices that would benefit you and your family the most. For many people, talking to a lawyer about end-of-life issues can be uncomfortable; however, most people who complete the process are rewarded with a sense of relief and certainty that their wishes will be carried out.

15-1. Overview of Lifetime and Post-Mortem Distributions of Your Assets

What if You Do Not Have a Will?

If you do not have a plan in place to give away your assets at your death, such as a will or a funded trust, your property will be disposed of through a process called intestacy or intestate succession. This, like probate, is a court proceeding wherein your estate is "administered." Colorado law dictates who will receive your property if you die without a will. For example, if you are married when you die and have no surviving issue (children or their descendants) or parents, your spouse will receive all of your estate.

If you are not married at the time of your death, any of your children (whether biological or adopted) will receive all of your property in equal shares. If you have no spouse or children, your parents will receive your property. If your parents have died, your brothers and sisters will receive your property. If you have no living family or relatives, then by default the State of Colorado will get your property.

What if You Do Have a Will?

If you have a will, a court proceeding is necessary to administer your estate. This process is called probate. Probate also happens if you die without a will. Probate is the legal process by which your property is collected and distributed according to your will. During probate, your property is managed by an administrator called a "personal representative." Generally, a personal representative manages everything without extensive court involvement. You should appoint a personal representative in your will. If you do not have a will or if your will fails to appoint a personal representative, the court will appoint one for you. Similarly, if you have a minor or disabled adult child and do not have a will or your will fails to appoint a guardian, the court will appoint a guardian for your child. If the court appoints a personal representative or a guardian, the person named may not be the person you would have chosen; therefore, it is important to review your will to ensure you have a personal representative appointed.

If, at the time of your death, you own real property or if your estate includes personal property valued at more than $60,000, and if these assets do not pass to another person through a survivorship interest, then your will must be probated (or an intestate court proceeding must take place) to pass your property on to your heirs (see the discussion on "Survivorship Interests" in this chapter). The probate process usually takes about 6 to 12 months and is much simpler and less expensive in Colorado than in many other states. However, probate may take longer than 12 months, depending on the size and complexity of the estate.

Small Estate Affidavit

If your estate does not include any real estate interests, or more than $60,000 of property that does not pass through survivorship, your assets may be transferred through a small estate affidavit without any court involvement.

Transfer of Assets Other than Through Probate

The following is a list of legal techniques used to pass property to your intended beneficiaries. This section is meant to describe the different techniques and does not necessarily advocate for one over another.

Trusts

Property held in trust will pass under the terms of the trust rather than through probate. There are many types of trusts. Trusts can be revocable or irrevocable and can be designed to be effective during your lifetime or at your death. Trusts will be discussed in greater detail in section 15-3, "Types of Estate Planning Techniques," in this chapter.

Survivorship Interests

Holding property with another person under a survivorship interest, such as joint tenancy, is sometimes used as an inexpensive alternative to a will or trust. A survivorship interest may be applied to both real and personal property. However, there may be pitfalls to this transfer method both during life and at death, including problems with creditors, taxes, and the lack of control. Generally, attempting to use joint ownership to avoid having an estate plan is faulty logic, as there is substantial risk involved with this type of planning. Also, a will is still necessary in the event both joint owners die simultaneously. (See section 15-2 of this chapter, "Ownership of Property," for more information on survivorship interests and options to joint tenancy, such as life estates.)

Payable On Death (POD) and Trustee Accounts

POD and trustee accounts are other alternatives to wills and intestate succession for bank accounts. Such an account is treated like a normal bank account during the lifetime of the account owner, sometimes called the trustee. On the account owner's death, any funds in the account will be automatically distributed to recipients, or beneficiaries, designated by the account owner. The beneficiaries have no control over the account during the owner's lifetime. Contact your bank if you wish to set up an account in this manner. Before doing so, however, remember that there are pitfalls to this transfer method, just as with survivorship interests.

Securities Registered to Transfer On Death (TOD)

This device for transferring stocks and bonds at death to named beneficiaries works like a POD bank account. It has similar advantages and disadvantages.

Beneficiary Deed

Title to an interest in real property may be transferred on the death of the owner by recording, prior to the owner's death, a beneficiary deed designating a beneficiary for the property. The transfer is effective only on the death of the owner, and the owner can revoke or cancel a beneficiary deed by recording a proper revocation prior to his or her death. The advantage of using such an instrument is that the designated transferee, or the person you wish to transfer the property to, can be changed during your lifetime, and creditors of the proposed transferee cannot attach the property during your lifetime. There can be disadvantages to beneficiary deeds in the context of Medicaid planning. It is important to talk to an attorney prior to using a beneficiary deed.

Life Insurance

Life insurance proceeds pass to whomever you have named to receive those benefits; that person is the beneficiary. The insurance company will have a record of the beneficiary you chose when you purchased your policy. You also should keep a record of the current beneficiaries of each life insurance policy for your own files.

You have the option to change the beneficiary at any time. You must tell your insurance company in writing if you wish to do this. Most insurance companies provide a form to change the beneficiary. It is also wise to name another person as an alternate, or contingent, beneficiary in case your first beneficiary dies before you do. A beneficiary may be the personal representative of your estate, though this can have unfavorable consequences if your estate has a substantial number of creditors; or the trustee of a living trust, which is sometimes referred to as a revocable or *inter vivos* trust. All beneficiary designations should be coordinated with your overall estate plan since the insurance company will pay the policy proceeds to the named beneficiary, even if your will says someone else should receive the money.

Retirement Accounts

There are numerous types of retirement accounts. There are IRAs, 401(k) and 403(b) accounts, and others. With these types of accounts, the proceeds pass upon your death in accordance with the beneficiary designation you create with the holder of the account. The beneficiary designation rules are similar to those with life insurance as discussed above.

Estate Taxes

Congress and the President finally reached a compromise on the estate tax in the waning days of 2010. They passed H.R. 4853 on a "bi-partisan" basis, which changed the estate tax for decedents dying in 2010, 2011, and 2012, and also made changes to the gift and generation-skipping tax provisions for those years. The estate tax exemption is at $5,000,000, and assets over $5,000,000 will be taxed at 35 percent. Congress and the President also included a new concept for married couples called "portability." This means any unused exemption at the first spouse's death can be used by the surviving spouse. There are some planning uncertainties with portability because it is new, and there are some pitfalls due to unintended consequences that portability can cause. Because the estate tax is reinstated, there is a stepped-up basis adjustment for a decedent's assets at the date of death. The carry-over basis system of 2010 is no longer in effect.

Because this tax structure is only effective through the end of 2012, Congress and the President have created more uncertainty for people trying to plan their estates. In 2013, the $1,000,000 exemption level returns, and assets over $1,000,000 will be taxed at 55 percent. This makes estate planning difficult, so it is especially important to discuss your estate plan with an estate planning attorney. There are planning options available during 2011 and 2012 that take advantage of the high exclusion amount by gifting assets.

We are hopeful that Congress will again address the issue of the estate tax before the end of 2012, although, due to the fact that 2012 is an election year, it may be impossible to effect meaningful, long-term reform. As always, it is important to consult with an attorney to design a plan that is best for you.

Gifts

You can make a gift to be effective during your lifetime, called an *inter vivos* gift, and one that is effective upon death, called a testamentary gift. A lifetime gift is a voluntary transfer of personal or real property. The person giving the property, called the donor, receives nothing in return. The donor must intend to make the gift. For a lifetime gift to be completed under the law, the gift must be delivered and the person receiving the gift must accept the gift. You cannot force a person to accept a gift he or she does not want.

Once a lifetime gift is given, it cannot be taken back unless the person receiving the gift agrees and actually returns it. To make a gift that is to become effective upon death, you may use a will, trust, or other special mechanism, such as a beneficiary deed or payable on death account.

A lifetime gift must be delivered to be valid. For example, suppose you want to give a special ring to your niece. If you put a note on it saying, "this ring is for my niece when I die," the gift will not be valid because it was not delivered to your niece during your lifetime.

If you want to give something that is very large, such as a piano, you may do so by symbolic delivery. Symbolic delivery occurs when you give something that represents what you actually want to give, such as a written description of the item or a model of it. To make a lifetime gift when you are unable to physically transfer the possession of the gifted item, you need to document the gift in writing.

Sometimes a person may be too sick to give the actual gift item. In this situation, a constructive delivery means the person receiving the gift is given the means of receiving the gift. For example, you may give that person the keys to a safety deposit box or to a car.

If there is a dispute, the court will decide whether the donor intended to make a gift, whether there was delivery, and whether the gift was accepted. Again, putting your intentions in writing is always a good idea.

When giving a gift of personal property, real property, or money, you may need to file a gift tax return. Currently, you can give $13,000 to any one person per year without paying a gift tax. If you give more than $13,000 to one person in a year, you may have to report the gift on a gift tax return. Whether you are required to file a gift tax return depends upon your other assets, prior gifts, etc. Most likely you will not have to pay tax on the gift; however, you should consult your attorney or your accountant if you make a large gift to an individual or group of individuals in any single year.

15-2. Ownership of Property

In Colorado, you may hold title to real property in several different ways. Real property refers to land, as well as to whatever is erected or growing upon or affixed to that land. Ownership of what lies underground, such as mineral rights, water, oil, mining rights, etc., may or may not be a part of the real property interest you own. You can actually separate the rights to the property above ground from the rights of the property interest below ground. You can even restrict the use of the above-ground property rights through easements.

The way property is titled is important because it affects what happens to the property during your lifetime and upon your death. The principal types of ownership are:

1) Sole ownership;

2) Tenancy in common;

3) Joint tenancy (with right of survivorship); and

4) Life estate.

You should know what type of ownership you have for all of your property. This will tell you what your rights are concerning property that you fully or partially own.

Sole Ownership

If you own property solely in your name, you own all of the rights to that property. You can use it, rent it, sell it, or give it away. If you want to transfer property that is solely in your name to a person or entity on your death, then you may do so by a will, trust, or beneficiary deed. If you do not designate whom you want to receive your property (through a will, trust, or beneficiary deed), the property will pass to your legal heirs at your death by the laws of intestacy.

Tenancy in Common

If you own property with another person, then by law you own that property as a tenant in common unless the ownership document states otherwise. A tenant in common is a person who owns a percentage of the entire property. For example, if two parties purchase property, and each has contributed equally to the purchase, then the parties can agree that each owns one-half, or 50 percent, of the property. You may sell or gift this one-half interest to others. You also may transfer this interest upon your death to others through a will or trust.

If you are a tenant in common, you may appoint a specific person or persons in your will to receive your interest or it will become part of the residuary or balance of the estate. If your interest does not pass under the terms of your will, then your interest will pass to your heirs by the laws of intestacy. The other tenants in common do not become the owners of your interest on your death. Upon your death, the person(s) appointed receives your interest in the property from your estate. That person(s) will then hold your interest in the property with the other tenants in common.

Tenants in common who cannot agree on how to sell or manage the property usually have to go to court to settle their differences.

Joint Tenancy (with Right of Survivorship) for Real and Personal Property

In Colorado, persons may hold real and personal property with a right of survivorship. Usually joint tenancy is used to hold real property, but sometimes people use it for personal property such as in bank and investment accounts. Creating a right of survivorship is a way of managing property. A right of survivorship assures that when the owner dies, the remaining co-owner(s) will automatically receive the deceased owner's share of the property. For example, a husband and wife often hold property together in joint tenancy with this right of survivorship. Upon the death of either the husband or wife, the survivor will be the exclusive owner of the property.

You also may hold title with someone other than your spouse. You and the other owner will hold property with the right of survivorship. Friends, relatives, and business partners use this form of ownership when they want to own property jointly, but ensure the survivor will receive the interest in the property to the exclusion of the deceased owner's relatives or heirs. This allows the property to pass to the survivor(s) on death.

The party who dies first cannot transfer by will the property that is held subject to a right of survivorship. Holding title in joint tenancy will supersede the provisions in the will, which may try to dispose of the property interest. If you own property in this manner and you want to pass that property to a particular person (other than the person with whom you hold the property in joint tenancy) or entity, you will need to sever the joint tenancy.

Creating a right of survivorship requires special language when used in a deed, trust, or will. Creating a right of survivorship in a deed has many possible legal consequences. Some of the legal consequences are the following:

▶ If you sign a deed transferring real property to yourself and someone other than your spouse, and you and this other person have the right of survivorship, then you may have made a gift. This may require you to file a federal gift tax return.

▶ Once you sign the deed, you cannot take the property back. You will have trouble selling or mortgaging the property without the agreement and signature of the other person you have named on the deed.

▶ The property held with a right of survivorship passes to the survivor. Even if you name someone else to receive property in your will or trust, the titling of the property will control who receives it.

There are also some risks in creating a right of survivorship:

▶ If you name someone as a joint tenant with the right of survivorship on a bank account, then that person can take part or all of the money out of the account without your permission.

▶ A right of survivorship may cause the property to go to someone other than your intended heirs.

▶ Sometimes a creditor of the other person you named on your property with a right of survivorship can take all or part of that property to pay debts.

▶ There may be adverse gift and/or estate tax consequences to titling property in joint tenancy.

It is also important to point out that titling property in joint tenancy as an alternative to an estate plan is generally not a good idea. An estate plan encompasses more than simply passing property; however, joint tenancy can be used as a technique within the estate plan.

Life Estate for Real Property

If you own a life estate interest in real property, then you are one of the owners of the property, together with the person or persons who own the interest after you die. This other person is referred to as the remainderman. Owning a life estate interest means you can live in or possess the property until you die, although you have the responsibility to take care of the property, pay the taxes, etc. When you die, the property passes to the remainderman. You may create a life estate by transferring the property to a third party and retaining the right to live on the property for your lifetime and receive any income generated by that property during your lifetime.

For example, if you want to give your property to a friend or to your child, but you want to live on that property or receive income from that property until your death, then you would create a life estate. You would do so by deeding the property to your friend or your child, the remainderman, to have it upon your death, and reserving a life estate to yourself in the deed.

You also may create a life estate by a will or trust. For example, suppose you want your friend, Harry, to own the property. When Harry dies, you want the property to pass to your brother, Bill. You can let Harry keep the property until his death by creating a life estate for Harry in your will or trust. On Harry's death, you can have the property go to Bill, the remainderman.

There are other ways that a person can hold title other than those described. If you have any questions about the nature and extent of property ownership, you should talk to a lawyer.

15-3. Types of Estate Planning Techniques

Wills

A will is a statement that describes how your assets will be given away after you die. A will lets you give anything you own, including real estate, cars, business holdings, money, and personal property, to anyone you want after your estate debts are paid. A will also may state whom you want as the guardian of a minor or disabled adult child. In a will, you can appoint a personal representative (executor or administrator) to complete your affairs after your death. Wills provide substantial flexibility for leaving your assets to whomever you choose.

Colorado recognizes holographic wills. A holographic will is a will written in the decedent's own handwriting and signed by the decedent. While holographic wills are recognized in Colorado, they are not preferred because of authenticity issues.

If you wish to make a will, other than a holographic will, you must meet these minimum legal requirements:

▶ You must be at least 18 years old.

▶ You must be of sound mind. This means you must understand what property you have to give and to whom you are giving this property after your death.

▶ You must be making a will because you want to make a will and not because someone is forcing you to do it.

▶ The will must be in writing (typed) and dated.

▶ You must sign the will. If another person is signing for you because you cannot, he or she must sign the will at your request and in your presence.

▶ Two disinterested witnesses must sign the will in your presence, and certify that you signed the will voluntarily and were of sound mind, or your signature must be acknowledged by a notary public.

You may prepare your own will; however, it is not recommended. There are certain restrictions to giving away your property. For example, your will cannot give away property you own in joint tenancy with right of survivorship if the other joint owner survives you. (See section 15-2 of this chapter, "Ownership of Property," for more information on the transfer of real property.) In addition, your will cannot give away property that has a named beneficiary, such as the proceeds of life insurance policies. To change the beneficiary designation on property with a named beneficiary, you must fill out a change of beneficiary form with the company holding the property. Simply giving the property away through your will is not sufficient.

Also, while Colorado law generally gives you broad freedom to give away your estate as you desire, it is important to keep in mind that a surviving spouse has a right to a percentage of the deceased spouse's estate, if the surviving spouse is disinherited by his or her husband or wife. This right is referred to as an elective share. Depending on the number of years a husband and wife were married, the surviving spouse is entitled to a specific percentage of the deceased spouse's estate. If this is something you may be concerned about, it is best to see an attorney to discuss your options. Because some of the restrictions on giving away property can be confusing, it is a good idea to review your will periodically to make sure it reflects your wishes, especially after any financial or other changes in your life.

Trusts

A trust is an arrangement where real or personal property is held by one person, called the trustee, for the care or benefit of another person, the beneficiary. There are basically two types of trusts: those created at your death, referred to as testamentary trusts, and those you create during your lifetime, usually referred to as living trusts, revocable trusts, or *inter vivos* trusts. A testamentary trust is set up in your will, and takes effect only after your death and after your estate has been administered. Testamentary trusts, like living trusts, can be established to save estate taxes and to manage assets for minor or disabled adult children. Because testamentary trusts become effective after death, they are useful in situations where asset management is not needed during life.

A living, or *inter vivos*, trust may be revocable or irrevocable, and it may be funded or unfunded. A funded living trust is an alternative to a will and to probate. In a funded living trust, a person, the settlor, puts property and money into his or her trust during his or her lifetime for his or her benefit and possibly for the benefit of other family members. An unfunded living trust typically receives assets through a simple "pour-over will" following the settlor's death.

Most people who are able to manage their own financial affairs usually name themselves as trustee of living trusts they establish. The trustee's duties are to invest the trust assets and make the assets and income available to the settlor/beneficiary during his or her life. Such a trust is almost always revocable, meaning that the settlor can revoke or amend the trust as long as he or she is able.

In situations where the settlor is also the trustee and he or she becomes disabled, alternate trustees are usually named in the trust to assume trustee responsibilities, the most important of which is providing for the financial needs of the disabled settlor/beneficiary. A settlor will usually name a spouse, adult child, relative, friend, or bank as alternate trustees. When the settlor/beneficiary dies, the trust often terminates, and the successor trustee will distribute the trust property to the beneficiaries, similar to the distributions in a will. In many situations, however, living trusts will continue for the benefit of the settlor's spouse and children and terminate at a later date.

Benefits of Using a Trust

A living trust has several advantages if it is set up properly and fully funded, meaning all the settlor's assets are placed in trust. These are listed below.

First, a fully funded trust can reduce or eliminate the need for probate upon the death of the settlor. While this is a significant reason in many states, Colorado's probate process is relatively simple and inexpensive.

Second, a Colorado resident who owns real property in another state can put that real estate into a living trust and thereby reduce or eliminate the need for probate in the other state. This is an especially important reason when the probate system in the other state is expensive and cumbersome.

Third, a living trust may avoid the need for a conservatorship for the settlor if he or she becomes legally disabled and the settlor has funded his or her trust. However, a living trust cannot avoid a guardianship proceeding, because the trustee of a living trust cannot make medical or care decisions for the settlor unless the trustee is the named agent for the settlor under a separate medical power of attorney. (See Chapter 24, "Medical Advance Directives," and Chapter 26, "Guardianship of Adults," for more information on guardianships and health care powers of attorney.)

Fourth, the terms of a living trust are generally private, unlike a will where the document is delivered to the court as part of the probate proceeding. For instance, many individuals may not want the "world" to know the terms of their distributions to their heirs, as would be the case with the use of a will deposited with a court.

Fifth, trusts are a good tool for tax planning. Some trusts are designed specifically to minimize federal estate tax. The terms of the trust dictate the distribution of the trust assets to utilize the currently effective estate tax exemption, or use the marital deduction to avoid any tax at the first spouse's death. There are also trusts that are designed to be funded with specific assets, like a residence or life insurance, that can create favorable tax consequences for the settlor and the beneficiaries.

Finally, trusts can be used to accomplish asset protection for individuals and their beneficiaries. Third-party asset protection trusts can be created for beneficiaries. This type of trust protects an inheritance from a beneficiary's creditors, a beneficiary's divorce, or a spendthrift beneficiary. First-party asset protection trusts can provide some creditor protection for individuals, but these trusts must be set up with a great deal of care, as there can be unfavorable consequences if they are set up incorrectly.

If the trust is not drafted correctly, significant harmful tax liabilities may occur. Generally, you should not try to create your own trust or purchase a preprinted living trust. Preparing and managing the living trust can be more expensive in Colorado than a will and probate. Initially, living trusts and wills with testamentary trusts are usually more expensive to prepare and manage than wills without trusts; however, the expense up front may save your estate future expenses.

Pet trusts have become increasingly popular as part of an estate plan. Often, people are concerned about the well-being and care of their pets after they die. One of the most famous pet trusts of recent history was Leona Helmsley's trust for her dog, Trouble. In her will, she established a $12 million trust to benefit Trouble.

A pet trust can be established in either a will or a trust, and can benefit one pet or many pets. The idea behind a pet trust is to appoint a person or organization to care for your pet and establish a trust fund to finance the care of your pet. The trust will continue after your death until the pets pass away and the remaining funds, if any, will be distributed to a contingent beneficiary named in the trust. If you would like to establish a trust for a pet, you will need to work with an attorney to coordinate the pet trust with your estate plan.

Changing Your Will or Living Trust

A will or living trust that meets all of the requirements described earlier is valid until you revoke it. You may revoke either a will or a living trust at any time. A will or living trust that is valid in another state is also valid in Colorado, so simply moving to another state does not revoke a will or trust.

If you change your mind about a particular distribution of your property, or if circumstances force you to otherwise change your will or living trust, you can create a codicil to your will (a document amending your will) or a trust amendment to change your living trust. The codicil or trust amendment must be signed and witnessed with the same formalities as your original will or living trust. While a codicil or trust amendment provides you with a convenient method for making minor changes to your will or living trust, significant modifications may require redrafting the original document. You should never write on your will or living trust after it is executed. Such writing may not be legally effective and may invalidate the entire document. Always consult an attorney about how to change your will or living trust.

Power of Attorney

A power of attorney gives another person the legal authority to manage some or all of your financial affairs. A power of attorney is created when a person, called the principal, gives someone else, called the attorney in fact or agent, written permission to act on the principal's behalf. The attorney in fact does not have to be a lawyer and may be a spouse, relative, or friend.

A power of attorney can give the attorney in fact authority to manage most of the business that may otherwise require the principal's presence or signature. For example, if you are physically unable to go to the bank, you could give someone the power to deposit and withdraw money from your account. The principal also could create a limited power of attorney. This grants permission to the agent to perform only certain acts. In other situations, the principal could create a general power of attorney. This grants permission to the agent to handle all financial affairs.

A power of attorney does not take away the principal's rights to make his or her own decisions about financial matters. The principal can end the power of attorney at any time by simply telling the agent in writing. The principal should send copies of the termination notice to anyone with whom the agent may need to conduct business, such as the bank. A power of attorney ends automatically when the principal dies.

The principal must be mentally competent to grant a power of attorney. The power of attorney must be in writing and signed. It also should be notarized, but it does not need to be witnessed. If a power of attorney is used to transfer real property, it must be recorded in the Clerk and Recorder's Office in the county where the property is located.

In Colorado, the principal may state in the document that the power of attorney is durable. This means that it continues to be valid even if the principal becomes incapacitated. If no such statement is contained in the document, then the power of attorney stops being valid when the principal becomes incapacitated. If the principal has stated in the document when the power is to end, then the power will be effective only until the ending date. However, the principal may revoke the power of attorney at any time as long as he or she is not incapacitated. You should only give a power of attorney to someone you trust completely. (See Chapter 24, "Medical Advance Directives," for more information on the medical durable power of attorney.)

Transferring Ownership Interests of Real Property During Your Lifetime

Deeds

If you want to transfer your interest in real property, you must do so in writing. The document used to transfer your interest is called a deed. There are four types of deeds in Colorado:

1) General warranty deeds;

2) Special warranty deeds;

3) Bargain and sale deeds; and

4) Quit claim deeds.

A general warranty deed tells the person to whom the property is being sold or transferred that you are warranting the title and making other warranties about the property. A warranty means a representation as to the title of the property. This means you will guarantee the title except for any conditions specifically listed in the deed.

A special warranty deed is similar to a general warranty deed, but does not give all the warranties that a general warranty deed gives.

A bargain and sale deed transfers whatever title or interest you may have at the time of the transfer or later acquire. However, it does not give any warranty that your title is good.

A quit claim deed, on the other hand, only transfers whatever title you may have at the time of the transfer.

You must give the deed to the person receiving the property. A deed will not be effective if you fill it out, sign it, and keep it in the desk drawer or other place for safe keeping. If you want to give your real property to someone, you must complete the deed properly. You must sign the deed in front of a notary public. You must give the deed to the person you want to receive the property or you may record the deed in the Clerk and Recorder's Office in the county where the property is located. Once you give your property to someone else, it becomes theirs, and you cannot take it back.

There are a few practical matters you should know about completing a deed:

▶ The property legally must be described by lot and block numbers, if it is located in a subdivision.

▶ It must be described by metes and bounds or a sectional description if not in a subdivision. A tax lot number or street address is not enough.

▶ The deed must state what was given or paid, called consideration, for the property. If the property is a gift, the deed can say that the consideration is love and affection.

▶ Never sign a deed someone else has prepared for you, unless you know and understand the results.

▶ Once a deed has been received or delivered, it must be recorded with the county clerk and recorder where the property is located.

All deeds, mortgages, contracts, and other writings concerning ownership interests in real property should be recorded. This protects you and the person receiving the property. If you do not record a deed when you are purchasing property, the seller could sell the property again to someone else and you would lose the property. An unrecorded deed also could create problems with transferring the property in the future, because upon selling the property one requirement is that you are the rightful owner. If you have not recorded the deed, then you are not the owner of record.

Funeral Issues

Your specific wishes for your own funeral arrangements are best done in writing. To avoid any problems, you should communicate your wishes to your family or loved ones in advance. If you leave the original of this writing in your safety deposit box, then you also should have a copy outside of the box and known to your family or loved ones. This is because the safety deposit box is very often not opened until after the funeral has been held.

Colorado law provides that you may execute a Declaration Instrument (Declaration) that gives your specific instructions for disposition of your last remains and your funeral arrangements. The Declaration needs to be in writing, dated, and signed by you. It can be inserted in your last will and testament, or it can simply be any separate writing making your Declaration as to your wishes. The Declaration also can be made within a prepaid funeral, burial, or cremation contract with the mortuary or crematorium. In the Declaration, you may specifically direct the arrangements for disposition of your remains and any ceremonial arrangements to be performed after your death. Or, you can direct that the person you name in the Declaration has the authority to make all those arrangements.

If you wish to provide for cremation, be sure your wishes are communicated to all of your family, and that your wishes are properly documented in your will or declaration. If not, and if any family member objects, the funeral home usually will not allow cremation.

As a pre-planning option, you may wish to make arrangements directly with a funeral home. However, it is very important to let a loved one know you have purchased a funeral and burial plan from a specific funeral home. This allows the loved one to carry out your wishes.

Generally, you may purchase a revocable (can be changed) or irrevocable (cannot be changed) funeral and burial plan. An advantage to an irrevocable funeral and burial plan is that it is an exempt asset if you are attempting to qualify for Medicaid.

If you decide to exercise a pre-planning option, be sure to read all of the documents carefully to confirm you are getting exactly what you paid for. It is very important to check for competitive rates. It also is very important to be sure there will not be any additional charges to your estate. The main reason for obtaining a prepaid funeral and burial plan is to pay all of the costs in advance.

If you are receiving state public assistance, such as financial aid payments, or medical assistance, such as Medicaid, you may be eligible to receive a limited contribution of state funds to assist with the expenses of the funeral, burial, or cremation.

To apply for assistance with funeral, burial, or cremation expenses, and to determine whether you are eligible for such assistance after your death, your family should contact the county Department of Social Services that was handling your case during your lifetime.

15-4. Additional Information

General Advice

You should keep an up-to-date, itemized list of all your property and debts. This includes insurance policies, securities, bank accounts, real estate, jewelry and artwork, business interests, pension plans, IRAs, and other retirement benefits. You should keep this list with your other important documents, like your will, trust documents, and powers of attorney. You should record where you maintain a safe deposit box and where you keep your important documents. You also should list your current financial advisors, your attorney, and your accountant on a piece of paper and keep it with your list of property. Give a copy of this list to your personal representative, successor, trustee, relative, or friend you trust, and to your attorney or financial advisors. Giving people who will be involved with your estate administration a list of where your documents are kept will help them gather the appropriate information to uphold your wishes.

A letter regarding your funeral wishes and any prepaid arrangements should be given to whoever you think will be involved with your funeral, as this will ensure that your family will know your wishes.

Guardianship and Conservatorship Proceedings

Under certain circumstances, a guardian or conservator may need to be appointed for an individual (see Chapter 25, "Conservatorship of Adults," and Chapter 26, "Guardianship of Adults," for additional information).

15-5. Resources

Colorado Bar Association Brochures
(303) 860-1115
www.cobar.org; Go to "For the Public," then "Public Legal Education," then "Educational Materials/Brochures."

Brochure Titles:

▶ What to Do When Someone Dies

▶ So Now You Are a Personal Representative

▶ So Now You Are a Conservator

▶ So Now You Are a Guardian

▶ So Now You Are a Trustee

▶ Probate in Colorado

▶ Living Trusts

▶ Estate Planning

Metro Volunteer Lawyers

An organization of the Denver Metro-area bar associations where lawyers volunteer to take certain categories of civil cases for indigent people. Intake for the cases is done by Colorado Legal Services.

> Mailing address:
> 1905 Sherman St., Ste. 400
> Denver, CO 80203
> (303) 837-1313
> www.metrovolunteerlawyers.org

Colorado Legal Services

For Denver, Adams, Jefferson, Douglas, and Arapahoe counties, call (303) 837-1313. This will be answered by voice mail; please stay on the line for information. (See Chapter 5 under "Resources," section 5-6, for other Legal Aid Offices.)

> 1905 Sherman St., Ste. 400
> Denver, CO 80203
> (303) 837-1321
> www.coloradolegalservices.org

Metropolitan Lawyer Referral Service

> (303) 831-8000 (Metro Denver/Boulder)
> (970) 226-2455 (Ft. Collins)
> (877) 283-8145 (Toll-free)
> www.mlrsonline.org

Colorado Department of Revenue

> 1375 Sherman St.
> Denver, CO 80261
> (303) 238-7378
> (800) 659-2656 (TTY)
> www.colorado.gov/revenue

Chapter 16

Estate and Succession Planning for Farmers and Ranchers

Marianne Blackwell, Esq.*
William M. Sheets*
Office of Gift Planning
University Advancement
Colorado State University

SYNOPSIS

16-1. Economic Background of Farm and Ranch Estate and Tax Planning

Prior to the 1950s, farmers and ranchers in the United States were primarily concerned with upgrading farming practices to do a better job of food and fiber production, often to provide food just for their own families. In the fairly agrarian society of the 1950s, the total U.S. population was about 150 million and farmers made up 12.2 percent of the labor force. One farmer supplied approximately 15.5 persons in the U.S. their agricultural food source, and there were about 5.4 million farms in the country.[1] From the 1950s forward, many new technologies, including those developed within the framework of the

---

[1] *A History of American Agriculture, 1607-2000* (ERS-POST-12.) (Sept. 2000). Washington, D.C.: U.S. Department of Agriculture, Economic Research Service.

land-grant universities,[2] became available to the American farmer and rancher and, as a result, farm and ranch size began to grow. During these post-1950s decades of tremendous technological and productivity growth, farmers and ranchers invested greater capital into their agribusinesses. Farm acreage was consolidated into larger production units.[3]

In the 1970s, farmland values began to increase, accelerating throughout the decade, reaching record land prices in the early 1980s.[4] In many cases, farmland and ranch land values more than doubled. Inflation became a major force for landowners to deal with, as speculators moved into the land markets trying to seek shelter or a "hedge" against the erosion of buying power due to an oversupply of dollars. Subsequent increases in land and other farm property values made many farmers and ranchers millionaires. (Most of their wealth was merely on paper, as they were in many cases land rich and cash poor.) As our population became more concentrated in urban and suburban living centers, agrarian statistics changed significantly. In the 1990s, farmers accounted for 2.6 percent of the U.S. labor force, with only 2.1 million farms in existence. Farmers had become more productive, however: one farmer supplied approximately 100 persons their food source.[5]

Although most farmers and ranchers enjoyed the benefits of inflation in their property values and their technologically enriched farm and ranch industries, this increase in success and wealth brought new concerns such as property ownership options, business entity selection, estate and retirement preparation, and succession planning. This chapter attempts to address some of the issues surrounding farm and ranch ownership and the special concerns relating to estate planning for the farmer and rancher. Any comprehensive estate, retirement, or succession plan will be influenced by the decisions made in these matters, and one should be attentive to the consequences of these choices.

---

[2] Land-grant universities (also called land-grant colleges or land-grant institutions) are institutions of higher education in the U.S. that have been designated by each state to receive the benefits of the Morrill Acts of 1862 and 1890. The Morrill Acts funded educational institutions by granting federally controlled land to the states. The mission of these institutions, as set forth in the 1862 Act, is to teach agriculture, military tactics, the mechanic arts, and home economics, not to the exclusion of classical studies, so that members of the working classes might obtain a practical college education. Land-grant universities maintain state cooperative extension offices throughout the country; thus, they are a tremendous resource for the agricultural community.

[3] In 1950, the average acres per farm was 216; in 1992, the average acres per farm was 461. In 1950, the number of U.S. irrigated acres was 25,634,869. In 1992, there were 49,404,000 irrigated acres.

[4] Farm income, grain prices, interest rates, return on other investments, and 1031 exchanges are often mentioned as reasons for the increase.

[5] *Supra*, n. 1. For comparison, in 2006, Colorado had 30,700 farms and ranches, with an average farm size of 1,000 acres. *High Plains Journal*, Dec. 10, 2007, Article 2007-50.

16-2. Property Ownership and Transfer

Property may be owned by one person or by two or more persons concurrently. The two most important types of co-ownership are joint tenancy and tenancy-in-common. The method selected may affect both the size of one's estate and the estate and inheritance tax consequences. Everyone should always consider the federal estate tax exemption limits (and future changes to these exemptions) and the values of their estates when deciding how to hold property, but farmers and ranchers should be even more vigilant of these matters, due in great part to constantly shifting property values.

Joint Tenancy

In a joint tenancy, all co-owners are equally entitled to the use, enjoyment, control, and possession of the land, or its equivalent in rents and profits. The best-known characteristic of joint tenancy is the right of survivorship. Upon the death of one joint tenant, the decedent's rights pass immediately to the surviving tenant(s). Death of a joint tenant does not affect title, as the title is vested equally in all joint tenants rather than individually. Many persons, and particularly married couples, hold or own much of their property as joint tenants with the right of survivorship. According to common law, joint tenancy must feature "four unities": time, title, interest, and possession. Joint tenants must acquire title at the same time, be named in the same deed, hold exactly equal interests, and be entitled to equal rights of possession.[6]

When a joint tenant dies, the decedent's interest passes immediately and automatically to the surviving joint tenant(s). Jointly owned property does not go through probate when a joint tenant dies.[7] The property does not pass according to the property owner's will, nor does it descend to one's heirs according to state law. The decedent's interest merely disappears, and the entire ownership remains in the hands of the surviving joint tenant(s). Joint tenancy ensures the surviving spouse of a fair share of the marital property, and the property passes free of the claims of unsecured creditors. Disadvantages of joint tenancy may arise if marital difficulties occur, or if one of the parties has obligations or responsibilities (such as children) resulting from a previous marriage.

With regard to estate planning, the passing of jointly held property to a surviving spouse may not allow the decedent's federal tax exemption to be fully utilized. Since the property is simply passed on, it is not included in the value of the decedent's estate and therefore cannot have the exemption made against it. For this reason, many estate planning practitioners recommend against holding property in joint tenancy with rights of survivorship, especially for estates that exceed or may potentially exceed the estate tax exemption.

---

[6] C.R.S. § 38-11-101.

[7] An exception occurs when both or all of the joint tenants are involved in simultaneous deaths. The property now goes through probate because there is no surviving joint tenant.

Tenancy-in-Common

Tenancy-in-common is an estate in land held by two or more persons with only the unity of possession. Unlike joint tenancy, tenants-in-common may hold varying size interests, may take title at different times, and may receive their interests through different deeds. But each is entitled to the undivided possession of the property, according to their proportionate share and subject to the rights of possession of the other tenants. Upon the death of a tenant-in-common, there is no right of survivorship. The decedent's interest passes according to his or her will or the state law of descent and distribution.

Any farmer and rancher must look at his or her overall estate plan to determine if the property he or she owns is held appropriately to permit all allowable tax advantages. Professional advisors will assist in this determination and should be utilized for estate planning purposes as well as property acquisition opportunities.

16-3. Choice of Business Entity

Business, including ranches and farms, can be structured in a variety of ways. While sole proprietorship may work for the size of your farm or ranch, it may be advantageous to select a more complex form of business entity. Reduction of taxes, limiting liability, raising capital, expanding operations, bringing a family member or other person into your operations — these are just some of the objectives a business owner must consider when determining how his or her business is best owned. The possible forms of doing business are numerous.[8] The four most basic forms are sole proprietorship, general partnership, corporation (C and S varieties), and limited liability company. Consultation with a professional advisor is crucial to provide help with entity selection.

Sole Proprietorship

Simply put, a sole proprietor is defined as going into business for oneself. The business is not distinct from one's personal tax and liability concerns. No state registration is needed, and the business owner has total control over his or her business operations. When the sole proprietor dies, the business is terminated, without need for formal documentation or procedure. The sole proprietor reports all business income and losses on his or her individual tax return.[9] The largest drawbacks are that the person has no shield from liability and non-business assets can be sought after to settle debts.

---

[8] For example, limited partnerships, registered limited liability partnerships, joint ventures, business trusts, and others.

[9] There is a separate Schedule F for farms and ranches, but this is part of the individual's Form 1040.

Partnership

Like a sole proprietorship, a partnership requires no formal creation documentation.[10] A partnership begins when two or more people start doing business together. Partners are responsible for each other's actions, business debt, and obligations, including court judgments, jointly and severally. A partnership does not pay taxes on profits. The Internal Revenue Service (IRS) considers partnerships to be "pass-through" or "flow-through" entities: the income or losses from the business flow through to the individual partners who then report these items on their individual tax returns. The partnership is required to file an annual Form 1065, which provides information on the entity to the IRS, and each partner attaches Schedule K-1 to his or her Form 1040, setting out each partner's share of profits and losses.

Corporations

A corporation is a legal entity, separate from its owners and managers. It is created by state statute with the filing of articles of incorporation with the Colorado Secretary of State and is governed by the laws of Colorado.[11] A corporation may either be a "C" corporation or an "S" corporation. All corporations are C corporations unless they elect to be treated as an S variety. The election is solely a tax matter; under state law, the election of C or S makes no difference.

The biggest advantage of conducting business as a corporation is the aspect of limited liability or corporate shield. This protects the business owners and shareholders from personal liability for corporate debts and obligations so that only the corporate assets are used to pay corporate debts. To maintain this shield, the corporation must conduct itself separately from the personal affairs of its owners. There should be corporate formalities, such as adequately funding the corporation, maintaining separate books and records and bank accounts, no commingling of personal and corporate assets (unless they can be designated as investments to fund the corporation), holding regular meetings of the shareholders and directors, formally issuing stock, and others.

A corporation is the only type of business that must pay its own income taxes on profits. However, any justifiable business cost can be deducted as an expense. Net corporate income is taxed to the corporation even if it is retained as earnings or paid out as dividends to its shareholders. Corporations have favorable tax treatment in the form of lower rates, but shareholder dividends face double taxation, taxed once at the corporate tax rate and again as ordinary income to the shareholder (but corporate losses do not flow through to be taken by the shareholders).

---

[10] A partnership agreement, however, is a recommended plan. In the absence of an agreement, there are state statutes that govern partnership relationships. Uniform Partnership Law, C.R.S. §§ 7-60-101, *et seq.*

[11] Colorado Corporations and Associations Act, C.R.S. §§ 7-90-101, *et seq.*

S corporations are a hybrid form of entity, combining the legal characteristics of a C corporation and the tax treatments of a partnership. In this type of corporation, with few exceptions, the business profits, losses, credits, and deductions pass through the corporation to the owners, who report them on their own Form 1040 returns. There are no taxes owed at the entity level, and profits and losses are proportionately allocated based on the ownership interest of the shareholders.

Limited Liability Company (LLC)

S corporations and limited partnerships have been increasingly replaced as the entity of choice by the LLC.[12] In an LLC, members can retain their limited personal liability while still performing the business affairs of the company. LLCs do not require the formal management of a corporation, but members still should be aware to shield the LLC from liability by keeping separate books, records, and bank accounts; keeping the LLC adequately funded; and best practices would dictate drafting an operating agreement (similar to corporate by-laws). LLCs are taxed like partnerships, meaning flow-through of profits and losses to the members. Single-owner LLCs are treated as sole proprietorships by the IRS and do not file a separate return. The owner reports all income and losses on Schedule C of his or her Form 1040. Like a partnership, a multiple-member LLC is required to file an informational tax return, Form 1065, and provide each member with a Schedule K-1 to report his or her share of profits and losses.

Overall, the LLC provides simplicity and flexibility and the pass-through feature could help save taxes (a corporation and its shareholders are subject to double taxation on the gain from a sale of land, if ever any farm/ranch property must be sold). If your plan is to include multiple shareholders and/or investors in your business operations, or if you have employees to whom you offer benefits, a corporation might work best: a corporation can deduct the cost of health insurance premiums, reimbursement of medical expenses, etc., but in an LLC, only a portion of these types of expenses can be deducted.

As stated, every farmer and rancher will have different objectives to meet when selecting the entity by which they want to conduct business. If employees are working in a farm or ranch operation, it would make good sense to protect one's personal assets in the event of accident or death by structuring the business as a corporation or limited liability company. A simple and small farm or ranch operation may work well as a sole proprietorship or partnership. Consultation with a professional advisor will assist one in determining the appropriate vehicle to use.

---

[12] See the Colorado Limited Liability Company Act at C.R.S. §§ 7-80-101, *et seq.*

16-4. Estate Planning

The fundamentals of estate planning are really no different for farmers and ranchers than they are for individuals in the non-farm world. However, retirement and succession planning perhaps have special significance in that farm and ranch households are often affected by savings and retirement policies in ways that are different from the rest of the U.S. households. For example, farm operators are typically older than the majority of the U.S. workforce.[13] Healthcare, medical improvements, and technological advances in farming equipment and techniques have all contributed to this phenomenon, not to mention that farming is becoming popular as a part-time, retirement activity.

In addition to the issue of age, farmers and ranchers often have several income sources and different forms of wealth and savings habits as compared to the general population. Increased personal savings, land and equipment holdings, contributions through self-employment taxes, off-farm income,[14] less reliance on Social Security — all of these factors contribute to a different setting for farmers and ranchers and their retirement and estate planning.

Getting Started

There are required basics for anyone contemplating estate planning. Planning strategies for farmers and ranchers can also include:

▶ Create and maintain an up-to-date, itemized list of all property and debts, including, but not limited to, insurance policies, securities, bank accounts, real estate (farm and other), farm and recreational equipment, jewelry and artwork, business interests, pension plans, IRAs, and other retirement benefits.

▶ Consult with appropriate advisors (an estate planning attorney, CPA, or financial advisor) to begin creating a will or trust (or maintaining existing documents) and planning for and managing your asset base and tax (income, gift, and estate) considerations. Maintain a written list of your current financial advisors, attorney, and accountant, and keep it with your list of property. Give a copy of this list to your personal representative, successor, trustee, relative, or friend you trust, and to your attorney or financial advisors.

▶ Consider drafting and safeguarding certain powers of attorney, including a health care power of attorney and directive to physicians.

---

[13] Over one-fourth of all farmers and about half of all agricultural landlords are age 65 or older, compared with only about 3 percent of the overall U.S. labor force. *Amber Waves* (April 2005), a publication of the U.S. Department of Agriculture, Economic Research Service. In 2002, the average age of a Colorado farmer was nearly 54 years. *High Plains Journal*, Dec. 10, 2007, Article 2007-50.

[14] Off-farm income — outside business interests, wages, salaries, interest and dividends, pensions, annuities, military retirement, unemployment, Social Security, veterans' benefits, other public retirement and public assistance programs, and rental income from nonfarm properties — can account for up to 90 percent of total farm household income. *Amber Waves* (April 2005), a publication of the U.S. Department of Agriculture, Economic Research Service.

▶ Create a viable estate management plan, considering the exemption limits for passing along assets free of transfer taxes. As of February 2012, the date this chapter was updated, the taxable estate exemption threshold is $5 million (up from $3.5 million in 2009) for an individual or $10 million for a couple for both estate and gift tax levies, with a top tax rate at 35 percent for estates above these levels. These extensions are only for two years and will expire at the end of 2012. With this in mind, consider the following.

- Coordinate the marital deduction and the estate tax credit. Simply leaving everything to your spouse is not always the best estate planning, especially if your estates exceed the limits of this tax credit. Remember that each spouse is entitled to the estate tax exemption, and all efforts should be made so that both spouses are allowed to take their credit, if needed. When property passes directly to a surviving spouse (such as when property is held in joint ownership with rights of survivorship), then the decedent's estate will not get benefit of the exemption and it is therefore wasted. The unlimited marital deduction (property passes to surviving spouse without any estate tax) should be used in coordination with the estate tax credit to ensure that as much property passes to heirs and the surviving spouse without imposition of any estate taxes.[15]

▶ Keep in mind the special-use valuation tax election available to farmers and ranchers under I.R.C. § 2032A. This provision allows an executor to value real property according to its actual use, rather than its highest or best use. Allowing valuation at its actual use can result in a lower estate value, thus potentially lowering taxes. The 2012 special use valuation limit is $1 million.[16]

▶ Obtain values for your assets from qualified appraisal agents. Assets to be valued include real estate, farm equipment, machinery and other inventory, homesteads, vehicles, supplies, and any tangible asset with value.

▶ If you own real property in multiple states, you need an estate plan in each state. For example, an estate with ranch land in Colorado and Nebraska needs probate proceedings in each state to transfer or convey that property to heirs. In this situation, a trust is the best tool: no probate is needed, and the trustee can dispose of or manage multiple-state real estate.

---

[15] Appreciating land values and increasing farm sizes have led to a larger share of farm estates being subject to the federal estate tax. In 2006, approximately 2 percent of all estates in the U.S. owed federal estate taxes, but approximately 4 percent of all farm estates and nearly 18 percent of commercial farm estates owed estate taxes. *United States Department of Agriculture, Farm Bill Forum.*

[16] To qualify for the I.R.C. § 2032A limit, (1) the net value of the business property must be at least 50 percent of the decedent's gross estate and at least 25 percent of the decedent's adjusted gross estate (the gross estate reduced by certain deductible debts, expenses, claims, and losses); (2) the decedent must have transferred the business to specified close family relatives; and (3) the decedent or family members must have used the qualifying property for five of the eight years prior to the decedent's death. Qualified heirs must use the farm or business property for 10 years after the decedent owner's death.

▶ Record whether and where you maintain a safe deposit box and where you keep your important documents.

▶ Provide instructions regarding your funeral wishes and any prepaid funeral plans to whoever will be involved in making these arrangements.

▶ Consider charitable transfers to accomplish estate planning goals, whether they be a charitable remainder trust, a charitable lead trust, a charitable gift annuity, or outright gifts to charities and family members.

Some Estate Planning Transfer and Tax Reduction Strategies

Conservation Easements

A conservation easement is a restriction or encumbrance placed on property that protects the property from certain types of development, often preserving the ecological and open-space values of the land. It is a legally enforceable land preservation agreement between a landholder and either a governmental agency (a municipal, county, state, or federal entity) or a qualified not-for-profit land trust organization. Conservation easements are voluntary and allow the landowner to continue to privately own and manage the land and potentially receive significant state and federal tax advantages by donating the conservation easement. Perhaps of even greater value to a farmer or rancher, by creating this type of environmentally friendly restriction, they have contributed to the public good by preserving the conservation values associated with their land for future generations.

To gain tax advantages from granting a qualified conservation easement on their land, farmers and ranchers must obtain a written appraisal report from a qualified appraiser.[17] Additionally, farmers and ranchers wishing to obtain a conservation easement must now apply for a tax credit certificate from the Colorado Division of Real Estate[18] and be subject to individual and state limits for the tax credit amounts.

In the last several years, the Colorado Conservation Easement Tax Credit program has come under scrutiny from the Colorado Department of Revenue and the IRS.[19] Several other states have similar programs, but Colorado's history of generous tax credits, and

---

[17] Beginning on July 1, 2011, conservation easement appraisers must be Licensed Certified General Appraisers and comply with specific conservation easement-related education requirements.

[18] See www.dora.state.co.us/real-estate/conservation/documents/TCC_Application_Guidence.pdf for assistance in applying for this Certificate, as well as for additional information.

[19] "Colorado is seeking repayment of $15 million of tax credits granted as part of an innovative incentive program to save endangered lands. And that amount is likely to grow as part of a massive audit the Colorado Department of Revenue has undertaken to determine whether the tax credits were overvalued or were claimed on lands that weren't endangered. The Revenue Department's investigation, one of the largest it has ever undertaken, is looking at more than 10,000 tax returns claiming the credits since 2001. During that time, more than $274 million of conservation credits were claimed from Colorado's treasury alone. The Internal Revenue Service and the state's divisions of real estate and security also are investigating the credits, the people who received them and the appraisers who valued the land." *Rocky Mountain News*, "State Disputes $15 Million of Tax Credits," Jerd Smith, Dec. 8, 2007.

especially the sale or transfer of these tax credits, concerned those tax regulatory agencies.[20] The State of Colorado created an Oversight Commission[21] to review conservation easement laws, applications, and appraisals of these easements.[22] As a result, legislation was passed in 2010 that changed the rules and limits with regard to conservation easements, especially the availability of tax credits. In light of these new laws and requirements, anyone considering granting a conservation easement should consult with an attorney to determine the current legal status of these types of encumbrances.

Installment Sales

When selling real property and receiving one or more payments in subsequent years, the taxpayer may report the sale as an installment sale. This allows the taxpayer to defer the recognition of gain over many years and save taxes.[23] Under federal tax law, a farmer who sells development rights to his or her land and receives payment for the sale in installments would be taxed each year only on the capital gain from the sale he or she receives during that tax year. The farmer would not be required to pay taxes on the full capital gain in the sale year, although the farmer could elect to do so if he or she wished, even if he or she is receiving payment in installments.

The installment land contract (ILC) is also a method of effecting a sale. An ILC is a contract for delayed delivery of a deed providing for periodic payments over a term of years, similar to a promissory note. It is distinguished from the typical real estate buy-sell contract in that the buy-sell contract does not usually contain provisions for installment payments. The ILC is merely intended to hold the deal for a short period until the condition of title is completed and title is delivered to the buyer. Installment land contracts are more prevalent during periods of "tight" money or when a property is difficult to finance conventionally. Oftentimes a person with little or no cash for a down payment will be permitted to take possession of property under an installment land contract providing for monthly payments to the seller. The seller will still hold "legal" title, and the buyer will possess "equi-

---

[20] Colorado is one of three states that allow the sale or transfer of tax credits. *Id.*

[21] *See* C.R.S. § 12-61-721.

[22] In 2008, Colorado's appraiser statutes were amended by the passage of HB 08-1353, the Conservation Easement Bill, to prevent abuses of the state's land preservation tax credit program. This legislation created a nine-member Conservation Easement Oversight Commission, whose members are appointed by the governor. From this commission, legislative changes were made to the Conservation Easement Tax Credit Program and HB 10-1197 was introduced. Under the new law, "Notwithstanding any other provision of this section, for income tax years commencing during the 2011, 2012, and 2013 calendar years, a taxpayer conveying a conservation easement in 2011, 2012, or 2013 and claiming a credit pursuant to this section shall, in addition to any other requirements of this section, submit a claim for the credit to the Division of Real Estate in the Department of Regulatory Agencies. The Division shall issue a certificate for the claims received in the order submitted." The legislation also limits the impact to the state budget to $22 million annually in certificates authorized (in 2008, $63 million in tax credits were claimed). See www.dora.state.co.us/real-estate/conservation/taxcredit for current updates to the allowed tax credits by the Division of Real Estate, as well as for links to the Tax Credit Certification Application process; see also C.R.S. §§ 39-22-522(2.5) and 12-61-722.

[23] *See* 26 U.S.C. § 453.

table" title. Farmers and ranchers with equitable title can still use the property as needed while the conditions to complete the final purchase are met.

16-5. Succession Planning

Succession planning is a continuous process to transfer knowledge, skills, labor, management, control, and ownership between the generations. Decisions regarding ownership of assets; choice of business entity; and estate, retirement, and tax planning are all part of the overall plan for succession. Successful farm and ranch generational transfer depends in great part on the financial aspects of the farm or ranch operations, as well as the personal aspects. So many factors come into play when handing down a business — expectations and goals of both older and younger generations can be similar or quite different. As with any business transaction, open communication is essential and sharing these expectations and goals is crucial to a successful transition.

Recent surveys provide some alarming statistics. Only 1 percent of family-owned farm and ranch businesses in North America are transferred to a third generation. Another report shows that 30 percent of all family-owned farm and ranch businesses have not considered a successor, with only 63 percent having done so after the owner has reached age 65. Another recent survey shows that more than 58 percent of farm and ranch business owners list inadequate succession planning as the biggest threat facing their business.[24]

Handing It All Down

As difficult as it may be, it is important to envision the day when you no longer will be in charge of your farm or ranch. You could leave your heirs and your business vulnerable to considerable estate taxes and management upheaval if a succession plan is not created.

Typically, succession planning entails several steps: (1) determining the practicality of transferring your business (*i.e.*, are your farm or ranch operations sufficiently viable for this transfer to make sense?); (2) choosing a successor (is there a family member, friend, or employee who is willing to succeed into your responsibilities and take on the new ownership role and responsibility?); (3) beginning the transfer of ownership and management to the successor; and (4) finalizing the transfer of ownership and management responsibilities to the successor. Typically, the process of succession planning is stretched out over several years, as a moderately paced transition provides the best environment for the bottom line and overall stability of the operations.

Experts in the field of succession planning suggest using these best practices:

▶ Set a target date as your last day as primary decision-maker on the farm or ranch, and start shifting responsibilities ahead of time. You want to be able to oversee the transition while you are still there.

---

[24] *Amber Waves* (April 2005), a publication of the U.S. Department of Agriculture, Economic Research Service. For additional economic research, see www.ers.usda.gov/publications.

▶ Assist in the development, training, and education of your successors along the way and keep them fully informed of your work. Schedule regular meetings to review finances (including debt and revenue updates and forecasts), workload expectations and schedules, employee issues, important non-farming topics, and equipment and supply, to name a few.

▶ Work with professional advisors to complete any transfer of assets and debt restructuring, review and modify (if necessary) existing business structures, and review or finalize any other legal and financial transfer requirements. Consider having a buyout agreement in place if multiple successors are involved.

▶ Set goals and expectations that take into consideration the needs of your successor, including family time, lifestyle, work habits, and the successor's expectations and goals.

▶ Decide with your successor whether to offer an incentive to retain key employees after the transition.

▶ Consider off-farm family members' needs and expectations. Provide for buying out a family member's interest, if necessary (*e.g.*, sons or daughters who are not on the farm or ranch, but with whom you wish to share your inheritance).

▶ Review the asset protection and liability insurance needs of your business operations.

Some Additional Tax Saving Devices

Trusts

Trusts are extremely helpful tools to use during estate and succession planning. They can be valuable in administering the orderly transfer of assets and management to heirs. Trusts, including charitable trusts, may be used to shelter capital gains tax and provide greater cash flow for the retirees that in some cases may be used in wealth replacement strategies. Trustees can add valuable assistance as an objective third party to issues that arise within families during and after succession transition. Goals of trust creation can be numerous: replacing wealth, providing for a special-needs beneficiary and/or minor children, avoiding probate (especially if real property is owned in many states), providing for a beneficiary or spouse without financial management skills, keeping your estate private, protecting assets, organizing business assets into one vehicle, and allowing for flexible distribution of property, among others.

Charitable trusts might work well for your estate and succession plans as well. Charitable trusts can achieve multiple goals, including removing assets from large estates, providing an income stream to you or other beneficiaries with the remainder left to a charity of your choice, fulfilling your philanthropic goals and desires, passing along assets to heirs with reduced transfer costs, potentially providing you with a significant charitable deduction for the value of assets transferred into a charitable trust, establishing a means by which you can create a philanthropic legacy or family foundation, and passing along your values to your heirs. Some trusts, like the charitable lead trust, allow you to transfer income-producing assets into this type of trust, which provides an income for the charity for a term of years, and the remaining assets in the trust can be transferred free of generation-skipping and other transfer taxes, if the trust is properly set up.

Gifts

In 2012, the limit for tax-free gifting is $13,000 per person per year or $26,000 for husband and wife combined. Using this annual gift tax exemption can be particularly important in cases where the value of the estate of a farmer and/or rancher exceeds the estate tax applicable exclusion amount available to both spouses. These gifts can serve several purposes: perhaps providing "early" inheritance to those non-farm family members, establishing educational trusts for grandchildren, funding a wealth replacement, creating an irrevocable life insurance trust, and more.

16-6. Conclusion

A good estate and succession plan can save farm and ranch families thousands of dollars in estate taxes, income taxes, and administrative costs. Many farmers and ranchers wait too long to begin their financial, business, and estate plans, to the detriment of their families and heirs. Some of the concepts discussed above may not apply to your farm or ranch operations, but they are typical of issues facing all business owners in today's world, including the agribusiness owner. We intended this chapter to provide an overview of the many business issues facing the farmer and rancher, knowing before we started that we could not address them all adequately. Our hope is that it will give you thoughts and ideas to take to your professional advisors and develop an estate or succession plan that meets all of your and your family's needs, goals, and expectations. Peace of mind is a wonderful thing.

---

* The Office of Gift Planning at CSU cultivates, designs, facilitates, and stewards planned gifts to the University, and works with donors who contribute non-cash gifts (appreciated stocks, real estate, etc.). In our efforts, we use a variety of financial tools and techniques for giving, including bequests, charitable gift annuities, charitable remainder trusts, and charitable lead trusts. All planned gifts require the assistance of one or more qualified specialists: an attorney, certified public accountant, estate planning specialist, trust officer, and/or an insurance agent can be involved as we work with donors to accomplish their charitable goals.

In addition, we provide education to our donors through marketing and outreach efforts that include advertisements, publications, brochures, website information, e-newsletters, public speaking presentations, and the like. We consider it absolutely essential to make our office a resource for folks who are contemplating a deferred gift or have any questions concerning their estate planning goals. Additionally, we supply technical expertise to our colleagues in the development staff and work closely with them if they have a donor who is considering a planned gift.

Chapter 17

Annuities

Rebecca L. Franciscus, Esq.
Enforcement Division Staff Attorney
Denver Regional Office
U.S. Securities and Exchange Commission

SYNOPSIS

Variable annuities have become a part of the retirement and investment plans of many Americans. This chapter provides a general description of annuities with special focus on variable annuities, including what they are, how they work, and the charges you will pay. Before buying any variable annuity, however, you should find out about the particular annuity you are considering. Request a prospectus from the insurance company or from your financial professional, and read it carefully. The prospectus contains important information about the annuity contract, including fees and charges, investment options, death benefits, and annuity payout options. Additionally, you should compare the benefits and costs of the annuity to other variable annuities and to other types of investments, such as mutual funds. Moreover, be prepared to ask your insurance agent, broker, financial planner, or other financial professional lots of questions about whether a variable annuity is right for you.

17-1. What Is an Annuity?

An annuity is a contract between you and an insurance company under which you make a lump-sum payment or series of payments. In return, the insurer agrees to make periodic payments to you beginning immediately or at some future date. Annuities typically offer tax-deferred growth of earnings and may include a death benefit that will pay your beneficiary a guaranteed minimum amount, such as your total purchase payments.

17-2. Types of Annuities

There are generally two types of annuities: fixed and variable. In a **fixed annuity**, the insurance company guarantees that you will earn a minimum rate of interest specified in the annuity contract during the time that your account is growing. The insurance company also guarantees that the periodic payments will be a guaranteed amount per dollar in your account. These periodic payments may last for a definite period, such as 20 years, or an indefinite period, such as your lifetime or the lifetime of you and your spouse.

In a **variable annuity**, by contrast, you can choose to invest your purchase payments from among a range of different investment options, typically mutual funds. You may direct allocations of your money into separate accounts. The rate of return on your purchase payments, and the amount of the periodic payments you will eventually receive, will vary depending on the performance of the investment options you have selected.

Variable annuities differ from mutual funds in several important ways, such as:

▶ Variable annuities let you receive periodic payments for the rest of your life (or the life of your spouse or any other person you designate). This feature offers protection against the possibility that, after you retire, you will outlive your assets.

▶ Variable annuities have a death benefit. If you die before the insurer has started making payments to you, your beneficiary is guaranteed to receive a specified amount — typically at least the amount of your purchase payments. Your beneficiary will get a benefit from this feature if, at the time of your death, your account value is less than the guaranteed amount.

▶ Variable annuities are tax deferred. This means you pay no taxes on the income and investment gains from your annuity until you withdraw your money. You may also transfer your money from one investment option to another within a variable annuity without paying tax at the time of the transfer. When you take your money out of a variable annuity, however, you will be taxed on the earnings at ordinary income tax rates rather than lower capital gains rates. In general, the benefits of tax deferral will outweigh the costs of a variable annuity only if you hold it as a long-term investment to meet retirement and other long-range goals.

An **equity-indexed annuity** is a special type of annuity. During the accumulation period — when you make either a lump-sum payment or a series of payments — the insurance company credits you with a return that is based on changes in an equity index, such as the S&P 500 Composite Stock Price Index. The insurance company typically guarantees a minimum return, but guaranteed minimum return rates vary. After the accumulation period, the insurance company will make periodic payments to you under the terms of your contract, unless you choose to receive your contract value in a lump sum.

17-3. Regulation of Annuities

Fixed annuities are not securities and are not regulated by the Securities and Exchange Commission (SEC). Check with the Colorado Division of Insurance regarding regulation of fixed annuities (see section 17-6, "Resources," for more information). Variable annuities are securities regulated by the SEC. Equity-indexed annuities combine features of traditional insurance products (guaranteed minimum return) and traditional securities (return linked to equity markets). Depending on the mix of features, an equity-indexed annuity may or may not be a security. Currently, the typical equity-indexed annuity is registered with the state insurance commissions, and is not registered with the SEC.

17-4. How Variable Annuities Work

A variable annuity has two phases: an **accumulation phase** and a **payout phase**. During the **accumulation phase**, you make purchase payments, which you can allocate to a number of investment options. For example, you could designate 40 percent of your purchase payments to a bond fund, 40 percent to a U.S. stock fund, and 20 percent to an international stock fund. The money you have allocated to each mutual fund investment option will increase or decrease over time, depending on the fund's performance. In addition, variable annuities often allow you to allocate part of your purchase payments to a fixed account. A fixed account, unlike a mutual fund, pays a fixed rate of interest. The insurance company may reset this interest rate periodically, but it will usually provide a guaranteed minimum (*e.g.*, 3 percent per year).

During the accumulation phase, you can typically transfer your money from one investment option to another without paying tax on your investment income and gains, although you may be charged by the insurance company for transfers. If you withdraw money from your account during the early years of the accumulation phase, however, you may have to pay "surrender charges," which are discussed below. In addition, you may have to pay a 10 percent federal tax penalty if you withdraw money before the age of 59½.

> **Tip:** Your most important source of information about a variable annuity's investment options is the prospectus. Request the prospectuses for the mutual fund investment options. Read them carefully before you allocate your purchase payments among the investment options offered. You should consider a variety of factors with respect to each fund option, including the fund's investment objectives and policies, management fees and other expenses that the fund charges, the risks and volatility of the fund, and whether the fund contributes to the diversification of your overall investment portfolio. The SEC's online publication, *Mutual Fund Investing: Look at More Than a Fund's Past Performance*, provides information about these factors. Another SEC online publication, *Invest Wisely: An Introduction to Mutual Funds*, provides general information about the types of mutual funds and the expenses they charge. (See section 17-6, "Resources," for links to the SEC's website.)

At the beginning of the **payout phase**, you may receive your purchase payments plus investment income and gains (if any) as a lump-sum payment, or you may choose to receive them as a stream of payments at regular intervals (generally monthly). The choice regarding how you receive payments is called a **settlement option.** Moreover, the **maturity date** is the latest date on which you can begin receiving payments from your annuity under any of the settlement options available to you. The date shown on the **specifications page** of your contract is automatically set as the date when you *must* begin receiving payments from your contract.

If you choose to receive a stream of payments, you may have a number of choices of how long the payments will last. As mentioned above, under most annuity contracts, you can choose to have your annuity payments last for a period that you set (such as 20 years) or for an indefinite period (such as your lifetime or the lifetime of you and your spouse or other beneficiary). During the payout phase, your annuity contract may permit you to choose between receiving payments that are fixed in amount or payments that vary based on the performance of mutual fund investment options.

The amount of each periodic payment will depend, in part, on the time period that you select for receiving payments. Be aware that some annuities do not allow you to withdraw money from your account once you have started receiving regular annuity payments.

In addition, some annuity contracts are structured as **immediate annuities**, which means that there is no accumulation phase and you will start receiving annuity payments right after you purchase the annuity.

> **Caution:** Withdrawals prior to age 59½ may be subject to 10 percent federal tax penalties.

The Death Benefit and Other Features

A common feature of variable annuities is the **death benefit**. If you die, a person you select as a beneficiary (such as your spouse or child) will receive the greater of (1) all the money in your account, or (2) some guaranteed minimum (such as all purchase payments minus prior withdrawals).

Some variable annuities allow you to choose a "stepped-up" death benefit. Under this feature, your guaranteed minimum death benefit may be based on a greater amount than purchase payments minus withdrawals. For example, the guaranteed minimum might be your account value as of a specified date, which may be greater than purchase payments minus withdrawals if the underlying investment options have performed well. The purpose of a stepped-up death benefit is to "lock in" your investment performance and prevent a later decline in the value of your account from eroding the amount that you expect to leave to your heirs. This feature carries a charge, however, that will reduce your account value.

Variable annuities sometimes offer other optional features, which also have extra charges. One common feature, the **guaranteed minimum income benefit**, guarantees a particular minimum level of annuity payments, even if you do not have enough money in your account (perhaps because of investment losses) to support that level of payments. Other features may include **long-term care insurance**, which pays for home health care or nursing home care if you become seriously ill.

Caution: You will pay for each benefit provided by your variable annuity. Be sure you understand the charges. Carefully consider whether you need the benefit. If you do, consider whether you can buy the benefit more cheaply as part of the variable annuity or separately (*e.g.*, through a long-term care insurance policy).

Tip: You may want to consider the financial strength of the insurance company that sponsors any variable annuity you are considering buying. This can affect the company's ability to pay any benefits that are greater than the value of your account in mutual fund investment options, such as a death benefit, guaranteed minimum income benefit, long-term care benefit, or amounts you have allocated to a fixed account investment option.

Variable Annuity Charges

You will pay several charges when you invest in a variable annuity. Be sure you understand all the charges before you invest. **These charges will reduce the value of your account and the return on your investment.** Often, they will include the following:

▶ **Surrender charges.** A **surrender charge** is a type of sales charge you must pay if you sell or withdraw money from a variable annuity during the "surrender period," which is a set period of time that typically lasts six to eight years after you purchase the annuity. Surrender charges will reduce the value of, and the return on, your investment. Generally, the surrender charge is a percentage of the amount withdrawn, and declines gradually over a period of several years, known as the "surrender period." For example, a 7 percent charge might apply in the first year after a purchase payment, 6 percent in the second year, 5 percent in the third year, and so on until the eighth year, when the surrender charge no longer applies. Often, contracts will allow you to withdraw part of your account value each year — 10 or 15 percent of your account value, for example — without paying a surrender charge.

▶ **Mortality and expense risk charge.** This charge is equal to a certain percentage of your account value, typically around 1.25 percent per year. This charge compensates the insurance company for insurance risks it assumes under the annuity contract. Profit from the mortality and expense risk charge is sometimes used to pay the insurer's costs of selling the variable annuity, such as a commission paid to your financial professional for selling the variable annuity to you.

▶ **Administrative fees.** The insurer may deduct charges to cover record-keeping and other administrative expenses. This may be charged as a flat account maintenance fee (perhaps $25 or $30 per year) or as a percentage of your account value (typically around 0.15 percent per year).

▶ **Underlying Fund Expenses.** You will also indirectly pay the fees and expenses imposed by the mutual funds that are the underlying investment options for your variable annuity.

▶ **Fees and Charges for Other Features.** Special features offered by some variable annuities, such as a **stepped-up death benefit**, a **guaranteed minimum income benefit**, or **long-term care insurance**, often carry additional fees and charges.

▶ **Initial sales loads**, or fees for **transferring** part of your account from one investment option to another, may also apply.

Tip: You should ask your financial professional to explain to you all charges that may apply. You can also find a description of the charges in the prospectus for any variable annuity that you are considering.

Tax-Free "1035" Exchanges

Section 1035 of the U.S. tax code allows you to exchange an existing variable annuity contract for a new annuity contract without paying any tax on the income and investment gains in your current variable annuity account. These tax-free exchanges, known as 1035 exchanges, can be useful if another annuity has features that you prefer, such as a larger death benefit, different annuity payout options, or a wider selection of investment choices.

You may, however, be required to pay surrender charges on the old annuity if you are still in the surrender charge period. In addition, a new surrender charge period generally begins when you exchange into the new annuity. This means that, for a significant number of years (as many as 10 years), you typically will have to pay a surrender charge (which can be as high as 9 percent of your purchase payments) if you withdraw funds from the new annuity. Further, the new annuity may have higher annual fees and charges than the old annuity, which will reduce your returns.

Caution: *If you are thinking about a 1035 exchange, you should compare both annuities carefully. Unless you plan to hold the new annuity for a significant amount of time, you may be better off keeping the old annuity because the new annuity typically will impose a new surrender charge period. Also, if you decide to do a 1035 exchange, you should talk to your financial professional or tax adviser to make sure the exchange will be tax free. If you surrender the old annuity for cash and then buy a new annuity, you will have to pay tax on the surrender.*

Other Tax Considerations

Other investment vehicles, such as IRAs and employer-sponsored 401(k) plans, also may provide you with tax-deferred growth and other tax advantages. For most investors, it will be advantageous to make the maximum allowable contributions to IRAs and 401(k) plans before investing in a variable annuity.

In addition, if you are investing in a variable annuity through a tax-advantaged retirement plan (such as a 401(k) plan or IRA), you will get *no additional tax advantage* from the variable annuity. Under these circumstances, consider buying a variable annuity only if it makes sense because of the annuity's other features, such as lifetime income payments and death benefit protection. The tax rules that apply to variable annuities can be complicated; before investing, you may want to consult a tax adviser about the tax consequences to you of investing in a variable annuity.

Bonus Credits

Some insurance companies are now offering variable annuity contracts with "bonus credit" features. These contracts promise to add a bonus to your contract value based on a specified percentage (typically ranging from 1 to 5 percent) of purchase payments. Frequently, insurers will charge you for bonus credits in one or more of the following ways:

▶ **Higher surrender charges.** Surrender charges may be higher for a variable annuity that pays you a bonus credit than for a similar contract with no bonus credit.

▶ **Longer surrender periods.** Your purchase payments may be subject to surrender charges for a longer period than they would be under a similar contract with no bonus credit.

▶ **Higher mortality and expense risk charges and other charges.** Higher annual mortality and expense risk charges may be deducted for a variable annuity that pays you a bonus credit. Although the difference may seem small, over time it can add up. In addition, some contracts may impose a separate fee specifically to pay for the bonus credit.

Before purchasing a variable annuity with a bonus credit, ask yourself — and the financial professional who is trying to sell you the contract — whether the bonus is worth more to you than any increased charges you will pay for the bonus. This may depend on a variety of factors, including the amount of the bonus credit and the increased charges, how long you hold your annuity contract, and the return on the underlying investments. You also need to consider the other features of the annuity to determine whether it is a good investment for you.

> *Caution:* Variable annuities with bonus credits may carry a downside, however: higher expenses that can outweigh the benefit of the bonus credit offered. You should also note that a bonus may only apply to your initial premium payment, or to premium payments you make within the first year of the annuity contract. Further, under some annuity contracts, the insurer will take back all bonus payments made to you within the prior year or some other specified period if you make a withdrawal, if a death benefit is paid to your beneficiaries upon your death, or in other circumstances.

> *Tip:* Take a hard look at bonus credits. In some cases, the "bonus" may not be in your best interest.

> *Remember:* Variable annuities are designed to be long-term investments, to meet retirement and other long-range goals. Variable annuities are not suitable for meeting short-term goals because substantial taxes and insurance company charges may apply if you withdraw your money early. Variable annuities also involve investment risks, just as mutual funds do.

17-5. Questions to Ask Before Investing

Questions to Ask When Purchasing Variable Annuities

Variable annuities combine features of insurance and securities investments. They can be an important part of your retirement and investment plans, but it is important to make sure they are right for you. **Before you purchase an annuity, request a prospectus from the insurance company or from your financial professional, and read it carefully.** The prospectus contains important information about the annuity contract, including fees and charges, investment options, death benefits, and annuity payout options. You should compare the benefits and costs of the annuity to other variable annuities and to other types of investments, such as mutual funds.

Recently, the SEC issued a report on how these products are sold. Based on the problems we've seen, here are some important questions we recommend that you ask before purchasing a variable product.

> ▶ Might I need this money in the next few years? Variable products are long-term investment vehicles. They aren't appropriate if you'll need your money in the short term because substantial taxes and insurance company charges may apply if you withdraw your money early.

> ▶ Am I willing to take the risk that my account value may decrease if the underlying mutual fund investment options perform badly?

▶ Do I understand the features of the variable annuity? Do I understand all of the fees and expenses that the variable annuity charges?

▶ If a variable annuity offers a bonus credit, will the bonus outweigh any higher fees and charges that the product may charge?

▶ Are there features of the variable annuity, such as long-term care insurance, that I could purchase more cheaply separately?

▶ Do I have enough money right now to purchase this product? Because variable products are long-term investments, it can be dangerous to your financial health to mortgage your home in order to purchase a variable annuity. If a salesperson pressures you to do so, call the SEC or another agency listed in section 17-6, "Resources."

▶ Am I being urged to purchase a variable annuity or variable insurance in my IRA, 401(k), or other retirement account? One key benefit to purchasing variable products is the fact that earnings on the invested money accumulate tax deferred. But these tax benefits are of no value if you're purchasing the product in your IRA, 401(k), or other retirement account because those accounts are already tax-advantaged. Make sure that the features you're buying are worth the money you're paying.

▶ Does the firm recommend this product to all its customers? Everyone has different investment objectives. Variable products are not "one size fits all." Be careful if a salesperson recommends one product to all customers. That may mean the product isn't right for you.

▶ What will I lose if I exchange this product? If a salesperson is urging you to exchange your variable product for a new contract, you'll need to compare both products carefully, because:

- The guaranteed death benefit of the new product may be less than the old;

- You may have to pay a "surrender charge" to get out of the old product;

- The new product may impose higher annual fees and a new surrender charge; and

- The new product may impose a new surrender charge period.

Remember: Variable annuity contracts typically have a "free look" period of 10 or more days, during which you can terminate the contract without paying any surrender charges and get back your purchase payments (which may be adjusted to reflect charges and the performance of your investment). You can continue to ask questions in this period to make sure you understand your variable annuity before the "free look" period ends.

Questions to Ask the People Who Sell Investments or Provide Investment Advice

Financial professionals who sell variable annuities have a duty to advise you as to whether the product they are trying to sell is suitable to your particular investment needs. Don't be afraid to ask them questions, and write down their answers, so there won't be any confusion later as to what was said.

> **Tip:** Check the background of your financial professional: you can verify your broker's disciplinary history by checking the Central Registration Depository (CRD) either through the Colorado Division of Securities or the Financial Industry Regulation Authority (FINRA). You can also find out about investment advisers and whether they are properly registered by reading their registration forms, called the "Form ADV." You can view an adviser's most recent Form ADV online by visiting the SEC's website. (See section 17-6, "Resources," for more information.)

▶ Are you registered with our state securities regulator? Have you ever been disciplined by the SEC, a state regulator, or other organization (such as FINRA or one of the stock exchanges)?

▶ What training and experience do you have? How long have you been in the business? What other firms have you been registered with? What is the status of those firms today?

▶ Have you personally been involved in any arbitration cases? What happened?

▶ How long has your firm been in business? How many arbitration awards have been filed against your firm?

▶ What is your investment philosophy?

▶ Describe your typical client. Can you provide me with some names and telephone numbers of your long-term clients?

▶ How do you get paid? By commission? Amount of assets you manage? Another method? Do I have any choices on how to pay you?

▶ Do you make more if I buy this annuity (or stock, or bond, or mutual fund) rather than another? If you weren't making extra money, would your recommendation be the same?

▶ Are you participating in a sales contest? Is this purchase really in my best interest, or are you trying to win a prize?

▶ You've told me what it costs me to buy this stock (or bond, or mutual fund); how much will I receive if I sell it today?

▶ If your financial professional changes firms, ask if he or she was paid to change firms. Do you get anything for bringing me along?

17-6. Resources

U.S. Securities and Exchange Commission
  Office of Investor Education and Advocacy
  100 F St., NE
  Washington, D.C. 20549
  (800) SEC-0330
  www.sec.gov

  Denver Regional Office
  1801 California St., Ste. 1500
  Denver, CO 80202
  (303) 844-1000

Colorado Division of Insurance
  1560 Broadway, Ste. 850
  Denver, CO 80202
  (303) 894-7499 (metro-area)
  (800) 930-3745 (statewide)
  www.dora.state.co.us/insurance/index.htm

Colorado Division of Securities
  1560 Broadway, Ste. 900
  Denver, CO 80202
  (303) 894-2320
  www.dora.state.co.us/securities/index.htm

Colorado Attorney General/AARP ElderWatch Hotline
  (800) 222-4444

Local District Attorneys Offices

Metro Area District Attorney Offices or Fraud Hotlines:
  Adams and Broomfield counties: (303) 659-7720
  Arapahoe, Douglas, Lincoln, and Elbert counties: (720) 874-8500
  Boulder County: (303) 441-3700
  Denver County: (720) 913-9179 (Fraud hotline)
  Jefferson and Gilpin counties: (303) 271-6800

Financial Industry Regulatory Authority (FINRA)
The largest non-governmental regulator for all securities firms, including sellers of variable annuities, doing business in the United States. As of June 2007, FINRA is the combination of the National Association of Securities Dealers (NASD) and the New York Stock Exchange (NYSE) regulatory bodies. Call for a free Central Registration Depository (CRD) broker check at (800) 289-9999.
  www.finra.org
  www.SaveAndInvest.org/index.htm

Chapter 18

Philanthropy and Planned Giving

Marianne Blackwell, Esq.*
William M. Sheets*
Office of Gift Planning
University Advancement
Colorado State University

SYNOPSIS

18-1.   About Philanthropy

18-2.   What Are Planned Gifts?

18-3.   Types of Planned Gifts and the Advantages to the Donor

18-4.   Conclusion

18-5.   Resources

18-1. About Philanthropy

Throughout life, you may have been asked to make donations to individuals or charities, and, after considerable discerning thought, may have given to those to which you felt a connection. However, now in the "golden years," you may be asked to consider a different type of gift: your legacy. What can you leave the next generation? This question may not be as difficult to answer as: *How* will you leave your gift to the next generation? The decision about "how" to leave a legacy gift may seem more complex at first glance. After all, financial gifts given throughout your lifetime probably came from your income, but now you are making a decision about giving from your accumulated wealth. This chapter is designed to provide some insight into philanthropy as an activity and as a philosophy, help you find information about your favorite charity, and provide you with options with which to plan your gift.

One of the best essays written on the topic of deciding how one should engage in appropriate philanthropy comes from the book, *Philanthropy: Voluntary Action for the Public Good*, by Robert L. Payton. It is an essay on friendship, charity, the human condition, and the methods and values of science and morals. Payton's reflections on reason and emotion in philanthropy are inspired by Thomas Jefferson's famous letter to Maria Cosway entitled,

"A Dialogue Between My Head and My Heart," in which Jefferson theorizes that common sense and emotion can often be at odds as we consider charitable intent and acts. Payton postulates that even today, we all have conflicts in deciding how and when and to whom to give — conversations between our Head and our Heart. What gift makes sense in today's world, where homelessness, famine, and constant human needs are worldwide and ever-present? Will my gift make a difference? Can I be sure that my gift will be used appropriately? We present a part of the essay here to stimulate your thoughts about how to evaluate the question of determining your giving nature.

From Payton's essay:

Beyond friendship, in our less personal relations in society at large, Jefferson counsels against the misleading influence of narrow self interest. The Head leads us astray when it intrudes in the affairs of the Heart. He illustrates his theme with the example of a weary soldier seeking a lift on the back of Jefferson's carriage. Jefferson's self interest advises against it: His Head argues that there will be other soldiers further on; eventually we'll put too much of a burden on the horses. Jefferson rides on, but his conscience gets the better of him: It may not be possible to help everyone, his Heart pleads, but we ought to help those we can. The logic of compassion wins out, but too late, because when Jefferson turns back to find the soldier, the soldier has taken another road.

The Center on Philanthropy at Indiana University describes philanthropy in a less complex way:

It's a powerful feeling, helping others.

You've felt it: The "warm glow" that comes when you do something good for someone else.

You feel it every time you give money to a cause you believe in. But it radiates just as strongly when you volunteer at a community event, participate in a service club, take food to a sick neighbor, or help out a friend.

This feeling is an expression of your concern for others rather than yourself. Of wanting to help fill a need, solve a problem, make life better for someone else. In short, of wanting to take action, voluntarily, for the public good.

This is philanthropy.

Philanthropy is personal and private. Everyone will have a different philosophy and follow his or her own Heart or Head, or both. We hope you enjoy the journey as you come to a decision regarding your own charitable path.

18-2. What Are Planned Gifts?

Planned gifts are a variety of charitable giving methods that allow donors to express their personal values by integrating charitable, family, and financial goals. Making a planned, charitable gift usually requires the assistance of a knowledgeable advisor such as an attorney, financial planner, or CPA to help structure the gift. Planned gifts can be made with cash, but many planned gifts are made by donating assets such as stocks, real estate, insurance, or business interests — the possibilities are endless. Planned gifts can provide valuable tax benefits and/or lifetime income for donors, spouses, or other loved ones. The most frequently made planned gifts are bequests to charities, made through wills. Other popular planned gifts include charitable trusts and charitable gift annuities.

The advantages of planned gifts are many, but some of the more popular reasons for establishing this type of gift are:

1) Providing a life income to the donor;

2) Removing assets from one's estate to lessen the estate tax burden;

3) Avoiding or mitigating capital gains taxes by gifting appreciated, long-held property;

4) Receiving a charitable tax deduction;

5) Turning low or non-income-producing assets into higher income payouts;

6) Fulfilling one's charitable intent by supporting a favorite charity; and

7) Providing a charitable gift, receiving tax benefits, *and* also maintaining control of the asset during one's lifetime.

18-3. Types of Planned Gifts and the Advantages to the Donor

Bequests

The basic, easiest, and most popular planned gift is a bequest. Experts say that nearly 80 percent of all planned gifts to charities are in the form of a will provision or a bequest. A charitable bequest is a provision in your will that designates a charity as a beneficiary. Bequests can either be specific (leaving a certain asset or a set sum of money to the charity) or general (leaving a percentage of your estate to the charity). Most charities will help you with the bequest language you'll want to use in your will. It is important to include enough information in the bequest so that your estate administrator will know to which charity or charities you want your gift directed.

The greatest advantage to leaving a bequest to charity is that you, the donor, maintain control over your assets until your death. For this reason, charities consider bequests to be *revocable* or incomplete in nature — that is, the gift is not absolute. If the estate's assets cannot support payment of the bequest to a charity, there is no legal obligation on the part of the estate to make payment. Or, the donor can change his or her beneficiaries during his or her lifetime and can remove a charity (or any other beneficiary) from his or her will. As in all other types of planned gifts, a bequest can be designated to be used for any purpose that the donor wishes, so long as the gift is not to be used for any intention that is in violation of the law. If you have a particular use to which you would like your bequest directed, the charity will be most pleased if the terms of your intentions are set forth specifically in your will provision. Without such specific language, the charity may not be able to fully realize your plans — and the charity will want to use your gift in the way that you intended. If acceptable to you, all charities would appreciate the opportunity to know of your bequest provision and charitable intentions while you are still living; you could send them the entire will or simply the pages with their particular gift noted thereon. It would be up to you, of course, if you wanted to be publicly thanked and recognized for your future gift by the charity, or you could remain anonymous if that is more comfortable for you.

Retirement Plan Gifts

Another way to provide a planned gift to a charity is to include your favorite non-profit organization in your retirement plan documents. You can designate a charity as a beneficiary of your individual retirement account (IRA), 401(k), or other qualified retirement plan. In many regards, if a person is charitably inclined, it is preferable to fund such gift with this type of asset because the proceeds from these accounts are, at death, considered income in respect of a descendent (IRD). This tax law concept is generally defined as taxable income earned but not received prior to death. No matter who the beneficiary is, the income, when received, will be taxed to the beneficiary as it would have been taxed to the decedent. Generally, inherited property is not included in an heir's taxable income, but if a family member receives an IRD asset, he or she will be subject to income tax when the gift is distributed. (An exception to this rule is that beneficiaries who inherit Roth IRA funds do not have to pay taxes on the dollars.) Here are some examples of IRD assets:

- ▶ Non-qualified stock options;
- ▶ Distributions from IRAs and retirement plans;
- ▶ Profit-sharing plans;
- ▶ Deferred compensation;
- ▶ Deferred capital gain on installment sales;
- ▶ Accrued interest on savings bonds;
- ▶ Commissions earned but not received at death (*e.g.*, real estate, insurance, or brokerage);
- ▶ Remaining payments from lottery winnings (if you took a cash payout);
- ▶ Accounts receivable or unpaid fees from people or companies for whom the decedent provided services (*e.g.*, doctors, attorneys, accountants, etc.);
- ▶ Grain in storage, harvested crops, or bales of hay; and
- ▶ Uncollected salaries, wages, bonuses, commissions, vacation pay, and sick pay of a cash-basis employee.

When a donor provides at death for a direct transfer from his or her retirement account to a qualified charity, however, the entire value of the IRD assets will go to the charity tax free. In addition, the donor's estate receives a charitable estate tax deduction for the entire amount of the gift. Making a gift of IRD can be quite easy. For example, a donor could make to a charity a specific bequest of U.S. savings bonds owned at death, or the donor can simply change the beneficiary designation on his or her retirement account — *e.g.*, IRA, 401(k), 403(b), or defined contribution plan.

Your retirement plan administrator can furnish you with the appropriate designation of beneficiary forms to complete. As in a will bequest, you can authorize a portion or percentage of your retirement assets to be shared by any combination of charities and/or other heirs.

Gifts of Appreciated Stock

By donating securities held long-term (more than one year) to a charitable organization, you can avoid capital gains tax on the appreciation and receive a charitable deduction for the full fair market value of your donation. If your estate will be subject to federal estate tax, removing assets from your estate can also save estate taxes. Here is an example of the advantages of giving appreciated stock versus the gift of money:

Giving Appreciated Stock

Value of stock gift (28% tax bracket) = $25,000

Your basis (what you paid for it) in the stock = $5,000

Expected gain from the sale of the stock = $20,000

Savings by contributing the stock to charity:

$25,000 charitable deduction (savings of $7,000 in income taxes
($25,000 x 28%))

$3,000 capital gains tax savings (15% x $20,000)

NET COST OF GIFT = $15,000 ($25,000 - $7,000 - $3,000)

Giving Cash

Value of gift (28% tax bracket) = $25,000

$25,000 charitable deduction (savings of $7,000 in income taxes
($25,000 x 28%))

NET COST OF CASH GIFT = $21,000 ($25,000 - $7,000 + $3,000)

Life Income Gifts

Charitable Gift Annuity (CGA) and Deferred Charitable Gift Annuity (DCGA)

A charitable gift annuity is a contract between a donor and the issuing charity. This is often the gift of choice when a guaranteed present income or future income is desired. In this gift option, typically a gift of cash or securities is transferred to the charity of the donor's choice in exchange for a contractual life income paid to the donor or donors at least annually, or deferred to a later date in the case of a DCGA. The income is guaranteed by the issuing charity, and the donor can name himself or herself sole annuitant or designate a second annuitant, usually a spouse. A gift annuity can also be purchased on behalf of another party — for example, an adult child. If the CGA is a two-life annuity, the payout will continue until the death of the second annuitant. A portion of the gift is invested by the charity and used to provide income for life, and the remaining portion qualifies as a present-interest gift to the charity, which then entitles the donor to a charitable tax deduction. Some charities require that annuitants be of a certain age — say, 65 — before they can enter into any gift annuity. Some charities also have a minimum dollar amount to fund a CGA.

The American Council on Gift Annuities (ACGA) sets suggested maximum rates for CGAs and DCGAs. The ACGA reviews the rates and can change them periodically, depending upon the current interest rates and current mortality tables. The majority of charities use the rates recommended by the ACGA, and these rates are incorporated into charitable CGA software programs. The annuity payout rate will be determined by the age or ages of the annuitants, although some charities deviate from the suggested rates. (Be careful that a charity that does not use the suggested rates has sufficient assets to pay for a higher rate.) In the case of a DCGA, the rate is set at the time the gift is made, but the rate is reflective of what the software program projects the appropriate payout rate will be when the annuitant begins to take payment. Almost all charities that offer gift annuities use software programs that automatically calculate the rate. You can easily request an illustration that will include your variables of amount of gift and age(s) of annuitant(s). This illustration or projection will clearly show the charitable deduction, payout rate, and annuity payment.

Technically, a CGA/DCGA is part gift and part sale, or a *bargain sale*. Think of it as two separate transactions: a gift to the charity and then the purchase of an annuity. The gift portion is the value of the property transferred to the charity minus the present value of the annuity. The sale portion is the present value of the annuity. The payout of any gift annuity depends on the asset that was transferred to the charity. So, some of the annuity payment will be tax free, some might be return of capital gain income, and some might be ordinary income. The following is helpful to know:

▶ *If the donor contributes cash*: The annuity payment is part tax-free return of principal and part ordinary income, for the duration of the annuitant's life expectancy.

▶ *If the donor contributes appreciated, long-term property*: The annuity payment is part tax-free return of principal, part return of capital gain income, and part ordinary income — all for the duration of the donor's life expectancy. Another way to look at it: if a donor transfers this kind of property to fund the gift annuity, he or she is deemed to have sold a portion of the property to the charity and the donor can then spread the capital gains over his or her life expectancy (as opposed to incurring the full amount of the capital gains tax if the same property was sold on the open market and not given to charity).

Another component to consider in a CGA or DCGA is the Internal Revenue Service (IRS) discount rate, which is used to determine the charitable deduction. The rate is the annual rate of return that the IRS assumes the gift assets will earn during the gift term. The IRS discount rate is published monthly and is announced on about the 20th of the month that precedes the month to which the rate will apply. It equals 120 percent of the annual midterm rate, rounded to the nearest 0.2 percent. The annual midterm rate is the annualized average yield of Treasury instruments over the past 30 days that have remaining maturities of three to nine years.

Basically, the higher the discount rate, the higher the charitable deduction will be, and vice versa. In calculating the charitable deduction, a donor is entitled to use the rate for the month in which the gift is made or the rate of either of the two previous months, so the timing of a CGA or DCGA can become important. If the charitable deduction is important to the donor, he or she may want to wait until the discount rate is at an acceptable percentage. At the time this chapter was updated (February 2012), the IRS discount rate was 1.4 percent. The discount rate is reflective of the economy, and because of the ongoing economic challenges, the rate has dropped to its lowest numbers ever. In the past 13 years, the rate reached its highest point of 8.2 in July and August 1996. Lower federal interest rates mean lower IRS discount rates, which, consequently, mean lower charitable tax deductions for CGA or DCGA annuitants. But the upside of a lower discount rate is that the tax-free portion of a gift annuity's payment is maximized.

If all of this sounds very complicated, it really is not! The CGA or DCGA is a very popular planned gift option. To belie your fears, let us sum up the benefits of this type of gift, which may be attractive to you:

- ▶ It yields income for life (fixed payments).
- ▶ The donor can select the starting date of the income.
- ▶ It gives the possibility of one or two income beneficiaries.
- ▶ It is a guaranteed contractual agreement — payment is an absolute obligation of the issuing charity.
- ▶ The donor desires to make a present gift to a favorite charity.
- ▶ The donor can turn low or non-producing assets into higher-return assets by establishing a charitable gift annuity with cash or securities.

Here is a list of the current rates as of February 2012:

One Life		Two Lives	
Your Age	**Rate of Return**	**Your Ages**	**Rate of Return**
50	3.7%	50/55	3.3%
55	4.0%	55/60	3.7%
60	4.4%	60/65	4.0%
65	4.7%	65/70	4.4%
70	5.1%	70/75	4.8%
75	5.8%	75/80	5.3%
80	6.8%	80/85	6.1%
85	7.8%	85/90	7.3%
90+	9.0%	90/95+	8.8%

The rate of return is slightly lower for two lives because the period of payment generally is longer.
These rates are subject to change. Please check with your charity for current rates offered.
Please be advised that not all organizations offer CGAs at the above ages and rates.

Here's an example of how a gift annuity can work:

Donor profile:

Mr. Brown, aged 72, currently owns $25,000 in highly appreciated stock, which is producing low dividends; he purchased the stock over one year ago for $10,000. With retirement approaching, Mr. Brown is considering ways to secure his future income.

Strategy to reduce capital gains:

Mr. Brown establishes a $25,000 charitable gift annuity by donating his highly appreciated stock to a charity.

Financial Benefits:

Annuity: $25,000

Annuity Payout: 5.4%

Annual Payout for Life: $1,350

Immediate Charitable Tax Deduction: $9,674.50 (assumes a 1.6 percent IRS discount rate)

A great advantage of funding a charitable gift annuity with a donation of highly appreciated stock is the reduction of capital gains tax liability. The 15 percent capital gains tax is eliminated on the gift portion of the transfer. Although he will have some capital gains tax spread out over his life expectancy, Mr. Brown avoids an immediate payment of $2,250 in capital gains tax (15 percent of the gain) that would be due if he sold the securities.

Charitable Remainder Trust (CRT)

A charitable remainder trust is a separate trust arrangement between a donor and a trustee chosen by the donor, and will always involve a legal document establishing the terms of the trust. The trustee can be a bank or trust company, brokerage firm, an individual, a charity, or even the donor. Under the terms of the CRT, the donor reserves the right to receive payment from the trust or can provide for payment to other beneficiaries. When the trust is dissolved (often at the death of the donor or surviving beneficiaries), the remaining principal is distributed to the charity or charities named by the donor who established the trust. A CRT is an *irrevocable* planned gift; that is, the donor cannot change his or her mind once the trust is established and he or she receives the corresponding charitable tax deduction. The beneficiary charities can be changed, but the trust remainder will be paid out to a charitable organization or else punitive tax results will occur. As with all planned gifts, if you are considering a CRT, be sure to seek the advice of your advisors, including tax consultants and attorneys.

To fund a CRT, cash, securities, real property, or other assets are transferred into a trust. The trustee manages the trust assets and pays the donor's beneficiaries a fixed income for life or for a term of years. CRTs come in a variety of forms, including a fixed income annuity trust, in which the annual income never changes, and a unitrust, in which the assets are valued each year and the income is paid according to the trust's value. CRTs can even be designed to hold real estate and pay no income, but once the real estate is sold, the trust flips into a life income trust.

Most banks and trust companies that serve as trustees require a minimum of $100,000 to establish this type of planned gift. The administrative costs for managing charitable trusts can be quite high, usually a percentage of the trust's assets. Because the CRT is considered a separate entity, it must file a tax return and can be responsible for other reporting duties, which can make the cost of maintenance too high for smaller-sized accounts below $100,000. Further, preparing the CRT documents can run into a few thousand dollars. So, the CRT is certainly not for everyone. The benefits of a CRT, though, especially a unitrust, are numerous: these trusts are extremely flexible, can be established with high payout rates, can be used to provide maintenance and support for a surviving spouse, can turn low or non-producing assets into higher payout assets, can receive additional assets during the life of the CRT (in the case of a unitrust), and more. Here is a comprehensive list of the advantages of this type of gift:

▶ The donor retains the right to receive income for his or her life, the lives of others, or for a specified term of years.

▶ There is the possibility of multiple beneficiaries.

▶ Assets transferred into the CRT can be sold and reinvested in higher income-producing assets.

▶ The donor has the ability to choose the trustee (and can self-trustee, if desired).

▶ A CRT preserves the principal of one's assets while generating life income.

▶ The donor can elect to receive a fixed income based on the original value of assets transferred or an income based on the value of the assets recalculated each year (annuity trust versus unitrust options).

▶ The donor can continue to fund the CRT if it is a charitable remainder unitrust (CRUT) (assets revalued each year). If the CRT is established as a fixed income trust (a charitable remainder annuity trust), the donor cannot make additional gifts to the trust in the future.

▶ The donor receives a charitable income tax deduction in the year that he or she funds the CRT or makes any additional contribution (CRUT).

▶ The donor chooses the amount of the payment (generally, a percentage of the initial gift amount or value of assets).

▶ The trustee can tailor the investment strategy of the CRT and the taxable character of the income to meet the unique needs of the donor.

▶ The donor can choose one or more charitable organizations to share in the trust principal upon termination of the CRT and reserves the right to change any charity.

▶ The donor can change the frequency and timing of the payments (monthly, quarterly, semi-annually, or annually).

▶ The donor can reduce potential estate taxes by removing the assets from his or her estate.

▶ The donor can avoid/mitigate capital gains tax by funding the trust with appreciated property.

A CRT can be an excellent strategy to use with illiquid assets, and CRTs come in several varieties. Consider the following example. John and Jane Green, ages 72 and 70, jointly own undeveloped land that is currently valued at $550,000 and has a cost basis (the price they paid for the property) of $70,000. They are in a 35 percent tax bracket, and property taxes run $10,000 per year. They owe nothing on the property and are in a 15 percent capital gains bracket. The property does not produce any income. If they sold the property, the Greens would incur capital gains of $480,000. Therefore, their capital gains tax would be $72,000 if they sold the land.

The Greens learned that they could convert the property to new income with favorable tax benefits using a charitable remainder flip unitrust. They transferred the land to a 5 percent flip unitrust, retaining a joint and survivor income interest. When the land is sold, the trust holding the property "flips" to a regular CRT unitrust and the proceeds from the land sale are reinvested in assets that produce an income for the Greens. When the trust is dissolved, the remaining assets will go to a charity of their choice.

By transferring the land to a flip unitrust, the Greens accomplished the following:

▶ Made an irrevocable gift to one or more of their favorite charities;

▶ Avoided an immediate capital gains tax of $72,000;

▶ Generated new income once the property was sold;

▶ Received a substantial charitable income tax deduction in the year of the transfer; and

▶ Reduced probate expenses and potential estate taxes by removing the property from their probate estates.

Charitable Lead Trust (CLT)

A charitable lead trust is like a mirror image of the charitable remainder trust. In this gift option, a donor transfers property to the lead trust, which pays a percentage of the value of the trust assets, usually for a term of years, to the charity of the donor's choice. At the end of the trust term, the remaining assets in the trust and any growth it has realized are passed onto the donor or his or her designated beneficiaries. Donors use lead trusts to accomplish the following:

▶ Accelerate an income tax charitable deduction for future charitable gifts into the current tax year (qualified grantor lead trust);

▶ Pass property to heirs and beneficiaries at reduced transfer tax cost (qualified nongrantor lead trust); and

▶ Make charitable gifts beyond the federal income tax charitable contribution ceilings.

There are two types of charitable lead trusts: the *grantor lead trust* and the more popular *nongrantor lead trust*. A grantor lead trust provides the donor with a charitable income tax deduction for the present value of the payments the charity is to receive from the trust. The donor continues to be taxed on the income earned by the trust each year — including the amounts distributed to the charity. At the end of the trust term, the trust assets are returned to the donor or other designated beneficiaries. To avoid any negative tax result, lead trust donors often fund grantor trusts with tax-exempt securities.

In the other type of lead trust, a nongrantor trust, the donor is not treated as the owner and neither reports income earned in the trust nor receives an income tax deduction for the charity's lead interest. The goal of a nongrantor lead trust, however, is not to get an income tax deduction, but to significantly reduce or even eliminate either the gift or estate transfer tax on the value of the assets used to fund the trust. Like the grantor lead trust, at the end of this CLT's term, the assets remaining in the trust are distributed, usually to children or grandchildren. Any appreciation of the value of the trust will avoid gift and estate taxes (transfer taxes) when they are eventually received by beneficiaries.

Obviously, a CLT, either a grantor or nongrantor variety, is not for everyone. They require extensive tax and legal expertise, and usually benefit those with serious gift and estate tax considerations. A CLT can be a terrific option if a donor has an income-producing asset that will increase in value over time, the donor does not need the income from the asset, and the donor wants the asset back eventually. Here are some of the CLT advantages:

▶ The donor receives a gift and estate tax deduction for the assets transferred to the trust (qualified grantor lead trust).

▶ CLT property can be transferred to the ultimate beneficiaries at a low transfer cost.

▶ Appreciation of the value of the trust will avoid gift and estate taxes (transfer taxes) when eventually received by the beneficiary (nongrantor lead trust).

▶ Management of transferred assets can be carried out by an institutional trustee, such as a bank or trust department.

▶ It is the best option if the donor has a moderate to large taxable estate.

▶ The trust will hold assets with growth and income potential outside of the donor's estate.

▶ The donor desires to pass certain assets to heirs or keep them in his or her estate, but also has charitable intent and wants to benefit his or her favorite charity.

Retained Life Estate Deed: Personal Residence or Farm

You can donate your personal residence, farm, or vacation home to the charity of your choice while retaining the right to live on and use the property for life, or for a fixed term of years. This arrangement is called a *retained life estate*. In exchange for this type of planned gift, you receive an immediate income tax deduction. The amount depends on the value of the property and your age (and the age of any other person given life use). In addition, you retain the right to rent your home or make improvements to it. You continue to have responsibility for maintenance, insurance, and property taxes. The advantages of this type of planned gift could be attractive for a donor who does not plan to leave the property to his or her heirs, who has taxable income and could benefit from a charitable deduction, and who wants to benefit his or her favorite charity. Here is a list of the benefits of making a retained life estate gift:

▶ The donor receives an immediate income tax deduction for the value of the property minus the present value of the retained life estate.

▶ The donor can retain full use of the property during his or her lifetime.

▶ The donor can reduce gift and estate taxes that would be owed by his or her heirs by removing assets from his or her probate estate.

▶ The donor can make a gift now, while retaining the right to use the property.

▶ The donor can immediately benefit a charity of his or her choice.

Obviously, this type of gift will work best for donors who have no plans or desire to pass their residence, farm, or vacation home to their heirs, or who have no heirs to whom they wish to leave the property.

Here's an example of how a retained life estate gift works. Ellen, aged 65, a widow, deeds her home to XYZ Charity, though she plans to live there for the rest of her life. The market value of the property is $200,000 (the house, $160,000, and the land, $40,000). Using the required IRS table to discount the gift based on Ellen's life expectancy and future depreciation of the house, her accountant determines her income tax deduction to be in excess of $70,000, which she can take the year of her gift, plus she can carry over any excess deduction over an additional five tax years. Ellen remains in the property until her death or she moves, and retains all incidents of ownership.

18-4. Conclusion

Hopefully, this chapter has enticed you to think about your giving nature and brought about such questions as: Do I want to give to charity? Can I afford to give? How much should I give? Is my charity worthy of a gift? What about my heirs? In the event that you have come to a "Heart and Head" conclusion that charitable giving, especially the gift of a legacy, is something you would like to pursue, the options that gift planning provide are numerous. Although by no means a complete explanation or listing of all the varieties of planned gifts, we provide here a starting point we hope you will find helpful.

18-5. Resources

In today's society, there are more complexities than Thomas Jefferson could ever have anticipated. Fortunately, modern technology gives us an opportunity to evaluate charitable organizations through a variety of resources. Some of those resources are listed here for your convenience:

Charity Navigator
Charity Navigator, America's premier independent charity evaluator, works to advance a more efficient and responsive philanthropic marketplace by evaluating the financial health of over 5,300 of America's largest charities.
www.charitynavigator.org

U.S. National Better Business Bureau
A project of the BBB Wise Giving Alliance, give.org evaluates charities based on financial and management practices. This is the only major site that names charities that do not meet standards.
www.give.org

JustGive Guide
JustGive maintains a database of screened and approved charities, organized by subject. A good choice for donors more interested in giving to a particular cause rather than a particular charity.
www.justgive.org

American Institute of Philanthropy Charity Watch

This website provides names and ratings for top-rated charities only. Lesser-rated organizations can be found in their print publication, "Charity Rating Guide."

    www.charitywatch.org/toprated.html

GuideStar

The idea here is to provide enough information for donors to make their own judgments. The database includes all IRS-registered tax-deductible charities, comprising over 700,000 organizations. Some listings do not provide full data. You can find interesting information on this site, such as charity CEO and director salaries.

    www.guidestar.org

American Red Cross

For over 130 years, Red Cross volunteers have been guided by a single principle: to help people in need, regardless of race, religion, gender, or national origin. The Red Cross has been there, and will continue to be there, for disaster victims in need of food, clothing, and shelter.

    www.redcross.org

Network for Good

Network for Good is an e-philanthropy site where individuals can donate, volunteer, and get involved with the issues they care about.

    www.networkforgood.org

---

* The Office of Gift Planning at CSU cultivates, designs, facilitates, and stewards planned gifts to the University, and works with donors who contribute non-cash gifts (appreciated stocks, real estate, etc.). In our efforts, we use a variety of financial tools and techniques for giving, including bequests, charitable gift annuities, charitable remainder trusts, and charitable lead trusts. All planned gifts require the assistance of one or more qualified specialists: an attorney, certified public accountant, estate planning specialist, trust officer, and/or an insurance agent can be involved as we work with donors to accomplish their charitable goals.

In addition, we provide education to our donors through marketing and outreach efforts that include advertisements, publications, brochures, website information, e-newsletters, public speaking presentations, and the like. We consider it absolutely essential to make our office a resource for folks who are contemplating a deferred gift or have any questions concerning their estate planning goals. Additionally, we supply technical expertise to our colleagues in the development staff and work closely with them if they have a donor who is considering a planned gift.

Chapter 19

Estate Planning For Non-Traditional Families

Elizabeth A. Bryant, Esq.
Elizabeth A. Bryant, P.C.

Erica Johnson, Esq.
Ambler & Keenan, LLC

Elizabeth Mitchell, Esq.
Ambler & Keenan, LLC

SYNOPSIS

19-1. Estate Planning Issues for Non-Traditional Families

Estate planning is a term that is often misunderstood. In this article, it means not only planning for health and financial issues that may arise during life, but also planning for the distribution of assets at death. Estate planning is important for everyone, but it is especially important for those in the lesbian, gay, bisexual, and transgender (LGBT) community and those opposite sex couples who choose not to marry (collectively referred to as "partners"). Where the law does not recognize one's committed relationship, the need to proactively plan is paramount.

The State of Same-Sex Marriage in our State

Same-sex couples are currently allowed to marry in many countries around the world. In the United States, same-sex marriages are legal in Massachusetts, Connecticut, Iowa, New Hampshire, New York, Vermont, Washington, the District of Columbia, and the Indian nations in Washington state and Oregon. In addition, approximately 18,000 marriages were performed in California in 2008 before a legal challenge was made, the final outcome of which is still pending.

California, Delaware, New Jersey, Oregon, Nevada, and Illinois have some form of domestic partnerships or civil unions.

Maine, Maryland, and Wisconsin have laws that provide some of the same rights as marriage for same-sex couples.

Hawaii has reciprocal beneficiaries contracts that are similar to Colorado's Designated Beneficiary Agreements, which are explained in section 19-4.

Maryland and Rhode Island recognize same-sex marriages performed in other states.

However, *none* of these marriages, domestic partnerships, or civil unions are legally recognized in Colorado. Currently, Colorado's constitution provides that a marriage in Colorado is recognized legally only if the marriage is between one man and one woman. No same-sex marriages are recognized in Colorado.

Common Law Marriage

Opposite sex couples that choose not to marry often have questions about whether or not they are in a common law marriage. There is a discussion of common law marriage in Chapter 13, "Family Relationships."

Reasons People Do Not Complete Estate Plans

The reasons people do not do estate planning are usually the same for all communities, whether traditional or non-traditional. Not understanding the process, procrastination, believing that one doesn't have enough assets to require planning, or the feeling that "it isn't going to happen to me," are just a few of the reasons that are often heard.

What Happens When There Is No Estate Plan

Before deciding *not* to do any estate planning, it is important to understand what can happen if no estate planning is done. Following are some examples of what can happen if there are no estate planning documents in place.

If There is No Durable Power of Attorney for Property in Place

If someone in Colorado is unable to make his or her own financial decisions, and there is no durable power of attorney for property (also called a durable financial power of attorney) that names a person to act on his or her behalf, a court must appoint what is known as a conservator. Who the court will appoint is governed by Colorado law. In general, the priority list for appointment of a conservator is as follows:

1) A spouse;

2) A person designated in a Designated Beneficiary Agreement (discussed in section 19-4);

3) Parents;

4) Adult children; or

5) An adult the person has lived with for the past six months.

While it is possible for a non-married partner to be appointed conservator using the priority shown above, the other people with higher priority may object. Even though the partner has the legal ability to apply to the court to be appointed conservator, there is a mandated review process and court hearing that must still be completed before a conservator is appointed. Once appointed, the conservator must make annual reports to the court. The delay and expense associated with the conservatorship process can be avoided with the execution of a durable financial power of attorney, which appoints the partner to make financial decisions. Durable financial powers of attorney are discussed in more detail in section 19-3.

If There is No Will or Trust in Place

When someone dies without a will or a trust, and has assets in their name (those that are not jointly owned and those without a beneficiary designation or payable on death designation), what happens with these assets is determined by Colorado law according to what are called the intestacy statutes. Probate is required to distribute these assets. Colorado's intestacy statutes list to whom the assets are to be distributed under probate, in the following order:

1) A spouse;

2) A person granted the right to inherit under a Designated Beneficiary Agreement (see section 19-4);

3) Issue (children or descendants of deceased children);

4) Parents;

5) Siblings or descendants of deceased siblings; or

6) Grandparents or descendants of deceased grandparents.

Not included in the list are a partner, a favorite charity, or a best friend. If a person does not want the intestacy statutes to say what will happen to their assets, a Will or a Trust is needed.

I Only Have Personal Property Items

Many times, people feel as though they do not have an "estate" so they do not need to do an "estate plan." However, this is a trap for those in non-traditional relationships. Even if your estate is made up only of the tangible personal items you and your partner have accumulated over the years, you need to create a plan for where those items are to go upon your death. With a legally recognized marriage between a man and a woman, when one spouse dies, all of the tangible items are presumed to be owned jointly, and therefore they automatically transfer to the surviving spouse. In a non-traditional relationship that does not qualify as a legal marriage, this is not the case. When a partner dies, his or her tangible personal items do not transfer automatically to the surviving partner. They transfer under the intestacy laws, often to the deceased partner's children, parents, or siblings. This can be very distressing to the surviving partner, and is probably not what the deceased partner wanted. A will or a Designated Beneficiary Agreement can avoid this scenario.

I Own Everything Jointly With My Partner

When two partners own an asset in joint tenancy, if one of them dies, the entire asset transfers to the surviving partner. This transfer by operation of law at one partner's death may seem like the easiest answer to many partners' concerns. However, there are a number of issues and potential problems that can arise when using joint tenancy.

These issues surface primarily where one partner owns an asset and wishes to change the sole ownership to joint ownership with his or her partner. As an example, let's look at the concerns where one partner owns a home, and wants to put his or her partner on the title as a joint owner. The following considerations must be addressed.

Partners are not allowed to make unlimited, tax-free gifts to each other the way that spouses are allowed under federal law. If Partner A owns the home and adds Partner B to the property title, Partner A has made a gift of one-half of the equity in that property to Partner B. If that gift is over the annual gift exclusion amount (currently $13,000), Partner A is required to file a gift tax return with the IRS. If partners are considering any type of transfer between them, they should consult with their tax professional before doing so.

Most mortgages in this country have a "due on transfer" clause. If the owner transfers any interest in the property to someone not on the mortgage without the mortgage company's permission, the lender can demand full payment of the mortgage debt immediately. There is a federal law called Garn St. Germaine that exempts such transfers between spouses, but this does not apply to partners. Partners need to check with their mortgage company before transferring the ownership of property from one partner to both partners.

Adding a partner to the title of property as a gift may also cause unfavorable capital gains tax issues.

If a property transfers to the surviving partner automatically at the death of the first partner, the first partner's children or other family and friends will not receive any of the property when the surviving partner dies, unless the surviving partner makes a will or trust or otherwise provides that the property will be split between both partners' families at the second partner's death. This can be an unintended consequence of owning a property as joint tenants.

In summary, transfers and gifts should not be made before consulting with a tax and/or legal professional familiar with these issues.

19-2. Colorado and Federal Laws Affecting Non-Traditional Families

Second Parent Adoption

As of 2007, Colorado allows second parent adoptions. In a second parent adoption, it is not necessary for the two parents to be married to each other, as is the case with stepparent adoptions. Therefore, two partners can now both be the legal parents of a child. The result is that both partners will have the same rights and obligations associated with being a parent under Colorado law.

In order to seek a second parent adoption, the child must have only one sole legal parent, and that parent must consent to the adoption. If the second parent is found by the court to qualify to adopt, the end result will be a new birth certificate for the child naming two mothers or two fathers.

State Employee Domestic Partner Benefits

Colorado now offers domestic partner benefits to same-sex partners of state employees. These domestic partner benefits do not apply to opposite-sex partners. The partner must be over the age of eighteen and must be the same sex as the state employee. The partners must have shared an exclusive committed relationship for at least one year, and they must have the intent that their relationship will last indefinitely. The two must not be related by blood, and neither of them can be married to another person. For information about the benefits offered and the procedure for obtaining those benefits, employees should speak with their specific employers.

One item of note is that employees should also speak with their tax professionals prior to enrolling their partners for benefits. As with all same-sex partners insuring their partners, if the employer is paying for the benefits, the value of the benefits is taxable income to the employee partner.

Employment Non-Discrimination

Colorado has added sexual orientation, real or perceived, to the list of characteristics for which a person may not be discriminated against at work. This includes areas of hiring, firing, harassment, and compensation. Additionally, the definition of sexual orientation was written to include one's gender status. If someone believes they have been a victim of discrimination based on their sexual orientation or gender status, they should contact a qualified employment law attorney. The LGBT Center of Colorado has a legal helpline for issues of employment discrimination based on sexual orientation, gender identity or gender bias, and HIV status (call (303) 282-6524 to reach this helpline).

Pension Protection Act

In the past, if a partner died and left his or her 401(k), 403(b), or 457 plan to his or her partner (or any non-spouse), the surviving partner, rather than having the opportunity to withdraw the proceeds over his or her life expectancy, had to withdraw the 401(k) proceeds immediately, or in some cases, over a five year period. In many instances, this created a major income tax burden on the surviving partner in the year(s) in which the money had to be withdrawn.

With the passing of the Pension Protection Act and additional IRS action in 2010, custodians of these types of retirement plans must now allow a non-spouse beneficiary, such as a partner, to make a direct trustee-to-trustee transfer of the retirement plan proceeds to an inherited IRA. If done correctly, the surviving partner would then be allowed to spread the distributions from that inherited IRA out over his or her life expectancy, thereby spreading out the income tax burden over that same time period.

It is important to note that there are several traps that could be triggered if this process is not carried out correctly. Therefore, if a surviving partner is due to inherit his or her deceased partner's retirement plan, he or she should contact a tax advisor prior to taking action to claim the plan proceeds.

Federal Estate Tax

The federal estate tax is a tax on a deceased person's estate if the estate is over the limit set by federal law for the year in which the person died. In 2012, that limit is $5,000,000. Under current law, the limit is set to go down to $1,000,000 per person on January 1, 2013. The details of estate taxes are beyond the scope of this chapter. However, one area of frustration to those in same-sex relationships is that they are not able to benefit from what is known as the unlimited marital deduction.

As a married couple, federal law allows a spouse to leave an unlimited amount to his or her spouse at death, without the estate being subject to estate tax. The limits set forth above do not apply if the estate is being left to a spouse. Same-sex marriages are not recognized by federal law, and therefore, when a partner dies, his or her estate will be subject to the estate tax if it is over the estate tax limit. Additionally, if the estate is given to the surviving partner, and that partner is then over the estate tax limit at his or her death, the estate will be taxed again. Unless the federal government recognizes same-sex marriages, this unlimited marital deduction will not be available to same-sex partners, even if they are legally married in another country or in a U.S. state that recognizes same-sex marriages.

19-3. Important Documents

Wills or Trusts

A thorough overview of wills and trusts is provided in Chapter 15, "Estate Planning: Wills, Trusts, and Your Property." For the purposes of those in the LGBT community and those who are in non-married partnerships, the importance of having a will or a trust is based on the fact that the laws that apply when someone dies without a will or trust (intestacy laws) do not provide for one's partner or for charitable gifts. Colorado's intestacy laws are described in section 19-1.

Durable Power of Attorney for Property

A durable power of attorney for property (also called a financial power of attorney) allows a person (the principal) to appoint someone else (the agent) to make financial decisions for the principal. When referring to a power of attorney, the word "durable" means that the document remains valid during any period that the principal is incapacitated. There are non-durable powers of attorney. However, when the power of attorney is not durable, if the principal becomes incapacitated, the document is no longer effective, and the agent has no power to make decisions. Therefore, in most cases, a durable power of attorney is appropriate.

A good power of attorney should not only appoint a primary agent, but should appoint a successor agent, and, if possible, a back-up to the successor agent. Then, if the primary agent is unable or unwilling to act, the next agent can take over, and if the next agent is unable to act, the second successor agent can take over.

The document should set out when the power of attorney will become effective. There are three primary ways a power of attorney will become effective:

1) The power of attorney may be effective only upon the incapacity of the principal. Therefore, if the principal is not incapacitated, the agent has no power. In this case, the power of attorney document must define how incapacity is to be determined. In most cases, this can be done by a court determination, or upon obtaining the written opinion of a doctor or doctors that the principal lacks the capacity to handle his or her own financial affairs. If the power of attorney is valid upon incapacity, the agent will also need a HIPAA release in order to obtain a doctor's statement that the principal is incapacitated (HIPAA releases are explained below).

2) The power of attorney may be effective at the time the principal signs it. In this instance, the agent can act on behalf of the principal as soon as the power of attorney is signed by the principal.

3) The power of attorney may also be a hybrid power of attorney. This type of power of attorney provides that if the agent is the spouse or partner, the powers are granted immediately, but as to the successor or second-successor agent, the powers are not granted unless the principal become incapacitated.

In 2010, Colorado passed a law that potentially limits the powers of an agent who is not a spouse, descendant, or ancestor of the principal. Therefore, it is important that a power of attorney appointing an agent who is not a spouse, descendent, or ancestor of the principal be reviewed and possibly updated to comply with the new law.

Finally, many powers of attorney for property nominate the appointed agent as the court-appointed conservator in the event the principal would need a court-appointed conservator.

Medical Power of Attorney

A medical or healthcare power of attorney allows a person (the principal) to appoint someone else (the agent) to make medical decisions for the principal in the event the principal is unable to make such decisions for himself or herself.

As with a financial power of attorney, a medical power of attorney should name successor and second successor agents if possible.

Some medical powers of attorney cover the issue of whether the agent may make organ donations for the principal upon death. Additionally, many nominate the appointed agent as the court-appointed guardian, in the event the principal would need a court-appointed guardian.

When the agent appointed is not a blood relative, the power of attorney should specifically state that the agent will be able to visit the principal in any healthcare facility. President Obama signed a presidential memorandum banning discrimination against hospital visitors based on sexual orientation. However, it is still the best practice to specifically include such visitation rights in the medical power of attorney.

Living Wills

A living will is also referred to as an advance directive. A living will is designed to allow the principal to state his or her directions with regard to whether he or she would like to have life-sustaining procedures implemented or continued in the event the principal is declared to have a terminal condition or be in a persistent vegetative state.

Colorado's living will statute provides that two physicians must determine, in writing, that the principal is terminally ill or in a persistent vegetative state. If that determination is made, then the living will directs the physicians to carry out the principal's wishes regarding life-sustaining procedures. Some living wills direct that a certain number of days must pass where the principal is unable to effectively receive or evaluate information or communicate decisions before any decision is made to withdraw life-sustaining procedures, and some living wills direct that life-sustaining procedures should never be withdrawn. A living will also allows the principal to state his or her wishes with regard to whether artificial nutrition and hydration are to continue, if they are the only procedure still being provided.

The living will is legally binding on healthcare providers, and can diminish the possibility of a battle concerning such issues between the principal's partner and the principal's family of origin.

Declaration of Last Remains

A declaration of last remains allows the principal to make a legally binding written statement regarding what is to happen to his or her last remains. Burial or cremation are the two most common directions. The declaration also allows the principal to appoint an agent and successor agents to have the burial or cremation carried out. Under Colorado law, such written statement, signed by the principal, is legally binding on the funeral home. As with so many other statutes, the law regarding last remains declarations provides a list of agents that have the power to make such decisions if someone dies without having made a written statement regarding their wishes. The priority list to be able to make these decisions does not include a committed partner. It is as follows:

1) Personal representative;

2) Spouse;

3) The person granted such power in a Designated Beneficiary Agreement;

4) A majority of adult children;

5) A majority of parents and guardians;

6) A majority of siblings; or

7) Anyone that will take on the responsibility.

In order to ensure that a partner is able to make these decisions, a written statement signed by the principal should be used. The statement need not be in a separate document; it may be a part of another document, such as a will or power of attorney.

HIPAA Release

The Health Insurance Portability and Accountability Act of 1996 (HIPAA), a federal law, provides that doctors and other healthcare providers may not share a patient's medical information or medical records with anyone other than the patient. This can be very problematic if the patient has family or friends that need such information. While spouses are not exempt from HIPAA privacy laws, it is sometimes the case in practical settings that healthcare professionals will share medical information about a patient with his or her spouse. Since same-sex couples are not allowed to marry under the laws of Colorado, this willingness to share information does not always extend to unmarried partners. Therefore, any thorough estate plan needs to include a HIPAA release, allowing the release of medical records and information to the partner, and other friends or family members, if desired.

19-4. Colorado's Designated Beneficiary Agreement

A New Estate Planning Tool

Another estate planning tool for Colorado citizens who are not married is a document called a Designated Beneficiary Agreement (DBA). The adoption of DBAs in Colorado became effective on July 1, 2009. A DBA permits unmarried adults to give each other certain rights and appoint each other for certain roles. This section will explain the requirements for making a valid and enforceable DBA, discuss what rights the DBA can confer, and discuss what must be done to revoke or override the rights conferred in a DBA. It will also explain the benefits of a DBA, as well as point out its significant limitations.

Although a DBA has been generally viewed as an estate planning tool for non-traditional couples (same-sex couples who cannot marry and opposite-sex couples who choose not to marry), its application is much broader and can include unmarried friends and relatives, such as an unmarried parent and his or her unmarried adult child.

Who Can Enter Into a DBA and What Makes a DBA Valid and Enforceable?

First, there can only be two parties to a DBA, and both parties must satisfy *all* of the following criteria: both must be at least eighteen years of age, both must be competent to enter into a contract, and both must enter into the DBA without force, fraud, or duress. Additionally, neither party may be married to anyone, and neither party may be a party to another DBA with a different person.

If both parties meet all of the criteria listed in the previous paragraph, then additional criteria must be satisfied. The DBA form must be in "substantial compliance" with the standard form set forth in the Colorado statutes. It must also be properly completed, signed, acknowledged by a notary, and recorded with the county clerk and recorder in a county where one of the parties to the DBA resides. A copy of a DBA form is included as Exhibit 19B, and a downloadable DBA can be found online at www.designatedbeneficiaries.org.

What does "substantial compliance" mean? A DBA is in substantial compliance if it includes the disclaimer contained in the box at the top of the DBA form in Exhibit 19B, the instructions and headings about how to grant or withhold a right or protection, the statements about the effective date of the DBA and how to record the agreement, and the notarized signatures of the two parties. If the DBA does not contain all of these requirements it may be invalid, so you should either use the form provided in Exhibit 19B or go online to print and complete the form from www.designatedbeneficiaries.org.

What Rights Can Be Conveyed With a DBA?

There are sixteen distinct rights and protections set forth in a DBA. Six of the rights listed on the DBA are rights that people already have under Colorado law, with or without a DBA. These are the right to: (1) jointly acquire, own, and transfer title to property; (2) be designated as a beneficiary in a will, trust, or for non-probate transfers; (3) be designated as a beneficiary and recognized as a dependent in a life insurance policy; (4) be designated as a beneficiary and recognized as a dependent in a health insurance policy (if the health insurance policy is an employer-sponsored group plan, check if the employer allows such coverage); (5) be designated as a beneficiary in a retirement or pension plan; and (6) act as a proxy decision-maker or surrogate regarding medical decisions.

Eight of the rights are statutory rights that are usually given in a will, trust, or medical power of attorney, and can now be given in a DBA. These are the right to: (1) inherit real or personal property from the other designated beneficiary when there is no valid will or trust; (2) petition and have priority for appointment as personal representative, guardian, or conservator for the other designated beneficiary; (3) visit the other designated beneficiary in a hospital, nursing home, hospice, or similar care facility; (4) initiate a formal complaint regarding alleged violations of the other designated beneficiary's rights as a nursing home patient; (5) receive notice of withholding or withdrawal of life-sustaining procedures from the other designated beneficiary; (6) challenge the validity of a living will of the other designated beneficiary; (7) act as agent for the other designated beneficiary to make, revoke, or object to anatomical gifts; and (8) direct the disposition of last remains of the other designated beneficiary.

The remaining two rights are new statutory rights that, until July 1, 2009, were only available to a spouse or dependent children. These are the right to: (1) have standing to receive benefits pursuant to the Workers' Compensation Act of Colorado in event of the death of the other designated beneficiary while on the job; and (2) have standing to sue for the wrongful death of the other designated beneficiary.

Know the Rights You Are Granting and Carefully Complete the DBA Form

You need to know that a DBA is presumed to grant all of the rights listed in the statutory form *unless* the parties to the DBA explicitly withhold a right or protection. If there are some rights that you *do not* want to give the other party, you *must* withhold the rights by initialing the line in the form next to the right to be withheld. As with any document that grants legal rights, it is essential for you to carefully and fully complete the form.

When is a DBA Effective?

Currently, a DBA is effective as of the date and time received for recording by the county clerk and recorder of the county where one of the designated beneficiaries resides. A DBA can be delivered or mailed, along with a filing fee in cash or check. The clerk and recorder must issue two certified copies of the DBA showing the date and time the office received the DBA for recording. The filing fee will vary with each county, so you should call the clerk in advance to find out the amount of the check to include. It is also a good idea to include a pre-addressed and stamped envelope for the return of the document to you.

Can a Valid DBA be Revoked or Terminated?

There are several ways to revoke or terminate a valid DBA. One way is when one of the designated beneficiaries unilaterally records a Revocation of Designated Beneficiary Agreement form (revocation) with the county clerk and recorder of the county where the DBA was originally filed. A copy of a revocation form is included as Exhibit 19C. Revocation is effective as of the date and time the revocation is received for recording by the county clerk and recorder. The clerk is to issue a certified copy of the revocation to the designated beneficiary recording the revocation and must mail a certified copy of the revocation to the other designated beneficiary at that party's last-known address.

Another way to revoke a valid DBA, or a portion of a valid DBA, is for a designated beneficiary to sign a legal document that conflicts with all or a portion of the DBA, such as a will or a beneficiary designation form for a life insurance policy. A DBA is revoked upon the marriage of either of the designated beneficiaries. A valid DBA is also terminated upon the death of a designated beneficiary; however, a right or power conferred upon the living designated beneficiary survives the death of the deceased designated beneficiary. Thereafter, the surviving designated beneficiary may enter into a new DBA with a different person, as long as the other requirements of the law stated above in "Who Can Enter Into a DBA and What Makes a DBA Valid and Enforceable?" are met.

What Is the Effect of a DBA on Any Existing Estate Planning Documents I Have?

A DBA does not override documents you may already have, or subsequently enter into, such as a will, trust, medical power of attorney, or a beneficiary designation under a life insurance policy or retirement asset. Said another way, a valid legal document entered into before or after a DBA is recorded that conflicts with all or a portion of the DBA causes the DBA, in whole or in part, to be replaced or set aside.

If I Have a DBA Do I Need Other Estate Planning Documents?

It is essential to understand that a DBA does not replace the need to prepare other estate planning documents. The DBA is a Colorado document and it is unclear whether it will be honored out of the state of Colorado, so if you travel outside the state, you still need documents such as a medical power of attorney. Be aware that a DBA is limited in scope, as it only allows a party to name one decision-maker, whereas a medical power of attorney names successor agents. Additionally, the DBA does not appoint an agent to handle the financial affairs of the other designated beneficiary, so having a current financial power of attorney is essential if you want someone to be able to make financial decisions for you. Finally, while the DBA does provide intestacy rights between the two parties, it cannot provide for the simultaneous death of both parties.

If I Have Other Estate Planning Documents, Why Would I Want a DBA?

One reason is that a DBA is the only way for two unmarried persons to seek workers' compensation benefits if either of them dies at work. Another reason is that a DBA may give both parties the right to sue for the wrongful death of the other designated beneficiary. If you are in an opposite-sex relationship, you might want a DBA to provide evidence that you are not in a common law marriage.

Does Having a DBA Mean that I Don't Have to Do Anything Else with My Assets?

A DBA does not automatically designate the other party as a beneficiary of contractual benefits, such as life insurance or retirement assets, or create co-ownership of real estate. If you want the other party to a DBA to be the designated beneficiary of your life insurance or retirement assets, you *must* complete and sign a separate beneficiary designation form for those assets. If you want the other party to a DBA to be a current co-owner of any property you own, you need to add that person to the title of the property. You should seek help from an attorney to make sure it is done correctly or you may cause problems with the title, which a court may have to correct. Be aware that adding someone to the title of your property may have unintended tax consequences.

What Happens at the Death of a Party to a Valid, Unrevoked DBA?

If the deceased party to the DBA has given the right of intestate succession to the other party, then that surviving party is technically an heir of the deceased party, and has the right to challenge a will or trust document of the deceased party. If the personal representative has actual notice or actual knowledge that there is a valid, unrevoked DBA in existence, the surviving party must be identified as an heir on the documents submitted to the court to open the deceased party's probate, and must be notified if a probate is opened. The personal representative will also need to search the county clerk and recorder's records in any county where the personal representative has actual knowledge that the deceased party was domiciled for the three years prior to the deceased party's death, to determine whether there is a valid, unrevoked DBA in existence.

So Should I Prepare and Sign a DBA?

A DBA is an additional estate planning tool for Colorado citizens who are not married, and may be a document you should prepare. But, it does not provide all of the protections and benefits most people need, both during lifetime and after death, and should not be relied on as the only document you need to have. It is really a document to reinforce the other life and estate planning documents (powers of attorney, wills, and trusts) you should have in place to ensure your wishes are known and can be legally enforced.

19-5. Medicaid Issues Unique to Unmarried Couples

Medicaid regulations establish eligibility requirements for single persons and married couples qualifying for Medicaid, but do not address unmarried couples or LGBT couples applying for Medicaid. As a result, persons applying for Medicaid who are part of an unmarried couple or an LGBT couple are treated as single individuals. There are several additional factors about which partners should be concerned when it comes to resources (assets), gifting, income, and estate recovery.

Resource Requirements

Medicaid regulations divide assets into two categories: countable assets and exempt assets. Exempt assets include the principal residence (with equity of up to $525,000), one automobile, household goods and personal effects, the cash value of life insurance policies if the face value does not exceed $1,500, cemetery plots, and irrevocable pre-paid burial and funeral plans. All other assets are countable, and an individual is limited to $2,000 in countable assets.

When a married person is applying for Medicaid in order to pay for care in a skilled nursing or assisted living facility and that person's spouse remains at home, the spouse at home is known as the "community spouse." The community spouse can keep a total of $113,640 in countable assets. See Chapter 2, "Medicaid," for more information.

If the individual applying for Medicaid benefits is part of an unmarried or LGBT couple, often his or her assets are held jointly with the partner. This presents a problem for Medicaid planning because jointly held assets count towards the $2,000 resource limitation for an individual. As a result, the assets must be separated and held individually by each partner.

Under Medicaid regulations, the presumption is that the joint assets are owned equally by each partner. During the Medicaid process, this could result in a substantial loss of assets for the partner not needing Medicaid benefits, because half of the assets will be transferred to the Medicaid applicant and may be spent on skilled nursing care. If the partner not needing Medicaid benefits can prove that he or she contributed more than half of the assets to the joint account, it is possible to divide the account based on the amount of the contribution. Either way, the assets will need to be titled differently, and the couple should be advised about the Medicaid and tax implications of changing title on assets.

Gifting

Most assets held by unmarried and LGBT couples are held jointly. If a Medicaid applicant simply removes his or her name from a joint account, it constitutes a gift for Medicaid purposes. The problem with making such a gift, or transfer, is that any gift made within five years of applying for Medicaid (otherwise known as the look-back period) will trigger an ineligibility period (a period of time that Medicaid will not pay for care).

If an account is held jointly by a married couple, removing the name of the Medicaid recipient does not trigger an ineligibility period. Therefore, it is important that unmarried and LGBT couples understand that re-titling assets could cause an ineligibility period for Medicaid and plan for a way to pay for the cost of skilled nursing care during the ineligibility period.

Income

When a Medicaid recipient is receiving care in a facility, all of his or her income is paid to the facility each month except for that recipient's personal needs allowance of $50. If the Medicaid recipient is married, a portion of the Medicaid recipient's income can be transferred to the community spouse each month to assist with the expenses of the spouse who is still living at home. This amount transferred to the community spouse each month is known as the minimum monthly maintenance needs allowance (MMMNA). However, Medicaid regulations do not allow for such a transfer of income from the Medicaid recipient to the non-married partner who does not need Medicaid benefits.

The inability to transfer a portion of the Medicaid recipient's income to the partner still living at home can create a problem for that partner if his or her income is not enough to cover the monthly expenses. The couple is essentially changing from a two-income family to a single income family, which may force the partner not needing Medicaid benefits to sell the primary residence or reduce or eliminate expenses.

Estate Recovery

Upon the death of the Medicaid recipient, the Colorado Department of Health Care Policy and Financing will recover against the Medicaid recipient's estate in an effort to be repaid for the benefits paid to the Medicaid recipient. If the Medicaid recipient is married, there are spousal impoverishment protections that prevent Medicaid from recovering against the primary residence. However, no such protections are in place for non-married or LGBT couples. Depending on how the primary residence is titled (in joint tenancy or tenancy-in-common), this could create a situation where the partner not needing Medicaid is forced to sell the primary residence to pay what is owed to Medicaid.

While federal regulations allow the states to provide an exception to estate recovery if there is an unmarried or GLBT partner living in the primary residence, the states are not required to grant that exception.

Medicaid is an extremely complicated area of the law for anyone, but especially for those who are not married. A legal professional with expertise in Medicaid should be consulted as early as possible when planning for Medicaid in order to avoid many of the pitfalls summarized above.

19-6. Resources

Administration on Aging
www.aoa.gov/AoARoot/AoA_Programs/Tools_Resources/diversity.aspx#LGBT

American Society on Aging
LGBT Aging Issues Network (LAIN)
71 Stevenson St., Ste. 1450
San Francisco, CA 94105-2938
(800) 537-9728
(415) 974-9600
www.asaging.org/lain

DRCOG
Ombudsman Office: LGBT Training/Project Visibility for Assisted Living and Nursing Homes. Publishes an LGBT Elder Resource Guide.
Denver Regional Council of Governments
(303) 455-1000
www.drcog.org/documents/LGBT_ElderResourceGuide.pdf

Family Caregiver Alliance
LGBT Caring Community Program and Online Support Group.
    785 Market St., Ste. 750
    San Francisco, CA 94103
    (415) 434-3388
    (800) 445-8106
    www.caregiver.org

To subscribe to the LGBT Caregiver Online Support Group, visit:
    http://lists.caregiver.org/mailman/listinfo/lgbt-caregiver_lists.caregiver.org

Gay and Lesbian Medical Association
    1326 18th St. NW, Ste. 22
    Washington, DC 20036
    (202) 600-8037
    info@glma.org
    www.glma.org

Lambda Legal Defense Fund
    National Headquarters
    120 Wall St., 19th Fl.
    New York, NY 10005-3904
    (212) 809-8585
    www.lambdalegal.org

National Center for Lesbian Rights (NCLR)
    870 Market St., Ste. 370
    San Francisco, CA 94102
    (415) 392-6257
    www.nclrights.org

National Resource Center on LGBT Aging, a program of SAGE
    (212) 741-2247
    www.lgbtagingcenter.org

National Gay and Lesbian Task Force
    1325 Massachusetts Ave. NW, Ste. 600
    Washington, DC 20005
    (202) 393-5177
    www.thetaskforce.org/issues/aging

Old Lesbians Organizing for Change (OLOC)
    P.O. Box 5853
    Athens, OH 45701
    (888) 706-7506
    www.oloc.org

Project Visibility: A Training to Understand the Strengths and Needs of LGBT Elders
Audience: assisted living residences, nursing homes, and all senior care providers.
Boulder County Aging Services
www.projectvisibility.org
(303) 441-3583

Services and Advocacy for GLBT Elders (SAGE)
305 Seventh Ave., 6th Fl.
New York City, NY 10001
(212) 741-2247
www.sageusa.org

The Center
*Denver's GLBT community center for over 30 years. Includes programs for LGBT seniors as the
SAGE of the Rockies affiliate.*
1301 E. Colfax Ave.
Denver, CO 80218
(303) 733-7743
www.glbtcolorado.org

Transgender Aging Network
P.O. Box 1272
Milwaukee, WI 53201
(414) 559-2123
www.forge-forward.org/TAN

Other Online Resources and Reports:

▶ www.lgbtlongtermcare.org — Video about concerns about long-term care and the
LGBT community and "Stories from the Field" from the National Senior Citizens Law
Center

▶ www.metlife.com/mmi/research/still-out-still-aging.html#findings

▶ www.thetaskforce.org/downloads/reports/reports/MakeRoomForAll.pdf

▶ www.thetaskforce.org/downloads/reports/reports/CaregivingAmongOlderLGBT.pdf

▶ http://sageusa.org/uploads/Advancing%20Equality%20for%20LGBT%20Elders%
20%5BFINAL%20COMPRESSED%5D.pdf — "Improving the Lives of LGBT Older
Adults," March 2010

Exhibit 19A.
Information from SAGE at The Center

The Center
www.glbtcolorado.org

The Center is proud to recognize and affirm that our community is made up of a wonderful diversity of LGBT people of all ages. Understanding that folks have different interests, strengths, needs, relationships, and resources as they get older, The Center offers programming designed especially for people over 50.

Over the past decade, an active and committed group of advocates has drawn increasing attention to the often neglected issues of growing old as a gay man, a lesbian, a bisexual, or a transgendered person. Gay and Gray in the West was an organization begun very informally that eventually produced three significant conferences in Denver that helped to articulate these issues locally, and that ultimately led to the creation of a full-fledged program at The Center.

In 2009, The Center became an affiliate of SAGE (Services and Advocacy for GLBT Elders), the nation's oldest and largest organization dedicated to the older members of the LGBT community, and our program was officially named SAGE of the Rockies. Our program embodies the principles and values of SAGE as reflected in all we have to offer.

The services offered through SAGE of the Rockies include a variety of exciting, educational, and helpful ways to get involved as an older LGBT adult. Whether planning for the future (housing, finances, legal issues, health care), having a good time (social events, intergenerational opportunities, travel), or finding help when you need it (caregiver support groups, referrals to safe and quality community services, educational presentations), SAGE of the Rockies is here for you.

We know from experience that when we come together and speak as a united voice, we can make things happen to negate the effects of ageism and homophobia. We are a whole generation of change-makers (the 60's, Stonewall, LGBT Pride, response to HIV/AIDS) and we haven't stopped yet. Now we have new fronts needing our attention, like safe places to live and receive care, affordable housing, laws that protect against discrimination and harm, and being treated equally with other older (and married) people when it comes to benefits and service eligibility. SAGE of the Rockies gives us that voice.

SAGE (Services and Advocacy for GLBT Elders) of the Rockies

Imagine you are a 70-year-old GLBT person and you are not completely open about your sexuality and/or gender identity. You have been told for the past 50 years that you are sick, a sinner, depraved, or that you are mentally ill. You are estranged from your family, you do not have children, if you are partnered you do not realize the rights granted to married couples and you are statistically more likely to age alone. You will likely NOT access community services. You are invisible within the GLBT community. You are not afforded many of the protections enjoyed by heterosexual citizens.

This past May, SAGE served an 83-year-old man who had just lost his wife of over 50 years. He cried as he told of his two grown sons in Denver; he knows he is gay and had no idea what his options were. He was invited to join our art therapy group and the Tuesday morning men's coffee group. After several weeks he joined 20+ other SAGE men as they sat and talked about old cars, current events, their children and grandchildren, religion, and places to feel safe. He also joined our Storytelling Through Writing group. In July, this beautiful man marched as a proud military veteran in the annual PrideFest parade. This power of community and affirmation is making a difference in the lives of our GLBT elders every day.

At SAGE we also offer social gatherings, grief groups for surviving partners, a written storytelling opportunity, cultural outings, spirituality and wisdom workshops, coming out support groups, writer's workshops, and more. Work on housing options, legal issues, financial planning, and training health providers and senior agencies about the specific cultural histories of GLBT elders is well under way. With the help of several community partners such as Jewish Family Service, Kaiser Permanente, and the Area Agency on Aging (DRCOG), we are doing important work on behalf of the 50+ GLBT population in Denver and Colorado.

Our mission at SAGE of the Rockies is to build programs to serve the unique needs of the aging GLBT population and to promote successful aging. We hear repeatedly from participants in SAGE programs that they have formed friendships and connections that are improving their quality of life and that we are saving lives.

Exhibit 19B.
Designated Beneficiary Agreement

DESIGNATED BENEFICIARY AGREEMENT

DISCLAIMER

Warning: while this document may indicate your wishes, certain additional documents may be needed to protect these rights.

This designated beneficiary agreement is operative in the absence of other estate planning documents and will be superseded and set aside to the extent it conflicts with valid instruments such as a will, power of attorney, or beneficiary designation on an insurance policy or pension plan. This designated beneficiary agreement is superseded by such other documents and does not cause any changes to be made to those documents or designations.

The parties understand that executing and signing this agreement is not sufficient to designate the other party for purposes of any insurance policy, pension plan, payable upon death designation or manner in which title to property is held and that additional action will be required to make or change such designations.

The parties understand that this designated beneficiary agreement may be one component of estate planning instructions and that they are encouraged to consult an attorney to ensure their estate planning wishes are accomplished.

We, _____, who resides at _____, referred to as Party A,
     (Full Name)   *(Street Address, City, State, Zip)*

and _____, who resides at _____, referred to as Party B,
     (Full Name)   *(Street Address, City, State, Zip)*

hereby designate each other as the other's Designated Beneficiary with the following rights and protections granted or withheld as indicated by our initials:

*To grant one or more of the rights or protections specified in this form,
initial the line to the left of each right or protection you are granting.*

*To withhold a right or protection, initial the line to the right
of each right or protection you are withholding.*

A DESIGNATED BENEFICIARY AGREEMENT SHALL BE PRESUMED TO GRANT ALL OF THE RIGHTS AND PROTECTIONS LISTED IN THIS FORM UNLESS THE PARTIES TO THE AGREEMENT EXPLICITLY EXCLUDE A RIGHT OR PROTECTION.

To **grant** a right or protection, initial:

Party A   Party B

To **withhold** a right or protection, initial:

Party A   Party B

The right to acquire, hold title to, own jointly, or transfer inter vivos or at death real or personal property as a joint tenant with me with right of survivorship or as a tenant in common with me;

The right to be designated by me as a beneficiary, payee, or owner as a trustee named in an inter vivos or testamentary trust for the purposes of a nonprobate transfer on death;

The right to be designated by me as a beneficiary and recognized as a dependent in an insurance policy for life insurance;

The right to be designated by me as a beneficiary and recognized as a dependent in a health insurance policy if my employer elects to provide health insurance coverage for designated beneficiaries;

The right to be designated by me as a beneficiary in a retirement or pension plan;

The right to petition for and have priority for appointment as a conservator, guardian, or personal representative for me;

The right to visit me in a hospital, nursing home, hospice, or similar health care facility in which a party to a designated beneficiary agreement resides or is receiving care;

The right to initiate a formal complaint regarding alleged violations of my rights as a nursing home patient as provided in section 25-1-120, Colorado Revised Statutes;

To grant one or more of the rights or protections specified in this form, initial the line to the left of each right or protection you are granting.

To withhold a right or protection, initial the line to the right of each right or protection you are withholding.

A DESIGNATED BENEFICIARY AGREEMENT SHALL BE PRESUMED TO GRANT ALL OF THE RIGHTS AND PROTECTIONS LISTED IN THIS FORM UNLESS THE PARTIES TO THE AGREEMENT EXPLICITLY EXCLUDE A RIGHT OR PROTECTION.

To **grant** a right or
protection, initial:

Party A   Party B

To **withhold** a right
or protection, initial:

Party A   Party B

_____   _____   The right to act as a proxy decision-maker or surrogate decision-maker to make medical care decisions for me pursuant to section 15-18.5-103 or 15-18.5-104, Colorado Revised Statutes;   _____   _____

_____   _____   The right to notice of the withholding or withdrawal of life-sustaining procedures for me pursuant to section 15-18-107, Colorado Revised Statutes;   _____   _____

_____   _____   The right to challenge the validity of a declaration as to medical or surgical treatment of me pursuant to section 15-18-108, Colorado Revised Statutes;   _____   _____

_____   _____   The right to act as my agent to make, revoke, or object to anatomical gifts involving my person pursuant to the "Revised Uniform Anatomical Gift Act", part 1 of article 34 of title 12, Colorado Revised Statutes;   _____   _____

_____   _____   The right to inherit real or personal property from me through intestate succession;   _____   _____

_____   _____   The right to have standing to receive benefits pursuant to the "Workers' Compensation Act of Colorado", article 40 of title 8, Colorado Revised Statutes, in the event of my death on the job;   _____   _____

_____   _____   The right to have standing to sue for wrongful death in the event of my death; and   _____   _____

_____   _____   The right to direct the disposition of my last remains pursuant to article 19 of title 15, Colorado Revised Statutes.   _____   _____

This Designated Beneficiary Agreement is effective when received for recording by the county clerk and recorder of the county in which one of the designated beneficiaries resides. This Designated Beneficiary Agreement will continue in effect until one of the designated beneficiaries revokes this agreement by recording a Revocation of Designated Beneficiary form with the county clerk and recorder of the county in which this agreement was recorded or until this agreement is superseded in part or in whole by a superseding legal document.

_____   _____
Signature of Designated Beneficiary, Party A   *Signature of Designated Beneficiary, Party B*

_____   _____
Date   *Date*

State of Colorado
County of _____

This document was acknowledged before me on _____.

[SEAL]

My commission expires: _____.

_____
Signature of Notary Public

Exhibit 19C.
Revocation of Designated Beneficiary Agreement

REVOCATION OF
DESIGNATED BENEFICIARY AGREEMENT
This revocation form must be recorded in the same county as the Designated Beneficiary Agreement form it revokes.

I, _____, residing at _____.
 (Full Name)   *(Street Address, City, State, Zip)*

entered into a Designated Beneficiary Agreement on _____, with the following person:
 (Date)

_____, whose last known address is:
 (Full Name)

_____
 (Street Address, City, State, Zip)

in which I designated such person as a Designated Beneficiary. This Designated Beneficiary Agreement was

recorded on _____, in the County of _____.
 (Date)

The indexing file number of the Designated Beneficiary Agreement is _____.

I hereby revoke that Designated Beneficiary Agreement, effective on the date and time that this revocation is received for recording by the Clerk and Recorder of _____ County.

_____   _____
 (Signature)   *(Date)*

State of Colorado
County of _____

This document was acknowledged before me on
_____.   [SEAL]

My commission expires: _____.

_____
 Signature of Notary Public

This revocation of beneficiary agreement was recorded in my office on _____, at _____ o'clock, and pursuant to section 15-22-111, Colorado Revised States, I mailed a copy of this revocation of beneficiary agreement to _____ at the address contained in this revocation of beneficiary agreement.

Clerk and Recorder of _____ County
By: _____

Chapter 20

Reverse Mortgages

Doni Dolfinger
Paulette Wisch, CML
Universal Lending Corporation

SYNOPSIS

Many senior homeowners realize that their greatest financial asset is the equity or money they have accumulated in their homes. If they want to use this money, for whatever reason, they consider either selling the home or borrowing against it. The problem with selling is, they still need a place to live and may not want to rent. The problem with borrowing may be the difficulty in making the mortgage payments. Another option might be a reverse mortgage, which allows the homeowner to live in the home without a monthly repayment to the lender. This often misunderstood option is not as complicated as it is made out to be.

20-1. What Is a Reverse Mortgage?

A reverse mortgage is a special type of mortgage loan designed for homeowners who are 62 years of age and older. It is a loan against the home that does not have to be paid back as long as the homeowner lives in the home.

Proceeds received from a reverse mortgage are considered proceeds of a loan instead of income; therefore, you do not pay income taxes on the money you receive. There are also no restrictions on how you choose to spend your money. A few ideas might be to:

▶ Increase monthly income;

▶ Hire in-home help;

▶ Eliminate a house payment;

▶ Update the home;

▶ Pay off credit cards;

▶ Pay for long-term care insurance; or

▶ Purchase a second home.

20-2. Traditional Mortgage Versus Reverse Mortgage

With a traditional mortgage, you qualify for and borrow a large sum of money based on factors such as your income, job history, and credit worthiness. The lender wants to make sure that you will be able to repay the loan by making monthly installment payments. If payments are not made, the lender can foreclose and you could be forced out of your home.

The reverse mortgage works quite opposite from a traditional loan. You are not required to make monthly payments. Because of this, your income or credit score is not typically a factor in qualifying for the loan. A reverse mortgage is seen truly as a collateral loan, with only one payment required. This payment is made when you move, sell, or die. It can be paid from the sale of the house (the remaining equity goes to you or your heirs) or your heirs may choose to refinance it and keep it.

20-3. Eligibility, Responsibility, and Repayment

When considering a reverse mortgage, it is important to know if you are eligible, how much money you qualify for, and if the programs you are looking at help you accomplish your goal. If your goal is to pay off your $45,000 mortgage and the reverse mortgage provides you with $100,000, you can leave the balance in the line of credit or you can receive payments. If you are short of funds, you may want to wait until the variables are more favorable or you may bring in the difference from other assets or savings.

How Much Money Can I Get With a Reverse Mortgage?

The money that you qualify for is based on the following factors:

▶ The age of the borrower(s);

▶ The current interest rate;

▶ The appraised value of the home; and

▶ The lending limits (on the HECM program).

Eligibility Requirements

▶ ALL homeowners *must* be 62 years or older. At least one of the homeowners must live in the home as his or her principal residence.

▶ All homeowners must agree to attend a one-on-one educational meeting on reverse mortgages with an approved counselor. After speaking with the counselor, you will receive a certificate. Your lender will need the original signed certificate in order to process your loan.

▶ The home must be owned free and clear or have a mortgage balance that can be paid off by the proceeds of the reverse mortgage or by the homeowner. As explained earlier, the homeowner may choose to bring cash in to make up a shortage.

▶ The property can be a single-family home or a one- to four-unit dwelling on most programs.

▶ Townhomes, approved condominium units, planned unit developments (PUDs), and some manufactured homes qualify on most programs.

Responsibilities of the Homeowner

▶ Keep property taxes current.

▶ Maintain adequate homeowners' insurance.

▶ Maintain the property in good condition.

▶ Use the home as your primary residence.

Choices on Your Payment Plans

Although there may be other reverse mortgage products available, the FHA-Insured program (also called a Home Equity Conversion Mortgage, or HECM) has been the most popular nationwide for the past 20 years. An experienced reverse mortgage lender will offer you several options. You choose the one that best fits your needs. With the FHA-Insured program, you are able to adjust your payment plan as your life situation changes. You may change your plan as many times as needed for a small fee of $20 per change. The exception to this is the fixed-rate plan, which is a closed-end loan and cannot be changed.

FHA-Insured Options

▶ *Tenure Payments.* The lender pays you equal monthly payments for as long as at least one homeowner is living in the home. This monthly payment continues even if the loan balance grows higher than the value of the home. (Tenure payments are not available on all programs.)

▶ *Term Payments.* The lender pays you equal monthly payments for a pre-determined period of time. Even after the last payment ends, you still remain the homeowner. No repayment is required for as long as you are living in the home. (Term payments are not available on all programs.)

▶ *Line of Credit.* With a line of credit, you may access your money as needed. The remaining balance in your line of credit grows in value over time. There is no fee to withdraw money from your account. Once your withdrawal request has been made, the lender has five business days to deposit it to your account. (Not all programs have line of credit growth.)

▶ *Initial Draw or Lump-Sum Cash Advance.* Lump-sum withdrawal allows for immediate cash at loan disbursement (three business days after closing). You may choose to draw all or a portion of the money available to you. If you have an existing mortgage or property lien, these would be paid at loan disbursement.

▶ *Combination.* You may choose a combination of the above plans. (Not available on all programs.)

When Is the Reverse Mortgage Repaid?

A reverse mortgage becomes due and payable when the last living homeowner sells, dies, or moves away. If needed, a homeowner can be away from the home for 12 months due to health reasons.

The total loan amount owed is the amount of money the lender has disbursed to you, plus interest and fees accrued during the life of the loan. You, or your estate, are legally required to pay back *only* the balance due on the loan. All money (equity) left after the loan is repaid belongs to you or your estate.

The reverse mortgage is repaid in one payment, either from the sale of the house or by other assets. If the amount owed is more than the sale of the house, *the remaining debt is paid by the insurance fund.* You, or your heirs, have no personal liability.

Interest Rate Information

Reverse mortgages, like traditional mortgages, are tied to a specific index that may be tracked by the public. They are usually based on the LIBOR (London Inter Bank Offering Rate) plus the investor margin. Once your loan closes, changes in interest rates do not affect the amount of money that you originally qualified for. Even if you choose the variable rate option, your payment will only change if you change it. If, for example, you receive $850 a month, you will get that for your chosen term unless you change the plan.

Interest rates are determined by the program. Remember, one size does not fit all. Each program has pros and cons. A knowledgeable lender will be able to explain them so you can make an educated decision about which reverse mortgage would be best for you.

20-4. HECM (Reverse Mortgage) for Purchase

Effective January 1, 2009, the FHA added an HECM (Reverse Mortgage) for Purchase enhancement. HECM stands for Home Equity Conversion Mortgage. HECM mortgagors can now purchase a home with reverse mortgage proceeds. This saves the customer money, as it is a "one close" transaction.

▶ Transactions may be completed on a single-family home, a duplex, a triplex, or a fourplex, so long as the owner lives in the dwelling.

▶ Additional monetary investment must come from cash on hand or from the sale or liquidation of the mortgagor's assets.

▶ The lender must verify the source of all funds.

▶ No bridge loans are allowed.

▶ If the property is new, a Certificate of Occupancy must be issued.

▶ Customers must occupy the property within 60 days of closing.

20-5. HECM Saver

FHA introduced the HECM Saver product in September 2010. The Saver product was designed for the purpose of lowering upfront loan closing costs for borrowers who want to borrow a smaller amount than what would be available with a standard HECM product. In the standard reverse mortgage, the upfront mortgage insurance premium is 2 percent of the value of the home. If the HECM Saver is chosen, the mortgage insurance premium is 0.01 percent. This means that, on a $200,000 home, the premium would drop from $4,000 to $20. On reverse mortgages all fees can be financed into the loan.

The HECM Saver is a great product for people who are concerned about preserving equity and who need a smaller amount of cash.

20-6. Pros and Cons

Pros

▶ You remain in title to the home.

▶ You decide how you would like to spend your money.

▶ There are no monthly payments required. Your lender cannot foreclose on you for non-payment because there is no monthly repayment required.

▶ There is no pre-payment penalty on most reverse mortgages.

▶ A reverse mortgage is an insured loan. You (or your heirs) are guaranteed never to owe more than the value of the home.

▶ There are several choices in how you can receive your money.

▶ The money you receive is considered proceeds of a loan, not income; therefore, it does not affect Medicare, Social Security, SSI, or Medicaid. (Note: It is important to know and follow your benefit program rules to maintain your eligibility for certain programs.)

Cons

▶ Your loan balance gets larger, not smaller, because you are not making payments; however, interest and fees accrue and add to the balance owing. If you want to leave the home free and clear to the heirs, you should not choose a reverse mortgage.

▶ Reverse mortgages may be desirable for someone planning to stay in their home because of the initial costs. The longer you stay, the more cost effective the loan, just like a traditional loan.

▶ There are adjustable and fixed rate reverse mortgages. Obviously, the adjustable rate loans will change according to the program chosen. The fixed rate loan would guarantee the rate for the life of the loan.

▶ The adjustable rate offers many different options to remove proceeds from the loan and interest is charged only on what is taken. If the fixed rate is chosen, all the money must be taken at the time the loan is completed.

20-7. Awareness and Education

Many homeowners have not had a mortgage or loan against their home for many years. It is important to know what to expect from the lender and how to get your questions answered. Gathering information is fairly easy. Classes are often provided on reverse mortgages, free booklets from AARP are available, and, of course, approved counselors are a great resource.

▶ *Counseling.* Counseling is mandatory for all reverse mortgage programs. This is a one-on-one session with an approved counselor to review the legal and financial implications of the reverse mortgage, as well as any other alternatives that may be available. As part of your session, you will be given a Certificate of Borrower Counseling. If you choose to go forward with an application, you must provide the original copy of the certificate to your reverse mortgage lender. This certificate may expire in 180 days.

▶ *Application.* This is when you sign all the paperwork to get the loan started. Typically, your reverse mortgage specialist will meet you at your home or his or her office to explain each page in great detail. You will receive a copy of all the paperwork you sign. If you have completed your counseling, the lender will need the *original* counseling certificate and photocopies of other documents such as homeowners' insurance. Your lender will let you know what they require for application.

▶ *Appraisal.* An appraisal will be ordered to determine your home's value. You should receive a copy of the appraisal at or prior to closing. The appraised value of your home will be used for the final loan calculations. The FHA reverse mortgage requires that your home meets FHA guidelines. The appraiser will determine if any repairs are required on your home. In many cases, if repairs are needed, they can be completed within six months after your loan closing.

▶ *Processing and Underwriting.* There are many things happening behind the scenes while your loan is in process. Your lender will order the appraisal, title work, credit report, flood certification, lien payoffs (if applicable), homeowners' insurance verification, etc. After receiving all the pertinent data, the lender sends your loan package to underwriting for final loan approval. When your loan is ready for closing, your loan specialist will contact you to determine which payment plan you have selected. Processing typically takes three to six weeks, depending on your lender.

▶ *Loan Closing and Disbursement.* Now it is time to sign the final closing documents. This typically takes place in your home, the lender's office, or the title company office. If you want your lawyer to review your documents, notify your lender so it may provide them in advance of your closing. You will receive copies of all the paperwork you sign to retain for your personal records. After closing, you have three business days in which to cancel the loan, if you so choose. After this three-day period passes, the loan is in place and the funds are disbursed. (The three-day cancellation period only pertains to refinances, not purchases.)

20-8. Frequently Asked Questions

Q: What is so unique about this program?
A: There are no required monthly payments – *none*.

Q: Can I make payments if I want to?
A: Yes, and any payments you make will increase the amount of equity that will be left when the home is sold.

Q: Who is eligible for a reverse mortgage?
A: You and any co-borrowers must:

> ▶ Be at least 62 years of age;
> ▶ Live in the home as a primary residence;
> ▶ Speak with the approved counselor; and
> ▶ Have equity in the home.

Q: Do I have to own my home free and clear?

A: No. Even if you have an existing loan, in many cases, reverse mortgage proceeds can be used to pay the debt.

Q: May I use a reverse mortgage to buy a new home?

A: Yes, but working with an experienced reverse mortgage lender is key. There may be additional steps required. Your lender can walk you through this process.

Q: Will I have to pay fees?

A: No out-of-pocket fees are usually required. Closing costs, origination fees, and mortgage insurance (if required) can be financed by the loan. Ask your lender if it charges any up-front fees; some lenders may ask you to pay for the appraisal up front, while others ask you to pay it only if your loan does not close.

Q: Is there a charge for the required FHA Counseling?

A: Some counseling agencies do charge and some *do not*. The maximum is $125. When you set your appointment, ask your counselor if the agency charges any fees.

Q: Are there any ongoing fees after closing?

A: Yes, there are typically mortgage insurance fees (on the HUD program), as well as interest accrual and sometimes servicing fees, but you are not required to pay them; they are added to your loan balance.

Q: I know I will be charged interest, but on what?

A: Interest is charged only on the amount disbursed to you or on your behalf and is added to your loan balance each month.

Q: Is this a fixed rate loan?

A: There is a fixed rate option available; however, the interest rate is higher than the variable rate. The fixed rate program also requires that the homeowner take a full disbursement of funds (no line of credit or monthly payments).

Q: What is helpful when "shopping" for a reverse mortgage lender?

A: You should shop for a knowledgeable, experienced lender who can accurately complete your loan in a reasonable time frame and offer you more than one program. Ask your lender how long they have offered reverse mortgages and how many they personally have done. You may want to ask for references and speak with a previous customer they worked with and who has had their reverse mortgage for a while. Are they a member of the Better Business Bureau? Are they a member of the National Reverse Mortgage Lenders Association?

Q: Can I sell my home whenever I want?

A: Yes – and you keep whatever money is left over after you pay off your loan balance. Most programs have *no* prepayment penalty. Have your lender confirm this in writing or show you where it is in your paperwork.

Q: If I take a reverse mortgage, who owns my home?
A: *You* remain the owner of the property.

Q: What are my/our responsibilities?
A: You and/or your spouse must live in the home, keep the property in good repair, and make sure your taxes and homeowners' insurance are current.

Q: Is money from a reverse mortgage taxable?
A: No, money from a reverse mortgage is considered loan proceeds and therefore is not taxable income.

Q: What if my property is in a revocable trust?
A: Property in a revocable trust usually qualifies. The lender will need a copy of the trust to see that it meets the program guidelines. If it does not, oftentimes your lawyer can modify it so that it meets the program guidelines and you may leave the property in the trust.

Q: Are there restrictions on how I use the money?
A: No. It is your money and your decision on how to spend it.

Q: What if my house needs repairs?
A: You find the contractor or handyman, get the estimate, and the repairs can be completed after your loan is finalized. Money will be reserved from your loan for these repairs, and you will have up to six months to complete them. (Repairs cannot be more than 15 percent of the value of the home.)

Q: When is my loan due?
A: When you and/or your spouse no longer live in the home as a primary residence.

Q: Are reverse mortgages safe?
A: Yes. You or your heirs are guaranteed never to owe more than the value of the home at the time of sale.

Q: Can I sell whenever I want to?
A: Absolutely. It is no more difficult to sell a home with a reverse mortgage than to sell a home with a traditional mortgage.

Q: Will my heirs owe anything if I die?
A: *No*, reverse mortgages have insurance to guarantee that you would never leave a debt to your heirs. When you die, the house goes to your estate. The reverse mortgage is repaid from either the sale of the house or other assets, and the remaining equity goes to your estate. If the house does not repay the loan, it is paid by the insurance fund, *not* your heirs.

Q: If my home appreciates in value, who gets that money?
A: You or your estate are legally required to pay back only the balance due on the loan. Again, all money left after the loan is repaid belongs to you or your estate.

Q: What if I have to go to a nursing facility?

A: You can be gone from the property for up to one year because of illness and the loan is not affected.

Q: Will this affect Social Security, Medicare, or Medicaid?

A: Money from a reverse mortgage will not affect Social Security or Medicare. Even if you are getting Medicaid, Supplemental Security Income, or Old Age Pension, you may qualify. You must abide by program guidelines to avoid termination of benefits.

20-9. Real-Life Examples

Lois had her home paid free and clear, and then her daughter needed some money because of a divorce. Lois secured a traditional loan on her home to help her daughter, who promised to help with the payments. When her daughter did not help her, Lois could not keep up with the payments and was in danger of losing her home. She applied for and completed the reverse mortgage, and, with the proceeds, paid off her previous mortgage in time to rescue the home from foreclosure.

When Betty's husband died suddenly, she was in shock. She and Bill had been getting by on their fixed incomes, and when Bill died, her Social Security benefits were reduced and the loan on the house still had to be paid. Betty researched reverse mortgage programs and decided the FHA-Insured program was the right one for her. She obtained the reverse mortgage and used part of the proceeds to pay off the home loan. With the balance of the proceeds, she is receiving $400 a month to offset the loss of income, and she left $35,000 in her line of credit that she can use as needs arise.

Mr. and Mrs. Meyers wanted to purchase a "winter" home in Texas, where many of their family members lived. Based on their ages of 66 and 68, and the value of their primary Colorado residence of $225,000, they qualified for $120,000 through the reverse mortgage. This amount enabled them to easily purchase their winter retreat in which they plan to live three to four months a year. They now own both properties without the financial burden of mortgage payments on either property.

Grace, who is 98, said, "I saved for my retirement, I just didn't think I would live this long." As Grace aged, she used all of her savings to hire home care, as she was adamant she would not go to a nursing home. When she was 98, her savings was gone, so she secured a reverse mortgage and was able to remain in her home, with care paid for by utilizing the equity she had in her home.

20-10. Resources

Colorado is fortunate to have many good reverse mortgage counselors. Here are some of the local counselors for your convenience. You may look at the entire list on the FHA website, www.hud.gov.

The HUD-approved housing agencies listed below provide assistance to renters, homebuyers, and homeowners requiring housing information. They are not HUD offices. Any of these agencies will conduct the required informational session for the FHA insured reverse mortgage.

City of Aurora Community Development Division
9898 E. Colfax Ave.
Aurora, CO 80010
(303) 739-7900
www.auroragov.org (Click on "Living Here," then "Housing and Community Resources.")

Northeast Denver Housing Center
1735 Gaylord St.
Denver, CO 80206
(303) 377-3334
www.nedenverhousing.org

GreenPath Debt Solutions
1247 Riverside Ave.
Fort Collins, CO 80524
(800) 550-1961
www.greenpath.com

Money Management International
Telephone Counseling Only:
(866) 490-9438
www.moneymanagement.org

Grand Junction Housing Authority
1011 N. 10th St.
Grand Junction, CO 81501
(970) 245-0388
www.gjha.org

Consumer Credit Counseling Service
Telephone Counseling Only:
5265 N. Academy Blvd., Ste. 1000
Colorado Springs, CO 80918
(719) 598-2227
www.cccs.net

Consumer Credit Counseling Service of Pueblo
200 W. 1st St., Ste. 302
Pueblo, CO 81003
(719) 542-6620
www.cccs.net

Helpful Reverse Mortgage Websites

National Reverse Mortgage Lenders Association
www.nrmlaonline.org

Federal Housing Administration
U.S. Department of Housing and Urban Development
www.hud.gov

Fannie Mae
www.fanniemae.com

AARP
www.aarp.org

Colorado Housing Counseling Coalition
www.housingcounseling.com

Loan Calculations
http://reversemortgage.org

Chapter 21

Assisted Living and Nursing Home Issues

Heather M. Porreca*
Jennifer Reeves*
Area Agency on Aging
Denver Regional Council of Governments

SYNOPSIS

21-1. Introduction

The purpose of this chapter is to provide information to help you select an appropriate assisted living residence or nursing home for yourself or your loved one. In this chapter, we provide:

▶ A description of the Ombudsman Program;

▶ An overview of the long-term care options in Colorado;

▶ A description of the type of care that is provided at assisted living residences and nursing homes;

▶ Factors you should consider when evaluating and selecting an assisted living residence or nursing home; and

▶ Resources to help you in selecting an appropriate resident-centered care setting.

Selecting an appropriate long-term care facility for yourself or a loved one can be confusing and stressful. The selection process is challenging because it often occurs at a time of crisis, sometimes without time to prepare. Additionally, most people are not familiar with the available long-term care options, the services that are provided, or the rights and legal protections that are available to residents of assisted living facilities or nursing homes. We will refer to the people who live in assisted living residences or nursing homes as "residents" to reflect that for most individuals the long-term care facility is their home.

The Ombudsman Program is an important resource as you choose the long-term care facility that best meets your needs. It is a free, nationwide advocacy program for residents of assisted livings and nursing homes who might feel powerless and vulnerable. Every long-term care facility in Colorado has an ombudsman assigned to visit and investigate complaints from family and residents. Ombudsmen are required to visit assisted living residences at least once every three months and nursing homes at least once a month. Long-term care ombudsmen are responsible for educating residents, family members, and care providers about the rights that residents have been granted under federal and Colorado law. (A complete list of residents' rights appears at the end of this chapter as Exhibit 21A.) Ombudsmen are resident advocates who take the perspective of residents when resolving issues. Their work is funded by federal grants under the Older Americans Act. They are frequent visitors to assisted living residences and nursing homes, and are trained to identify issues affecting resident rights. Ombudsmen are ideally suited to provide information to consumers when selecting long-term care facilities.

21-2. Long-Term Care Facilities

Long-term care facilities are broadly divided into two groups: assisted living residences and nursing homes. Smaller assisted living residences are also referred to as personal care boarding homes or simply PCBHs. In this chapter, we will use the term "assisted living residences" or "assisted livings" to include personal care boarding homes and assisted living residences.

Assisted Living Residences

An assisted living residence is a residential community that provides room, board, and at least the following services: personal care services, protective oversight, social care, and regular supervision available on a 24-hour basis. Personal care services include a physically safe environment, supervision, and assistance with activities of daily living (often referred to as ADLs) such as medication administration, bathing, dressing, and toileting. Protective oversight includes monitoring the needs of residents to ensure that they receive the services and care necessary to protect their health, safety, and well-being. At a minimum, staff at assisted livings must be present at all times. Some assisted living residences, known as secured facilities, also have locked doors to prevent residents with dementia from leaving the building. Some assisted living communities specialize in providing care to residents with dementia, who tend to wander. These communities may identify themselves as secured or locked environments.

There are approximately 571 assisted living residences in Colorado. There are over 278 assisted living residences in the Denver metro area alone. Assisted living residences range in size from 3 to 274 residents. The smaller assisted living residence may have a home-like aspect, whereas the large assisted livings have amenities such as common areas, dining rooms, theaters, libraries, and spa-like facilities. The most common reasons for admission to assisted living residences are medication management; eating, bathing, and dressing assistance; and the need for supervision without requiring the skilled nursing care available at nursing homes.

Assisted living residences with more than three residents who are not related to the owner of the facility are required to be licensed by the Colorado Department of Public Health and Environment. Facilities that accept Medicaid payments must also be certified by the Colorado Department of Health Care Policy and Financing. In Colorado, assisted living residences are surveyed by the Colorado Department of Public Health and Environment at least annually. The results of the survey are available to the public and accessible on the Colorado Department of Public Health and Environment website. (See section 21-6, "Resources.")

Staffing

Staffing at assisted living residences and nursing homes differs in relationship to the needs of the residents. Assisted livings often try to provide a home-like environment while providing 24-hour non-medical supervision. In smaller homes, it is common for the owner to be directly involved with resident care. Larger communities, by contrast, have an administrator who is responsible for the overall management and daily operations of the facility, and various staff members provide direct resident care.

Assisted living residences are required to have at least one staff member onsite whenever residents are present, 24 hours a day. There are no state-mandated staffing requirements or staff-to-resident ratios for assisted living residences. Rather, an assisted living residence must employ the type and number of care providers necessary to operate the home in compliance with Colorado Department of Public Health and Environment regulations. However, if the facility accepts Medicaid, the federal government requires a staffing ratio of 1 staff member to every 10 residents during the day, and 1 staff member to every 15 residents at night. The staffing ratio for a secured environment is one staff member to every six residents. Staffing at assisted living residences generally includes Qualified Medication Administration Persons (QMAPs), whose responsibility it is to distribute medication to residents. There has been an increase in assisted living residences having either a Licensed Practical Nurse (LPN) or Registered Nurse (RN) on staff. They typically are given the title "wellness coordinator." They oversee the medication program and the QMAPs. As of

November 1, 2008, all assisted living communities are required to have on site at all times at least one staff member who has been trained in cardiopulmonary resuscitation (CPR) and first aid. They are also required to have training in lift assistance.

Nursing Homes

Nursing homes, sometimes called skilled nursing facilities, provide skilled nursing care, rehabilitative services, or health-related care and services to chronically ill individuals, including those with chronic mental illnesses. Many nursing homes also offer short-term care (often called respite care), extended care rehabilitative services, and special locked units or neighborhoods for people with Alzheimer's disease or other types of dementia. Some nursing homes have expertise in caring for individuals with brain injuries, behaviors that occur after a stroke or as a result of dementia, wound care, drug and alcohol addictions, or specific diseases such as multiple sclerosis or various mental illnesses. Many people mistakenly think that nursing homes only provide care to elderly adults, but nursing homes serve people, regardless of age, who have chronic illness and need long-term care. It is not unusual to have young residents who have suffered brain injuries, or who are morbidly obese, living in the same facility with elderly residents who have dementia, chronic obstructive pulmonary disease, or who are mentally ill.

There are approximately 214 nursing homes in Colorado, 87 of which are located in the Denver metro area. They range in size from 30 to 240 residents. Nursing homes, like assisted living residences, are inspected or surveyed annually by the Colorado Department of Public Health and Environment (CDPHE). Additionally, the CDPHE may enter the facility at any time to investigate complaints that are made by residents, families, ombudsmen, members of the public, or anyone concerned about the care residents are receiving at the nursing home. The CDPHE survey results and complaint investigations are required to be posted within the nursing home and available for public inspection at any time.

The trend in nursing homes and assisted livings is to move away from an institutional model to a resident-centered model of providing care. Facilities associated with the Eden Alternative or the Pioneer Network, or identifying themselves as embracing "culture change," are most likely to meet the needs of the residents as individuals rather than forcing the resident to fit into the needs of the nursing home staff and administration. A nursing home or assisted living that emphasizes culture change views life in a nursing home as a time of continued growth. Culture change facilities work to empower the resident to take control over his or her care and believe that spontaneity and creativity are ways to reduce boredom and depression. (See section 21-6, "Resources," for more information about culture change. The Eden Alternative website has a list of Eden-certified communities in your area.)

Like assisted living residences, nursing homes vary in size and type of amenities available. Some nursing homes have large common areas, private dining rooms appropriate for family gatherings, recreational facilities, libraries, gardens, and small general stores. Facilities may also offer use of their transportation vehicles to take residents to medical treatments and social outings. Nursing homes are required to meet all the care needs of the resident, including health, social, and recreational needs. The social worker should be an internal advocate for residents living in nursing homes. Loved ones should know the administrator, director of nursing, social worker, and the resident's CNAs by name and by face.

The Centers for Medicare and Medicaid Services offer ratings for nursing homes nationwide on the Nursing Home Compare website. This can be a useful tool during the process of selecting a nursing home. See Section 21-6, "Resources." The rating system gives each nursing home a rating between one and five stars. Nursing homes with five stars are considered to have above-average quality, while nursing homes with one star are considered to have quality that is below average. The ratings are based on the health department inspections, staffing, and quality indicators such as the prevalence of pressure sores on residents' bodies or changes to residents' mobility.

Staffing

Staffing at nursing homes is more standardized to meet the regulatory requirements of the state and federal governments. Staff are divided into departments that are responsible for meeting the needs of the residents. Nursing homes are required to have a nursing home administrator who is responsible for the overall operations of the facility. The nursing home administrator must be licensed by the State of Colorado and identified by the initials "NHA" after his or her name. The name of the administrator and medical director are available at the Colorado Department of Public Health and Environment's website. (See section 21-6, "Resources.")

All medical care at the nursing home must be provided under the supervision of a physician. Each facility is required to have a medical director, a physician who formulates and directs overall policy for medical care in the nursing home. The director of nursing (DON) supervises nursing services and must be a registered nurse; he or she is responsible for supervising the entire nursing staff, including nursing supervisors and certified nurse aides. Nursing supervisors are either registered nurses or licensed practical nurses. Their responsibility is to supervise the care that is provided during the shifts for one section or unit of the nursing home facility.

Certified nurse aides (CNAs) provide most of the personal care for residents, including assistance with bathing, eating, dressing, and assisting the resident in and out of bed. CNAs comprise about 80 to 90 percent of the nursing staff and perform some of the most difficult and strenuous work done in nursing homes. They must complete a state-approved training and competency evaluation program. Colorado requires certified nurse aides to have at least 75 hours of training. It is not unusual to see temporary or agency-certified nurse aides or licensed practical nurses at nursing homes. Nursing homes should strive to have consistent staffing with minimal use of agency or temporary staff. CNAs provide the majority of direct care to the resident; thus, it is important that residents and their families become familiar and comfortable with their care providers.

21-3. Six Key Steps to Selecting a Good Assisted Living Residence or Nursing Home

In this section, we discuss how to select the right facility that will be the best fit for you or your loved one. These issues include identifying the individual's needs, knowing what to look for in a facility, observing and talking with residents and staff, becoming informed about the facility's management, understanding the payment schedule, and reviewing the contract or admission agreement.

We suggest that you contact your local Ombudsman Program when starting your facility search; contact information is provided at the end of this chapter. Ombudsmen are required to visit assisted living residences quarterly and nursing homes monthly, so your local ombudsman will be able to assist you in finding a facility that best fits your or your loved one's needs.

Step 1: Identify your needs or the needs of your loved one.

How old are you or your loved one?

When contacting facilities, it is important to ask up front if they have an age requirement. Some assisted living residences only accept people who are 65 or older. However, there are facilities that serve a younger disabled population as well. Most nursing homes accept residents regardless of age if the facility can meet their care needs.

What size facility is appropriate for you or your loved one?

Assisted living residences can range from 3 to 274 residents. Nursing homes range from 30 to 240 residents. Generally, larger facilities offer more amenities and services to the resident.

What geographical area would you or your loved one prefer?

For some individuals, the location can be the determining factor when selecting a long-term care facility.

What level of care do you or your loved one require?

This is vital in determining whether a person is appropriate for an assisted living residence or nursing home. Ask yourself the following questions: Are you or your loved one incontinent of bladder or bowel? Can you get in and out of bed without assistance (transfer)? Are you able to walk without assistance (ambulate)? Do you require a special or therapeutic diet (usually ordered by a doctor)? Does your loved one have a history of wandering or become physically or verbally combative?

Do you or your loved one have special needs?

Ask yourself: Is your loved one in a motorized wheelchair? Does your loved one have a gastric feeding tube (G-tube)? Does your loved one require bariatric care (obesity)? Nursing homes typically provide a special/therapeutic diet; however, assisted livings are not required by regulation to provide this service. Similarly, some nursing homes do not have the wide door openings, lifts, or beds required to care for morbidly obese residents. If your loved one is insulin dependent, verify that the assisted living community will manage and administer the insulin injections.

What facility is going to be the best fit for you or your loved one?

Some communities specialize in caring for a specific population, such as individuals with Alzheimer's disease or dementia, multiple sclerosis, mental illness, or brain injury. If a person has been diagnosed with Alzheimer's disease or dementia, it sometimes is necessary to place the individual in a secured assisted living residence or a secured unit in a nursing home. This is usually determined with the guidance of a physician.

How will you or your loved one pay for the long-term care needs?

Both assisted livings and nursing homes accept a variety of payment sources, including Medicaid, Medicare, long-term care insurance, and private pay. It is important to note that Medicare pays for long-term care only under specific circumstances. (See Chapter 2, "Medicare.") Medicaid assisted livings are referred to as alternative care facilities (ACF).

Step 2: Know what to look for when you visit the prospective facility.

We advise that you visit prospective facilities at least twice. The first visit should be scheduled with the admissions office. The second visit should be unannounced, perhaps in the evening. You need to know what to look for when you make your visits. Here are a few things to consider:

Is the facility clean?

Does the facility appear to be clean? Do you smell any odors? You should not smell urine in any long-term care facility. This indicates a lack of attentiveness from the staff.

Get permission to view a resident's room, bathroom, and shower.

Is the room clean, comfortable, and home-like? Do you observe personal photos, mementos, or furniture? Are the closets adequate? Will you or your loved one share a room? Is there space for toiletries and personal items? Does the bathroom have grab bars and an easily accessible shower?

Do the residents have privacy?

Is there access to a telephone in a private area? Is there space to meet with family and friends?

Can you easily find posted instructions on how to contact the local ombudsman, the county health department, adult protection services, and the Medicaid office (if applicable)?

Step 3: Observe and talk with residents and staff members.

Are the residents clean and well groomed?

Are the residents up and active during the day?

Are residents engaged in activities and interacting with one another? Ask to see the activities scheduled for the month. Pay attention to the number of activities that are offered during the weekends. Residents often comment that there is not enough to keep them busy over the weekend.

How is transportation provided?

Does the facility provide transportation to and from medical appointments? Does the facility provide transportation to outside activities?

Visit with the residents.

Ask the residents about the care they receive. Ask if they would recommend the facility to others.

Try to visit during a meal and look at the dining area.

Does the posted menu reflect what the residents are eating? Are the residents served their meals promptly? Are staff attentive and offering residents assistance?

Observe interaction between residents and staff.

Do residents respond well to the staff members? Do staff members seem to respect and enjoy the residents? Are staff members wearing their identification badges? Ask if the nursing home or assisted living community participates in culture change principles of resident-centered care. This should be reflected in resident-staff interaction. Do staff members appear hurried or rushed? Does the nursing home appear to have adequate staffing? Nursing homes are required to post in a public place the number of Certified Nurse Aids, Licensed Practical Nurses, and Registered Nurses on duty for every shift. During your visit, verify that the posting is accurate.

How do the staff members address the residents?

Does the staff address the residents with respect? It is usually not appropriate to address adults as "honey" or "sweetie."

Do staff members respect the residents' privacy?

Are the staff members knocking on the resident's door and waiting for a response before entering? Are privacy curtains pulled and/or doors closed when providing personal care to the resident?

Is water available at the residents' bedsides?

Are cups available and can residents easily get a drink of water?

Does the staff respond promptly to requests for assistance?

A request for assistance should be responded to within a few minutes. Are call lights within the resident's reach? Some assisted livings do not have a call light system; however, staff must respond promptly to residents' needs.

Ask about the staff training.

How much training does each staff member receive? Who provides the training? Does the staff receive training specific to the needs of the community it serves, such as multiple sclerosis, Alzheimer's disease or dementia, or mentally ill residents? Ask about the staff turnover rate. Ask if the facility utilizes a consistent staffing method. Consistent staffing is a scheduling practice where the same care providers work with the same residents so that the staff can anticipate the residents' needs. If an assisted living community, ask if the staff is up to date on their CPR and first aid training.

Do the staff members acknowledge your presence?

If you are visiting without a tour guide, someone should tactfully inquire about your presence at the facility. This is an informal, yet effective, security measure.

What does the facility do to promote resident-directed care or culture change?

Do residents get up and go to bed when they want to? Are residents involved in their own care planning? Are there open dining hours? Is the facility Eden-certified?

Step 4: Become informed about the facility's management and administration.

Is the long-term care facility licensed?

If you are considering an assisted living, it is important to know if the facility is licensed. Any facility providing care to three or more unrelated adults must be licensed by the state. All nursing homes are licensed by the state and federal government. Licensing information is available on the Colorado Department of Public Health and Environment website, listed in section 21-6, "Resources."

Read the most recent state survey.

Assisted living residences and nursing homes are inspected every year. The comprehensive inspection is known as a survey and is conducted by the Colorado Department of Public Health and Environment. Facilities are required to make the survey available to residents and visitors, and it is also available online at the Colorado Department of Public Health and Environment's website (see section 21-6, "Resources"). Contact your local Ombudsman Program to help explain the facility's survey.

Is the facility locally owned or part of a large national organization?

It is useful to understand the ownership of the facility. This could reflect how responsive the facility will be to your concerns or complaints.

How long has the administrator been at the facility?

Beware of frequent changes in key administrative positions or ownership, including the administrator or executive director, director of nursing, and social worker. Contact your local ombudsman for information regarding staff changes.

Step 5: Understand the facility payment system.

Understand the daily rate.

Some assisted livings offer a "menu" of services that detail costs associated with each service provided. Other assisted living residences will assess residents and assign them a "rating" and base the cost of services on where they fall in a spectrum. For nursing homes, ask to see an itemized list of the daily charges and clarify the billing procedures for additional items such as incontinence pads, toothpaste, rubber gloves, and tissues.

What types of payments are accepted?

The most common types of payment are Medicaid, Medicare, long-term care insurance, and private pay. It is crucial to know that Medicare will cover rehabilitation only. (See Chapter 2, "Medicare.")

Can you use your own pharmacy?

Some assisted living residences will charge an extra monthly fee if the resident chooses to use a different pharmacy. This should be explained at the resident's admission. Nursing home residents have the right to purchase pharmaceuticals from the pharmacy of their choice, but they must ensure that they are delivered in a timely manner.

Step 6: Read the contract or admission agreement completely and thoroughly.

Remember: this is a binding legal document. Arbitration clauses are becoming more common in admission agreements. By signing an arbitration agreement, you are waiving your right to sue the facility if you are not satisfied with the care your loved one receives. Consult with an attorney if you have questions.

Review the facility admission policy.

It is very important to review the facility's admission criteria/policy. This policy should include what resident care a facility can and cannot accommodate. Prior to admission, the facility should conduct an admission assessment to identify the care needs of the future resident.

Understand the facility discharge policy.

Just like the admission policy, it is vital to understand the facility discharge policy. Discharge practices are regulated by state and federal regulations. This policy should explain how and why discharge notices are issued and clearly state that the notice must be in writing. Ask the question: Under what circumstances could my loved one be asked to leave?

Read and understand all facility policies and procedures.

These may include a bed-hold policy, termination clause, the type of transportation that will be provided and at what rate, therapeutic diets that are offered and at what rate, emergency protocols, and evacuation plans. Some facilities will ask relatives of potential residents to assume responsibility for expenses that are not paid in full by the resident. Before agreeing to be held financially liable, you should consult an elder law attorney.

21-4. Conclusion

Selecting a long-term care facility is a challenging process. In conjunction with the steps outlined here, the Ombudsman Program is an important resource available to assist you and your loved one in the selection process. The service is free to residents and their families. Ombudsmen help ensure the health, safety, welfare, and rights of residents living in long-term care facilities, and all complaints are kept confidential. If a problem does develop after admission, you can contact your local ombudsman for assistance and information.

21-5. Common Acronyms

AAA. Area Agency on Aging.

ACF. Alternative Care Facility.

ADL. Activities of Daily Living.

ALR. Assisted Living Residence.

CNA. Certified Nurse Aide.

DON. Director of Nursing.

LPN. Licensed Practical Nurse.

PCBH. Personal Care Boarding Home.

QMAP. Qualified Medication Administration Persons.

RN. Registered Nurse.

SNF. Skilled Nursing Facility.

21-6. Resources

Colorado Culture Change Coalition
www.coculturechange.org

State Ombudsman
Colorado State Ombudsman
The Legal Center for People with Disabilities and Older People
455 Sherman St., Ste. 130
Denver, CO 80203-4403
(303) 722-0300
(303) 722-3619 (TTY)
(800) 288-1376
www.thelegalcenter.org

Denver Regional Council of Governments — Area Agency on Aging (DRCOG)
Ombudsman Program for Adams, Arapahoe, Broomfield, Clear Creek, Denver, Douglas, Gilpin, and Jefferson counties
1290 Broadway, Ste. 700
Denver, CO 80203
(303) 455-1000
www.drcog.org

Colorado Department of Public Health and Environment (CDPHE)
Health Facilities and Emergency Medical Services Divisions
4300 Cherry Creek Dr. S.
Denver CO 80246-1530
(303) 692-2000
(800) 866-7689
www.healthfacilities.info
www.cdphe.state.co.us/hf/ncf/index.html

The Eden Alternative
www.edenalt.org

The Pioneer Network
www.pioneernetwork.net

Nursing Home Compare
www.medicare.gov/nhcompare

Alzheimer's Association — Colorado Chapter
455 Sherman St., Ste. 500
Denver, CO 80203
(303) 813-1669
(800) 272-3900 (24-hour Helpline)
(866) 403-3073 (TDD)
www.alz.org/co

---

* This chapter was previously written by Ayodele Labode, J.D., M.S., and Heather M. Porreca.

Exhibit 21A.
Residents' Rights

When it becomes necessary for a person to enter a long-term care facility, it shall be the responsibility of all the staff at the facility to promote and protect the following rights of the person.

1. The right to be treated with respect and dignity.

2. The right to privacy, including communication by mail or phone.

3. The right not to be isolated or kept apart from other residents.

4. The right not to be sexually, verbally, physically, or emotionally abused, humiliated, intimidated, or punished.

5. The right to be free from neglect.

6. The right to live free from involuntary confinement or financial exploitation, and to be free from physical or chemical restraints.

7. The right to have personal possessions secured.

8. The right to voice grievances and recommend changes in policies and services.

9. The right to receive 30-days' notice of transfer or discharge, which must include reason, effective date, location, and appeal rights.

10. The right to reasonable use of the telephone.

11. The right to have visitors and the right to privacy during such visits.

12. The right to information about the rights, services, and rules, communicated in an understandable language.

13. The right to make decisions and choices regarding care and treatment in the management of personal affairs, funds, and property.

14. The right to exercise choice in attending and participating in religious activities.

15. The right to be reimbursed at an appropriate rate for work performed on the property for the benefit of the administrator, staff, or other residents in accordance with the resident's care plan.

16. The right to 30-days' written notice of changes in services provided by the facility, including, but not limited to, changes in charges for any or all services.

17. The right to have outside advocates, including members of community organizations whose purpose includes rendering assistance to the residents.

18. The right to wear clothing of the residents' choice.

19. The right to choose to participate in social activities.

20. The right to receive services in accordance with the resident agreement and care plan.

Exhibit 21B.
Assisted Living and Nursing Home Checklist

Step 1: Identify your needs or the needs of your loved one.

- How old are you or your loved one?
- What size facility is appropriate for you or your loved one?
- What geographical area would you or your loved one prefer?
- What level of care do you or your loved one require?
- Do you or your loved one have special needs?
- What facility is going to be the best fit for you or your loved one?
- How will you or your loved one pay for the long-term care needs?

Step 2: Know what to look for when you visit the prospective facility.

- Is the facility clean?
- Get permission to view a resident's room, bathroom, and shower.
- Do the residents have privacy?
- Can you easily find posted instructions on how to contact the local ombudsman, the county health department, the adult protection services, and the Medicaid office (if applicable)?

Step 3: Observe and talk with residents and staff members.

- Are the residents clean and well groomed?
- Are the residents up and active during the day?
- How is transportation provided?
- Visit with the residents.
- Try to visit during a meal and look at the dining area.
- Observe interaction between residents and staff.
- How do the staff members address the residents?
- Do staff members respect the residents' privacy?
- Is water available at the residents' bedside?
- Does staff respond promptly to requests for assistance?
- Ask about staff training.
- Do the staff members acknowledge your presence?
- Does the facility promote resident-centered care or culture change?

Step 4: Become informed about the facility's management and administration.

- Is the long-term care facility licensed?

- Read the most recent state survey.

- Is the facility locally owned or part of a large national organization?

- How long has the administrator been at the facility?

Step 5: Understand the facility payment system.

- Understand the daily rate.

- What types of payments are accepted?

- Can you use your own pharmacy?

Step 6: Read the contract or admission agreement completely and thoroughly.

- Review the facility admission policy.

- Understand the facility discharge policy.

- Read and understand all facility policies and procedures.

Exhibit 21C.
Colorado Area Agencies on Aging Regions

REVISED 8/27/10   COLORADO AREA AGENCIES ON AGING REGIONS

1 Sandra Baker, AAA Director
  Single Entry Point (SEP)
Northeastern Colorado Association of
 Local Governments
231 Main Street, Suite 211
Fort Morgan, CO 80701
Phone: 970.867.9409
Fax: 970.867.9053
Email: sbaker@necalg.com
Website: www.NortheasternColorado.com
Northeastern Region
Counties: Washington, Yuma, Logan,
Morgan, Phillips, Sedgwick
SUA Contact: Peggy Spaulding 303.866.2867

2-A Margaret A. Long, AAA Director
Larimer County Office on Aging
Larimer County Human Services
2601 Midpoint, Suite 112
Fort Collins, CO 80524
Phone: 970.498.7750
Fax: 970.498.7605
Email: mlong@larimer.org
Website: www.larimer.org/seniors
Northeastern Region
Counties: Larimer
SUA Contact: Peggy Spaulding 303.866.2867

2-B Eva Jewell, AAA Director
  Single Entry Point (SEP)
Weld County Area Agency On Aging
P.O. Box 1805
315 C. N. 11th Ave.
Greeley, CO 80631
Phone: 970.346.6950
Fax: 970.346.6951
Email: EJewell@co.weld.co.us
Website: www.co.weld.co.us
Northeastern Region
Counties: Weld
SUA Contact: Peggy Spaulding 303.866.2867

3-A Jayla Sanchez-Warren, AAA Director
DRCOG Area Agency on Aging
1290 Broadway, Suite 700
Denver, CO 80203
Phone: 303.455.1000
Fax: 303.480.6790
Email: jswarren@drcog.org
Website www.drcog.org
Northeastern Region
Counties: Adams, Arapahoe, Broomfield,
Clear Creek, Denver, Douglas, Gilpin, Jefferson
SUA Contact: Todd Coffey 303.866.2750

3-B Sherry Leach, AAA Director
Boulder County Aging Services Division
P. O. Box 471
3482 North Broadway
Boulder, CO 80306
Phone: 303.441.3570
Fax: 303.441.4550
Email: bcaaa@bouldercounty.org
Website: www.bouldercountyseniors.info
Northeastern Region
Counties: Boulder
SUA Contact: Audrey Krebs 303.866.2846

4 Guy Dutra-Silveira, AAA Director
Pikes Peak Area Agency on Aging
15 South 7th Street
Colorado Springs, CO 80905
Phone: 719.471.2096
Fax: 719.471.1226
Email: gdutra@ppacg.org
Website: www.ppacg.org
Southern Region
Counties: El Paso, Park, Teller
SUA Contact: Audrey Krebs 303.866.2846

5 Terry Baylie, AAA Director
East Central Council of Governments
P. O. Box 28
128 Colorado Avenue
Stratton, CO 80836
Phone: 719.348.5562, ext. 5
Fax: 719.348.5887
Email: baylie@prairiedevelopment.com
Website: http://ecaaa.tripod.com
Northeastern Region
Counties: Cheyenne, Elbert, Kit Carson, Lincoln
SUA Contact: Peggy Spaulding 303.866.2867

6 Celestino Santistevan, AAA Director
  Single Entry Point (SEP)
Lower Arkansas Valley Area Agency on Aging
P.O. Box 494
13 West Third St Room 110
La Junta, CO 81050
Phone: 719.383.3166
Fax: 719.383.4607
Email: celestino.santistevan@state.co.us
Website: www.oterogov.com
Southern Region
Counties: Baca, Bent, Crowley, Kiowa, Otero,
Prowers
SUA Contact: Peggy Spaulding 303.866.2867

7 Virginia Jimenez, Aging Program Admin
Pueblo Area Agency on Aging
Southern Region
2631 E. 4th Street
Pueblo, CO 81001
Phone: 719.583.6110
Fax: 719.583.6323
Email: virginia.jimenez@co.pueblo.co.us
Website: www.co.pueblo.co.us
Southern Region
Counties: Pueblo
SUA Contact: Audrey Krebs 303.866.2846

8 Frances Valdez, AAA Director
South-Central Colorado Seniors, Inc.
P.O. Box 639
1116 3rd Street
Alamosa, CO 81101
Phone: 719.589.4511
Fax: 719.589.2343
Email: francesv@qwestoffice.net
Website: No website
Southern Region
Counties: Alamosa, Conejos, Costilla, Mineral,
Rio Grande, Saguache
SUA Contact: Todd Swanson 303.866.2651

DISTRIBUTION FOR PUBLIC USE

9 Christina Knoell, AAA Director
San Juan Basin Area Agency on Aging
P.O. Box 5456 (450 Lewis Street, B1)
Pagosa Springs, CO 81147 – Western Region
Phone: 970.264.0501
Fax: 1.888.290.3566
Email: christinaknoell@sjbaaa.org
Website: www.sjbaaa.org
Counties: Archuleta, Dolores, LaPlata,
Montezuma, San Juan
SUA Contact: Todd Swanson 303.866.2651

10 Lee Bartlett, AAA Director
Region 10 Area Agency on Aging
Drawer 849
300 N. Cascade Ave.
Montrose, CO 81402 – Western Region
Phone: 970.249.2436
Fax: 970.249.2488
Email: lee@region10.net
Website: www.region10.net
Counties: Delta, Gunnison, Hinsdale, Montrose,
Ouray, San Miguel
SUA Contact: Audrey Krebs 303.866.2846

11 Dave Norman, AAA Director
Associated Governments of Northwest Colorado
P.O. Box 20000-5035
510 29 1/2 Road
Grand Junction, CO 81502 – Western Region
Phone: 970.248.2717
Fax: 970.248.2702 or 970.248.2849/2883
Email: dave.norman@mesacounty.us
Website:
http://www.humanservices.mesacounty.us/index.cfm?id=160
Counties: Garfield, Mesa, Moffat, Rio Blanco, Routt
SUA Contact: Todd Swanson 303.866.2651

12 Jean Hammes, AAA Director
Northwest Colorado Council of Governments
Alpine Area Agency on Aging
P.O. Box 2308
249 Warren Ave.
Silverthorne, CO 80498 – Western Region
Phone: 970.468.0295
Fax: 970.468.1208
Email: aaa12@nwc.cog.co.us
Website: www.nwc.cog.co.us
Counties: Eagle, Grand, Jackson, Pitkin, Summit
SUA Contact: Todd Swanson 303.866.2651

13 Steve Holland, AAA Director
Upper Arkansas AAA – Southern Region
139 East 3rd Street
Salida, C0 81201-2612 – Southern Region
Phone: 719.539.3341
Fax: 719.539.7431
Email: s-holland@qwestoffice.net
Website: www.upperarkansasareaagencyonaging.org
Counties: Chaffee, Custer, Fremont, Lake
SUA Contact: Todd Swanson 303.866.2651

14 Jim Davis, AAA Director
Huerfano/Las Animas Area Council of Governments
d/b/a South Central Council of Governments AAA
300 Bonaventure Avenue
Trinidad, CO 81082 – Southern Region
Phone: 719.845.1133
Fax: 719.845.1130
Email: jdavis@sccog.net
Website: www.sccog.net
Counties: Huerfano, Las Animas
SUA Contact: Audrey Krebs 303.866.2846

Chapter 22

Hospital Discharge Planning: Advocating for Seniors' Medicare Rehabilitation Benefits

Michele M. Lawonn, J.D., P.T.
Medical-Legal Advocates, LLC

SYNOPSIS

22-1. Discharge Planning

Seniors can best advocate for their rights to Medicare Parts A and B rehabilitation benefits by understanding the Medicare guidelines and medical systems, knowing the appropriate rehabilitation admission criteria, and then making an informed choice regarding all the available options for their rehabilitation. Seniors, their families, and their healthcare advocates also need to be willing to appeal any adverse decision that inappropriately terminates rehabilitation benefits or seeks to deny reimbursement for Medicare Parts A and B benefits. An excellent Medicare resource organization is the Center for Medicare Advocacy, Inc., at www.medicareadvocacy.org.

Acute-care hospital discharge planning begins almost *immediately* upon your admission to the hospital. Medicare defines "discharge planning" and states the requirements for conducting discharge planni0ng. Its purpose is "to ensure a timely and smooth transition to the most appropriate type of . . . setting for post-hospital or rehabilitation care." Seniors and their families or other health care advocates need to communicate as soon as appropriate with the discharge planner, so seniors' needs and concerns are considered in discharge plans.

Discharge planning usually is conducted with a multi-disciplinary team approach and includes input and discharge recommendations from the patient's physicians; nurses; and physical, occupational, and speech therapists (speech-language pathologists). Information and recommendations are given to the senior's hospital discharge planner (who usually has a nursing or social work background), to arrive at reasonable options for the safe discharge of the patient. These options are then discussed with the senior and his or her family or other health care advocate. It is *highly* recommended that the senior have an advocate assist him or her with discharge planning and that he or she is present during the discussions with the discharge planner.

The discharge plan provides recommendations regarding a senior's medical and rehabilitation needs for discharge from the hospital. Its purpose is to ensure seniors receive continuity of medical care and all the services they need pursuant to "Health Insurance for the Aged and Disabled," Title 42, Chapter 7, Subchapter XVIII of the Social Security Act.

There are many variables in insurance coverage that a senior 65 years old or older may have. *See* Chapter 3, "Health Insurance Beyond Medicare." Many Colorado seniors choose to assign their Medicare Part A and Part B benefits to a private organization or insurance company and obtain benefits under Medicare Part C, or "Medicare Advantage." These Medicare Advantage plans may not always afford seniors their legally entitled rehabilitation benefits, in spite of the obligation for Medicare Advantage plans to provide at a minimum the same coverage for skilled nursing facilities (SNF), home health care, and Part B rehabilitation services as are provided under original Medicare Parts A and B. This chapter is limited to discussing original Medicare Parts A and B fee-for-service coverage and encourages Medicare Advantage beneficiaries to investigate the rehabilitation benefits of their plans.

22-2. Patient Discharge Planning Factors

The discharge planner and the discharge planning team consider numerous patient risks and other factors in making their recommendations. These include, but are not limited to:

▶ Insurance coverage and Medicare eligibility. To trigger Medicare Part A benefits, the senior must be admitted as an in-patient and be *hospitalized for three consecutive calendar days*, not kept on "observation" status. If a senior is on observation and meets the "in-patient criteria," his or her status must be changed to "in-patient admission" in order to trigger eligibility for Medicare Part A rehabilitation benefits. Clarify admission status and the date of admission with the hospital in order to determine this threshold criteria;

▶ Cognitive status, especially his or her judgment and safety awareness abilities;

▶ Fall history and risk for future falls;

▶ Age;

▶ Level of independence in ambulation and ADLs (activities of daily living) prior to hospital admission;

▶ Living situation (*i.e.*, lives alone or lives with a family member, spouse, or friend);

▶ Where he or she lives (*i.e.*, in a house, condominium, townhouse, mobile home, assisted living facility, senior independent apartment (with or without meal availability), or skilled nursing facility);

▶ Egress/ingress into living quarters (*i.e.*, stairs, elevator, ramp, hand railings);

▶ Support and resources available to senior from family, friends, and community;

▶ Wound and skin care needs (*i.e.*, decubitus ulcers or potential for development);

▶ Infectious disease processes (*i.e.*, need for intravenous antibiotics);

▶ Nutrition, feeding tubes to provide nutrition, and availability of meal service;

▶ History of being compliant or non-compliant with medical treatment/medications; and

▶ Medical diagnosis and complexity, including, but not limited to, having cancer and receiving chemotherapy and/or radiation; end-stage renal disease and receiving dialysis; chronic obstructive pulmonary disease (COPD) and needing pulmonary treatments and oxygen; cerebral vascular accident (stroke), closed-head injury, or subdural hematoma with extensive rehabilitation needs; morbid obesity; multiple sclerosis; cardiac complexity, including coronary artery bypass graft, pacemaker implantation, myocardial infarction, and atrial fibrillation (a-fib); total joint replacements; and fractures, including location and weight-bearing status (amount of weight allowed) on legs and arms.

22-3. Discharge Options

Options for discharge from the acute care hospital include:

▶ Skilled nursing facility (SNF);

▶ In-patient rehabilitation facility (IRF);

▶ Long-term acute care hospital (LTAC), also known as critical access hospital;

▶ Home with home health services;

▶ Hospice care in the home or in a facility;

▶ Home with outpatient rehabilitation facility services;

▶ Home or SNF with Medicare Part B skilled rehabilitation services; or

▶ Home without rehabilitation services.

SNF Rehabilitation Facility

Skilled Nursing Facility (SNF) or Post-Hospital Extended Care Services

Medicare Part A hospital insurance benefits provide up to 100 days of in-patient extended care benefit coverage. Days 1 to 20 are covered at 100 percent for all costs. This includes all skilled nursing expenses; all physical, occupational, and speech therapies; use of durable medical equipment such as wheelchairs, walkers, and special beds; and all other ancillary services such as supplemental oxygen. Days 21 to 100 require a 2012 daily co-insurance charge of $144.50. Most supplemental or Medigap insurance plans cover this co-insurance charge; seniors are urged to purchase these insurance policies.

A beneficiary does not have an absolute right to payment for 100 days of skilled nursing or skilled rehabilitation services. Rather, skilled rehabilitation services are reimbursed if they are deemed "reasonable" and "medically necessary" and require the skills, knowledge, and judgment of a professional therapist.

The criteria necessary to be eligible for Medicare Part A benefits for an SNF are as follows:

▶ A three-day minimum, medically necessary, in-patient hospitalization is required as an admitted patient and not on observation status. This is the most important triggering event for Medicare Part A rehabilitation benefits eligibility. Days are counted from midnight forward, must be consecutive, and the day of discharge does not count. For example, if a senior is admitted to the hospital at 11:50 p.m. (2350), these 10 minutes count as one required day;

▶ Admission to the SNF is within 30 days of hospital discharge (though there are a few exceptions to this rule);

▶ The senior must require skilled nursing care or skilled rehabilitation services, or both, on a daily basis. The "daily" skilled rehabilitation services or therapy requirement is met if skilled services are provided for five days per week. Most SNFs in the Denver metro area provide skilled therapy services a minimum of five days per week;

▶ The skilled services are for treatment of a condition that was treated in the hospital or that arose while in the SNF for treatment of a condition for which the senior was hospitalized in the qualifying stay;

▶ The SNF must be a Medicare-certified facility, and the "bed" must be deemed a Medicare-certified bed; and

▶ A physician must certify the need for skilled rehabilitation services.

Discharge Planning

Discharge planning also is done at the SNF, to determine appropriate and safe placement for the senior after skilled nursing and rehabilitation services are no longer deemed reasonable and medically necessary.

The senior and his or her health-care advocates need to maintain frequent and open communication with the SNF rehabilitation personnel so that they are informed as to the senior's progress and expected discharge date and plan. SNFs are required to develop a post-discharge plan of care to ensure a safe and orderly discharge. Frequently, a physical or occupational therapist performs a home safety assessment in advance of the senior's discharge to determine the senior's discharge and adaptive equipment needs, home egress and ingress accessibility, and overall mobility and safety concerns in the senior's home.

If the SNF determines that the senior no longer qualifies for skilled services and the facility wants to transfer the senior to a non-Medicare certified bed (*i.e.*, end Medicare Part A benefits and/or change rooms), the senior must be given a two-day notice of transfer that outlines his or her appeal rights. The senior has the right to refuse a transfer from a skilled to a non-skilled bed.

The Medicare Benefit Policy Manual states that beneficiaries receiving Medicare Part A in an SNF will not lose their coverage and may leave the facility for an outside pass or a short leave of absence for the purpose of attending a special religious service, holiday meal, family occasion, car ride, or for a trial visit home. It is not, by itself, evidence that the individual no longer needs to be in an SNF for the receipt of required skilled care. However, the beneficiary needs to get his or her physician to order and permit this outside pass, which is usually limited to approximately four hours.

In-Patient Rehabilitation Facility

Patients who have Medicare Part A benefits and meet the in-patient rehabilitation facility (IRF) admission criteria may be transferred to or admitted directly to an IRF. IRFs provide intensive three hours per day rehabilitation services in an in-patient setting.

To pass the criteria for admission to an IRF, the senior must:

▶ Be able to tolerate three hours per day, five days per week, of skilled rehabilitation services, including physical, occupational, and speech and language therapy; be able to benefit from rehab; and agree to participate in the rehab program. The senior is allowed three days under PPS (the Prospective Payment System) to ramp up to a tolerance of three hours per day of therapy;

▶ Need at least two skilled therapy services;

▶ Have good rehabilitation potential to achieve a higher functional level;

▶ Have the physical and cognitive capacity to benefit from the rehab program;

▶ Presently have or be in need of skilled rehabilitation services;

▶ Have a physician who agrees with transfer to acute rehab when medically stable and there is documentation in the senior's medical record;

▶ Have no scheduled surgery or procedure that would require a readmission to an acute care hospital prior to his or her rehabilitation program completion;

▶ Have documentation of his or her pre-admission status and living situation;

▶ Require 24 hours per day of skilled nursing and physician care; and

▶ Have received a rehabilitation diagnosis that is one of the 60 percent Rule categories, or the IRF has beds to take the patient if outside of the Centers for Medicare and Medicaid Services (CMS) rehabilitation impairment categories (the 60 percent Rule requires IRFs to fill 60 percent of their beds with patients having one of the 13 diagnoses listed below as either a primary or secondary diagnosis).

CMS 60 Percent Rule Impairment Categories for IRF Admission Eligibility

An in-patient rehabilitation facility must fill 60 percent of its beds with only these 13 patient diagnosis and impairment categories in order to be in compliance and maintain its IRF status:

▶ Cerebrovascular accident (recent or old cerebrovascular accident (CVA), thrombosis, hemorrhage, or embolism of the brain, *i.e.*, stroke);

▶ Spinal cord injury (paraplegia or quadriplegia);

▶ Congenital deformity (spina bifida);

▶ Amputation;

▶ Major multiple trauma (multiple fractures, fracture with internal injury);

▶ Hip fracture (femoral head or neck);

▶ Brain injury (obstructive hydrocephalus, closed head injury, open head injury, brain tumor, encephalopathy, West Nile complications);

▶ Neurological disorder (*i.e.*, multiple sclerosis, muscular dystrophy, amyotrophic lateral sclerosis (ALS), Huntington's disease, Guillian-Barré, Parkinson's disease, post-polio syndrome, motor neuron diseases, polyneuropathy);

▶ Burns;

▶ Active polyarticular rheumatoid arthritis, psoriatic arthritis, and seronegative arthropathies;

▶ Systemic vasculidities with joint inflammation;

▶ Severe or advanced osteoarthritis (osteoarthritis or degenerative joint disease):

  ▪ Must involve two or more major weight-bearing joints with joint deformity and substantial loss of range of motion (elbow, shoulders, hips, or knees and cannot count a joint with a prosthesis);

  ▪ Atrophy of muscles surrounding the joint;

  ▪ Significant functional impairment of ambulation and other ADLs;

▶ Knee and hip joint replacement if:

  ▪ Bilateral (both sides);

  ▪ The person is morbidly obese and has a Body Mass Index (BMI) over 50; and/or

  ▪ The person is age 85 or older.

Seniors with cardiac and respiratory compromises and medically complex patients may be precluded from the availability of medically necessary intensive in-patient rehabilitation under this 60 percent Rule.

Seniors with these types of impairments now can be included only in the "other 40 percent" of admissions to IRFs, rather than counting in the 60 percent mix. As health care insurances generally follow Medicare guidelines, this rule change may adversely affect people of all ages in obtaining intensive rehabilitation in an in-patient rehabilitation hospital. The trend easily may be toward the use of skilled nursing facilities for the rehabilitation of all adults.

Discharge Planning

This is very similar to that of discharge from a skilled nursing facility. Also, like discharge from an SNF, an expedited appeal process may apply. *See* section 2-3, "Appeal Rights," in Chapter 2, "Medicare."

Long-Term Acute Care Hospital (LTAC)

LTACs generally accept patients who tend to be very medically complex and who are expected to need acute care in-patient hospitalization for at least 25 days. LTACs are in the same Medicare Part A payment category as acute care in-patient hospitals and in-patient rehabilitation facilities. The benefit period is 60 days without a co-insurance charge, an additional 30 days with the $289 per day co-insurance, and the possibility to tap into the lifetime reserve of 60 days at $578 per day.

Home Health Care Services

Either Medicare Part A or Part B can reimburse post-hospital home health care services. If the threshold three-day, medically necessary, in-patient hospitalization has occurred to trigger Medicare Part A benefits and the senior has Part A, it will reimburse for home health care services.

Reimbursement is under Medicare Part B if the senior has this insurance coverage and has not been hospitalized for three days or at all. Home care services must commence within 14 days of discharge from the in-patient hospital or SNF. The patient must be "homebound" or "confined to home" to be eligible for home health services, which are limited to reasonable and necessary intermittent skilled nursing care; physical, occupational, and speech therapy; and home health aide services. "Homebound" is defined as follows:

> An individual shall be considered to be "confined to his home" if the individual has a condition, due to an illness or injury, that restricts the ability of the individual to leave his or her home except with the assistance of another individual or the aid of a supportive device (such as crutches, a cane, a wheelchair, or a walker), or if the individual has a condition such that leaving his or her home is medically contraindicated. While an individual does not have to be bedridden to be considered "confined to his home," the condition of the individual should be such that there exists a normal inability to leave home and that leaving home requires a considerable and taxing effort by the individual.

Any absence of an individual from the home attributable to the need to receive health care treatment, including regular absences for the purpose of participating in therapeutic, psychosocial, or medical treatment in an adult day-care program that is licensed or certified by a State, or accredited, to furnish adult day-care services in the State shall not disqualify an individual from being considered to be "confined to his home." Any other absence of an individual from the home shall not so disqualify an individual if the absence is of infrequent or of a relatively short duration. For purposes of the preceding sentence, any absence for the purpose of attending a religious service shall be deemed to be an absence of infrequent or short duration.

Skilled rehabilitation services must be provided by a Medicare-certified home care agency, pursuant to the patient's care plan and ordered by the patient's physician. After the initial assessment, home therapy visits are usually scheduled one to four times per week.

Home health care agencies must provide a Medicare beneficiary a pre-deprivation written notice of its intent to cut back or terminate services, whether the reason for that change is a Medicare coverage determination, lack of physician certification, a home health agency's unwillingness to provide services for business reasons unrelated to coverage, or sheer caprice. These mandatory two-day Home Health Advance Beneficiary Notices (HHABNs) must explain the procedure for seeking review of the termination or cutback in services. If you do not agree with this termination of services, call the Quality Improvement Organization (QIO), Colorado Foundation for Medical Care ((800) 727-7086 or (303) 695-3300) to file an expedited appeal.

Hospice Care

Hospice care benefits are covered under the Medicare Part A hospital insurance benefit if the patient has Medicare Part A and has chosen to elect this benefit. Patients are entitled to two 90-day election periods, followed by an unlimited number of 60-day periods. Hospice care is concerned about maintaining the patient's quality of life as he or she approaches death.

Medicare will pay for a consultation visit with the hospice medical director or other hospice physician, if the patient is terminally ill and has not yet elected the hospice benefit. Eligibility for hospice care includes situations where:

▶ The patient's attending physician and the hospice medical director or other hospice physician certify that the patient is terminally ill and has six months to live if the terminal illness runs its normal course. For any subsequent 90- or 60-day periods, only one physician needs to do the certification;

▶ The patient signs a hospice benefit election form with the hospice of choice, choosing hospice care over regular Medicare Part A covered benefits for the terminal illness; and

▶ A Medicare-approved hospice program provides hospice care.

It is important to note that a "Do Not Resuscitate" order is not required in order to receive hospice care, nor must the patient be "homebound" to receive hospice.

The following services are provided by hospice care:

▶ Physical, occupational, and speech therapy skilled services for purposes of symptom control or to enable the senior to maintain functional skills;

▶ Physician services and nursing care;

▶ Durable medical equipment such as hospital bed and wheelchair rental, commode chair, raised toilet seat, or walkers;

▶ Pain-relieving and all other medications (*Note*: Medicare Part D changes some of these reimbursements);

▶ Home health aides and homemaker services;

▶ Medical social worker and case manager services;

▶ Spiritual, grief, and loss counseling;

▶ General in-patient hospital care, not for treatment of terminal illness;

▶ Respite care covered for five consecutive days; and

▶ Bereavement care.

Room and board costs in a hospice facility (or an SNF) generally are not a covered benefit unless the beneficiary requires general in-patient or respite care. However, Medicaid covers these costs for Medicaid beneficiaries.

Discharge Planning

Hospice Medicare regulations require that, prior to "any termination of service, the provider of the service must deliver valid written notice to the beneficiary of the provider's decision to terminate services." This notice triggers the right to request an expedited determination by independent review.

A senior (hospice beneficiary) can be discharged under only three circumstances:

1) The senior moves out of the hospice provider's service area or transfers to another hospice provider;

2) The hospice provider determines that the senior is no longer terminally ill; or

3) The hospice provider determines, pursuant to its policy of discharge for cause, that the senior's behavior (or the behavior of other people in the senior's home) is disruptive, abusive, or uncooperative to the extent that delivery of care to the senior or ability of the hospice to operate effectively is seriously impaired.

The regulations regarding discharge for cause require the hospice provider to:

▶ Advise the senior that it is considering a discharge for cause;

▶ Make efforts to resolve the issues caused by the senior's behavior or home situation; and

▶ Show that this proposed discharge is not based upon the senior's use of hospice services nor his or her medical record.

Medicare Part B Rehabilitation Benefits

Medicare Part B rehabilitation benefits are available to the patient for skilled therapy rehabilitation services as follows:

▶ When the patient does not have a medically necessary, three-day in-patient hospitalization to trigger Medicare Part A benefits and he or she needs home health or outpatient rehabilitation therapy services (*e.g.*, the senior fell at home and sustained injuries, was seen and treated in the emergency room, and then was sent home with a prescription for home health or outpatient physical therapy);

▶ While the patient is a resident of an SNF or an assisted living facility or lives in the community, and skilled rehabilitation services are deemed medically necessary, as there has been a change in functional status; and

▶ After an SNF patient exhausts his or her Medicare Part A rehabilitation benefits of 100 days, and skilled rehabilitation services continue to be deemed reasonable and necessary (for example, the senior sustained a cerebrovascular accident with profound deficits).

The Balanced Budget Act of 1997 changed reimbursement for Medicare Part B outpatient rehabilitation benefits to an original total benefit of $1,500 for occupational therapy skilled services per year and a $1,500 total benefit for both physical and speech therapies per year. There has been a moratorium on these payment caps since 1998, and it was most recently extended through December 31, 2011.

As of March 2012, the cap for reimbursement of therapy applies, as there has been no further Congressional action. The 2012 maximum yearly capped reimbursement is now $1,880 for occupational therapy skilled services, as well as for combined physical and speech therapy skilled services. These caps do not apply to therapy services provided in hospital-based outpatient departments.

Allowing a reimbursement cap on outpatient Part B rehabilitation benefits has a detrimental effect on the majority of seniors, especially those seeking both physical and speech therapy skilled services in the same fiscal year. Seniors should consider contacting their elected representatives regarding these capped rehabilitation reimbursements and request that this problem be corrected permanently.

22-4. Rehabilitation

Rehabilitation skilled services include physical, occupational, and speech therapy. Therapy's primary goal is to facilitate the patient's return to his or her previous level of independent living and functioning.

Assuming the patient's medical status remains stable, there usually is a direct correlation between the amount, frequency, duration, and type of therapy services received post-hospitalization and the patient's potential to (1) stay as independent as possible, and (2) live in the least restrictive environment in his or her community. All therapy disciplines overlap in some manner, and they operate in a multi-faceted approach.

The emphases of the individual therapy disciplines include, but are not limited to, the following functions:

Physical Therapy

▶ Evaluates and facilitates the senior's ability to achieve safe and independent mobility in his or her environment;

▶ Assesses the senior's safety, judgment, and problem-solving skills. Facilitates the person's development and use of appropriate skills during the performance of all functional tasks;

▶ Assesses the senior's need for durable medical equipment such as a wheelchair, cane, walker, crutches, or other assistive device; tub/shower bench; raised toilet seat; and adaptive equipment such as grab bars and home ramp access;

▶ Facilitates the senior's development of independently and safely performed functional skills, which include, but are not limited to:

- The ability to get in and out of bed;

- Transferring between bed and a wheelchair;

- Walking without risk of falls, with or without an assistive device;

- Transferring to the toilet; and

- Independent mobility outdoors in his or her community;

▶ Facilitates the achievement of functional leg, arm, and trunk strength and mobility;

▶ Facilitates the achievement of functional sitting and standing balance;

▶ Evaluates the senior for use of pain management modalities; and

▶ Conducts pre-discharge home safety evaluations and assesses a home's need for modifications and adaptive equipment.

Occupational Therapy

▶ Evaluates and facilitates the senior's ability to perform independent activities of daily living (ADLs), which include, but are not limited to:

- Feeding with or without adaptive equipment;

- Hygiene and care of teeth, mouth, and hair;

- Toileting;

- Safe toilet, bed, tub/shower bench, and wheelchair transfers;

- Bathing;

- Independent dressing of upper and lower body, with or without adaptive equipment; and

- Safely done household skills such as cooking and cleaning.

▶ Occupational therapy, like physical therapy, facilitates the senior's development and use of appropriate safety and judgment during the performance of ADLs and all functional skills;

▶ Administers the Allen Cognitive Assessment tool to assess and predict the appropriate level of care needed by the patient post-discharge;

▶ Assesses the senior's need for durable medical equipment and adaptive equipment such as grab bars, tub/shower bench, hand-held shower, raised toilet seat, reacher, dressing aides, eating and food preparation aides, wheelchairs, and seating systems;

▶ Facilitates the achievement of functional sitting and standing balance;

▶ Facilitates the achievement of functional arm and trunk strength and mobility; and

▶ Conducts pre-discharge home safety evaluations and assesses a home's need for modifications and adaptive equipment.

Speech and Language Therapy

▶ Evaluates and facilitates the senior's cognitive development, including judgment, safety, and processing skills;

▶ Evaluates and facilitates the senior's ability to regain language and communication skills;

▶ Facilitates the senior's use of communication devices such as the telephone, signboards, and computer-assisted communication;

▶ Evaluates the senior's ability to swallow liquids and food safely and without risk of aspiration, and makes dietary recommendations for adapted eating;

▶ Facilitates the senior's ability to regain independent swallowing and eating abilities; and

▶ Conducts specialized swallow tests such as barium swallow.

22-5. Appeals

Beneficiaries are required to receive written notice of termination of services, noncoverage, and cutbacks in coverage pursuant to Medicare Parts A and B. This notice should set forth the appeal procedure. Appeals are time sensitive. See Chapter 2, "Medicare," for the discussion on appeals of adverse decisions. Beneficiaries are *strongly* encouraged to file an appeal on any denied and terminated services pursuant to Medicare Parts A and B, and to submit physicians' supporting documentation of "medical necessity" for these services.

The Medicare appeal procedure and forms can be found at www.medicare.gov, and the Colorado Senior Health Insurance Assistance Program (SHIP) through the Colorado Division of Insurance offers seniors appeal filing assistance. SHIP can be reached at (888) 696-7213.

22-6. Conclusion

Negotiating the Medicare maze of rules and regulations, with its constantly changing legislative landscape of operating policies, is indeed a challenge. However, by knowing the rules and especially the critical triggering eligibility criteria for seniors' rights to Medicare Parts A and B rehabilitation benefits, seniors will obtain these benefits. Vigilant advocacy by the senior and his or her healthcare advocate will increase the senior's probability of success at returning to his or her previous level of independent functioning and living situation.

22-7. Resources

The Center for Medicare Advocacy, Inc.
National non-profit organization and excellent Medicare resource.
National office:
P.O. Box 350
Willimantic, CT 06226
(860) 456-7790
www.medicareadvocacy.org

Washington, D.C. office:
1025 Connecticut Ave. NW, Ste. 709
Washington, D.C. 20036
(202) 293-5760

Centers for Medicare and Medicaid Services
7500 Security Blvd.
Baltimore, MD 21244
www.cms.hhs.gov

Colorado Foundation for Medical Care
23 Inverness Way E., Ste. 100
Englewood, CO 80112-5708
(303) 695-3300
www.cfmc.org

Colorado Senior Health Insurance Assistance Program (SHIP)
Offers seniors appeal filing assistance.
1560 Broadway, Ste. 850
Denver, CO 80202
(888) 696-7213
(303) 894-7499
(800) 930-3745
www.dora.state.co.us/insurance/senior/senior.htm

Colorado Gerontological Society and Senior Answers and Services
Provides counseling regarding health insurance issues, Medicare, etc.
>3006 E. Colfax Ave.
>Denver, CO 80206
>(303) 333-3482
>www.senioranswers.org

Medicare Claims and Helpline
>(800) 633-4227
>(877) 486-2048 (TTY)
>www.medicare.gov

Chapter 23

Powers of Attorney

Shari D. Caton, Esq.*
Poskus, Caton & Klein, P.C.

SYNOPSIS

23-1. Introduction to Powers of Attorney

Whether young or old, you should decide who will make medical and financial decisions for you in case you become incapacitated by a debilitating physical disease or mental impairment, whether permanent or temporary. In order to give legal effect to your decision, you should prepare a document granting someone the legal ability to act on your behalf. The legal document is called a durable power of attorney.

What is a power of attorney?

Essentially, a power of attorney is a legal document that grants legal rights and powers by a person (the "principal") to another (the "agent" or "attorney-in-fact") to make decisions on behalf of the principal. The agent has the obligation to make decisions based upon the preferences of the principal and the authority granted in the document. An agent may not override the wishes of the principal.

What is a durable power of attorney?

A "durable" power of attorney permits an agent to make decisions even if the principal becomes incapacitated. Powers of attorney signed after January 1, 2010, are durable unless the document provides that it is terminated by the incapacity of the principal. Documents signed before January 1, 2010, must contain language stating "this power of attorney shall not be affected by disability of the principal," "this power of attorney shall become effective upon the disability of the principal," or similar words to confirm the intent for the power of attorney to continue despite the principal's subsequent disability or illness.

Why should I have a durable power of attorney?

If you become incapacitated because of an accident or illness, your agent can immediately step in and make decisions for you without going to court to obtain a guardianship and/or conservatorship. Guardianship and conservatorship proceedings may be expensive, public, and time consuming. By preparing a durable power of attorney in advance, you decide who will make your decisions and, by doing so, you may save your family the stress and expense of petitioning the court.

How do I create a power of attorney?

Any adult who understands what he or she is doing can create a power of attorney by writing down exactly what he or she wants the agent to do. Once the document has been prepared, it should be signed and notarized.

Because a power of attorney should be tailored to your particular circumstances, it should be written by an attorney to ensure that your intentions are clearly expressed. If you choose not to hire an attorney, the Colorado "Statutory Form Power of Attorney" is probably the best form to use. This form is provided as Exhibit 23A of this chapter.

When does a power of attorney take effect?

When a power of attorney takes effect depends on what the document directs. There are two primary ways a power of attorney takes effect. The first is referred to as a "springing power," which means the document will take effect only when an event described in the instrument takes place. Typically, this is when the principal is incapacitated as determined by a licensed physician. The second type is a "standing power" that takes effect as soon as it is signed by the principal. Some powers of attorney may blend these two concepts. For example, a principal may direct that a power of attorney is "standing" if the principal's spouse is acting as agent; however, if the spouse cannot act, the successor agent's power may be "springing." All powers of attorney signed after January 1, 2010, are considered "standing" powers if they are silent as to the effective date.

Does a power of attorney take away a principal's rights?

A power of attorney does not take away a principal's rights to make decisions. An agent simply has the power to act along with the principal in accordance with the authorization set forth in the document. Only a court, through a guardianship and/or conservatorship proceeding, can take away a principal's rights.

Can a principal change his or her mind?

A principal may change his or her mind and revoke a power of attorney at any time, so long as the principal has capacity. All a principal needs to do to revoke a power of attorney is send a letter to the agent notifying the agent that his or her appointment has been revoked. From the moment the agent receives a revocation letter, he or she can no longer act under the power of attorney. The principal should also send a copy of the revocation to any institution or person that may have received notice of the original power of attorney, such as doctors or banks. Otherwise, those individuals or institutions may continue to rely on the power of attorney until given notice of the revocation.

State law automatically revokes the principal's appointment of a spouse as an agent when a petition for divorce, legal separation, or annulment is filed, unless the power of attorney provides otherwise. However, if a successor agent is named in the document, the power of attorney would remain in effect for the principal with the successor agent.

Whom should I name as my agent or attorney-in-fact?

The agent selected to act under a power of attorney should be a trusted individual. Common choices for agents are a spouse, an adult child, a sibling, or a trusted friend. Some principals choose professional fiduciaries to serve as agent. Either way, it is always recommended to ask the person you want to name for permission to name them as an agent to ensure that they are willing to accept the appointment.

When does an agent accept appointment?

Except as otherwise provided in the power of attorney, a person accepts appointment as an agent under a power of attorney by exercising authority or performing duties as an agent, or by any other assertion or conduct indicating acceptance.

What are an agent's duties?

Unless otherwise stated in the power of attorney, an agent that has accepted appointment must act in accordance with the principal's reasonable expectations to the extent that they are actually known, and must otherwise act in the principal's best interest. The agent must act within the scope of authority granted in the power of attorney, in good faith, with care, competence, and diligence. The agent must also keep detailed records of all receipts, disbursements, and significant transactions taken under the power of attorney.

Can a principal hold an agent liable for the agent's actions?

An agent is a "fiduciary," meaning the agent must act with the highest degree of good faith on behalf of the principal. The agent must follow any and all instructions given by the principal. If the principal's wishes are not specific, then the agent is free to do what is in the best interest of the principal. The agent must act in accordance with the principal's best interest, not the agent's interests. If an agent fails to act in accordance with the principal's wishes or in the principal's best interest, the agent can be held liable for his or her actions.

Can the agent be reimbursed for expenses and compensated for work?

Unless otherwise stated in the power of attorney document, an agent may be reimbursed for reasonable expenses and compensated for his or her work. If a principal would like to ensure that his or her agent will be reimbursed for expenses and compensated for work, especially an agent who is a close family member, the principal should include this direction in the power of attorney.

What if a principal appoints multiple agents?

A principal may appoint more than one agent, but this is not usually recommended. Having more than one agent as a decision-maker can create a circumstance in which the agents do not agree on a particular course of action. When agents do not agree, a court may have to resolve the dispute. It is usually better to appoint only one person to be the decision-maker or to provide a tiebreaking mechanism in the document. Nonetheless, if multiple agents are appointed, the principal can allow them to act independently or require them to act in unison, depending upon how the power of attorney is worded. Unless the document provides otherwise, each co-agent may exercise its authority independently. In either case, multiple agents should regularly communicate to make sure their actions are consistent.

What is a successor agent?

A successor agent is the person named to serve as your agent if your first choice for agent cannot serve due to death, incapacity, resignation, or refusal to accept the office of agent. Unless the document provides otherwise, if a named agent is unable or unwilling to serve as agent, the next person in line under the document becomes agent.

No one can take over as agent under a power of attorney unless the principal names a successor agent (or agents) in the document or if the principal authorizes the agent to appoint a successor agent. If neither is possible, and the principal has become incapacitated, it may be necessary to petition the court for appointment of a guardian and/or conservator. Therefore, it is always best to name at least one successor agent in your power of attorney.

What do I do with my power of attorney document?

You should give your original power of attorney to the agent you appoint and keep a copy of the document for yourself with your other important papers. Additionally, you may want to provide banks or doctors with copies of the power of attorney to keep for their files.

What if I think someone is misusing a power of attorney?

Although having a power of attorney has many advantages, the primary disadvantage is that it gives an agent the opportunity to take advantage of the principal. Financial exploitation, which includes the illegal or unauthorized use of an individual's funds, property, or resources for profit or advantage, is not uncommon and requires prompt reporting. If you suspect that an agent is misusing a power of attorney, you should take immediate action.

If you suspect your agent is misusing your power of attorney, you should immediately request an accounting, revoke the power of attorney, and notify any people or institutions that may have been given a copy of the document. If you suspect someone else's agent is misusing a power of attorney or if you suspect that a principal was coerced to sign a power of attorney the principal did not (or could not) understand, you should contact Adult Protective Services to report your concerns.

Any interested person can also go to court in the county where the principal resides (or in the county where the guardian and/or conservator resides if one has been appointed) to control the agent or to request that the court replace the agent with a guardian or conservator or both. If an agent has misused a power of attorney, the court can force the agent to return any stolen assets.

What if my agent wants to resign?

An agent may resign according to the terms and conditions stated in the power of attorney. The agent must notify, in writing, the principal, the guardian and/or conservator (if any), any successor agent named in the document, and all reasonably ascertainable third parties who might be affected by the resignation. However, if the principal is incapacitated and there is no guardian, conservator, co-agent, or successor agent, the agent may resign by giving notice to the principal's caregiver, another person the agent reasonably believes has sufficient interest in the welfare of the principal, or to a government agency that has the authority to protect the principal.

When does a power of attorney terminate?

A power of attorney terminates when: (a) the principal dies (and the agent has knowledge of the death); (b) the principal becomes incapacitated, if the power of attorney is not durable; (c) the principal revokes the power of attorney; (d) the power of attorney provides that it terminates; (e) the express purpose of the power of attorney is accomplished; or (f) the principal revokes the agent's authority, or the agent dies, becomes incapacitated, or resigns, and the power of attorney does not provide for another agent to act under the power of attorney.

When does an agent's authority terminate?

An agent's authority terminates when: (a) the principal revokes the authority; (b) the agent dies, becomes incapacitated, or resigns; (c) an action is filed for the dissolution or annulment of the agent's marriage to the principal or for their legal separation, unless the power of attorney otherwise provides; or (d) the power of attorney terminates. Termination of an agent's authority is not effective until the agent has actual knowledge of the termination.

Is my power of attorney valid in other states?

A power of attorney is valid in any state, regardless of where the individual lived when the power of attorney was created. However, laws regarding powers of attorney vary from state to state.

2012 Senior Law Handbook

What is a limited power of attorney?

A Limited Power of Attorney, also known as a Special Power of Attorney, grants an agent the legal authority, in writing, to perform a specific act or acts on behalf of the principal. For example, if you do not want to grant an agent full control over your financial matters, but would like an agent to cash your checks, you can limit the agent's powers by preparing a Limited Power of Attorney.

What is the difference between a medical and a financial power of attorney?

A Medical Power of Attorney generally gives an agent the authority to make medical and personal decisions. A Financial Power of Attorney gives an agent authority to manage the principal's finances and property and to transact business on behalf of the principal. The following sections describe these two types of powers of attorney in greater detail.

23-2. Financial Powers of Attorney

A Financial Power of Attorney, also known as a General Power of Attorney or General Power of Attorney for Property, is a very flexible and inexpensive method of giving another person the legal authority to manage some or all of your financial affairs. The agent can do whatever the principal may do — withdraw funds from bank accounts, trade stock, pay bills, cash checks — except as limited in the power of attorney. When transacting business on behalf of the principal, the agent must use the principal's finances as the principal would for the principal's own benefit.

When an agent manages the finances for a principal, the most important rule for the agent is to maintain separate accounts. An agent should never commingle the agent's own funds with those of the principal. The easiest way for an agent to keep track of the basic financial records is to establish a separate checking account because the checks will act as receipts and the checkbook register as a running account. Likewise, the agent should avoid cash transactions whenever possible because such transactions are more difficult to account for and may be more heavily scrutinized. A principal should ensure that the agent understands that the agent has a legal obligation to furnish the principal, or his or her designee, with information about the agent's activities.

When an agent acts for the principal's benefit under a Financial Power of Attorney, the law holds the agent to the "prudent man rule," which means that the agent must exercise "due care" and manage the principal's funds not as if they were the funds of the agent, but with the care needed for managing funds of another. The agent should avoid speculative investments even if the agent would be willing to take more risk with his or her personal funds.

For all financial powers of attorney signed after January 1, 2010, the principal must state that the agent has certain powers, casually referred to as "hot powers." These "hot powers" include the power of an agent to create, amend, revoke, or terminate a trust; make a gift; create or change rights of survivorship; create or change a beneficiary designation; delegate authority granted under a power of attorney; waive the principal's right to be a beneficiary of a joint and survivor annuity, including a survivor benefit under a retirement plan; exercise various powers held by the principal in a fiduciary capacity; and disclaim or release property or a power of appointment. If the power of attorney does not include these "hot powers," then the agent lacks the authority to exercise any of these powers for the principal. The "hot powers" are listed as options in the statutory power of attorney form, Exhibit 23A.

As a word of caution, as previously mentioned, financial exploitation is not uncommon. The principal should be careful when empowering an agent through a Financial Power of Attorney. These documents are helpful tools and people should be encouraged to use them. However, a principal needs to carefully consider his or her choice of agent, monitor the agent, and consider other appropriate safeguards, such as including language in the document that allows successor agents or other family members to have some oversight of the agent currently serving.

23-3. Medical Powers of Attorney

A Medical Power of Attorney, also known as a Power of Attorney for Health Care, allows you to name an agent who will make health care decisions for you when you are not able to do so. In the document, you can give specific instructions to your agent about various issues like surgery, medical treatment, or the need for nursing home care. Unlike a living will, a Medical Power of Attorney's use is not limited to terminal illness or persistent vegetative state situations. Instead, the agent under a Medical Power of Attorney is authorized to make any health care decisions that the principal could make, with certain limitations, if the principal had capacity to do so. Although an agent acting under a Medical Power of Attorney may direct medical treatment while the principal is still medically capable of making his or her own medical decisions, it is uncommon. Typically, medical providers will look to the principal to make decisions relative to medical courses of action so long as the principal is able to provide informed consent. Nevertheless, no agent may consent to or refuse any proposed medical treatment for a principal over the principal's objection.

A Medical Power of Attorney can be as simple or as sophisticated as the principal and the principal's attorney wish to make it. In addition to the authority to make health care decisions, the principal can consider adding language that permits the agent to complete the documentation necessary for insurance, Medicare, Medicaid, and medical facility admissions. The document should also include language sufficient to satisfy the requirement of the Health Insurance Portability and Accountability Act of 1996, commonly known as "HIPAA." HIPAA is intended to ensure the privacy of medical information. Although an agent legally is entitled to access the medical records of the principal, by including specific HIPAA language which authorizes an agent to be considered a "personal representative" (the HIPAA term for an agent), the principal will ensure that the agent can discuss medical issues and access medical records so he or she can make informed decisions when the principal is unable to do so.

It is recommended that the principal discuss all medical issues and beliefs concerning medical treatment with his or her doctor and the agent under a Medical Power of Attorney, since the agent is required to follow the principal's wishes and intent as to medical care and treatment. If the principal's specific wishes are not known to the agent, the agent must act in accordance with the best interests of the principal as determined by the agent.

---

* Ms. Caton would like to thank the former authors of the *Senior Law Handbook* and the Colorado Bar Association power of attorney pamphlet authors for providing the basis for the chapter.

Exhibit 23A.
Sample Colorado Statutory Form
Power of Attorney for Property

STATE OF COLORADO
STATUTORY FORM POWER OF ATTORNEY

IMPORTANT INFORMATION

This power of attorney authorizes another person (your agent) to make decisions concerning your property for you (the principal). Your agent will be able to make decisions and act with respect to your property (including your money) whether or not you are able to act for yourself. The meaning of authority over subjects listed on this form is explained in the "Uniform Power of Attorney Act", part 7 of article 14 of title 15, Colorado Revised Statutes.

This power of attorney does not authorize the agent to make health care decisions for you.

You should select someone you trust to serve as your agent. Unless you specify otherwise, generally the agent's authority will continue until you die or revoke the power of attorney or the agent resigns or is unable to act for you.

Your agent is entitled to reasonable compensation unless you state otherwise in the special instructions.

This form provides for designation of one agent. If you wish to name more than one agent you may name a coagent in the special instructions. Coagents are not required to act together unless you include that requirement in the special instructions.

If your agent is unable or unwilling to act for you, your power of attorney will end unless you have named a successor agent. You may also name a second successor agent.

This power of attorney becomes effective immediately unless you state otherwise in the special instructions.

If you have questions about the power of attorney or the authority you are granting to your agent, you should seek legal advice before signing this form.

DESIGNATION OF AGENT

I _____ (name of principal) name the following person as my agent:

Name of agent: _____

Agent's address: _____

Agent's telephone number: _____

DESIGNATION OF SUCCESSOR AGENT(S) (OPTIONAL)

If my agent is unable or unwilling to act for me, I name as my successor agent:

Name of successor agent: _____

Successor agent's address: _____

Successor agent's telephone number: _____

If my successor agent is unable or unwilling to act for me, I name as my second successor agent:

Name of second successor agent: _____

Second successor agent's address: _____

Second successor agent's telephone number: _____

GRANT OF GENERAL AUTHORITY

I grant my agent and any successor agent general authority to act for me with respect to the following subjects as defined in the "Uniform Power of Attorney Act", part 7 of article 14 of title 15, Colorado Revised Statutes:

(INITIAL each subject you want to include in the agent's general authority. If you wish to grant general authority over all of the subjects you may initial "All preceding subjects" instead of initialing each subject.)

(_____) Real property
(_____) Tangible personal property
(_____) Stocks and bonds
(_____) Commodities and options
(_____) Banks and other financial institutions
(_____) Operation of entity or business
(_____) Insurance and annuities

(___) Estates, trusts, and other beneficial interests
(___) Claims and litigation
(___) Personal and family maintenance
(___) Benefits from governmental programs or civil or military service
(___) Retirement plans
(___) Taxes

(___) All preceding subjects

GRANT OF SPECIFIC AUTHORITY (OPTIONAL)

My agent MAY NOT do any of the following specific acts for me UNLESS I have INITIALED the specific authority listed below:

(CAUTION: Granting any of the following will give your agent the authority to take actions that could significantly reduce your property or change how your property is distributed at your death. INITIAL ONLY the specific authority you WANT to give your agent.)

(___) Create, amend, revoke, or terminate an inter vivos trust
(___) Make a gift, subject to the limitations of the "Uniform Power of Attorney Act" set forth in section 15-14-740, Colorado Revised Statutes, and any special instructions in this power of attorney
(___) Create or change rights of survivorship
(___) Create or change a beneficiary designation
(___) Authorize another person to exercise the authority granted under this power of attorney
(___) Waive the principal's right to be a beneficiary of a joint and survivor annuity, including a survivor benefit under a retirement plan
(___) Exercise fiduciary powers that the principal has authority to delegate, including powers to participate in the designation or changing of a fiduciary and powers to participate in the direction of a fiduciary in the exercise of the fiduciary's powers
(___) Disclaim, refuse, or release an interest in property or a power of appointment
(___) Exercise a power of appointment other than: (1) The exercise of a general power of appointment for the benefit of the principal which may, if the subject of estates, trusts, and other beneficial interests is authorized above, be exercised as provided under the subject of estates, trusts, and other beneficial interests; or (2) the exercise of a general power of appointment for the benefit of persons other than the principal which may, if the making of a gift is specifically authorized above, be exercised under the specific authorization to make gifts

(____) Exercise powers, rights, or authority as a partner, member, or manager of a partnership, limited liability company, or other entity that the principal may exercise on behalf of the entity and has authority to delegate excluding the exercise of such powers, rights, and authority with respect to an entity owned solely by the principal which may, if operation of entity or business is authorized above, be exercised as provided under the subject of operation of the entity or business

LIMITATION ON AGENT'S AUTHORITY

An agent that is not my ancestor, spouse, or descendant MAY NOT use my property to benefit the agent or a person to whom the agent owes an obligation of support unless I have included that authority in the special instructions.

SPECIAL INSTRUCTIONS (OPTIONAL)

You may give special instructions on the following lines:

_____

_____

_____

_____

_____

_____

_____

_____

EFFECTIVE DATE

This power of attorney is effective immediately unless I have stated otherwise in the special instructions.

NOMINATION OF CONSERVATOR
OR GUARDIAN (OPTIONAL)

If it becomes necessary for a court to appoint a conservator of my estate or guardian of my person, I nominate the following person(s) for appointment:

Name of nominee for conservator of my estate: _____

Nominee's address: _____

Nominee's telephone number: _____

Name of nominee for guardian of my person: _____

Nominee's address: _____

Nominee's telephone number: _____

RELIANCE ON THIS POWER OF ATTORNEY

Any person, including my agent, may rely upon the validity of this power of attorney or a copy of it unless that person knows it has terminated or is invalid.

SIGNATURE AND ACKNOWLEDGMENT

_____   _____

Your signature   Date

_____

Your name printed

_____

_____

Your address

_____

Your telephone number

State of _____)
) ss.
County of _____)

This document was acknowledged before me on _____, (Date) by
_____. (Name of principal)

(Seal, if any)

_____
Signature of notary

My commission expires: _____

This document was prepared by:

_____

_____

_____

IMPORTANT INFORMATION FOR AGENT

Agent's duties

When you accept the authority granted under this power of attorney, a special legal relationship is created between you and the principal. This relationship imposes upon you legal duties that continue until you resign or the power of attorney is terminated or revoked. You must:

(1)   Do what you know the principal reasonably expects you to do with the principal's property or, if you do not know the principal's expectations, act in the principal's best interest;

(2)   Act in good faith;

(3)   Do nothing beyond the authority granted in this power of attorney; and

(4)   Disclose your identity as an agent whenever you act for the principal by writing or printing the name of the principal and signing your own name as "agent" in the following manner:

(Principal's name) by (Your signature) as agent

Unless the special instructions in this power of attorney state otherwise, you must also:

(1)   Act loyally for the principal's benefit;

(2)   Avoid conflicts that would impair your ability to act in the principal's best interest;

(3)   Act with care, competence, and diligence;

(4)   Keep a record of all receipts, disbursements, and transactions made on behalf of the principal;

(5)   Cooperate with any person that has authority to make health care decisions for the principal to do what you know the principal reasonably expects or, if you do not know the principal's expectations, to act in the principal's best interest; and

(6)   Attempt to preserve the principal's estate plan if you know the plan and preserving the plan is consistent with the principal's best interest.

Termination of agent's authority

You must stop acting on behalf of the principal if you learn of any event that terminates this power of attorney or your authority under this power of attorney. Events that terminate a power of attorney or your authority to act under a power of attorney include:

(1)   Death of the principal;

(2)   The principal's revocation of the power of attorney or your authority;

(3)   The occurrence of a termination event stated in the power of attorney;

(4)   The purpose of the power of attorney is fully accomplished; or

(5)   If you are married to the principal, a legal action is filed with a court to end your marriage, or for your legal separation, unless the special instructions in this power of attorney state that such an action will not terminate your authority.

Liability of Agent

The meaning of the authority granted to you is defined in the "Uniform Power of Attorney Act", part 7 of article 14 of title 15, Colorado Revised Statutes. If you violate the "Uniform Power of Attorney Act", part 7 of article 14 of title 15, Colorado Revised Statutes, or act outside the authority granted, you may be liable for any damages caused by your violation.

If there is anything about this document or your duties that you do not understand, you should seek legal advice.

Chapter 24

Medical Advance Directives

Michael Kirtland, Esq.
Kirtland & Seal, L.L.C.

SYNOPSIS

Medical advance directives are legal documents that tell medical professionals and others about your desires concerning your medical treatment for use in the event you can no longer speak for yourself. The term "medical advance directive" most commonly refers to a living will, but the term may also include medical durable powers of attorney, cardiopulmonary resuscitation (CPR) directives, Do Not Resuscitate (DNR) orders, Medical Orders for Scope of Treament (MOST), and other directives concerning your care and disposition in the event your medical condition is terminal, and at or after the time of your death.

24-1. Living Wills

A living will, known in Colorado as an "Advance Directive for Medical/Surgical Treatment," is a document in which you express your preference as to how you wish to be treated in the event you are in a terminal condition or a persistent vegetative state and are also incapable of speaking for yourself concerning how you wish to be treated medically.

In 2010, the Colorado General Assembly passed a major update to Colorado's advance directive statutes. The purpose of the update was to modernize the 1989 statute, to recognize medical advances that have occurred since that time, and to allow for more flexibility in drafting living wills in Colorado. The new law does not change the basic philosophy of advance directives in Colorado, which is based upon the premise that competent adults should be permitted to accept or reject medical treatment in end-of-life situations, and to express those preferences in advance in writing.

The basic living will covers two end-of-life situations. The first of these is a terminal condition. A terminal condition means an incurable or irreversible condition for which the administration of life-sustaining procedures will serve only to postpone the moment of death. In other words, the medical professionals have determined they can take no other actions that will cure or improve your medical condition, and life-sustaining procedures may prolong your life somewhat, but not overcome your impending death. Life-sustaining procedures are medications, surgeries, or other medical therapies that would lengthen your remaining lifetime somewhat, but not reverse your medical condition. The second medical condition is a persistent vegetative state. The new law recognizes that the determination of whether or not a person is in a persistent vegetative state should be made by medical professionals, and not by attorneys and courts. As a result, the term is not defined in Colorado law, except to say that determination is based upon prevailing medical standards.

In either of these two end-of life situations, a Colorado living will permits the individual to select one of three choices. The first is to forego life-sustaining treatment. The second is to accept life-sustaining treatment, but only for a limited period of time. At the end of this period of time, determined by the individual in the living will, the individual's doctors will re-evaluate the individual, and if it is determined the individual remains in a terminal condition or a persistent vegetative state (which should always happen if the individual was correctly diagnosed previously), the life-sustaining treatment will be terminated. The third choice is to continue life-sustaining treatment as long as medically feasible.

In addition to expressing one's preference regarding life sustaining treatment, Colorado law permits the individual to express the desire to accept or withhold nutrition and hydration in a terminal condition or a persistent vegetative state. Under Colorado law, nutrition and hydration are treated separately from any other form of medical treatment. As with life-sustaining treatments, when determining one's preferences for provision of nutrition and hydration, the individual can express one of three preferences, as defined above.

The new law also permits a person to express individual medical instructions concerning other medical issues that they might face. The law now permits a person to list individuals with whom the person's doctor should discuss the person's medical situation, and provides language permitting the doctor to openly discuss the medical situation in light of the privacy requirements of the Health Insurance Portability and Accountability Act of 1996 (HIPAA). Finally, the new law includes language permitting an organ and tissue donation preference to be expressed in the living will. Organ and tissue donation is discussed more fully later in this chapter.

Under previous Colorado law, a sample living will was included in the statutes. The new law removes this sample form. This was done to permit more flexibility in using the various living will forms that have been developed in the last two decades.

Any competent adult may execute a living will. Under the new statute, the individual may also indicate whether an agent under a medical power of attorney may override the preferences expressed by the individual in the living will, or whether the agent under the medical power of attorney should be required to follow the directions contained within the living will.

Many people worry that if life-sustaining treatment, including nutrition and hydration, is withheld or withdrawn, they will suffer pain and discomfort as a result. The law in Colorado, and every other state, requires medical professionals to provide whatever medications or other treatments are necessary in order to make you as comfortable and pain free as is practical.

After you have executed your living will, you should provide a copy of the living will to any medical professional who keeps regular medical records on you. If you have multiple doctors, such as an internist, an orthopedic doctor, and so on, you should give a copy of your living will to each of these medical professionals. In all cases, provide them a copy of your living will to be placed in your medical files, but keep the original living will yourself, or provide it to your agent under medical power of attorney.

Federal law requires that, upon admission to a hospital, the hospital must ask you if you have a living will. You should bring your living will with you to the admissions process and let them make a copy for your medical file at the hospital. If you enter an assisted living facility or a nursing home, you should also provide a copy of the living will to the facility at the time of your admission.

Remember, so long as you are capable of making your own medical decisions, what you say at that time will determine what treatments you will or will not receive. The purpose of the living will is for you to express in advance what your wishes are, so that in the event you are unable to express your wishes, there is a written document telling the medical professionals and your family what your preferences are on the subject of terminal illness and persistent vegetative state situations.

Perhaps most important of all is for you to discuss with your loved ones your feelings, beliefs, and desires with regard to end-of-life treatment. The more your loved ones know about your desires, the more likely you are to receive the kind of medical treatment you wish to receive at the end of your life. Lawyers and doctors can provide support and expertise, but only you can provide your preferences. Take the time to speak with your loved ones and be open with them about how you feel on the subject of end-of-life treatment, life-sustaining procedures, and other issues concerning end-of-life matters.

You do not have to execute a new living will if you travel to or move to another state. However, as medical professionals are most comfortable with the living will form(s) commonly found in their state, if you stay for an extended period of time in another state (such as individuals who have a winter home in a warmer climate) or move to another state, it is a good idea to execute a new living will in a form that is commonly found in that state. For people who have two residences it is a good idea to have two living wills, each in the format commonly found in that state. HOWEVER: Be careful to ensure that the information in those two living wills is not in any way contradictory, or a court may invalidate both documents.

24-2. CPR Directives and DNR Orders

Cardiopulmonary resuscitation (CPR) directives and Do Not Resuscitate (DNR) orders are directives, signed by a doctor, that direct that in the event your heart stops or you stop breathing, you do not wish to have CPR or other methods of restarting your heart and breathing. These directives must be issued by a doctor. As such, you need to speak with your physician to obtain such a directive. Unless you have a signed CPR or DNR directive, the law in Colorado and the standards of medical practice will require medical professionals to make all reasonable efforts to restart your heart in the event it stops.

24-3. Medical Orders for Scope of Treatment

In 2010, the Colorado General Assembly passed a new law creating authority for a Medical Orders for Scope of Treatment (MOST) form. This law recognizes a growing trend in the various states to permit medical professionals to capture your wishes concerning end-of-life treatment preferences, and to allow that information to follow the patient from one health care facility to another, rather than requiring the information to be recreated and recompiled once the patient is admitted to the new facility. As with living wills and other advance directives, the purpose is to better ensure, in a written advance directive, that the wishes of the individual concerning his or her end of life medical treatment are known and followed.

The new statute does not make substantive changes to Colorado law or provide new alternatives for medical treatment. Rather, it simply places your wishes on one document, clearly identified in your medical records because of the bright green color of the form. The document is signed by you and your physician, thus making it a medical order in your medical records. It does not replace the living will; instead, the two documents work together to more fully capture your intentions concerning end-of-life treatment. Consistent with the living will statutes, the MOST statutes specifically say that nothing contained in the MOST form changes the accepted standards of medical practice and ethics.

The MOST form provides identifying information about the patient, and expresses the patient's preferences concerning end-of-life treatment, cardiopulmonary resuscitation (CPR), transfer to hospital facilities, and other end-of-life issues. Like the living will, it also provides for individualized instructions concerning these subjects.

To account for differences in moral or religious beliefs between the patient and the medical professionals treating the patient, the law provides that in the event the medical provider's moral convictions or religious beliefs conflict with the patient's instructions, the medical provider is required to effect the transfer of the patient to a medical provider or facility that is willing to comply with the MOST form.

Any competent person may execute a MOST form in conjunction with that person's doctor. Where a person is not competent to complete the form, an authorized agent under the person's medical power of attorney or a proxy under the medical surrogate statutes may complete the form on behalf of the incompetent person. The form may be revoked at any time and in any way that clearly indicates the executing person's intention to revoke the form.

Where the person has previously executed a living will, medical power of attorney, or other advance directives, those documents are to be kept with the MOST form in the patient's medical records. If there is an inconsistency between the documents, the most recently executed document will prevail.

24-4. Medical Power of Attorney

A medical power of attorney, sometimes known as a "Durable Medical Power of Attorney" or a "Power of Attorney for Health Care," is a legal document in which you appoint an "agent" to speak for you on the subject of medical treatment, in the event you are unable to speak for yourself. Unlike the living will, the medical power of attorney's use is not limited to a terminal condition or persistent vegetative state situations. The agent under the medical power of attorney is authorized to make any medical decision that you could make for yourself, with certain limitations, if you were mentally competent to do so. However, nothing in the medical power of attorney permits the agent to direct your medical treatment while you are still mentally capable of making your own medical decisions.

The medical power of attorney is called "durable" because it contains language within the document that directs that its authority should continue to be effective even in the event that you become legally or medically incompetent. Medical powers of attorney can be as simple or as sophisticated as you and your attorney wish to make them. However, at a minimum, the medical power of attorney needs to appoint an adult (defined in Colorado as a person 18 years of age or older) as your agent under the medical power of attorney. It is a good idea to include in the medical power of attorney an alternate or successor agent, in the event your primary named agent is deceased, unwilling, or otherwise unable to make medical decisions for you. It is not a good idea to appoint, and the medical community discourages appointing, co-agents, that is, two or more people who must act together to make medical decisions. The medical professionals much prefer to have one person with the authority to act.

Any properly written medical power of attorney today should include in it language sufficient to satisfy the requirements of the Health Insurance Portability and Accountability Act of 1996, commonly known as "HIPAA" (pronounced "HIP-ah"). HIPAA is intended to ensure the privacy of your medical information and to ensure that you have access to any medical information that medical professionals keep concerning you. Your medical power of attorney should include language that permits your agent to be considered a "personal representative" (the HIPAA term for an agent) for the purpose of discussing your medical records, conditions, and possible courses of medical treatment with the medical professionals. By including HIPAA language in the appointment of an agent under medical power of attorney, your agent can discuss your medical issues with the medical professionals, can make medical decisions when you are unable to do so, and can do such things as pick up medications for you at a pharmacy.

In addition to the basic elements of a medical power of attorney, you should consider adding language to your medical power of attorney to permit your agent to complete admission applications to medical facilities, assisted living facilities, and nursing homes; make applications for Medicare, Medicaid, and other medical insurance forms; and nominate and appoint a guardian.

Like the living will, you should provide a copy of your medical power of attorney to any medical professionals who keep medical records on you and provide a copy to any hospital, assisted living facility, nursing home, or other medical facility upon admission. You should keep the original of the medical power of attorney, or provide it to your agent. Additionally, as with the living will, it is an excellent idea to discuss your medical issues, your feelings and beliefs concerning medical treatment, and other related issues with your agent under the medical power of attorney and with your loved ones. It is the purpose of appointing an agent under the medical power of attorney that your agent should follow your wishes and intent as to medical treatment. The agent can only do so if he or she knows what you want.

You do not need to execute a new medical power of attorney in the event you travel to or move to another state, unless you wish to make changes to your medical power of attorney. To be safe, and to ensure your medical power of attorney meets the execution requirements of each state, you should have your medical power of attorney witnessed by two individuals unrelated to you, who are not in any way responsible for your medical care and medical bills, and have the medical power of attorney notarized.

Finally, authority to act under a medical power of attorney ceases upon the death of the principal, that is, the person who executed the medical power of attorney appointing the agent to act.

24-5. Organ and Tissue Donation

Under Colorado law, if you choose to, you may decide to donate your organs and/or tissue at the time of your death. This declaration to donate your organs or tissue may be done in a variety of methods, including making such a statement in your will, by making a direction on your driver's license, by declaration in a living will or a medical power of attorney, or by declaration in another written document such as an organ/tissue donation card or other similar written instrument. Be careful, however. While legally you can donate your organs and tissues through a statement in your last will and testament, there is a distinct possibility that no one will look at the terms and directions of your last will and testament until well after your death, including not until after your burial or cremation. So, while you can legally use a will to do this, it may not be the best choice available.

If you do not have a written declaration to donate your organs and tissue, or a written direction not to make such donation, then certain persons who survive you may make such donation of your organs and tissues. The authority to make such donation is in the following order of persons:

1) An agent of the decedent;

2) The spouse of the decedent;

3) Adult children of the decedent;

4) Parents of the decedent;

5) Adult siblings of the decedent;

6) Adult grandchildren of the decedent;

7) Grandparents of the decedent;

8) An adult who exhibited special care and concern for the decedent;

9) The persons who were acting as the guardians of the person of the decedent at the time of death; or

10) Any other person having the authority to dispose of the decedent's body.

As with all of these advance directive documents, it is a good idea to discuss your desires and beliefs with your loved ones so that they will know what you want done at the time of your death.

24-6. Disposition of Last Remains

We would all like to think that our relatives and loved ones will be in agreement as to what is to happen to our last remains at the time of our death. Unfortunately, it is quite possible that this will not be the case. As a result, Colorado has what is known as the Disposition of Last Remains Act.

Under this Act, you have the right to direct in writing who should control what happens to your last remains after your death. This direction must be in writing. If there is no such writing, your verbal directions do not have legal standing.

This written declaration may direct what you wish done with your last remains, that is, whether you wish to be buried, cremated, or have your remains donated to medical science. The declaration may also direct what funeral, religious, or other ceremonies you wish to have after your death.

If you do not have a declaration as to disposition of last remains, the individual who has authority to determine how to dispose of your last remains will be decided in the following order:

▶ The appointed personal representative or special administrator of your estate;

▶ The nominated personal representative under your last will and testament;

▶ Your surviving spouse;

▶ The majority decision of your adult children;

▶ The decision of your surviving parents or legal guardians;

▶ The majority decision of your adult siblings;

▶ Any person assuming legal and financial responsibility for the final disposition of your last remains; or

▶ The Office of the Public Administrator in your county.

24-7. Resources

Aging With Dignity
Distributor of "Five Wishes"
 P.O. Box 1661
 Tallahassee, FL 32302-1661
 (888) 5 WISHES ((888) 594-7437)
 fivewishes@agingwithdignity.org
 www.agingwithdignity.org

American Bar Association
Provides a Health Care Advance Directives booklet and form online:
 www.abanet.org/aging/publications/docs/shape_your.pdf

Caring Connections
National Hospice and Palliative Care Organization
Advocates for the rights of dying patients, provides legal information about end-of-life decisions, and offers counseling. State-specific free forms and instructions are available online.
 (800) 658-8898
 www.caringinfo.org

Colorado Hospital Association
 (720) 489-1630
 www.cha.com; click on "News & Publications," then "Publications" for a free copy of the brochure, "Your Right to Make Healthcare Decisions."

Chapter 25

Conservatorship of Adults

M. Carl Glatstein, Esq.
Glatstein & O'Brien LLP

SYNOPSIS

25-1. Introduction

What is a conservator? You may have heard the term, but do you understand what it means? A conservator is a type of trustee or fiduciary who is appointed by the court for an individual who is unable to manage his or her own financial affairs. Confusion arises because in some states, such as California, the term "conservator" is used interchangeably with the term "guardian." Other states, such as Texas and Florida, use the term "guardian" to also mean a conservator.

Colorado distinguishes between these two terms. Here, a conservator is placed in charge of a person's financial matters, while a guardian is placed in charge of the care and custody of a person and is responsible for making health care and placement decisions. Guardianship requires a determination of incapacity for an adult. (Minors need a guardian appointed because they are not legally competent until they reach age 18 — the age of majority.) Conservatorship, on the other hand, does not require that the person be found incapacitated or incompetent, although the two proceedings often go hand-in-hand.

It is important to understand that the appointment of a conservator affects a person's property rights, while the appointment of a guardian affects a person's civil liberties and personal freedoms. Since these are all constitutionally protected interests, they can only be taken away or limited by a court of competent jurisdiction, and only after due process is provided, which requires notice and a hearing. Certain safeguards are built into the law and the procedures required for imposing a conservatorship. The court retains jurisdiction over these matters and requires conservators to report on the finances of the protected person at least annually.

If the conservator is not acting in the best interest of the protected person, or is mismanaging the assets, the court may suspend or remove the conservator. The court may also impose a fine or surcharge, which means the conservator will have to repay the funds that were misappropriated. In some cases, the conservator may even be charged with a crime for taking advantage of an at-risk adult. Assuming the role and duties of a conservator is serious business and should not be done lightly.

25-2. Alternatives to Conservatorship

There are alternatives to conservatorship that should be considered first. Financial powers of attorney are very flexible and inexpensive. A power of attorney can give an agent the legal authority to manage the finances and act on behalf of the principal, who is the person granting the authority. However, at the time the principal signs the power of attorney, the principal must have sufficient capacity to know and understand what the document authorizes. If an individual is already incapacitated, or subject to undue influence, it may be too late to rely upon powers of attorney.

Forms for financial powers of attorney can be found in office supply stores, and many versions are available in software packages and on the Internet. However, relying upon powers of attorney without fully understanding their uses and potential for abuse can be penny-wise and pound foolish. While powers of attorney can be simple and useful tools, they can also wreak devastating results. An agent with a duly signed power of attorney can empty out your bank accounts, sell your investments, and even sell your house.

For limited purposes, a joint bank account may also be a simple alternative. With joint bank accounts, either party named on the title to the account may write checks, regardless of what the funds are used for. However, joint bank accounts, just like powers of attorney, may be abused. On top of that, when adding someone else's name to your account as a joint tenant, that person is entitled to ownership of everything in the account upon your death — regardless of what your will says.

With both financial powers of attorney and joint bank accounts, there is no court involvement and therefore no court oversight. It is very important to make sure that your agent or joint tenant understands the legal obligation to furnish you with information about his or her activities. It is also wise to make sure that a trusted friend or family member has the right to this information in the event of your incapacity or disability. Studies have consistently found that financial abuse of the elderly happens under the guise of a power of attorney. Unfortunately, most of this exploitation happens at the hands of family members.

This suggests that it may be wise to have several sets of eyes watching your financial affairs when you are no longer able to do so. You may also wish to consider turning to a professional fiduciary to take on this role. Often lawyers are needed to fix the damage done by trying to do things the easy way. By then it may be too late for the courts to do anything but preserve what's left of your assets.

Finally, one other alternative to conservatorship is the use of trusts. When creating a trust, you may designate who will be your trustee. You may even be your own trustee while you have the capacity and ability to manage your own assets. Upon your incapacity, a successor trustee can take over managing your assets. Trusts are also very flexible and can be used to hold specific assets or everything you own. Unlike conservatorships, trusts are private and generally only require court involvement if there are problems. However, there may also be significant tax ramifications in using a trust. Transferring your assets into trust may jeopardize your ability to qualify for Medicaid. Since there are often complex legal and tax matters involved, it is generally advisable to have an attorney work with you in the drafting and administration of the trust.

25-3. Court Process

A conservatorship is a legal proceeding, which is started by filing a petition for the appointment of a conservator. The filing fee with the court is $127 (in 2012). The person filing this pleading is the "petitioner" and is responsible for paying the filing fee. The person who is alleged to need the protection of a conservator is the "respondent" or "protected person." The petition is filed in the county where the respondent lives. A supporting doctor's letter should be attached to the petition. If the respondent is also incapacitated and no one has legal authority to make medical decisions for the respondent, a guardianship petition should be filed at the same time. This saves having to pay another filing fee later on. (See Chapter 26, "Guardianship of Adults," for more information.)

Many courts have packets of information with instructions for simple and uncontested conservatorships. More detailed information is also available on the Internet from the Colorado State Judicial Branch website at www.courts.state.co.us and by clicking on "Forms" then "Probate." Court staff are often very helpful, but remember, they cannot give legal advice. Often, family or friends may be able to follow the rules and file the pleadings without the assistance of counsel. However, if the respondent is objecting to the imposition of a conservator, an attorney must be appointed by the court to represent the respondent.

To further protect due process, the court will appoint a court visitor, who is required to meet personally with the respondent. The court visitor serves as eyes and ears for the court and files a written report. The court visitor tries to inform the respondent about the nature of the proceedings and interviews the respondent as to his or her wishes. The court visitor advises the respondent about the right to be present at the hearing, to cross-examine witnesses, to introduce testimony, and to have a medical or psychological evaluation performed. The court visitor also advises that the respondent has the right to be represented by counsel at his or her own expense. If the assets are insufficient, the representation is at the state's expense. If the respondent tells the court visitor that he or she wants an attorney, the court must appoint one. The fees charged by the court visitor must be paid by the petitioner prior to the hearing. In Denver, the court visitor charges a flat fee of $100. In other counties, an hourly fee may be charged.

Due process requires reasonable advance notice of the hearing. The respondent must be personally served with the notice of hearing and the petition for appointment of a conservator. Other interested parties must also be given advance notice, but this may be mailed. Interested persons include the respondent's spouse and all adult children, agents under powers of attorney, representative payees and other legal representatives, anyone the respondent has nominated to serve as conservator, and the respondent's primary care physician. If there is no spouse but the respondent has lived with someone during the previous six months, that person should be given notice as well. In the absence of immediate family, notice may have to be given to the closest relative by degree of kinship.

Without going into all the technicalities, at the hearing, the petitioner has the burden of proof to establish by clear and convincing evidence that the respondent is unable to manage his or her property due to some form of incapacity or deficit. The petitioner must also show that the respondent has assets which will be wasted or dissipated without proper management, or that the respondent or the respondent's dependents need funds for support, and that the appointment of a conservator will facilitate getting those funds.

25-4. Acceptance of Office

An individual nominated to serve as the conservator generally must submit an Acceptance of Office form. This requires the nominee to sign an affidavit disclosing any criminal history and judgments against him or her, among other things. The nominee is also required to submit a credit report, a name-based Colorado Bureau of Investigation criminal background check, and a copy of his or her driver's license or passport.

25-5. Responsibilities

Once an order of appointment is entered, the conservator has many duties and responsibilities. The court often requires the conservator to first obtain a fiduciary bond from an insurance company. The cost of the bond is payable out of the conservatorship assets. The purpose of the bond is to assure that the conservator faithfully carries out his or her duties and to preserve the assets covered by the bond. The bond company often reviews the accountings and reports that the conservator files more carefully than a court's staff has time to allow.

The conservator is required to file an inventory and financial plan within 90 days of appointment. The inventory is a snapshot of all the assets under the conservator's control as of the date of appointment. The financial plan is a budget that describes the protected person's monthly income and expenses, as well as how the assets under the conservator's control will be managed. Once this information is gathered, it should be possible to determine whether the protected person's income is sufficient to cover expenses, or whether assets will need to be sold to pay for his or her care. The financial plan should be reviewed and approved by the court, and should be followed faithfully. Failure to do so may create significant problems for the conservator, including removal or surcharge. If the protected person's situation changes, the financial plan should be amended and again approved by the court.

At least once a year, the conservator is required to file a conservator's report, detailing the income and expenditures over the past accounting period. The conservator's report provides a comparison between actual expenditures and the court-approved financial plan. It should be easy to determine at a glance whether the financial plan has been carefully followed and whether there have been extraordinary expenditures. The conservator's report should also indicate whether the financial plan is adequate to meet the protected person's needs or whether it should be amended.

25-6. Duties

A conservator is a type of fiduciary and has power and authority much like that of a trustee. Fiduciary duties include that of undivided loyalty to the person whose interests the conservator protects. The conservator may not engage in "self-dealing," which means profiting off the assets controlled. Although a conservator is entitled to reasonable compensation, family members often serve without pay. In any event, compensation paid to the conservator must first be authorized and approved by the court.

The conservator has a duty to exercise due care. The conservator must handle the conservatorship assets prudently, using reasonable care and caution in investing and managing the assets under the conservator's care. If there are sufficient assets to warrant investments, it may be prudent to rely upon a financial advisor to diversify and structure an investment portfolio, balancing risk and return. Sometimes it may be necessary to liquidate investments or even to sell the protected person's house. Any time there is a significant change in financial matters, it is advisable to seek court approval. This will limit the conservator's liability to the protected person and those who may inherit his or her estate.

25-7. Terminating Conservatorship

A conservatorship may need to terminate for various reasons: (1) the protected person may have regained capacity and no longer require assistance and oversight; (2) the protected person may have died; (3) the assets may have been depleted; or (4) if the conservatorship was for a minor, it is no longer needed when the minor becomes 21 years old. When such an event arises, the conservator is then required to prepare and file a final report and petition for the termination of the conservatorship. The final report covers the period since the last accounting and indicates what assets remain in the conservatorship to be distributed. After the death of the protected person, the conservator generally should take no action, other than to pay for funeral expenses and to preserve and protect the assets remaining, without obtaining a court order.

If the conservatorship terminated because the protected person is no longer incapacitated, then the assets should be transferred back into the name of the individual. If the conservatorship terminated because the protected person has died, then the assets are turned over to the personal representative of the individual's estate or as directed by the court. The conservator should ask the court to approve the final report, and then provide the court with proof that the assets have been distributed in accordance with the court's order. Once this is accomplished and the court is satisfied that the conservator has fulfilled all of the duties and obligations required, a decree of discharge will be entered, relieving the conservator of any further liability.

25-8. Resources

Colorado State Judicial Branch
Office of the State Court Administrator
101 W. Colfax, Ste. 500
Denver, CO 80202
(303) 861-1111
www.courts.state.co.us

Denver Probate Court
1437 Bannock St., Rm. 230
Denver, CO 80202
(720) 865-8310
www.denverprobatecourt.org

Chapter 26
Guardianship of Adults

Marcia G. O'Brien, Esq. (Retired)
Glatstein & O'Brien LLP

M. Carl Glatstein, Esq.
Glatstein & O'Brien LLP

SYNOPSIS

26-1. Guardianship Under Colorado Law

In Colorado, the court can appoint a guardian for either a minor or an adult who is deemed incapacitated. The person for whom a guardian is appointed is called the "ward." Different rules apply depending upon whether the ward is a minor or an incapacitated adult.

Each state has its own laws regarding guardianships and uses its own terminology, so do not be confused if you hear the term "guardian" used differently elsewhere. For example, in a number of states a guardian manages an individual's finances and makes decisions regarding his or her ward's physical health, safety, or self-care. That is not the case in Colorado, where a conservator is appointed to manage finances and property for a minor or an adult, unless there are limited assets and the ward does not have a conservator.

A person for whom a conservator is appointed is called a "protected person" in Colorado. It is possible for the court to appoint a guardian, a conservator, or both. The appointment of a conservator for an adult in Colorado is not a determination that the adult is incapacitated, as is the case when a guardian is appointed by the court. For a more complete discussion relating to conservatorships, please see Chapter 25, "Conservatorship of Adults."

26-2. When Does a Guardian Need to Be Appointed?

An incapacitated adult is defined in the Colorado Probate Code as an adult "who is unable to effectively receive or evaluate information or both or make or communicate decisions to such an extent that the individual lacks the ability to satisfy essential requirements for physical health, safety, or self-care, even with appropriate and reasonably available technological assistance."

This statute requires that a functional analysis be used in determining incapacity. The determination should not be based upon a particular diagnosis, although the court will want to know that information. Rather, the issue is whether the person can make decisions that are in that individual's best interest regarding his or her personal affairs. For example, if an adult is diagnosed with mild dementia but retains the ability to make decisions regarding his or her personal affairs that are in his or her best interest, that individual does not require a guardianship and a guardian will not be appointed.

The other important aspect of the definition of an incapacitated adult is its encouragement of the use of appropriate, reasonably available technological assistance. If such technological assistance enables an otherwise incapacitated adult to receive the information necessary to make decisions regarding his or her personal affairs that are in his or her best interests and/or to communicate such decisions, then a guardianship is unnecessary. For example, missing eyeglasses or hearing aids may make all the difference in whether a person can function independently.

26-3. Who Can Serve As a Guardian in Colorado?

Any person age 21 or older may be appointed as a guardian, regardless of whether that person is a resident of Colorado. Family members, professional guardians, volunteers, or in some counties, the Department of Human Services may serve as guardians. However, the nominated guardian must first submit for the court's review an Acceptance of Office form to which is attached a name-based criminal history check and current credit report.

There is a statutory priority for appointment as guardian, which sets forth that the court shall consider persons otherwise qualified in the following order of priority: (1) a currently acting guardian; (2) a person nominated as guardian by the respondent; (3) an agent under a medical durable power of attorney; (4) an agent under a general durable power of attorney; (5) the spouse of the respondent or a person nominated by a will or other signed writing of a deceased spouse; (6) an adult child of the respondent; (7) a parent of the respondent or an individual nominated by a will or other signed writing of a deceased parent; and (8) an adult with whom the respondent has resided for more than six months immediately before the filing of the petition. If good cause is shown, the court can appoint as guardian someone who has lower priority or no priority at all.

Under Colorado law, long-term care providers are prohibited from serving as guardian or conservator of a person for whom they provide care unless related by blood, marriage, or adoption. In addition, a professional guardian ordinarily will not be allowed to serve as both guardian and conservator, or as guardian and direct service provider, unless the court determines that good cause exists to allow the professional to serve in dual roles.

26-4. Types of Guardianships

Limited Guardianships

A limited guardianship restricts the guardian's authority to certain specified matters only. The underlying philosophy is that the guardian's powers should be no greater than necessary to see to the needs of that particular ward. If an unlimited guardianship is believed necessary, the petitioner (the person bringing a guardianship petition) will have to explain to the court's satisfaction why an unlimited guardianship is necessary. Otherwise, a limited guardianship will be ordered.

In fact, all guardianships are limited to the extent that a guardian may not initiate the commitment of a ward to a mental health care institution or facility except in accordance with the state's procedure for involuntary civil commitment. In essence, this means that the guardian has to follow Colorado mental health statutes when seeking psychiatric treatment or substance abuse treatment for the ward.

Emergency Guardianships

The court will appoint a guardian on an emergency basis only if it finds that substantial harm to a person's health, safety, or welfare is likely to result if an emergency guardian is not appointed, and no other person has authority to act under the circumstances. This means that there must be an imminent threat to the respondent. "Respondent" is the term for the individual for whom a guardianship is being sought.

26-5. Duties and Responsibilities of a Guardian

A guardian may make decisions for the ward as allowed within the scope of the guardian's authority, as set forth in the order of appointment issued by the court. The limitations on the guardian's authority should also be stated in the letters of guardianship that the court issues. The guardian is required to see that the basic daily personal needs of the ward for food, clothing, and shelter are met; however, the guardian is not personally responsible for paying for the ward's care.

Frequently, the scope of a guardian's authority includes determining where the ward should live, and arranging for and making decisions regarding the ward's care, medical treatment, and other services. However, if the ward has an agent under a medical durable power of attorney, the guardian may not revoke the medical durable power of attorney without an order of the court. The agent still has the legal authority to make medical decisions unless the court rules otherwise and revokes the power of attorney.

If no conservator is appointed and the ward has limited assets, the guardian may also need to address basic financial management issues for the ward. This is the exception to the general rule that a guardian does not manage the financial affairs for the ward. A guardian usually is allowed to manage the ward's government benefits if there is no conservator.

The guardian should make decisions after consulting with the ward, taking into account the ward's wishes and personal values, to the extent that it is reasonably possible to do so. The guardian should encourage the ward to participate in decision-making. The guardian's scope of duties and responsibilities should be crafted to reflect the ward's limitations. In addition to encouraging the ward to participate in decisions, the guardian should encourage the ward to act on his or her own behalf and to develop or regain the capacity to manage his or her own personal affairs. However, the guardian is ultimately responsible for making the decisions on behalf of the ward.

Within 60 days after appointment, a guardian's report must be filed with the court, which includes a personal care plan for the ward. A guardian's report form can be obtained online at www.courts.state.co.us and by clicking on "Forms." All guardian reports must be sent to the interested persons identified in the Order Appointing Guardian form who are to receive pleadings. The guardian's report addresses the ward's health, including his or her physical and mental condition, diagnosis, and prognosis; a personal care plan for the ward; plans for any therapies or treatments or other services; plans for future care; and any other issues that should be brought to the court's attention. Thereafter, the guardian must file annual reports with the court and interested persons as directed by the court.

The guardian must obtain prior permission from the court to move the ward out of Colorado. If the ward is to move permanently, consideration should be given to whether it would be in the ward's best interest to domesticate the guardianship (make the guardianship subject to the jurisdiction of the state where the ward plans to permanently reside), and whether a successor guardian who lives close to the ward's new home should be appointed. Likewise, if a ward is moving to Colorado from another state, it may be appropriate to domesticate the guardianship in Colorado. A guardian residing out-of-state can hire a local case manager to assist in carrying out the guardian's duties. If there is a significant change in the ward's condition, the guardian should file a status report with the court, sending a copy to all persons who are to receive pleadings as listed on the order of appointment.

26-6. The Appointment Process in Colorado

A petition for the appointment of a guardian is filed in the district court for the county in which the respondent lives. However, in the City and County of Denver, you will file in the Denver Probate Court. A petition can be filed by any person who is interested in the welfare of the respondent. There is a filing fee of $127 (in 2012), which is payable when the petition is filed. There is also a fee for the court visitor, which the petitioner is required to pay. This fee varies by county. Where neither the petitioner nor respondent has the ability to pay the fees, the court may order that the fees be waived. To request such a waiver, ask the court staff for the appropriate forms.

The petition for the appointment of a guardian should have attached to it an evaluation from a physician, psychologist, or other professional qualified to evaluate the respondent's alleged impairment. The evaluation should contain:

▶ A description of the nature, type, and extent of the respondent's specific cognitive and functional limitations;

▶ An evaluation of the respondent's mental and physical condition and, if appropriate, educational potential, adaptive behavior, and social skills;

▶ A prognosis for improvement and a recommendation as to the appropriate treatment or rehabilitation plan; and

▶ The date of any assessment or examination upon which the report is based.

If such a report is unavailable because the respondent refuses to be evaluated, the petitioner can file a request for an order that the respondent undergo an evaluation by an appropriately trained professional. Likewise, the respondent always has the right to request an evaluation through the court, or to obtain an evaluation by professionals whom the respondent selects.

The nominated guardian must file a name-based criminal history check, a current credit report, and a copy of his or her driver's license or passport, along with an Acceptance of Appointment form. If the nominated guardian lives out-of-state, an irrevocable power of attorney form also must be filed to allow the clerk of the court to accept service on behalf of an out-of-state resident.

When seeking the appointment of a guardian, there are specific notice requirements that must be followed. The respondent must be personally served and must appear at the hearing on the petition, unless the court excuses the respondent for good cause. Likewise, persons interested in the ward's welfare must receive notice of the guardianship hearing. You must carefully follow the notice requirements. As with any other important legal matter, if you do not understand the notice requirements, you should seek legal advice.

Once a petition has been filed with the court, the court will appoint a court visitor. The court visitor will meet with the respondent, the petitioner, the proposed guardian, and anyone else deemed necessary. The role of the court visitor is to act as the eyes and ears of the court, investigating whether a guardian should be appointed. The court visitor files a written report with the court, including a recommendation regarding whether a guardianship is necessary.

Every respondent has the right to legal representation. This is because the appointment of a guardian takes away some of the ward's legal rights, such as making decisions regarding the ward's personal affairs, medical care, and place of abode. One of the questions the court visitor asks the respondent is whether the respondent has a lawyer and, if not, whether the respondent wishes to have legal representation. The court must appoint a lawyer to represent the respondent if legal representation is requested by the respondent or recommended by the court visitor, or if the court determines that the respondent needs representation.

The respondent and the petitioner are required to attend the hearing, unless excused by the court for good cause. At the hearing, the respondent has the right to cross-examine witnesses and to call witnesses on his or her behalf. The petitioning party must establish by clear and convincing evidence the respondent's need for a guardianship. At the conclusion of the hearing, the court generally rules from the bench, announcing whether a guardian will be appointed for the respondent and the limitations applicable to the guardianship.

26-7. Compensation and Reimbursement of Expenses

A guardian is entitled to reasonable compensation for his or her services and reimbursement of expenses, payable from the ward's funds. Compensation paid to the guardian is treated as taxable income to the guardian and as a tax-deductible expense for the ward. Family members frequently serve without compensation, accepting only reimbursement of expenses for mileage, parking, and similar costs. There is no statutory schedule or criteria for a guardian's fee. Rather, the Colorado Probate Code in the Colorado Revised Statutes simply mandates that these fees must be fair and reasonable, leaving compensation to be determined on a case-by-case basis.

If family members receive compensation, it should be less than what professionals would receive. Professionals should seek compensation based upon their hourly rate for performing guardian services, which should be reasonable for the area. Contemporaneous time records, describing the services provided and time taken to perform those services, must be kept by all who seek compensation for their services as a guardian. A guardian is entitled to have legal representation, paid for with the ward's funds.

A guardianship may be modified by the court either to expand or to restrict the scope of authority of the guardian to reflect the ward's then-current condition. Before a modification will be granted, it must be established that the requested modification is in the ward's best interest. Through the use of a power of attorney, a guardian may delegate to another person, for a period not exceeding 12 months, any power regarding care, custody, or property of a ward, except the power to consent to marriage or adoption. This procedure should be utilized when a guardian is going out of town on vacation or otherwise may be unavailable.

26-8. A Guardian May Be Removed or Resign

A ward, or person interested in the welfare of a ward, may petition for removal of a guardian on the ground that removal would be in the best interest of the ward or for other good cause. A guardian may petition to resign. Either a petition to resign or a petition for removal may include a request for appointment of a successor guardian.

26-9. Termination of a Guardianship

A permanent guardianship most frequently terminates upon the death of the ward. At that time, the guardian should file a pleading advising the court that the ward has died. The court may also terminate the guardianship if the ward no longer meets the standard for establishing a guardianship.

In order to cut off the guardian's potential liability once a guardianship has terminated, the guardian should file with the court a petition for decree of discharge. Seeking a decree of discharge most commonly occurs in conservatorships, but the procedure is also available in guardianships. It is a prudent step where the guardianship was contested, issues were encountered that caused dissension, or there are disgruntled family members or other interested persons.

26-10. Resources

Colorado State Judicial Branch
Office of the State Court Administrator
101 W. Colfax, Ste. 500
Denver, CO 80202
(303) 861-1111
www.courts.state.co.us

Denver Probate Court
1437 Bannock St., Rm. 230
Denver, CO 80202
(720) 865-8310
www.denverprobatecourt.org

Department of Human Services
1575 Sherman St.
Denver, CO 80203
(303) 866-5700
www.cdhs.state.co.us

Chapter 27

Hospice and Palliative Care: Options for Care at the End of Life

Jennifer M. Ballentine, M.A.*
Life Quality Institute

SYNOPSIS

"Hospice was great for my husband, but quite frankly, it saved my life." "I've never met such caring people — they made a tough time almost a pleasure." "Honestly, I think Mom lived longer with hospice care than she would have without it!" These are the kinds of comments we hear every day from folks who have experienced hospice care. Ask around and you are likely to hear the same. After all, more than half of all Coloradoans who die receive hospice care. In a summary of survey results from 1,317 hospices across the country, compiled by the National Hospice & Palliative Care Organization in 2010, 98.3 percent of hospice patient family members said they would recommend hospice to others. That's amazing. Not even Geico has that kind of customer satisfaction!

Even so, many people and their families who could benefit from hospice care don't receive it — because they don't know about it or have inaccurate ideas about it; because they don't know it's fully covered by Medicare Part A, Medicaid, and most private insurance plans; because they wait too long and, in the crisis, don't have the information they need.

What exactly is "hospice," and how does it work? How is it paid for and how can you get it? And what is "palliative care," and how is it different from hospice? This chapter answers these questions and more.

27-1. What Is Hospice?

"Hospice" is not a place, like a nursing home or hospital. It is a way of caring for persons with terminal, or "end-stage," illness and supporting their families, provided by a specially trained team of professionals. The team works together and with the patient and family to maximize comfort and quality of life. The hospice approach emphasizes care for the whole person: body, mind, feelings, spirit, and relationships. In hospice, you are not "the gallbladder in room 232," but a person with a history, complex and important feelings, goals and dreams, family, and friends — and, by the way, a serious illness.

Most hospice patients receive care in whatever setting they call home. This includes nursing homes and assisted living residences. The idea is to maintain independence, familiar surroundings, and meaningful relationships for as long as possible. Hospice is not focused on curing the disease, but easing its distressing effects: pain, fatigue, nausea, dry mouth and skin, breathing difficulty, anxiety, sleeplessness, depression, and so on.

Hospice care is just as "aggressive" as curative care. Vigorous attention and sophisticated treatments and medications are used to maintain quality of life and comfort. Many persons enrolling in hospice experience a kind of "hospice bounce." One recent study showed that, on average, persons enrolled in hospice actually lived longer — some by weeks — than persons with the same diagnoses receiving curative treatment. And — like comic columnist Art Buchwald — about 16 percent of persons enrolled in hospice actually "graduate" and are discharged alive, in many cases because their condition has so improved, they are no longer considered "terminal."

27-2. How Can I Get Hospice Care?

Enrollment Criteria

In order to enroll in hospice, you must have a "terminal" illness and a life expectancy of six months or less, as certified by two physicians. This means that your attending or primary physician or any specialist involved in your care and a hospice medical director say that in their best professional judgment, your illness, if allowed to proceed without intervention, is likely to result in your death within six months. You must also agree to forego treatments that are intended for cure and not for comfort.

> *Note:* The enrollment criteria and other information about duration of care and coverage of costs in this chapter are specific to the Medicare Hospice Benefit. If you are covered by private insurance, criteria may differ. Be sure to check with the insurance agent or ask the hospice social worker to confirm your coverage.

Many hospices, however, have "open access" policies that offer a great deal of flexibility to allow and cover treatments that have traditionally been considered curative but can be "palliative" — that is, increase comfort or relieve pain. For instance, a hospice patient might receive "palliative radiation" to reduce the size of a tumor that is pressing on her spine in order to relieve pain or prevent paralysis.

Many hospices are now working to provide earlier access to hospice services by providing pre-hospice palliative care or transition programs. These programs allow patients and families to receive some of the services and symptom-management benefits of hospice care without formal hospice enrollment. Palliative care is covered in the second half of this chapter.

Duration of Care

Once you are enrolled in hospice, your condition is closely monitored. If your condition is progressing as expected, you may stay enrolled in hospice as long as needed. Initial coverage extends for 90 days from enrollment; after that, your situation is assessed again after another 90 days and then after each additional 60 days. Your enrollment is "recertified" as long as the basic hospice criteria are met — even long past six months. Sadly, less than 12 percent of hospice patients receive a full six months of care or more; right now, half of all hospice patients are enrolled for less than three weeks before death, some only for hours. This is not long enough to obtain the full benefit of the program of care, and many, many families find themselves saying, "I wish we'd done this sooner!"

> *Note:* Hospice enrollment is not a one-way street. If you don't like hospice care, wish to resume curative treatments, or get better, you can check out of hospice care (or "revoke") at any time. As long as criteria are met, you may re-enroll as well.

Getting a Referral to Hospice

There are many paths to hospice care. Each person's circumstances are unique. In general, however, the starting point for hospice care is the recognition that your illness cannot be cured or effectively managed. This may be a new diagnosis, coming as a shock after a brief period of illness or mildly worrisome symptoms. Or it could be a further development of an illness that has been controlled but not getting any better for some months or years. Or it could be that the illness has just outpaced available treatments. Most people these days do not die of classically "terminal" illnesses; rather, they suffer from longstanding chronic illnesses, sometimes several at once, that just gradually get worse over an unpredictable period of time.

This can make it difficult to get a hospice referral at the right time. Doctors may resist stating clearly that an illness has reached this "terminal" phase, or "end stage." In today's health care world, it seems there is always something more to try in search of a cure, and doctors are rightly committed to their patients' survival. However, even when an illness is clearly terminal, doctors can be very reluctant to answer the question, "How long do you think Mom has?" Honestly, they just don't know. A recent research study showed that when asked to make predictions about their patients' likely survival time, doctors typically overestimated by a factor of 5; that means they thought, in all good faith, that their patients would live 5 times longer than they actually did. And the better the doctor knew the person, the more he or she overestimated.

> *Tip:* If you have any question about whether hospice might be the right choice for you or your loved one, here's a good way to ask the question: "Would you be surprised if (Mom) were alive in a year?" If the answer is yes, a good follow-up question would be, "Would hospice be a good option for (Mom) now?" If the answer is yes, or even maybe, you now have a hospice referral.

If your illness has reached this stage, and if your own doctor is resisting the idea of hospice for whatever reason, you can ask for an evaluation by a hospice doctor as a first step. This evaluation can be done in the hospital, nursing home, or at home.

27-3. How Does Hospice Work?

During the evaluation or admissions interview, the physician or nurse can explain how hospice works. Here's an outline:

The Hospice Care Team

Hospice care is provided by a team of professionals:

A physician, who supervises the care, meeting regularly with the other members of the team to discuss the care plan and how things are going. Visits from the physician are likely to be infrequent, but he or she is closely monitoring your care and available for consultation at any time.

> **Note:** You don't have to give up your current doctor when you enter hospice. He or she can continue to supervise your care along with the hospice team. However, hospice doctors are specially trained in pain and symptom management and may have skills and "tools" other doctors lack.

A registered nurse, who visits you regularly, supervises the nurse's aide, and reports to the doctor and other team members. Just how often the nurse visits will depend on a lot of factors, but typically it's once or twice a week. The nurse, in consultation with the doctor, will work to relieve pain and other symptoms, including nausea, anxiety and depression, fatigue, skin irritations, problems with bowel and bladder function, and so on. Nurses keep a close eye on your mental and emotional health as well, and will alert other team members if difficulties arise.

A certified nursing assistant, who provides help with personal care, if needed. This includes bathing, dressing, hygiene, light food preparation (snacks), and so on.

A social worker, who can address social, emotional, practical, and financial challenges. For instance, social workers can help organize extra caregiving help; complete important financial or practical preparations for death; mediate family disputes; interpret insurance policies and obtain benefits; or provide support to your spouse or life partner, children, or other family members in distress.

A chaplain, who is specially trained to respond to the spiritual aspect of facing serious illness and the end of life. While chaplains may be ordained in or members of a particular religious tradition, they do not preach or promote any particular belief or faith. More than anything, they are expert listeners.

A volunteer, who can spend a few hours a week with you to give your family a break, do errands or laundry, prepare light meals, help with projects or tasks, or just visit.

Other specialists such as physical therapists or dieticians may be included, if needed. Some hospices even offer pet, aroma-, music, art, or massage therapy. All hospices have team members available 24 hours a day, 7 days a week, 52 weeks of the year. Help is only a phone call away at any time of the day or night.

> **Note:** The nurse and certified nursing assistant (CNA) will probably be the most frequent visitors. In fact, the nurse is the only team member that you must consent to see. The services of all the other team members are entirely optional and scheduled only as needed or desired. Everything is carefully tailored to individual needs and desires.

Hospice Care at Home and Other Options

As noted before, most hospice care is delivered to the person at home, including nursing homes and assisted living residences (ALRs). If or when a person cannot be at home, the hospice can arrange a place in a care facility — nursing home, ALR, or hospital — and continue to provide care there. For these patients and for long-time nursing home residents needing hospice care, the nursing home staff and the hospice team work together to coordinate the best combination of skilled nursing and hospice care. Likewise, hospices offer brief "respite stays" in care facilities for patients to give family caregivers a break or if they must go out of town or become ill themselves. Some hospices have dedicated, stand-alone residences to provide this inpatient care.

Hospice Care for the Family

Hospice considers the patient *and the family* to be under their care: all immediate family members, companions/life partners, and caregivers may ask for and receive attention and advice from members of the team. After the patient's death, family members are offered free grief counseling and bereavement care for up to 13 months. Many hospice agencies also offer grief education and support groups to the wider community.

> *Tip:* While all hospices must offer some form of bereavement support, pro-grams vary widely. Some hospices call or send periodic letters or newsletters; others offer group support meetings or individual counseling. And some offer educational programs on various aspects of grief, bereavement, and coping. A few offer special programs for children and teenagers, including summer camps. If grief support will be important to you or your family, be sure to ask about these services when you are making your choice of hospice.

Quality of Hospice Care

All hospices must be licensed by the state and adhere to state regulations for health care facilities. Hospices are not *required* to be certified by Medicare unless they want pay-ment from Medicare for services provided to beneficiaries. As a practical matter, then, a hos-pice that hopes to be in business very long must be certified by Medicare. This requires a survey, conducted by either state Health Department officials or Medicare-approved accred-iting organizations, to make sure that the hospice is operating according to the Medicare standards and state regulations. If you have concerns about quality, you may ask the hos-pice about their accreditation status or check for any survey deficiencies on the Colorado Department of Public Health and Environment website, www.cdphe.state.co.us/hf/hospice/index.html, or by calling the Health Facilities division, (303) 692-2800.

> *Note:* About six years ago, the National Hospice and Palliative Care Organi-zation launched its "Quality Partners" initiative, intended to improve and ensure the quality of hospice care across the nation. A "Quality Partners" mem-bership is an indication that a hospice has a special commitment to quality care. To determine membership of a facility, visit www.nhpco.org or call (800) 658-8898.

27-4. How Is Hospice Care Paid For?

Options for Coverage for Care

Hospice care is a fully covered Medicare Part A benefit for Medicare-enrolled persons, and most private insurance plans have a comparable hospice benefit. If you or your family member are not covered by Medicare or private insurance, Medicaid might be an option. Also, many hospices have a commitment to provide care regardless of a person's ability to pay, supported by community fundraising, donations, and grants.

The Medicare Hospice Benefit

For persons receiving hospice care under Medicare, the Medicare Hospice Benefit covers all services of the team and all medications, equipment and supplies, and care related to the terminal illness. There may be a modest copay for some drugs. Items and services not related to the terminal illness remain your responsibility. For instance, if you are enrolled in hospice for a diagnosis of cancer and have a fall and break a hip, the costs of treating the broken hip will not be covered by the Hospice Benefit, but likely will be covered by other parts of Medicare or your private insurance plan.

In some cases, room and board — whether in a nursing home, hospice residence, or hospital — are covered by the Medicare Hospice Benefit or private insurance. In other cases, these costs must be paid by you. Just when room and board is covered depends on the level of care you are receiving and the reason for your stay in the facility. Even over the course of a single stay, some days might be covered and some not. Most rooms in standalone hospice residences are private; some hospices offer shared rooms to reduce costs. Rates vary depending on location and level of care, but they tend to range between $200 and $700 per day.

Prior to enrollment in hospice, it's a good idea to have a thorough conversation with the admissions nurse or social worker on financial matters. Ask questions and get clear answers from the individual hospice agency about what benefits apply, what they cover and don't, room and board rates and charges, and any other resources that might be available.

> *Tip:* If you or a loved one are a veteran of the United States Armed Forces or National Guard, be sure to ask about Veterans Administration benefits and services. The Colorado Center for Hospice & Palliative Care Hospice—Veteran Partnership Workgroup has been working to inform hospices of veterans' issues and benefits, and the VA health care facilities of hospice services and benefits. There is good information on this topic on The Center's website at www.cochpc.org, or you can call (303) 694-4728 for more information.

27-5. How Can I Find Care and Choose a Hospice?

Hospice in Colorado

As of 2011 in Colorado, there are 59 hospice agencies providing care out of 82 locations to more than 17,000 people across the state. Eleven hospice agencies now have dedicated inpatient residences. About half of hospice programs in Colorado are independent not-for-profits, although the number of for-profit and national chain hospices is growing. A handful of hospices are run by the state or federal government.

About a third of Colorado's hospices are in urban areas, about a third in rural counties, and about a third in frontier regions. In urban areas, there may be a number of hospices from which to choose, while rural and frontier areas are often served by one agency (18 of 64 total Colorado counties in 2011). In 2011, only one Colorado county (Lake County) had no hospice patients receiving care under the Medicare Hospice Benefit. Each hospice organization has its own "flavor," admissions policies, and range of offerings beyond the core, mandated services.

Locating and Evaluating a Hospice

Just like any important decision in life, your choice of hospice should be made with care, based on up-to-date and reliable information, and after several deep breaths. Your doctor, hospital, or nursing home may recommend a particular hospice, but unless you live in an area served by only one agency, you do have a choice. Your top concerns should be quality and a good "fit" between you and the hospice staff and style.

There are two comprehensive resources for locating hospices in your area: Hospice Analytics' National Hospice Locator (www.hospiceanalytics.com) and the Colorado Department of Public Health and Environment (CDPHE; www.cdphe.state.co.us/hf/hospice/index.html). The National Hospice Locator allows you to search by state or zip code. You can compare agencies on several criteria: ownership type (nonprofit, for profit), agency type (free-standing, in a nursing facility, affiliated with a hospital), size (based on number of patients served daily), inpatient residence, state and national organization memberships, accreditation, and certification. The results provide contact information and direct links to agency websites. The CDPHE online directory lists all the hospices in the state, but does not provide any comparative criteria. Be aware that hospices tend to serve several counties, so if you do not find a hospice with an office in your city or town, there may be one nearby that serves your area.

> *Tip:* Hospice programs are very sensitive to how ethnic, cultural, and religious factors can influence a person's approach to death, funeral preferences, and the family's style of coping. Some agencies have gained special certifications in caring for members of particular cultural or religious communities; some have Spanish-speaking patient and family assistance or care teams and other non-English language interpreters; some have particular affinities with or historical ties to religious traditions. If these factors are important to you, be sure to ask about them when you talk to the hospice representative.

As noted earlier, hospice enrollment has some requirements, but a meeting with a hospice representative to get acquainted and discuss their services can be arranged at any time. If the hospice has a standalone residence, you may tour the facility. When you contact a hospice to discuss their services, here are some key questions you should ask:

▶ Are you certified by Medicare and/or accredited? How long have you been operating as a state-licensed and certified or accredited hospice?

▶ What services do you provide?

▶ What services are not covered by the Medicare Hospice Benefit? (If you will be covered by private insurance, ask if the hospice social worker can help you determine which services might not be covered by your policy. Likewise, if you do not have insurance, ask about Medicaid eligibility or the hospice's program for uninsured patients.)

▶ How can my or my loved one's current doctor(s) continue to be involved in my or my loved one's care?

▶ How often will the hospice team members visit?

▶ Will a volunteer be available to help?

▶ How do you respond to needs after hours and on weekends or holidays?

▶ What are our options if I or my loved one can't stay at home? Or what if my family needs a break?

▶ What are your room and board rates? When are these charges not covered by Medicare or my private insurance?

▶ If the patient now lives in a nursing home or assisted living residence, can you provide care there?

▶ What kind of support is available to the family/caregiver?

▶ In what ways do you provide bereavement care and grief counseling?

▶ Do you have special services for the members of my cultural/religious group? (If applicable.)

Hospice is a wonderful service to persons with end-stage illness and their families, but it's not for everyone. Some people don't "qualify" for hospice care, and some just aren't ready or never get the opportunity to shift from curative treatment to hospice care. Fortunately, there is an alternative: palliative care.

27-6. What Is Palliative Care?

Palliative (PAH-lee-uh-tiv) care is a relatively new kid on the block of American health care. It began growing rapidly in the mid-1990s and was granted official "sub-specialty" status by the American Board of Medical Specialties in 2006. Like hospice care, palliative care focuses on comfort rather than cure; aggressive treatment of distressing symptoms; and emotional, social, and spiritual support for patients and families. It involves a team of professionals addressing the needs and concerns of the whole person and family members. Unlike hospice, palliative care does not require a doctor's certification of life expectancy. It can be offered along with curative treatment, and it is not limited to "end stage" or "terminal" illness.

Other big differences between hospice and palliative care are that, right now, there is very limited insurance coverage for palliative care services and very few accepted standards and regulations governing them. Both of these issues are discussed more below.

27-7. How Can I Get Palliative Care?

Palliative care can begin at any point in the course of a serious illness and be provided side-by-side with treatment oriented toward cure. Right now, it is most commonly used when a person's illness has become very advanced but is not yet at the terminal stage. Many chronic conditions are well suited to this approach: COPD, congestive heart failure, Alzheimer's disease, multiple sclerosis, kidney or liver disease, Parkinson's, AIDS, cancer, ALS (Lou Gehrig's disease), diabetes, and others.

If you think you might benefit from palliative care, you should talk first to your primary physician, the hospitalist (the doctor overseeing your care in a hospital), or the specialist treating your illness to discuss what services might be helpful and available. You can also consult the National Hospice and Palliative Care Organization (www.nhpco.org or (800) 658-8898) or the American Academy of Hospice and Palliative Medicine (www.aahpm.org, go to the "Certify" tab, then select "HPM Physician Directory" or go to www.palliative doctors.org).

27-8. How Does Palliative Care Work?

Palliative care is a rapidly growing field; consistent models of care, standards, or even criteria defining in detail what it is and is not and what it does and does not provide have not yet been consistently adopted. As a result, there can be big variations in palliative care services and quality. In 2011, the Colorado Center for Hospice and Palliative Care, along with the Center to Improve Value in Health Care and Life Quality Institute, developed a set of guidelines to assist state surveyors in evaluating whether so-called "palliative care" services really offer what they should in the way that they should. At this writing, these guidelines (not regulations or requirements) are being reviewed by CDPHE; if adopted, they will help the state and consumers evaluate palliative care programs.

When you contact a provider for palliative care, be sure to get a clear and thorough explanation of just what is being offered. At its most basic, a palliative care service provides consultation with a specially trained doctor or nurse to develop a plan of care to provide comfort rather than cure and to address any areas of distress. More fully-fledged programs involve consultation with a full palliative care team and perhaps some limited follow up with or ongoing care of the person at home or in a health care facility.

In general, palliative care programs come in three styles from three different provider types: hospitals, hospice agencies, and nursing homes.

Hospital-Based Palliative Care

About 33 hospitals around the state offer palliative care consultation services, including University of Colorado Hospital, Aurora; the Veterans Administration; selected facilities in the Kaiser, Exempla, HealthOne, and Centura systems; Memorial Hospital, Colorado Springs; Denver Health Medical Center; Poudre Valley Hospital, Fort Collins; Boulder Community Hospital; Gunnison Valley Hospital, Gunnison; Parkview Medical Center, Pueblo; North Colorado Medical Center, Greeley; and The Children's Hospital, Aurora. The typical situation involves someone with a serious, advanced illness for which he or she is receiving continued curative treatment but is "wiped out" by the side effects, or the treatment is not working as well, fewer options are available, and a shift in goals of care should be considered. A palliative care consultation with a specially trained doctor or nurse — and, ideally, a social worker and chaplain — can identify symptoms that can be eased by palliative treatment. Beyond this, the consultation can help clarify goals and plans for the future management of the disease. In most hospital-based programs, however, there is no ongoing follow-up.

"Pre-Hospice" Palliative Care

Another type of palliative care program, often called "pre-hospice" or "transition," is offered by hospice agencies. In these programs, you can receive a palliative care consultation and a limited amount of follow-up without enrolling in hospice. This provides a real option for persons who are not quite ready for hospice from the standpoint of their personal goals or the progress of their illness. You can use the National Hospice Locator (www.hospiceanalytics.com) to find hospices in your area, then contact them to find out what palliative care services they offer.

Palliative Care in Long-Term Care

For better or for worse, many of us will likely spend some part of our final days in nursing facilities. Most elders who enter nursing homes for full-time residence die within two to three years of admission. Nursing homes have worked closely with hospices for many years to provide high-quality end-of-life care, but many are also now developing their own programs of palliative care.

More so than in the hospice or hospital setting, long-term care palliative care programs are subject to wide variation. In some cases, palliative or "comfort" care here simply means pain and symptom management performed under the guidance of a doctor who may or may not be well trained in palliative or end-of-life care. In other cases, it is very high-quality and full-spectrum end-of-life care up to and including the hospice phase. If you or a loved one reside in a nursing home and are a good candidate for palliative care, be sure you get a thorough explanation of just what this means at that facility and be sure your needs will be appropriately addressed.

Note: The Center to Improve Value in Health Care (CIVHC), in collaboration with Life Quality Institute and other organizations, has developed a set of "Best Practice" guidelines for palliative care in the long-term care setting. If your nursing home is not yet following these guidelines, they are available from both CIVHC (www.civhc.org; (720) 588-2095) and Life Quality Institute (www. lifequalityinstitute.org; (303) 398-6326).

27-9. How Is Palliative Care Paid For?

The other big difference between hospice and palliative care is that there is no Medicare Palliative Care Benefit. At this writing, Medicare will cover one visit from a hospice or hospital-based palliative care doctor. Some private insurers and managed care organizations (notably, Kaiser Permanente) are adding palliative care benefits. Hospice agencies offering palliative care programs often do so at their own loss or out of charitable monies. The Veterans Health Administration offers palliative care services at no extra charge to qualified persons. Palliative care can also be obtained through a few private practice doctors, advanced practice nurses, and nurse practitioners on a fee-for-service basis.

27-10. How Can I Find Palliative Care?

First, ask your physician. You can also ask your hospital or hospice agency of choice about their palliative care programs, or contact the National Hospice and Palliative Care Organization (www.nhpco.org) or the American Academy of Hospice and Palliative Medicine (www.aahpm.org).

27-11. How Can I Learn More?

If you would like to know more about hospice or palliative care, most hospice agencies are happy to answer your questions, and many can provide an informative presentation to your community group (place of worship, social club, workplace, etc.). Life Quality Institute offers frequent workshops and seminars on palliative care, medical decision-making, advance directives, and the challenges of caregiving. Life Quality Institute's website (www.lifequalityinstitute.org) has abundant resources on these topics as well. Call (303) 398-6326 for more information.

27-12. Conclusion

Hospice and palliative care are relative newcomers to medical care, but really they are new and improved forms of what medicine and health care has been about for thousands of years: caring for the sick, comforting the hurt, and supporting those who love them. Their shared goal is to help all persons live well at the end of life and never suffer needlessly.

27-13. Resources

National Hospice Locator
Offers a comprehensive directory of hospice agencies by state; also offers several comparative criteria, with contact information and direct links to agency websites.
> www.hospiceanalytics.com

Life Quality Institute
Offers community education on palliative and end-of-life care and the needs of caregivers, in particular the Creating Communities of Care program for organizing informal caregiving among neighbors, friends, and families.
(303) 398-6326
> www.lifequalityinstitute.org

The Iris Project
Offers community and professional education as well as private consultation on end-of-life care options, advance care planning, advance directives, caregiving, health care ethics, and more.
(303) 521-4111
> www.irisproject.net

The Colorado Advance Directives Consortium
Offers information on advance care planning and advance directives, including the Medical Orders for Scope of Treatment (MOST) program in Colorado. Template forms for medical durable power of attorney appointments, living will, CPR directives, and MOST forms are available, along with clear explanations of each tool and how to use it. Links to other resources and education are also provided.
> www.coloradoadvancedirectives.com

Colorado Center for Hospice & Palliative Care
Provides information on hospice, information on advance care planning, veterans resources, and education for hospice staff.
> (303) 694-4728
> info@cochpc.org
> www.cochpc.org

Colorado Health Care Association
The statewide association supporting nursing homes and assisted living residences. Can provide information on hospice and palliative care in the long-term care setting or specific information on skilled nursing facilities and assisted living residences.
> (303) 861-8228
> www.cohca.org

Center for Medicare & Medicaid Services
Offers a free booklet, "Medicare Hospice Benefits," which explains in detail coverage provided by Medicare and Medicaid for the costs of hospice care.
> 1-800-MEDICARE
> www.medicare.gov

Colorado Department of Public Health and Environment

Offers listings for all nursing and assisted living facilities and hospices in the state. To view detailed profiles, including survey results, go to www.cdphe.state.co.us/hf/index.html; select the facility type; click on "Get detailed profiles." Once you have located the facility you are interested in, click on its name and the survey results and other information will come up.

    (303) 692-2800

    www.cdphe.state.co.us/hf/hospice/index.html

National Hospice & Palliative Care Organization

Primarily geared toward professionals, but offers a toll-free help line, a Spanish language help line, and a searchable database of hospice agencies nationwide.

    (800) 658-8898 (toll-free help line)

    (877) 658-8896 (Spanish language help line)

    www.nhpco.org

Caring Connections

A national consumer-focused information source on all things end-of-life: state-by-state advance medical directives (living wills, etc.), caregiver resources, grief and bereavement support, information for businesses supporting employees involved in caregiving or grieving, and more.

    (800) 658-8898 (toll-free help line)

    (877) 658-8896 (Spanish language help line)

    caringinfo@nhpco.org

    www.caringinfo.org

GetPalliativeCare.org

An online resource for the public on palliative care nationwide, including a quick quiz to determine if palliative care is right for you and easily printed informational handouts. Information on Colorado-based providers is limited to hospitals, and only contact addresses and phone numbers are provided — no details on the services offered. Confirm any information with the facility itself.

    www.getpalliativecare.org

American Academy of Hospice and Palliative Medicine

Professional organization for providers of palliative medicine. List of Board certified palliative physicians provided on website: select "Certify" tab, then select "ABHPM Certified Physicians."

    www.aahpm.org

Excerpted and adapted with permission from How Hospice Can Save Your Life: A Guide to End-of-Life Care Options in Colorado, by Jennifer Ballentine, Life Quality Institute, forthcoming. © Jennifer Ballentine, 2008–2012.

Chapter 28

What to Do When Someone Dies: Responsibilities of the Personal Representative and Trustee Under Probate

Aaron L. Evans, Esq.*
Benson & Case, LLP

SYNOPSIS

Dealing with the loss of a loved one is difficult. It is our goal through this chapter to provide you with some important information that may hopefully make the days and weeks after the passing a little easier.

This chapter cannot relate everything you need to know. You should establish a relationship with your attorney early to ensure that all matters and questions are properly addressed. Seeking your attorney's advice before you act may help you avoid more costly legal fees later, and can ensure that you are protected from any liability. Your attorney should be able to provide you with very helpful information and explain the probate process to you.

28-1. Pronouncement of Death

Colorado requires a qualified medical professional to be notified and to make the official pronouncement of death. If your loved one dies at home:

▶ Call your physician or local hospital so they can come to certify the cause and approximate time of death.

▶ Follow any religious observances that your family member requested.

▶ Call family members who may wish to spend private time with your loved one before the mortuary removes the body.

▶ Turn off any electrical equipment attached to your loved one's body, but leave any tubes, etc., in place.

▶ Call your funeral director. He or she will remove the syringes, catheters, or tubes and transport the body to the mortuary.

▶ If it exists, find your family member's final arrangements plan to follow his or her final wishes with respect to whether a funeral, memorial service, cremation, organ donation, or whole body donation was desired. As much as possible, try to follow your loved one's plans. This will relieve you of the burden of making these decisions and will honor his or her last requests.

If your loved one dies in a hospital:

▶ The medical staff will assist you with paperwork if the body or organs are to be donated, or if there will be an autopsy performed.

▶ The medical staff can make the official pronouncement of death.

▶ The medical staff will coordinate with the mortuary or crematory for the arrangements to transport the body.

Call the Coroner

If the death occurs at home, you must call the coroner's office for the county in which the death occurs, or dial 911 if you want the support of emergency personnel. Paramedics will attempt resuscitation.

If you are using hospice care, do not contact the coroner's office or 911. Instead, call the hospice provider and they will handle these matters for you.

Notify Family and Friends

Ask family and friends to help you with some tasks, including notification of other family and friends.

The Red Cross will help you notify family members if the deceased was in the military or if the relative to be notified is in the military. The Red Cross will need the following information:

▶ Service member's full name;

▶ Rank/rating;

▶ Branch of service;

▶ Social Security number;

▶ Military address; and

▶ Information about the deployed unit and home base unit (applies to deployed service members only).

Follow the Deceased's Instructions

Look through the deceased's papers to find if he or she:

▶ Had a prepaid burial policy;

▶ Belonged to a memorial society; or

▶ Had written instructions regarding his or her arrangements for burial, cremation, and ceremonies the deceased did or did not want.

Note that these instructions could be legally binding even though they might be contrary to the wishes of others. If you have any questions about whether to follow them, contact a probate attorney or your mortuary.

Make Arrangements for the Deceased Person's Body

Arrange for the body to be picked up according to the coroner's instructions. Your funeral home or crematory will assist with this process.

28-2. What to Do One to Three Days After Death

Complete the Funeral and Burial Arrangements

Ask a trusted friend or family member to accompany you to the mortuary to advise and support you in making the funeral and burial arrangements. You may ask a clergy member to assist you.

Arrangements may include transfer to another location, burial, or cremation. If the deceased was a member of the Funeral Consumer Society of Colorado, you can obtain a lower rate on cremation or funeral services. Contact the Funeral Consumer Society of Colorado at (303) 759-2800. This also could be true for those who shop around. Cremation prices range from about $900 to $2,400 or more in the Denver metro area. Those prices should include the cost of the urn and other related services.

Note: Federal law requires price information to be given over the phone. Prices range a great deal, so you may want to compare prices.

If you have concerns that you cannot resolve with the funeral director or the management of the funeral home, contact the Funeral Service Customer Assistance Program at (800) 662-7666.

Financial Assistance

If the deceased was on public assistance, burial assistance may be available. Contact your local county Department of Social Services as soon as possible and ask for the Burial Assistance Department. There are strict spending limitations, so you must meet with Social Services prior to meeting with the mortuary. Total expenses of burial will be limited to qualify for the benefit.

If the deceased was in the military or is the spouse or dependent child of a person in the military, contact the VA cemetery or VA office. There may be burial benefits. The mortuary will call the VA at your request. Typically, unless the deceased was disabled due to service-related injuries, the only benefit a veteran receives is burial at a national cemetery.

Family Assistance

Choose someone to:

▶ Answer the phone calls from family members and friends and collect mail;

▶ Care for pets and plants, and tend to other household chores;

▶ Assist with lawn care or snow removal;

▶ Stay at home during the funeral and visit the home to guard against break-ins occurring when the family is at the funeral; and

▶ Prepare food for family and friends after the funeral.

Also, to reduce the likelihood of vandalism to the home or condominium, gather two or three electronic light timers so that lights, a radio, or TV will go on and off at appropriate times.

28-3. What to Do One to Ten Days After Death

Obtain Death Certificates

The most common and quickest way to obtain death certificates is through the funeral director. The cost is usually $10 for each death certificate. In order to estimate how many to order, you should estimate the number of different assets held by the deceased or institutions that will require a death certificate. Some examples of assets that will require an original death certificate are homes held in joint tenancy, stocks, bonds, and bank accounts.

If you do not order enough, you can get more death certificates later through the Vital Statistics Department for the county in which the death occurred or through the Colorado State Department of Public Health and Environment's Vital Records Office. The cost of a death certificate is $17.00 for the first copy and $10.00 for each additional copy.

Many people waste money by ordering too many death certificates: six to eight copies are usually adequate. Remember, you can always obtain more death certificates later, if needed.

In General

Contact the following persons or institutions:

▶ Police, to inform them that the house of the deceased will be vacant and to request that they occasionally check the house;

▶ Probate attorney, to set up a meeting to discuss the probate process, such as how to transfer assets, how to deal with heirs or devisees, and how to report taxes;

▶ Accountant or tax preparer, to assist with gathering information as to the deceased's assets owned and to determine what returns should be filed;

▶ Banks, to locate accounts and safe deposit boxes;

▶ Investment professionals, to obtain information as to assets owned by the deceased;

▶ Insurance agents, to discuss insuring the decedent's assets and to obtain necessary death claim forms for life insurance or other assets;

▶ Social Security at (800) 772-1213, to stop monthly deposits and learn about benefits;

▶ Veterans Affairs, to stop monthly checks and learn about benefits;

▶ Agencies providing pension services, to stop monthly checks and obtain claim forms;

▶ Guardian, conservator, or agent under a power of attorney, to notify of the death and the end of their responsibilities;

▶ Utility companies, to alter or discontinue service;

▶ Employer, to notify of death and learn about benefits;

▶ Newspapers and magazines, to stop subscriptions (you may consider asking for refunds of the unused portions of the subscriptions); and

▶ Post office, to forward mail (if necessary).

Avoid Unscrupulous People

In the period following the loss of a loved one, be careful before accepting any telephone solicitations, and be careful about volunteering personal information about the deceased to strangers over the phone. You may receive fraudulent invoices, so be sure to review invoices carefully for validity. Thieves read death notices and obituaries, so avoid stating the address and other private information about the deceased. Avoid any major lifestyle changes for a period to allow for reflection on how the loss will affect the surviving family and friends.

Veterans Benefits

The mortuary may assist you with the paperwork for VA benefits. For information on VA benefits, call the nearest VA office for benefits information and assistance.

Be prepared to identify the deceased's:

▶ Relationship to you;

▶ VA claim number;

▶ Date of birth;

▶ Date of death;

▶ Place of death;

▶ Surviving spouse or next of kin; and

▶ Medical history that bears on whether the death is service-related or not.

If you do not know the deceased's VA claim number, provide the service number and dates of active service.

Veteran's benefits may be available to the surviving spouse. Benefits may include a lump-sum death benefit, if the death was service-related; a continuing monthly payment; financial assistance with funeral expenses and cemetery plot; or burial of the deceased in a national cemetery. Ask for the "Federal Benefits for Veterans and Dependants" publication, or review the VA website at www.vba.va.gov/survivors/index.htm for more information about survivor benefits.

Social Security Benefits

For Social Security benefits, call the Social Security Administration immediately at (800) 772-1213. Your call will stop the monthly payments currently being received by the deceased. You must return the check for the month of death. If the deceased was receiving benefits by direct deposit (which is most likely the case), excess payments will, in time, be electronically withdrawn from the account.

Social Security monthly benefits are available to the surviving spouse, children under 18, and certain disabled children. Benefits include a lump sum death benefit (currently at $255 for a surviving spouse). Ask for the "Survivors Benefits" brochure or review the Social Security Administration's website at www.ssa.gov/pubs/deathbenefits.htm for more information about what to do when a beneficiary dies.

28-4. Personal Representative Duties Under the Probate Code

Your Duties in General

You have a duty to act impartially in regard to all parties to the estate. You have to treat each person the same. You have a duty to administer the estate with care, making sure to put the interests of the estate in front of your own interests in the estate.

As a personal representative, you are responsible for:

▶ Collecting and inventorying the assets of the estate;

▶ Managing the assets of the estate during the probate process;

▶ Paying the bills of the estate;

▶ Making distributions to the heirs or beneficiaries of the estate; and

▶ Closing the estate after all of the above responsibilities have been completed.

Prior to Appointment as Personal Representative

If you are nominated as the personal representative (also known as "executor") in a will, you have the power (before you are appointed by the court) to carry out written instructions of the deceased relating to the body, funeral, and burial arrangements. You may begin to protect the deceased's assets. Do not remove or distribute assets before opening the estate. Brochures are available from the Colorado Bar Association that explain the duties and responsibilities of a personal representative and how a personal representative is appointed when there is no will.

Search for the Will

The original will is usually in a safe place in the deceased's home, a safe deposit box, or an attorney's office. It is also possible that the will was lodged with the court for safe-keeping during the lifetime of the deceased. When the original signed will is found, lodge it within 10 days with the probate court in the county where the deceased lived. If you are only able to find a copy of the signed will, it may be possible to offer it for probate. However, the signed original will is preferred. If a will cannot be found, an attorney can help guide you through the intestate probate process. Also look for a handwritten list of instructions, a letter to family, or other similar documents. In Colorado, these documents may constitute a will.

Entering the Safe Deposit Box

Any person whose name is on the box may enter it at any time. An heir or beneficiary in a will can ask the bank to search for the will, a deed to a burial plot, or burial instructions. A representative of the bank will open the box in the presence of the heir or beneficiary and remove any will that is found. The bank will deliver the will to the court by certified mail, registered mail, or hand delivery, but first you should ask for a copy. After the will is filed with the court, the nominated personal representative can file a petition or application with the court to appoint her or him.

Search for Other Documents

The personal representative is the court representative who has the authority to search for any important documents. The search should include the home, office, place of business, and any safe deposit boxes. Meeting with advisors such as accountants, investment professionals, insurance agents, and attorneys is advised. Any information indicating that an asset exists or that bills are unpaid should be kept for use in the administration of the estate.

Items to look for:

▶ Funeral and burial plans;

▶ Safe deposit rental agreements and keys;

▶ Trust agreements;

▶ Nuptial agreements;

▶ Life insurance policies or statements;

▶ Pension, IRA, or retirement statements;

▶ Income tax returns for the past several years;

▶ Gift tax returns;

▶ Marriage, birth, and death certificates;

▶ Divorce papers;

▶ Military records and discharge papers;

▶ Certificates of deposit, bank statements, checkbooks, and check registers;

▶ Notes receivable and payable;

▶ Motor vehicle titles;

▶ Deeds, deeds of trust, mortgages, leases, and title policies;

▶ Stock and bond certificates and account statements;

▶ Bankruptcy filings;

▶ Partnership, LLC, or corporate agreements;

▶ Unpaid bills;

▶ Health insurance papers; and

▶ Papers regarding fraternal organizations or professional societies (some of these may offer benefits upon the death of their member).

Informal Versus Formal Probate

There are two types of probate: informal and formal. You should consult your attorney to decide which type of probate is right for your situation.

Informal probate happens when there is an uncontested will or, if there was no will, if all of the potential heirs of the estate agree on who should be personal representative and who the beneficiaries of the estate are. Filing an application for informal probate is usually less expensive than formal probate and takes less time. This is true because there is less court involvement.

Formal probate applies if the heirs and/or beneficiaries cannot agree on all the issues and need the court to decide for them. Formal probate is also necessary if the original will cannot be found.

Your Authority and Specific Duties

You will be issued "letters" from the court to say that you have been appointed personal representative. These letters are evidence that you have authority to act on behalf of the estate. You will need to show or send them to various third parties, such as banks, insurance companies, etc., when you are administering the estate.

Promptly after your appointment as personal representative, you should:

▶ Prepare a Notice of Appointment form, which is probably in the packet of forms you received from the court; send this to all who are interested in the estate, such as beneficiaries and unpaid creditors; and file proof with the court that this notice was sent. The notice form must be sent to all interested persons within 30 days of appointment to let them know the facts and ground rules regarding administration of the estate, including your name and address and the court in which the papers are filed.

▶ Set up an estate accounting system. This should be done at the beginning of your administration of the estate. For your protection, keep records of all financial transactions of the estate, and provide written accountings to the beneficiaries. This information will also be required for tax purposes. Keeping accounting records is very important and is often done incorrectly. In a supervised administration or with a formal closing, the accounting forms are also filed with the court.

Prepare a written inventory within three months to include the estate assets on a court-approved form. If you decide to close the estate formally, the inventory must be filed with the court. Otherwise, you can just give copies to interested parties. Maintain all documentation to support the values reported in the inventory.

Potential Liability as Personal Representative

As a personal representative, you may be liable to the beneficiaries for any loss to the estate and for any gain the estate should have realized but did not.

Situations in which a personal representative may be found liable include:

▶ You, for any reason, failed to exercise reasonable care and skill in managing the property of another;

▶ You negligently or intentionally did something that you *should not* have done, such as taken funds from the estate, failed to follow the will, or committed other actions that breached your fiduciary duty as personal representative; or

▶ You negligently or intentionally failed to do something that you *should* have done, such as properly inventoried the assets or failed to pay the heirs or beneficiaries of the estate.

This list is not exhaustive. It merely demonstrates some ways a personal representative can potentially incur liability. You should contact a probate attorney and seek his or her advice as to any potential problems that may arise.

Creditors

Following a death, certain creditors may be very aggressive. An important purpose of the probate administration is to provide an orderly process for dealing with all of the deceased's creditors. Try to avoid depleting the available cash on the first "squeaky wheels," because doing so can cause bigger problems later in the estate administration, and it can also expose the personal representative to a charge that he or she showed preference for a specific creditor over others.

28-5. Trustee Responsibilities

Your Duties in General

Once you have been named trustee, co-trustee, or successor trustee of a trust, there are certain duties to perform and rules to follow. Your authority as trustee comes from the trust itself, and your duties and powers should be described in the trust. Read the trust in detail, as it should answer many of your initial questions.

Your three basic duties to the trust and its beneficiaries are:

1) A duty of impartiality, not to favor the interest of one party over another;

2) A duty of undivided loyalty, not to put your own interest in a conflict with those of the trust; and

3) A duty to administer the trust with care and prudence.

You should consult your probate attorney or accountant as to any potential tax filings and other questions you may have regarding your duties as trustee.

Accounting

As trustee, you must set up and keep a set of trustee's books. These records must make a clear distinction between assets you handle as trustee and assets that are your own. Any mixing of the two is strictly prohibited. The frequency with which you must provide an accounting to the beneficiaries should be stated in the trust. If it does not say how often, then an accounting should be provided at least annually.

Trust Registration Statement

Colorado law requires all trusts to be registered with the probate court in the county where the trust is being administered. Registration should be done no later than 30 days after the trust is created. The trust registration statement should be amended or updated whenever there is a change in trustee or in the place of administration of the trust. There are court-approved forms for trust registration and amendment.

Potential Liability as Trustee

As the trustee, you may be liable to the beneficiaries for any loss to the trust and for any gain the trust should have realized but did not. The following are examples of ways in which a trustee may be found liable:

▶ If, for any reason, you failed to exercise the care and skill of a person of ordinary prudence in managing the assets of another;

▶ You negligently or intentionally did something that you should not have done, such as taken funds from the estate, did not follow the will, or took other actions that breached your fiduciary duty as trustee; or

▶ You negligently or intentionally failed to do something that you should have done, such as properly inventoried the assets or failed to pay the heirs or beneficiaries of the estate.

Again, this list is not all inclusive. It merely demonstrates some of the ways in which liability potentially may be incurred. Contact a probate attorney to seek his or her advice as to any potential problems that may arise.

28-6. Resources

Colorado Bar Association
(303) 860-1115 or toll-free (800) 332-6736
www.cobar.org

Colorado Department of Public Health and Environment
Vital Records Section
4300 Cherry Creek Dr. S.
HSVRD-VR-A1
Denver, CO 80246-1530
(303) 692-2230
www.cdphe.state.co.us/certs

Denver Probate Court
(720) 865-8310
www.denverprobatecourt.org

Funeral Consumer Society of Colorado
(303) 759-2800
www.funerals.org/affiliates/colorado

Funeral Service Consumer Assistance Program
(800) 662-7666

Social Security Administration
(800) 772-1213
www.ssa.gov

Department of Veteran Affairs
(800) 827-1000
(800) 829-4833 (TTY)
www.va.gov

---

* Based on a chapter originally written by Mark Masters, Esq., of Schmidt, Horen & Lockwood, L.L.P.

Chapter 29

Family Discussions, Decisions, and Dispute Resolution

Hon. John P. Leopold
JAMS

Rose Mary Zapor, Esq.
The Zapor Law Office, P.C.

SYNOPSIS

Difficult decisions must often be made as family members age. Because these decisions impact several generations and may require resources and expertise available only outside the family, they should not be put off.

These decisions are usually not about legal matters, yet the discussions may be emotional ones. If they are put off, legal issues could arise. When should a person stop driving? How will the family pay for a family member with special needs? When should you sell the family home? Surely, these decisions should not be left to the court. Family discussions are likely to be more productive if led by a professional who can ensure that everyone can be heard and can help the family identify important legal, financial, and medical questions, and help guide the decisions to be discussed.

29-1. Family Decisions

Families can use professional mediators to help them avoid court for many reasons, both for legal disputes such as probate of wills and for non-legal matters. Some of the non-legal issues that might be resolved through alternate dispute resolution are:

▶ Onset of dementia — Who will care for the family member? When is it time for full-time care?

▶ Caregiver burdens — How will the family handle respite care for the caregiver? Is the caregiver responsible for medical, personal, and financial decisions?

▶ Lifestyle changes — Is it time for Mom or Dad to move? Where? Can the family hire a caregiver and allow Mom or Dad to stay at home?

▶ Resident disputes — What to do if the care is not what was promised? What should the family do if there is a problem with a neighbor?

▶ Driving — When should Mom or Dad give up the keys? How is the family going to handle the loss of independence for the family member?

▶ Care disputes — The care provider will not listen to the family. Now what?

▶ Guardianship — Is Mom or Dad really incompetent, or does she or he just need some help? Who is best suited to make decisions?

▶ End-of-life decisions — When is it time to let Mom or Dad go? Should we use hospice? What about the hospital?

▶ Financial decisions — Should we use an accountant to handle the checkbook? Is there a need for a family member to account for the decisions made? Whose money is it, anyway?

▶ Estate matters — What if Mom or Dad has no will or power of attorney? What should the family do if there is a dispute about the estate?

29-2. The People Involved in the Decision

All of the family members should be present at the alternate dispute resolution sessions, even if they will not be providing care. Open discussions prevent misunderstandings.

Remember that only a court can take away a person's right to make his or her own decisions. A power of attorney does not allow a person to take away an elderly or disabled person's right to decide to leave a facility, fire a caregiver, or handle financial matters. Therefore, the elderly or disabled person has to be involved in the decision-making process. Even a person with dementia is able to make some decisions at times of lucidity, and the family should not assume that the person with dementia is not capable of participating or cannot participate.

If there are decisions to be made regarding residence, health, medication, or end-of-life issues, the family should choose a doctor or health care consultant with whom they all feel comfortable. This person would be involved in the decision-making process to provide information so that everyone would be able to make an informed decision.

29-3. Types of Alternate Dispute Resolution (ADR)

Disputes in elder law cases, like other cases that are filed in court, can be time-consuming and costly. In addition, the emotional toll on everyone involved often causes problems that last long after the trial, and possible appeal, have concluded.

Fortunately, you can use some well-respected services before you involve the courts or hire a lawyer. These services can spare considerable anxiety and challenges to family harmony. The general term for this process is alternate dispute resolution (ADR). There are many types of ADR available, some of which are explained below.

Arbitration

Arbitration resembles a trial before a judge, without a jury. Generally, either a single arbitrator or a panel of three arbitrators is selected to resolve a dispute.

Arbitration usually occurs when a contract or other agreement contains a provision or clause requiring this approach. Unless one of these circumstances exists, you cannot be forced to engage in arbitration.

In elder law cases, arbitration agreements may be found in trust documents. Contracts that address a wide number of issues may contain these clauses. If this is the case, the clause is almost always enforceable.

However, the parties may voluntarily agree to use either arbitration or to hire a retired district court judge to resolve their disputes without a contract clause or a court order (*see* C.R.S. § 13-3-111). In either situation, the parties generally pay the arbitrator or the retired judge for his or her services.

The courts have ruled that arbitration is "a favored means of dispute resolution." Colorado's version of the Uniform Arbitration Act (C.R.S. §§ 13-22-201, *et seq.*) provides that arbitration agreements are presumed to be "valid, enforceable and irrevocable."

If the document requires arbitration, it may specify whether there will be one or three arbitrators. If one arbitrator is to preside, the parties must agree as to who will serve as arbitrator.

If the arbitration is to be heard by three arbitrators, each party selects one arbitrator. Those two people then select the third arbitrator. That person serves as the chairperson of the "arbitration panel." Arbitrators are neutrals and cannot automatically vote in favor of the party who selected her or him.

Although arbitration hearings occur in a more relaxed setting than a courtroom, those who testify are placed under oath. Each side is permitted to ask questions of each witness. Exhibits are presented to the arbitrator(s) for consideration just as they would be in court.

Arbitrators' decisions are called "awards." The award may require someone to pay another person money, may direct that no money be paid at all, or may require one or all parties to perform certain acts. Even if no money is to be paid, the ruling is entitled an "arbitration award."

If you and the other parties agree to hire a retired district court judge to resolve your dispute, the Chief Justice of the Colorado Supreme Court must approve the appointment. If that happens, you cannot change your mind and ask to return to the court to which your case had been assigned. Decisions by a retired district judge, hired by the parties, can be appealed in the same way as the decision of any judge in Colorado, although there are some limitations.

Why would you want to arbitrate if you were not required to do so, or why would you hire a judge when you have full access to the courts?

If you use arbitration, you will know that the person you selected has fewer cases to decide than a district court judge. In addition, arbitration usually is a private matter. If your case is heard before a probate or district court judge, it will occur in a courtroom that is open to the public.

Family matters, such as elder law cases, tend to include some very personal matters. Judges are sensitive people and provide a professional and considerate environment for all cases. Arbitration can provide a level of privacy that is not permitted in court.

There are a number of individuals and organizations that offer arbitration services in Colorado and throughout the country. Arbitrators are trained and experienced people who are dedicated to giving the parties a complete and thoughtful hearing. Usually, the arbitration award is issued rapidly, often within 30 days after the arbitrator closes the hearing or receives the last written argument from a party.

Arbitration is a streamlined and effective way to resolve disputes. Hearings usually are set within a few months of the parties' submitting their documents to the arbitrator. The case often ends very quickly. As a result, the cost of arbitration can be less than the cost of a trial.

Arbitration agreements contain very specific language. If you face the prospect of arbitration, be sure to ask an attorney to review the document and explain the specific procedures you can utilize and those that you may be required to follow.

Mediation

Mediation occurs when parties to a dispute agree to ask a neutral person to consider the case and help them reach their own settlement. If you go to court, a judge or jury will decide who prevails and, in some instances, who will have to pay for some of the costs of the case. In mediation, you have a hand in negotiating an agreement.

Mediation is completely confidential and voluntary. This means that, if your efforts at settlement are not successful, neither the judge nor the jury will know anything that happened during your negotiations. This is a rule of law. It permits everyone to be completely open and candid without having to worry about what will happen in court if you do not reach an agreement.

Usually, the mediator asks each party to send her or him a "confidential settlement statement" about a week before the session. If you are not represented by an attorney and you are preparing this document, you should tell the mediator about the family member (whether living or deceased) as well as everyone else in your family. Explain how the dispute arose and what is at stake. Tell the mediator what your preferred result is. And help the mediator understand how you and those with whom you disagree reached the point of a court case.

At the conference, the mediator may ask all parties and their attorneys to meet in one room to review the procedures and to tell everyone there what is important to him or her. This can be an emotional time for everyone. It also lets you "get things off your chest" and move on to problem-solving with the air cleared.

After this initial meeting, the mediator may ask the parties to gather in separate rooms. She or he then will meet with each party to discuss her or his confidential statement and the comments at the joint meeting, and to learn more about the people with whom the mediator is then speaking.

Mediators may be "facilitative" or "evaluative." Facilitative mediators often hold more joint meetings, ask each party to consider the other's point of view in his or her presence, and try to help them move toward common ground. The mediator facilitates an agreement reached by all of the parties without evaluating the strength or weakness of the case in court.

Evaluative mediators will meet with the parties separately and offer their candid views about the "plusses and minuses" of each party's position, the potential risks of going to trial, and the mediator's experience with cases that are at least somewhat similar to the matter at hand. The mediator will also talk about the applicable law.

Neither facilitative nor evaluative mediation is a "better" approach. Some mediators may choose which technique is appropriate for the unique circumstances of the case he or she is mediating. When selecting a mediator, you can ask the office where the mediator works what technique(s) the mediator uses, and request that a mediator evaluate the case after facilitating a meeting.

You and the other parties in the case have to agree who or what service will provide mediation. Usually, the mediator charges an hourly fee and asks the parties to share that cost equally. Some offices charge a non-refundable case processing fee.

Enter mediation with an open mind. An experienced elder law mediator will be sensitive to the dynamics of a family dispute. While the mediator will not be a passive person, she or he should be respectful toward you and the dispute.

If a settlement is reached, the mediator will prepare a document often referred to as "Basic Terms of Settlement" or a "Memorandum of Understanding." You will be asked to sign this agreement. Upon doing so, it is binding and enforceable in court in the same way that a contract would be. If an attorney is involved and/or the matter has already gone to court, the attorney will draft a formal settlement document to be filed with the court.

As discussed earlier, mediation permits people to resolve their disputes with a great deal of input. No one "wins" or "loses" every issue. In the final analysis, having a hand in the settlement process usually makes each party feel better and permits them and their family member to move on with their lives, free from the expense and uncertainty of the courtroom.

Early Neutral Evaluation

This type of ADR involves two neutral evaluators who listen to both sides of the case, gather information, and then give their assessment of the case from a practical perspective.

The goals of Early Neutral Evaluation (ENE) are to:

▶ Enhance direct communication between the parties about their claims and supporting evidence;

▶ Provide an assessment of the merits of the case by a neutral expert;

▶ Provide a "reality check" for clients and lawyers;

▶ Identify and clarify the central issues in dispute; and

▶ Facilitate settlement discussions, when requested by the parties.

ENE aims to position the case for early resolution, if possible. The evaluators, a team of professionals experienced in family dispute resolution, host an informal meeting of clients and counsel at which the following occurs:

▶ Each side presents the arguments supporting their case (without regard to the rules of evidence and without direct or cross-examination of witnesses).

▶ There is time for rebuttal and additional information if needed.

▶ The ENE team identifies areas of agreement, gathers additional information, clarifies and focuses the issues, and encourages the parties to enter procedural and substantive stipulations.

▶ The ENE team meets without the parties and their attorneys present to evaluate the case and recommendations regarding further information and settlement options.

▶ While the ENE team is in caucus, the attorneys and parties have the opportunity to discuss settlement of any issues.

▶ The ENE team then presents feedback and recommendations to the parties and their attorneys.

▶ The parties and their attorneys caucus to discuss the recommendations.

▶ The parties and their attorneys provide feedback to the ENE team regarding acceptance or rejection of recommendations.

▶ If the parties and their attorneys request further settlement discussion, they engage in settlement discussions facilitated by the ENE team, often in separate meetings with each side. This process follows the procedure for mediation as outlined above. ENE teams are often specially trained in the ENE process.

The ENE team has no power to impose settlement and does not attempt to coerce a party to accept any proposed terms. The parties may agree to a binding settlement. If no settlement is reached, the case remains on the Court's docket. Teams usually include a man and a woman, and may be comprised of two mental health professionals or one mental health professional and one attorney.

Communications made in connection with an ENE session are treated in the same way as mediation and cannot be disclosed to anyone else not involved in the litigation, unless otherwise agreed to by all parties.

Family Group Conference

Often, families need to meet to make decisions that do not involve the elderly/disabled person's legal rights. Family members frequently become so entrenched in their positions that they talk "at" each other rather than "with" each other. When this happens, no one is listening.

A neutral third person can usually break the stalemate by providing an informal setting in which to discuss the problem. The neutral person can be anyone who is trusted by all of the family members — a religious leader, a mental health professional, a lawyer, or anyone other than a family member. A mental health professional can help the family distinguish current problems to be solved from past family conflicts. A lawyer can help the family, without representing any one family member, to distinguish what is truly a legal problem from what is a family spat. Mental health and legal professionals alike can suggest other solutions to be considered, help the family find outside referrals or sources of information, and move the dispute past the communication block.

A family group conference is a concept that developed in cultures that encourage families to work together to preserve the family unit and culture. A Family Group Conference (FGC) is a formal meeting that involves extended family members in a decision-making process when it is determined that a family member is in need of care and protection. The family member is still involved in the process, just as in all of the other forms of ADR. FGCs are used in many countries. In the United States, the process is also known as Family Guided Decision-Making. In Canada, the term Family Group Conference is used. In the Netherlands and Flanders, they are known as *Eigen Kracht Conferenties* ("Own Power Conferences").

The process that is normally followed is:

Information Sharing

▶ Begin the FGC with a ritual; for example, a prayer or song chosen by the family.

▶ The specific reason for meeting is stated and the purpose of the FGC is agreed upon.

▶ The agenda and procedure is agreed upon by the family.

▶ All invited participants (family and professionals) voice their understanding of the family's strengths and major concerns.

▶ Any legal issues are addressed, along with "non-negotiable" concerns regarding health or the law.

▶ The goal of this phase is to provide the participants with a complete picture of the family and the immediate safety needs of the specific family member.

Private Family Time

> ▶ All professionals attending the conference leave the room at this time.

> ▶ The family chooses a family member to continue the meeting and enforce the rules.

> ▶ The family addresses the non-negotiable concerns first, then addresses the most serious concerns shared by the group.

> ▶ A meal is shared among the family members.

> ▶ The goal of this part is for the family to use the strengths and resources they have to make decisions about the listed concerns.

Presentation of the Plan

> ▶ The family invites the professionals back into the room and presents the plan that was developed during private family time.

> ▶ The professionals review the pros and cons of the plan with the family, who will either accept the plan as it stands or modify the plan. If more information is needed to form an informed decision, the family will decide who will provide the information.

> ▶ If changes to the plan are needed, the facilitator can help guide the group through the process.

> ▶ Once the plan provides a safe, permanent, and caring environment, the family will then figure out a way to help support the family's plan.

29-4. For More Information

If your family needs more information regarding alternate dispute resolution, you may want to consult one of the following resources:

Mediate.com — Everything Mediation
This site has lists of mediators, both attorneys and mental health professionals, who are trained and experienced in various forms of mediation, including elder mediation, as well as articles on mediation and what you can expect.
> www.mediate.com

Colorado Bar Association
The Colorado Bar Association maintains lists of lawyers who conduct alternate dispute resolution.
> (303) 860-8115
> www.cobar.org

The Association for Conflict Resolution

The Association for Conflict Resolution is a national organization devoted to peaceful resolution of international, interpersonal, and family conflict. The Association of Conflict Resolution has a magazine with many articles devoted to various forms and uses of ADR.

> 12100 Sunset Hills Rd., Ste. 130
> Reston, VA 20190
> (703) 234-4141
> www.acrnet.org

The Center for Social Gerontology

The Center for Social Gerontology is a national organization devoted to promoting the individual autonomy of older persons and their well-being. One of their programs is to provide training for professionals and family members in dispute resolution involving older persons.

> 2307 Shelby Ave.
> Ann Arbor, MI 48103
> (734) 665-1126
> www.tcsg.org

Chapter 30

Programs, Services, and Resources for Older Adults

Lew Forester
The Senior Hub, Inc.

SYNOPSIS

30-1. Introduction

A wide range of programs and services are available for older adults to protect or enhance their health and well-being and to help them maintain safety and independence while living in the comfort of their own homes. These programs and services include everything from personal care services to free and low-cost home repairs, from Meals on Wheels to recreational and social opportunities. Services have increased and evolved over time to meet the needs of a rapidly growing older adult population. As the baby boomer generation continues to age, the need for services will expand and Congress will continue to enact legislation that will impact the variety and availability of resources and services in local communities. The Older Americans Act is one of many laws enacted to assist older adults in maintaining their health and well-being, and is the basis for local Area Agencies on Aging, discussed below.

Many of the programs and services that follow are not always well known or advertised, as they are most often provided by agencies that have a very limited budget for marketing and outreach and must direct most of their funding into providing the services. If you have difficulty locating a program, service, senior center, or senior organization in your area, call 211 (United Way Helpline) or contact your local Area Agency on Aging (see listings in Exhibit 8C appearing at the end of this chapter).

30-2. Area Agencies on Aging

An Area Agency on Aging (AAA) plans, coordinates, and funds services that enable seniors to live independently in their own homes. AAAs were established under the Older Americans Act in 1973 to respond to the needs of Americans aged 60 and over in every local community throughout the country. Services available through AAAs fall into five categories:

1) **Information and Access Services**, including information and referral, health insurance counseling, client assessment, care management, transportation, caregiver support, retirement planning, and education.

2) **Community-Based Services**, including employment services, senior centers, congregate meals, adult day services, and volunteer opportunities.

3) **In-Home Services**, including meals on wheels, homemakers, chore services, telephone reassurance, friendly visiting, energy assistance and weatherization, emergency response systems, home health services, personal care services, and respite care.

4) **Housing**, including senior housing for independent living and alternative living facilities, such as assisted living.

5) **Elder Rights**, such as legal assistance, elder abuse prevention programs, and ombudsman services for complaint resolution.

The services provided by AAAs across the country may vary and reflect the needs of the local communities they serve. Transportation and in-home care may be a priority in rural areas, for example, while Meals on Wheels and adult day services may be more of a priority in urban areas. AAAs continue to assess the needs of older adults in the communities they serve and adjust to meet these changing needs.

A list of Area Agencies on Aging for Colorado appears as section 11-6, "Resources," in Chapter 11, "Arm Yourself with Consumer Protection Information."

30-3. Adult Protective Services

Adult Protective Services (APS) provides assistance to at-risk adults whose health and well-being may be compromised or in danger due to abuse, neglect, or exploitation. In the Colorado Adult Protective Services statute, an at-risk adult is defined as

> an individual eighteen years of age or older who is susceptible to mistreatment or self-neglect because the individual is unable to perform or obtain services necessary for the individual's health, safety, or welfare or lacks sufficient understanding or capacity to make or communicate responsible decisions concerning the individual's person or affairs.

Mistreatment of an at-risk adult can include physical abuse, self-abuse, sexual abuse, neglect, confinement, financial exploitation, and other forms of exploitation. Physical abuse includes hitting, slapping, pushing, kicking, and confinement. Self-abuse is the infliction of injury to the adult by the adult's own volition, including suicide attempts, self-inflicted wounds, pulling out hair, etc. Neglect may include untreated medical conditions, malnourishment, dehydration, unclean appearance, bedsores, unsanitary conditions in the home, and being left alone for long periods of time when in need of supervision. Self-neglect may also include the above and may be caused by confusion, wandering, inability to communicate needs, and medication mismanagement.

To report suspected abuse, neglect, or exploitation: Call the county Department of Social Services where the at-risk individual lives and ask for Adult Protection intake. Have as many facts together as possible when you make the call, including names, addresses, phone numbers, dates, times, and the reasons you are making the call on this individual's behalf. If you are concerned about the welfare of an at-risk adult, you may also contact local police with your concerns and ask them to do a wellness check. They can then assess the situation and make a referral, if necessary, to Adult Protective Services. If the individual is in immediate danger, call 911.

What Adult Protective Services will do: APS staff will assess the individual's ability to make appropriate decisions for himself or herself and decide whether to open a case and make interventions on the individual's behalf. All at-risk adults have the right of self-determination and may refuse or reject protective services. A court must sometimes decide whether the individual is competent to make decisions for himself or herself. When given consent or appointed by the court, APS staff will investigate reports of abuse, neglect, and exploitation; remove at-risk adults from danger; and make arrangements for appropriate programs and services. If interventions are made, they are provided in a manner that will cause minimal disruption to the at-risk adult's life and ensure that his or her dignity and confidentiality are protected.

30-4. Senior Recreation Centers

Senior Recreation Centers may provide a number of different services depending upon the size and characteristics of the community they serve. Senior centers are a gathering place where older adults can participate in social, educational, fitness, and recreational opportunities.

Most all senior centers offer fitness classes, which may include aerobics, dance, yoga, tai chi, water fitness, etc. Most centers also offer various enjoyment/educational classes, including painting, pottery, jewelry-making, scrapbooking, cooking, computers, and languages. Many senior centers offer travel and outdoor recreation programs, as well as groups, clubs, and indoor games such as bingo, poker, pool, and bridge. Some senior centers may offer non-recreational programs, such as transportation services, congregate meal sites, and information and referral services. Again, classes and programs offered usually reflect the needs and interests of the local communities they serve.

Lists of senior recreation centers and other organizations serving seniors appear in Exhibits 8A, 8B, and 8C at the end of this chapter. As mentioned above, you may call 211 or your local AAA if your locality does not appear on this list.

30-5. Senior Service and Resource Organizations

A wide variety of programs and services of a non-recreational nature are offered by senior organizations and resource centers throughout the state. These services are vital to the health, safety, and well-being of older adults and may be funded entirely or in part by counties, municipalities, private foundations, and local Area Agencies on Aging.

As with senior recreation centers, senior resource organizations usually reflect and focus on the most significant needs of older adults in the communities they serve. Many of the programs and services listed in the section below may be offered by local senior resource organizations. Check the listings in Exhibits 8A, 8B, and 8C for senior resource organizations near you, or call 211 or your local AAA.

30-6. Key Programs and Services for Seniors

Adult Day Services: Provides care, activities, and meals for functionally impaired adults while their caregivers work or attend to other needs. Participants in the program are able to interact with peers in a social setting during the day, then return to the comfort of their own homes at night when family or other caregivers are present. This service is provided by both for-profit and non-profit agencies, and is often covered by insurance, Medicaid, or other public funds.

Benefits Check-Up: This program, developed and maintained by the National Council on Aging, connects seniors age 55 and over to financial benefit programs for which they may be eligible. Seniors with limited incomes may discover, for example, they are eligible for programs such as Old Age Pension or programs that pay all or part of their Medicare Part B premiums. Since 2001, millions have used Benefits Check-Up to find public benefits, veterans benefits, and programs to help pay for prescription drugs, health care, etc. Seniors can go online to www.benefitscheckup.org, enter the requested information, and receive a printout of benefits. They may also call (303) 629-4996 or (866) 550-2752 for assistance with this.

Care Management: A care manager can be an important resource to families and caregivers who are attempting to arrange for care or to access resources for their loved ones. This is often fully funded by Older Americans Act funds for seniors aged 60 and over. A care manager will arrange for a meeting with the client and interested family members, then conduct a full in-home assessment of the individual's strengths and needs. This will provide information on how well the individual is able to perform each of his or her activities of daily living, such as bathing, dressing, housework, money management, social needs, etc. A home safety assessment will also be conducted, and safety devices such as railings and grab bars may be arranged for. Once the care manager gathers this information, he or she will create a care plan, which will outline the services needed and who the providers will be. Help with necessary applications is also given. These providers may include meals on wheels, transportation, home health, volunteers, and any number of other services. The care manager will carefully monitor the delivery of services and make changes as needed. Care management greatly reduces the burden on loved ones and ensures the best possible, least restrictive care for the client.

Caregiver and Homemaker Services: Public funds are sometimes available to provide in-home care and/or homemaker services. As mentioned above, AAAs often fund these services in local communities. County Options for Long-Term Care agencies fund programs such as Home and Community Based Services (HCBS), which place caregivers in the homes of persons in need of help with activities of daily living. A Home Care Allowance (HCA) may also be available, which gives those in need of care a monthly allowance with which to pay someone for cleaning or caregiving. Some agencies provide free Respite Care, in which either a volunteer or paid staff is placed in the home for several hours or more per week to give the primary caregiver a respite, or break, from their duties.

Dental, Vision, and Hearing Services: A number of foundations, clinics, agencies, and service groups help pay for dentures and dental work, vision and glasses, and hearing and hearing aids, or provide services at a greatly reduced rate. Call 211 or your local senior organization for more information.

Employment Programs: Various agencies, such as AARP and county workforce centers, have programs that help seniors find employment. The Senior Community Employment Program (SCEP) is operated under Title V of the Older Americans Act. Seniors 55 and over are paid to perform up to 20 hours per week of community service in a training position in non-profit and governmental organizations while they learn new skills and pursue permanent employment.

Fall Prevention Services: Falls are the leading cause of injury deaths among older adults and the most common cause for hospitalization. Prevention may include home safety assessments and modifications, medications reviews, health assessments, and vision screenings. A number of free and low-cost programs and services are available to reduce or eliminate falls.

Forms Assistance: Seniors often are reluctant to apply for benefits for which they are eligible because of sometimes lengthy and confusing applications. Many senior resource organizations have staff who help seniors through the maze of paperwork necessary to receive benefits. County social services departments also have staff who help with applications for benefits such as food stamps, Medicaid, etc.

Free 911 Cell Phone: Some senior organizations and law enforcement agencies offer free cell phones for seniors. These cell phones are typically used and reconditioned and will only dial 911, so that seniors can dial for help in an emergency involving themselves or others. There is no contract or monthly service fee, as any working cell phone will dial 911.

Friendly Visiting and Telephone Reassurance: Volunteers are often available in local communities to make visits to homebound seniors who are isolated or in frail health. This provides regular social contact and helps to assure safety and well-being. Volunteers also provide telephone reassurance, whereby isolated seniors are called on a regular basis for socialization and to check on their well-being. This is also a great volunteer opportunity, and often connects homebound seniors looking for something to do with similar individuals. Check with your local senior organization for more information.

Handyman, Home Rehabilitation, and Weatherization Services: Many senior organizations offer low- to no-cost handyman services. Services may be performed by professionals or skilled volunteers. Many counties and municipalities offer housing rehabilitation programs where grants or low-interest loans are given to low-income homeowners to assist in repairing or replacing major housing systems that are potential health or safety concerns. Weatherization programs, which assist low-income homeowners in saving energy dollars by insulating homes, may also be available.

Information and Referral: Information on resources and services of all types is available through senior centers, resource centers, emergency assistance centers, social services agencies, Area Agencies on Aging, United Way (dial 211), and many other agencies. Often, an agency employs an information and referral specialist whose job is to identify needs, help solve problems, and make appropriate referrals.

Medical Equipment Lending: Programs are available that loan durable medical equipment, such as walkers, wheelchairs, bath benches, etc., free of charge to older adults recovering from surgery or temporarily in need of these items for health and safety. Call 211 or check with your local senior organization for details.

Nutrition Services: Services to help meet the nutritional needs of seniors include the following programs. *Meals on Wheels:* This is a nationwide program that may vary in services and scope from community to community. In general, volunteers deliver hot meals to homebound individuals who are unable to shop or prepare nutritious meals on their own. The daily contact by the volunteer also provides a wellness check and social contact for often frail, at-risk individuals. Costs are usually on a sliding scale. *Congregate Meals:* Group meals are provided free or at low cost at various sites, including schools, senior centers, and other public sites. Older adults are able to enjoy a nutritious meal in the company of others. *Other Food Programs:* Food banks, food stamps, and other programs are available to older adults living on limited, fixed incomes. Food banks usually serve geographical areas and have various days and hours of operation. Call 211 or your county social services department for a food bank in your area. Food stamp programs provide a regular monthly amount that may be spent on food-only items. Enroll for food stamps through your county department of social services. Government programs, such as the Commodity Supplemental Food Program (CSFP) may also be available on a monthly basis. Seniors are able to pick up government commodities at a site in their community, or have them brought to their house if they are homebound.

Personal Emergency Response Systems: A personal emergency response system (PERS) is an electronic device designed to let the user summon help in an emergency. This system has three components: a small radio transmitter or help button worn by the user, a console connected to the user's telephone, and an emergency response center that monitors calls. PERS may be purchased, rented, or leased and monthly service fees apply. As with any major purchase, it is important to check out several systems before you buy and to compare prices and features.

Property Tax Assistance: The *Colorado Senior Property Tax Exemption* is currently suspended (for 2010 and 2011 taxes payable in 2011 and 2012) due to shortfalls in the state budget. When this program is active, it is available to seniors aged 65 and over who have lived in their homes for at least 10 years or are the surviving spouse of someone who meets this requirement. The program exempts from taxation 50 percent of the first $200,000 of actual value of the residential property. Pending legislation may reinstate this program for 2013. Some other programs are listed here. *Disabled Veteran Exemption*: This is available to applicants who sustained a permanent disability while serving on active duty in the United States Armed Forces. Other eligibility requirements apply. Applications must be submitted to the Division of Veterans Affairs by July 1 each year. Call (303) 343-1268 for more information. *Property Tax Deferral*: This program is for Colorado residents who are 65 years of age or older or are in active military service. These individuals may defer or postpone payment of their property taxes by contacting their county treasurer's office. The state treasury will pay the taxes directly to the county for the taxes due that year. This loan (with interest) will be logged as a lien against the property, which is recovered when repaid or when the owner dies or the property changes hands. Applications for this program are available from your county assessor and should be submitted by April 1 each year. *Property Tax/Rent/Heat Rebate*: This program is for full-year Colorado residents who are age 65 or older, surviving spouses who are 58 years of age or older, or persons with disabilities. Income limits apply. Eligible individuals can receive this rebate even if they normally do not file any other income taxes. *Property Tax Work-Off Program*: Some taxing entities offer a property tax work-off program for citizens who are age 60 or over or who are physically or developmentally disabled. As an example, by volunteering in some local school districts, you may be able to work off up to $400 of your property taxes. Call your county assessor's office or local school district for more information on programs in your area.

Rent and Utility Assistance: Various non-profit and faith-based organizations offer rent, utility, and prescription assistance. Funding may come from a number of government and private sources. Call 211 or your local information and referral source for names and numbers of local agencies.

Resources for Pets: Pets are often vital companions for older adults, many of whom are homebound and have limited social contacts. Some agencies offer seniors the opportunity to adopt a pet free of charge. Other agencies offer spaying and neutering and other health services for pets for free or at low cost. Some food banks and other organizations often have pet food and other products available so that low-income seniors can provide for their pets. There are also for-profit businesses that come directly to the home for pet grooming, vaccinations, and other services.

Reverse Mortgage: A reverse mortgage is a loan against the home that does not need to be repaid for as long as the owner lives there. With a reverse mortgage, the equity or value of the home can be turned into a regular monthly cash advance or can be taken out in a single lump sum. Other options may also be available. Typically, nothing is repaid on the loan until the owner passes away, moves, or sells the home, at which time it will be repaid out of the equity or estate. The home remains in possession of the owner and may still be passed on to heirs. To be eligible for a reverse mortgage, seniors must be 62 or over and own and reside in the home. Many older adults living on limited, fixed incomes find a reverse mortgage an ideal way to increase monthly income and meet current needs. A number of lenders offer reverse mortgages, and loan and processing fees are involved. It is advisable to talk to at least two companies and compare fees and services offered. See Chapter 20, "Reverse Mortgages," for more information.

Senior Liaison Officers: Some law enforcement agencies employ a senior liaison officer, who will answer questions and concerns for seniors and provide information on frauds, scams, and guarding personal safety. They help to prevent seniors from being victims of crime and link them to other resources and agencies for assistance. Senior liaison officers often have a weekly presence in senior centers, shopping malls, and other public places.

Support Groups: In a support group, members give each other support, encouragement, and understanding about a similar problem, whether it be grief, caregiving, addiction, disease, etc. Support groups are usually led by a professional who offers encouragement and resources while allowing members to guide the conversation in a relaxed, non-threatening atmosphere. Most all groups are free of charge and provide a social connection for those experiencing loss or disease. A wide variety of support groups are available for seniors and their caregivers. Contact your local senior organization or mental health department for support groups in your area.

Tax Counseling: Many local senior organizations partner with the Internal Revenue Service to provide the Volunteer Income Tax Assistance (VITA) program. Trained volunteers from non-profit organizations provide free tax counseling and basic income tax return preparation for seniors, the disabled, and lower-income people. Many seniors who do not normally file are often unaware of rebates and refunds for which they may be eligible, such as rent, heat, and property tax rebates. This program is usually conducted at senior and other community centers during tax preparation season. Most locations offer electronic filing. To locate the nearest VITA site, call (800) 829-1040.

Transportation: Many local transportation districts have programs to serve disabled and frail individuals who are unable to use regular public transportation. Costs are minimal. Some senior organizations have government funding to provide free transportation to doctors, dentists, meal sites, food banks, or grocery stores. Some agencies serving seniors may also have volunteers who will provide free transportation.

Volunteer Opportunities — Senior Corps: Senior Corps is a nationwide program that connects adults aged 55 and over to a wide variety of volunteer opportunities in the communities in which they live. It offers three programs. The *Retired and Senior Volunteer Program (RSVP)* connects volunteers aged 55 and over with service opportunities in their communities that match their interests and skills. Volunteers are placed with schools, hospitals, food banks, and many other non-profit agencies. The *Foster Grandparent Program* connects volunteers aged 60 and over with children and young people with exceptional needs. Volunteers mentor, support, and offer guidance to vulnerable children. The *Senior Companion Program* matches volunteers aged 60 and over with adults in their community who have difficulty with the simple tasks of daily living. They may assist with shopping or light chores or just make friendly visits.

Exhibit 30A.
Colorado Senior Recreation Centers

Front Range — Denver Metropolitan Area

Arvada
North Jeffco Senior Center   (303) 425-9583
6842 Wadsworth Blvd.
www.apexprd.org

Aurora
Aurora Center for Active Adults   (303) 739-7950
30 Del Mar Cir.
www.auroragov.org

Brighton
Eagle View Adult Center   (303) 655-2075
1150 Prairie Center Pkwy.
www.brightonco.gov

Broomfield
Broomfield Senior Center   (303) 464-5526
280 Lamar St.
www.broomfield.org

Castle Rock
Castle Rock Senior Center   (303) 688-9498
2323 Woodlands Blvd.
www.castlerockseniorcenter.org

Commerce City
Commerce City Senior Center   (303) 289-3720
6060 E. Parkway Dr.
www.ci.commerce-city.co.us

Denver — City & County of Denver Recreation Centers
www.denvergov.org/recreation

Athmar Recreation Center   (303) 937-4600
2680 W. Mexico

Barnum Senior Center   (303) 937-4659
360 Hooker St.

College View Rec. Center 2525 S. Decatur St.	(303) 937-4630
Cook Park Recreation Center 7100 Cherry Creek S. Dr.	(720) 865-0610
Glenarm Recreation Center 2800 Glenarm Pl.	(720) 865-3380
Highland Senior Center 2880 Osceola St.	(303) 458-4868
La Alma Recreation Center 1325 W. 11th Ave.	(303) 572-4790
La Familia Recreation Center 65 S. Elati St.	(303) 698-4995
Martin Luther King Jr. Center 3880 Newport St.	(720) 865-0530
Montbello Recreation Center 15555 E. 53rd Ave.	(720) 865-0580
Montclair Recreation Center 729 Ulster Way	(720) 865-0560
Platt Park Senior Center 1500 S. Grant St.	(720) 865-0630
Quigg Newton Center 4430 Navajo St.	(303) 458-4899
St. Charles Rec. Center 3777 Lafayette St.	(303) 295-4462
Scheitler Recreation Center 5031 W. 46th Ave.	(720) 865-0640
Swansea Recreation Center 2650 E. 49th Ave.	(720) 865-0540
Twentieth Street Recreation Center 1011 20th St.	(720) 865-0520

Washington Park Recreation Center   (720) 865-3400
701 S. Franklin St.

Denver — Other Recreation Centers
Curtis Park Community Center   (303) 295-2399
929 29th Ave.
http://curtisparkcommunitycenter.services.officelive.com

Denver Indian Center   (303) 936-2688
4407 Morrison Rd.
www.denverindiancenter.org

Denver Inner City Parish   (303) 629-0636
1212 Mariposa St.
http://dicp.org

Jewish Community Center   (303) 399-2660
350 S. Dahlia St.
www.jccdenver.org

Mulroy Neighborhood Center   (303) 892-1540
3550 W. 13th St.

Our Savior's Senior Center   (303) 831-7023
915 E. 9th Ave.
http://oslcdenver.org

Salvation Army Red Shield Community Center   (303) 295-2107
2915 High St.

Salvation Army – West Adams   (303) 428-6430
2821 W. 65th Pl.

Schlessman Family YMCA   (720) 524-2750
3901 E. Yale Ave.
www.denverymca.org

Senior Support Services   (303) 832-1622
846 E. 18th Ave.
www.seniorsupportservices.org

Sunset Park Senior Center   (303) 297-0230
1865 Larimer St.
www.voacolorado.org

Westwood Community Center 1000 S. Lowell Blvd.	(303) 934-2181
Zion Senior Center 5151 E. 33rd Ave. www.zionbaptistchurchdenver.org	(303) 333-5746

Englewood
Malley Senior Recreation Center 3380 S. Lincoln St. www.englewoodgov.org	(303) 762-2660

Evergreen
Wulf Recreation Center 5300 S. Olive Rd. www.evergreenrecreation.com	(720) 880-1200

Golden
Golden Community Center 1470 10th St. www.cityofgolden.net	(303) 384-8100

Highlands Ranch
Recreation Center at Southridge 4800 McArthur Ranch Rd. www.hrcaonline.org	(303) 791-2500

Lakewood
Clements Community Center 1580 Yarrow St. www.lakewood.org	(303) 987-4820

Littleton Area
Douglas H. Buck Community Recreation Center 2004 W. Powers Ave. www.ssprd.org	(303) 797-8787
Foothills Park & Recreation District 6612 S. Ward St. www.ifoothills.org	(303) 409-2100

Northglenn
Northglenn Senior Center 11801 Community Center Dr. www.northglenn.org/seniors	(303) 450-8801

Parker
Parker Senior Center   (303) 841-5370
10675 Longs Way

Thornton
Thornton Senior Center   (303) 255-7850
9471 Dorothy Blvd.
www.cityofthornton.net

Westminster
MAC Center   (303) 426-4310
3295 W. 72nd Ave.
www.ci.westminster.co.us

Wheat Ridge
Active Adult Community Center   (303) 205-7500
6363 W. 35th Ave.
www.ci.wheatridge.co.us

Eastern Plains

Burlington
McArthur Senior Center   (719) 346-7986
350 Hollowell St.

Limon
Hub City Senior Center   (719) 775-2721
220 East Ave.

Northern Colorado

Boulder
www.bouldercolorado.gov

Boulder Senior Services East   (303) 441-4150
5660 Sioux Dr.

Boulder Senior Services West   (303) 441-3148
909 Arapahoe Ave.

Berthoud
Berthoud Community Center   (970) 532-2730
248 Welch
www.berthoudcolorado.com

Brush
Brush Senior Center   (970) 842-5046
710 Lincoln St.
www.brushchamber.org

Eaton
Legacy Senior Center   (970) 454-3411
1325 3rd St.
www.eatonchamber.org

Erie
Erie Community Center – Active Adults   (303) 926-2550
450 Powers St.
www.erieco.gov

Estes Park
Estes Park Senior Center   (970) 586-2996
220 4th St.
www.estesnet.com/seniorcenter

Fort Collins
Fort Collins Senior Center   (970) 221-6644
1200 Raintree Dr.
www.fcgov.com/recreation/seniorcenter.php

Fort Lupton
Fort Lupton Community Center   (303) 857-4200, x166
203 S. Harrison
www.fortlupton.org

Greeley
Greeley Senior Activities Center   (970) 350-9440
1010 6th St.
www.greeleygov.com

Johnstown
Johnstown Senior Center   (970) 587-5251
101 Charlotte St.
www.townofjohnstown.com

Lafayette
Lafayette Senior Center   (303) 665-9052
103 S. Iowa Ave.
www.cityoflafayette.com

Longmont
Longmont Senior Center   (303) 651-8413
910 Longs Peak Ave.
www.ci.longmont.co.us/sen_ctr

Loveland
Chilson Senior Center   (970) 962-2783
700 E. 4th St.
www.ci.loveland.co.us

Louisville
Louisville Senior Center   (303) 666-7400
900 Via Appia Way
www.louisvillerecreation.com

Nederland
Nederland Area Seniors, Inc.   (303) 258-0799
750 Peak to Peak Hwy.

Sterling
Heritage Senior Citizen Center   (970) 522-1237
821 N. Division Ave.

Wellington
Wellington Senior Center   (970) 568-7402
3800 Wilson Ave.

Southern Colorado

Alamosa
South Central Colorado Seniors   (719) 589-4511
1116 3rd St.

Calhan
Paulson Senior Center   (719) 347-2616
406 Cheyenne St.

Cañon City
Golden Age Senior Center   (719) 275-5177
728 Main St.

Colorado Springs
www.springsgov.com

Colorado Springs Senior Center   (719) 387-6000
1514 N. Hancock Ave.

Hillside Community Center   (719) 385-7900
925 S. Institute

Meadows Park   (719) 385-7940
1943 S. El Paso Ave.

Salvation Army Community Center   (719) 636-3891
908 Yuma
www.tsacs.org

Florence
Florence Community Center   (719) 784-6493
100 Railroad
www.florenceseniorcenter.com

La Junta
La Junta Senior Center   (719) 384-5991
601 Colorado Ave.
www.ci.la-junta.co.us/SeniorCenter.htm

Lamar
Lamar Senior Center   (719) 336-4072
407 E. Olive St.

Penrose
Penrose Senior Center   (719) 372-3872
405 Broadway
www.penrosechamber.com

Pueblo
Joseph H. Edwards Senior Center   (719) 545-8900
230 N. Union
www.srda.org

Rocky Ford
Rocky Ford Senior Center   (719) 254-6969
503 N. 9th St.

Salida
Senior Center of Salida   (719) 539-3351
305 F St.
www.salida.com

Trinidad
H.R. Sayre Senior Center   (719) 845-1133
1222 San Pedro Ave.

Woodland Park
Woodland Park Senior Center   (719) 687-3330
312 N. Center St.

Western Colorado

Aspen
Pitkin County Senior Center   (970) 920-5432
275 Castle Creek Rd.
www.aspenpitkin.com

Basalt
Eagle County Senior Center   (970) 927-6430
1400 E. Valley Rd.

Cedaredge
Cedaredge Community Center   (970) 856-3636
140 NW 2nd St.

Craig
Senior Citizen Center   (970) 824-3911
633 Ledford St.

Delta
Columbine Senior Services   (970) 874-7661
247 Meeker St.

Durango
Durango/La Plata Senior Center   (970) 382-6445
2424 Main Ave.
www.co.laplata.co.us

Hotchkiss
Hotchkiss Senior Citizens   (970) 872-3494
276 W. Main St.

Glenwood Springs
Lucy Huntly Senior Center (Colo. Mtn. College)   (970) 945-9117
1402 Blake Ave.

Grand Junction
Mesa County Senior Recreation Center   (970) 243-7908
550 Ouray Ave.

Gunnison
Senior Citizen Center   (970) 641-8060
200 E. Spencer Ave.

Montrose
Montrose Pavilion   (970) 249-7015
1800 Pavilion Dr.

Nucla
Nucla Senior Center   (970) 864-7278
386 Main St.

Olathe
Olathe Community Center   (970) 323-5391
115 Main St.

Paonia
Paonia Senior Center   (970) 527-3435
106 3rd St.

Parachute
Parachute Valley Senior Center   (970) 285-7216
540 N. Parachute

Steamboat Springs
Routt County Council on Aging, Senior Center   (970) 879-0633
1605 Lincoln
www.yampavalley.info

Rifle
Rifle Senior Center   (970) 625-1877
50 Ute Ave.

Exhibit 30B.
Senior Service and Resource Organizations

Front Range — Denver Metropolitan Area

AARP State Office, www.aarp.org/states/co	(866) 554-5376
AARP ElderWatch, www.aarpelderwatch.org	(303) 222-4444
Area Agency on Aging (DRCOG), www.drcog.org	(303) 455-1000
Benefits Check-Up, www.benefitscheckup.org	(303) 899-5582
Care Management Solutions of Lutheran Family Services, www.lfsco.org/care-management	(800) 579-9496
Catholic Charities — Senior Outreach	(303) 742-0828
Colorado Commission on Aging	(303) 866-2800
Colorado Division of Insurance, www.dora.state.co.us/insurance	(303) 894-7499
Colorado Fund for People with Disabilities, www.cfpdtrust.org	(303) 733-2867
Colorado Housing and Finance Authority, www.chfainfo.com	(800) 877-2432
Community Housing Services, www.chsico.org	(303) 831-1750
Denver Office on Aging, www.denvergov.org/aging	(720) 913-8477
Douglas County Senior Outreach Services, www.douglas.co.us	(303) 660-7519
Foster Grandparents Program, www.voacolorado.org	(303) 297-0408
Guardianship Alliance of Colorado, www.guardianshipallianceofcolorado.org	(303) 228-5382
Interfaith Community Services, www.ifcs.org	(303) 789-0501
Jewish Family Service, www.jewishfamilyservice.org	(303) 597-5000
Long-Term Care Ombudsman, www.thelegalcenter.org	(303) 722-0300
National Eldercare Locator, www.eldercare.gov	(800) 677-1116
Rebuilding Together Metro Denver, www.rebuildingdenver.org	(720) 524-0840
RSVP (Retired and Senior Volunteer Program) of the Denver Metro Area	(303) 297-0408
Senior Answers and Services, www.senioranswers.org	(303) 333-3482
Senior Assistance Center, www.seniorassistancecenter.org	(303) 455-9642
Senior Hub, Inc., www.seniorhub.org	(303) 426-4408
Seniors! Inc., www.seniorsinc.org	(720) 974-6701
Seniors Resource Center, www.srcaging.org	(303) 238-8151
Senior Support Services, www.seniorsupportservices.org	(303) 832-1622
Special Needs Trust Network, www.sntnetwork.org	(303) 331-4420

Northern Colorado

Boulder, Lafayette, and Louisville
Boulder County Aging Services,
    www.bouldercounty.org/cs/ag   (303) 441-3570
Boulder Senior Center East   (303) 441-4150
Boulder Long-Term Care Ombudsman   (303) 441-1173
Boulder County Aging Services
  Allenspark Nursing Clinic   (303) 747-2592
  Boulder Senior Services   (303) 441-3148
  Lafayette Senior Center   (303) 665-9052
  Longmont Senior Center   (303) 651-8411
  Louisville Senior Center   (303) 666-7400
  Lyons Senior Resources   (303) 823-9016
  Nederland Senior Resources   (303) 258-3068
  Niwot Senior Resources   (303) 652-3850
CareConnect, www.careconnectbc.org   (303) 443-1933
Circle of Care/Arts for Elders,
    www.circleofcareproject.org   (303) 449-8884
Guardianship Alliance   (303) 228-5382
Jewish Family Service, www.jewishfamilyservice.org   (303) 415-1025
Ombudsman Monitoring Program   (303) 441-3570
Project HOPE   (303) 441-3945
Retired Senior Volunteer Program (RSVP)   (303) 443-1933

Fort Collins
Aspen Club   (970) 495-8560
Eldercare Network, www.eldercarenet.org   (970) 495-3442
Elderly Outreach Program (Catholic Charities)   (970) 484-5010
Larimer County Office on Aging, www.larimer.org   (970) 498-7750
  Adult Resources for Care and Help   (970) 498-7757
  Answers on Aging (Senior Hotline)   dial 211
  Family Caregiver Support Program   (970) 498-7758
  Long-Term Care Ombudsman   (970) 498-7754 or (970) 498-7753
  Property Tax Work Off Program   (970) 498-7751
Pathways: Programs for Grief and Loss   (970) 663-3500
Poudre Valley Hospital Case Management,
    www.pvhs.org   (970) 495-8554
Volunteers of America (many programs for seniors)   (970) 472-9630

Fort Lupton
Catholic Charities   (303) 857-0521
Recreation Community Complex Coordinator   (303) 857-4200

Greeley

Area Agency on Aging, www.co.weld.co.us	(970) 346-6950
Catholic Charities Weld County	(970) 353-6433
Retired Senior Volunteer Program (RSVP)	(970) 351-2588

Longmont

Boulder County Aging Services Division	(303) 441-3570
Long-Term Care Ombudsman	(303) 441-3570
Outreach United Resource Center, www.ourcenter.org	(303) 772-5529
Senior Resource Specialist	(303) 651-8716
RSVP of Boulder County (many services for seniors)	(303) 772-2262

Loveland

Aspen Club	(970) 624-1860
Catholic Charities	(970) 663-1880
RSVP of Loveland	(970) 669-5460

Southern Colorado

Cañon City

Council of Governments, www.uaacog.com	(719) 275-8350
Upper Arkansas Council of Governments	
Area Agency on Aging, www.uaaaa.org	(719) 275-4979

Colorado Springs

El Paso Department of Human Services, http://dhs.elpasoco.com	(719) 636-0000
HealthLink 50+ Club	(719) 444-2273
Pikes Peak Area Agency on Aging, www.ppacg.org	(719) 471-7080
Pikes Peak Community Action Agency, www.ppcaa.org	(719) 633-8994
Senior Information and Assistance Center	(719) 471-2096
Senior Insurance Assistance	(719) 635-4891
Senior Resource Council, www.srccos.org	(719) 260-0744
Silver Key Senior Services, www.silverkey.org	(719) 884-2300

Monument

Tri-Lakes Cares, www.tri-lakescares.org	(719) 481-4864

Pueblo

Area Agency on Aging	(719) 583-6120
Adult Resources for Care and Help	(719) 583-6611
Long-Term Care Ombudsman	(719) 583-6110
Retired and Senior Volunteer Program (RSVP)	(719) 545-8900

Seniors! Inc.   (719) 553-0478
Senior Resource Development Agency, www.srda.org   (719) 545-8900
United Way of Pueblo, www.pueblounitedway.org   (719) 583-4455

Salida
Upper Arkansas Area Agency on Aging,
    www.uaaaa.org   (877) 610-3341 or (719) 539-3341

Western Colorado

Aspen
Pitkin County Senior Services,
    www.aspenpitkin.com/Departments/Senior-Services   (970) 920-5432

Carbondale
Senior Matters, www.carbondaleseniors.org   (970) 963-2536

Delta
Delta County Senior Resource Council, www.dcsrc.org   (970) 712-2295

Eagle
Rural Resort Retired Senior Volunteer Program   (970) 328-2610
Aging and Adult Services   (970) 328-8829

Glenwood Springs
Colorado Mountain College Lucy Huntley
    Senior Center   (970) 945-9117
High Country Retired Senior Volunteer Program   (970) 947-8462

Grand Junction
Center for Independence, www.cfigj.org   (800) 613-2271 or
    (970) 241-0315

Mesa County Supporting Our Seniors (SOS)   (970) 248-2722
RSVP Handyman Project, www.rsvpgrandjunction.org   (970) 243-9839

Rifle
Senior Housing   (970) 625-3974
Traveler Services   (970) 625-1366

Exhibit 30C.
Resource Directory — Denver Region Area Agency on Aging

RESOURCE DIRECTORY
FOR PERSONS 60 YEARS OF AGE OR OLDER

September 2011

DRC⊙G
DENVER REGIONAL COUNCIL OF GOVERNMENTS

AREA AGENCY ON AGING
1290 Broadway, Suite 700 Denver, CO 80203-5606

303-480-6700 *in metro Denver*
1-866-959-3017 *toll free outside metro Denver*
E-mail: *kroberts@drcog.org*
Web site: *www.DRCOG.NetworkofCare.org*

INFORMATION AND REFERRAL

Mile High United Way 211
City and County of Denver Governmental Services 311
AARP of Colorado...1-866-554-5376
Adams County/Senior Hub.. 303-426-4408
Arapahoe County/Aurora Senior Link..303-739-7960
Broomfield Senior Services (Community Center)........................... 303-464-5526
Clear Creek County/Project Support Senior Center............... 303-567-2382
Colorado Department of Human Services...General Information Line... 303-866-5700
....Aging and Adult Services....303-866-2800
Denver Commission on Aging... 720-913-8450
Douglas County/S.O.S... 303-660-7519
DRCOG Area Agency on Aging... 303-480-6700
.... Toll Free Outside Metro Denver 1-866-959-3017
....*www.DRCOG.NetworkofCare.org*
Gilpin County Senior Center... 303-582-5444
Jefferson County Aging and Adult Services............................... 303-271-1388
Jewish Family Service... 303-597-5000
Lutheran Family Services... 303-922-3433
Malley Senior Recreation Center... 303-762-2660
National Eldercare Locator.... 1-800-677-1116
Senior Reachout (Lakewood)... 303-987-4838
Seniors Inc. Help Program... 303-300-6900
Seniors' Resource Center (Metro Denver)................................ 303-238-8151
Senior Resource Center-Mountain Services (Evergreen).................. 303-674-2843
Volunteers of America Over 60 Services.................................... 303-297-0408

ADULT DAY PROGRAMS

Adult Care Supreme.. 303-922-6512
King Adult Day Enrichment Program 303-433-6887
ART Incorporated 720-323-2286
Centura Adult Day Program 303-964-2000
Chas. and Frances Johnson Adult Day Program 303-789-1519

1

Daybreak Adult Care Services 303-307-8855
Christian Living Communities 720-974-3555
Easter Seals Stroke Adult Day 303-233-1666
Elder Place 720-424-9288
Lana Adult Day Care 720-309-3953
Monaco Adult Day Care 303-333-2299
Morning Star Senior Day Program 303-326-8320
Parker Adult Day Care 303-873-1700
Prima Adult Day Services 720-524-9206
Prima 2 Adult Day Services 720-524-9206
Rocky Mountain Adult Day Care 303-691-2373
Royal Adult Day Center 303-307-4483
Sarah Care Adult Day Care Centers 303-221-7272
Senior Hub Adult Day Program 303-287-2400
Senior's Choice Adult Day Programs 303-344-0046
Seniors' Resource Center/Adult Day 303-238-8151
Skycliff Adult Day Program at Castle Rock 303-814-2863
Sunrise Adult Day Center 720-581-0388
Vermel's Adult Day Center 303-632-6449

CONSUMER AFFAIRS/LEGAL ASSISTANCE

AARP ElderWatch 1-800-222-4444
Colorado Civil Rights Division 303-894-2997
Colorado Consumer Line (Fraud, Complaints, etc) 1-800-222-4444
Colorado Legal Services Corporation
   Senior Citizens' Law Center .... (V/TDD) 303-837-1313
   Do –it-Yourself Legal Information Online .... *www.ColoradoLegal/Services.org*
Consumer Credit Counseling Service 1-866-889-9347
Economic Crime (D.A.'s office for Denver) 720-913-9179
Guardianship Alliance of Colorado 303-228-5382
Landlord/Tenant Disputes-Community Housing Services 303-831-1935
   Adams County 303-227-2075
   Jeffco Action Center 303-237-0230
Legal Center 303-722-0300
Metropolitan Lawyer Referral Service (normal cost) 303-831-8000

ELDER ABUSE

AARP ElderWatch 1-800-222-4444
Adult Protection .... Call the County Department of Human Services
Colorado Coalition for Elder Rights and Adult Protection 1-800-773-1366
DRCOG Long-Term Care Ombudsman
   (Nursing Homes/Assisted Living Facilities) 303-455-1000
Denver Center for Crime Victims Hotline .... 303-894-8000 or (V/TTY) 303-860-9555
Denver Center for Crime Victims Hotline in Spanish 303-718-8289
Victims Assistance Services for Older Adults
   (Jefferson/Gilpin Counties) 303-238-8151

2

EMPLOYMENT PROGRAMS

AARP Senior Community Service Employment Program (55+) 720-946-2901
Colorado Workforce Centers:
  Adams County Workforce Center (Main Office) 303-452-2304
  Arapahoe/Douglas County Workforce Center (Main Office) 303-636-1160
  Broomfield Workforce Center 303-464-5855
  Clear Creek County Workforce Center 303-567-3135
  Denver Workforce Development... 720-865-5619
  Douglas/Arapahoe Counties Workforce Center (Main Office) 303-734-5200
  Gilpin County Workforce Center .... 303-378-9342 or 303-567-3135
  Jefferson County Workforce Center 303-271-4742
Senior Community Service Employment Program:
  Seniors' Resource Center/Job Training Services 303-235-6982
Servicios de la Raza.. 303-458-5851

FINANCIAL/EMERGENCY ASSISTANCE

BenefitsCheckUp... *www.BenefitsCheckUp.org*
BenefitsCheckUp...or 1-866-550-2752 or 303-629-4996
St. Anthony Hospital serves older persons in the eight-county DRCOG Region:
  (Assist with Medicare Part D Prescription Drug Plan) .... 1-866-550-2752 or 303-629-4937
Catholic Charities Family Center 303-742-0828
Colorado Gerontological Society 303-333-3482
Colorado "Quest Card" Customer Services 1-888-328-2656
Colorado "Quest Card" Customer Services .... (TTY) 1-800-659-2656
County Departments of Human Services:
  Adams County Dept. of Human Services 303-287-8831
  Arapahoe County Human Services 303-636-1130
  Broomfield County Depart of Human Services 720-887-2200
  Clear Creek County Dept of Human Services 303-679-2365
  Denver County Dept of Human Services.. 720-944-3666
  Douglas County Dept of Human Services 303-688-4825
  Gilpin County Dept of Human Services 303-582-5444
  Jefferson County Division of Human Services..................................... 303-271-1388
Denver Indian Center 303-936-2688
Denver Urban Ministries 303-991-3977
Inter-Faith Community Services 303-789-0501
LEAP (Heating bill assistance)....Call the County Dept of Human Services
Salvation Army 303-295-3366
  Red Shield Center 303-295-2107
Colorado Gerontological Society 303-333-3482
Senior Assistance Center.. 303-455-9642
Senior Hub (Adams County).. 303-426-4408
Seniors Inc. (Money Management Program)... 303-300-6933
Seniors' Resource Center/Case Manager Program 303-238-8151
  Evergreen Program 303-674-2843
Servicios de la Raza.. 303-458-5851
Social Security and SSI Information 1-800-772-1213
Social Security Fraud Hotline 1-800-269-0271

Veterans' Affairs 303-343-1268
700 Club Operation Blessing 303-431-8295

HEALTH
Dental Services
Arapahoe County Senior Dental Program........................303-341-9370/303-761-1340
Colorado DHCA .... (Denver/Westminster/Arvada) 303-430-7399
Colorado Gerontological Society (Old Age Pension Dental Program) 303-333-3482
Community College of Denver (Dental Hygiene) 303-365-8338
Dentistry for the Handicapped.. 303-534-5360
Denver Health Medical Center Dental Program 303-602-8200
Donated Dental Services 303-534-5360
Salud Clinic (Commerce City) 303-286-8900
University of Colorado School of Dentistry.. 303-724-6900

Health Clinics
Adams County:
   Salud Clinic (Commerce City) 303-286-8900
   Visiting Nurse Association (Call for locations).................................. 303-744-6363
Arapahoe County:
   Littleton Clinic... 303-738-1124
   Visiting Nurse Association (Call for locations).................................. 303-744-6363
Clear Creek County:
   Chicago Creek Clinic 303-567-9201
   Clear Creek Nursing Service....................................303-567-3145 or 303-567-3147
   Meadows Family Medical Center 303-674-3117
   Mountain Family Health Center... 303-582-5276
Denver, City and County of:
   Denver Health Medical Center (Senior Plus services) 303-602-8154
   Women's Mobile Health – Mammogram, paps, breast exams 720-956-2035
Douglas County:
   Visiting Nurse Association (Call for locations 303-744-6363
Gilpin County:
   Mountain Family Health Center... 303-582-5276
Jefferson County:
   Centura Health – Senior Health Center 303-825-1234
   Family Practice Clinic (St. Joseph Hospital).................................... 303-318-2000
   P/SL Senior Citizens Health Clinic.. 303-869-2269
   University of Colorado Health Sciences Center (Medical Indigent)....... 303-372-8333

Hearing
Center for Hearing, Speech and Language 303-322-1871
International Hearing Society.. 1-800-521-5247
National Hearing Aid Bank (Hear Now) 1-800-648-4327
Audio Information Network of Colorado. 303-786-7777
Relay Colorado (Communication relay) 1-800-659-3656
Sign Language Associates (SLA) 303-321-6772
Sign Language Associates (SLA) .... V/TTY 303-321-6720

4

Hospice

Agape Hospice Services 720-482-1988
Beth Nehamah Hospice 303-766-7600
Colorado Community Hospice.................................. 303-546-7921
Denver Hospice Care Center, The.. 303-766-0050
Denver Hospice, The. 303-321-2828
Evercare Hospice.. 303-714-2400
Exempla Lutheran Hospice at Collier Hospice Center 303-425-8000
Hospice of St. John.. 303-232-7900
Hospice of Peace.. 303-561-5000
HospiceCare of Boulder and Broomfield Counties............................... 303-449-7740
Legacy Hospice 303-660-6107
Mt. Evans Hospice (Evergreen) 303-674-6400
Namaste Care Group, Inc. 303-860-9918
Odyssey Healthcare of Denver 303-561-1955
Porter Hospice 303-561-5100
Community Reach Center (Adams County).......................... 303-859-350
Trinity Hospice of Colorado... 303-799-5096
Visiting Nurse Association Hospice-at-Home...................................... 303-744-6363
VistaCare 303-639-9243

Medical Equipment

ATG Rehab... 303-781-1474
Assistance League of Denver 303-322-1688
Loan Closet (Broomfield resident)... 303-464-5526
Miracle on Wheels (Power wheelchairs) 1-800-749-8778
Senior Assistance Center 303-455-9642
Senior Solutions (Senior Hub/Adams County) 303-426-4408

Medication Management

RxAssist (St. Anthony Hospital Senior Program)......1-866-550-2752 or 303-629-4937

Mental Health

Arapahoe/Douglas County Mental Health.. 303-779-9676
Asian/Pacific Center.. 303-393-0304
Aurora Mental Health Center 303-617-2300
Boulder County Mental Health (Broomfield County) 303-466-3007
Community Reach Center (Adams County)... 303-859-3500
Haven Behavioral Senior Care of North Denver 303-288-7800
Lutheran Family Services... 303-922-3433
Mental Health Center of Denver (MHCD)... 303-504-6500
Jefferson County Center for Mental Health:
    (Jefferson, Clear Creek and Gilpin counties) 303-425-0300
Mental Health America of Colorado .... 1-800-456-3249 or 720-208-2220
Servicios de la Raza 303-458-5851
Suicide Prevention Hotline (24-Hour)... 1-800-SUICIDE

5

Prescription Assistance
AARP Pharmacy Service 1-800-456-2277
Aurora Inter-Church Task Force (Aurora residents) 303-360-0260
BenefitsCheckUp .. .. *www.BenefitsCheckUp.org*
Diabetics Care (Diabetic testing supplies) 1-800-500-6995
Metro CareRing.. 303-860-7200
RxAssist (St. Anthony Hospital Senior Program)....... 1-866-550-2752 or 303-629-4937
Senior Respiratory Solutions (Asthmatic) 1-800-398-9804
Seniors Inc.. 303-300-6900

Resource Organizations
ALS-Association Rocky Mountain Chapter (Lou Gehrig's Disease)............ 303-832-2322
Alzheimer's Association 303-813-1669
.... Alzheimer's HelpLine 1-800-272-3900
American Cancer Society 303-758-2030
American Diabetes Association 720-855-1102
American Heart Association/American Stroke Association 303-369-5433
American Lung Association 303-388-4327
Arthritis Foundation.. 303-756-8622
Brain Injury Association of Colorado.. 303-355-9969
Colorado AIDS Project... 303-837-0166
National Multiple Sclerosis Society-Colorado Chapter............................. 303-831-0700
Parkinson Association of the Rockies 303-861-1810
Rocky Mountain Stroke Association.. 303-730-8800

Vision
American Council of the Blind of Colorado.................1-888-775-2221 or 303-831-0117
Center for People with Disabilities 303-790-1390
Colorado Center for the Blind... 303-778-1130
Colorado Optometric Center 303-295-2402
Colorado Talking Book Library.. 303-727-9277
Division of Vocational Rehabilitation 303-866-2500
Eye Care America Senior's Eye Care Program 1-800-222-3937
Health S.E.T... 303-595-6633
Audio Information Network of Colorado........... 303-786-7777
Colorado Gerontological Society.. 303-333-3482
University of Colorado Eye Clinic... 720-848-2020

HEALTH INSURANCE
Centura Health Insurance Counseling for Seniors .... 1-800-544-9181 or 303-629-4940
Colorado Division of Insurance
Senior Health Insurance Assistance Program (SHIP)...Denver 1-888-696-7213
.... En Espanol......1-866-665-9668
Medicare Assistance (Claims, Entitlement, Appeals).......................... 1-800-633-4227
Medicare Fraud and Abuse Prevention Program 1-800-503-5190
HMO and Manage Care Appeals... 1-888-696-7213
Medicaid Eligibility.. Call County Department of Human Services

6

HOME MAINTENANCE

Aspen Design Renovation...303-345-7683
Broomfield Senior Services Volunteer Handyman Program........ 303-464-5526
Brothers Redevelopment (Home weatherization/improvement)................303-202-6340
Denver Urban Renewal Authority..303-534-3872
Sawicki Engineering (Home Improvement)...303-842-5109
Rebuilding Together (Adams and Arapahoe County)...........................303-217-2070
Senior Hub, Inc. (Adams County) 303-426-4408
Seniors' Resource Center..303-238-8151
Sun Power, Inc...303-382-1514
Volunteers of America - Safety of Seniors/Handyman Program..............303-297-0408

HOUSING

Colorado Division of Housing...303-866-2033
Community Housing Services..303-831-4046
HUD Locator...303-672-5343
Long-Term Care Facilities (DRCOG LTC Ombudsman Program) 303-455-1000
Section 8 Housing..(Contact Local Housing Authority)
Senior Housing Options 303-595-4464

Emergency Housing

Colorado Coalition for the Homeless 303-293-2217
Senior Support Services 303-832-1622
Mile High United Way - Shelter Hotline..303-561-2222

Housing Authority

Adams County Housing Authority 303-227-2075
Arvada Housing Authority 720-898-7494
Aurora Housing Authority...720-251-2100
Brighton Housing Authority 303-655-2160
Broomfield Housing Authority 303-438-6396
Colorado Housing and Finance Authority:
   (Low-Income Home/Renovation loans)..303-297-2432
Commerce City Housing Authority...303-289-3698
Denver Housing Authority 720-932-3000
Englewood/Sheridan Housing Authority...303-761-6200
Jefferson County Housing Authority..303-422-8600
Metro West Housing Solutions (Lakewood) 303-987-7580
Littleton Housing Authority 303-794-9608
Wheat Ridge Housing Authority 303-422-8600

IN-HOME AND RESPITE CARE

Call DRCOG for Information 303-480-6700
.... Toll Free Outside Metro Denver 1-866-959-3017

7

INCOME TAX PREPARATION
AARP (Call for site locations)..1-888-687-2277
Adams County Income Tax Assistance 303-654-6163
Colorado Department of Revenue (State tax information) 303-238-7378
IRS (Federal tax information)..1-800-829-1040
Seniors' Resource Center/VITA (Volunteer Income Tax Assistance) 303-238-8151

LONG-TERM CARE OPTIONS
Adult Care Management (Broomfield, Clear Creek and Gilpin Counties) ...303-439-7011
Long-Term Care Facilities/DRCOG Ombudsman Program 303-455-1000
Longterm Care Options:
   (Adams, Arapahoe, Douglas, Elbert and Denver Counties)....................720-974-0032
Options for Long-Term Care (Jefferson County)..303-271-4216

NUTRITION/MEALS
Broomfield County Home-Delivered Meals 303-464-5532
Food Bank of the Rockies...303-371-9250
Food Stamp information...........................Call County Department of Human Services
Hunger Free Hotline...720-382-2920
Littleton Cares, Inc (Meals on Wheels). 303-798-7642
Seniors' Resource Center/Evergreen 303-674-2843
VOA Dining Centers/Home-Delivered Meals 303-294-0111

ORGANIZATIONS FOR SPECIAL POPULATIONS
Asian Pacific Development Center..303-393-0304
Denver Indian Center...303-936-2688
Gay, Lesbian, Bisexual Community Center of Colorado 303-733-7743
Jewish Family Service 303-597-5000
Foreign Language Interpreter:
   Colorado Department of Health Care Policy & Financing 303-866-4008
   Denver Commission for People with Disabilities 720-913-8480
Senior Support Services (Homeless older adults).....................303-832-1622
Servicios de la Raza 303-458-5851
Southwest Improvement Council – SWIC (American Indian).....................303-934-2181
The Translation and Interpreting Center for Crime Victims 303-996-0976
Vietnamese Elderly Association of Colorado 303-922-3033

PERSONAL EMERGENCY
Gold Eagle Systems 303-770-2227
Health Watch 1-800-226-8100
Lifeline 1-800-LIFELINE
Pioneer Medical Systems 1-800-798-0626
Personal Alert 303-660-4853
ResponseLINK..303-805-5979

8

PET CARE
Denver Dumb Friends League (Emergency pet care/Adoptions)....(Ext. 0) 303-696-4941
Harrison Memorial Animal Hospital (Fixed-Income Pet Medical Service) ... 303-722-5800
Purina Pets for People ....Call local humane society

SENIOR CENTERS
Adams County
Aurora Center for Active Adults..303-739-7950
Brighton Senior Center 303-655-2075
Commerce City Senior Center 303-289-3720
Northglenn Senior Citizens Center..303-450-8801
Salvation Army-West Adams 303-428-6430
Senior Hub...303-426-4408
Thornton Senior Center 303-255-7850
Tri-Valley Senior Citizens Association 303-822-5855
Westminster Community Senior Center...303-426-4310

Arapahoe County
Aurora Senior Center..303-739-7950
Buck Community Recreation Center..303-794-9216
Malley Senior Recreation Center 303-762-2660
Tri-Valley Senior Citizens Association 303-734-1223

Broomfield, City and County of
Broomfield Senior Center..303-464-5526

Clear Creek County
Project Support Senior Center 303-567-2382

Denver, City and County of
Athmar Recreation Center 303-937-4600
Barnum Senior Center 303-937-4655
Carl Park Recreation Center...303-477-9251
Westwood Community Center..303-922-7701
Zion Senior Center 303-333-5746

Douglas County
Castle Rock Senior Center..303-688-9498
Parker Senior Center...303-841-5370

Gilpin County
Gilpin County Council on Aging...303-582-5444

Jefferson County
Clements Community Center 303-987-4820
Evergreen Recreation Center..303-674-6441
Foothills Park and Recreation District...303-987-3602
Golden Community Center (Front Porch)...303-384-8130
North Jeffco Community Recreation Center 303-425-9583

9

Seniors' Resource Center/Mountain Services (Evergreen) 303-674-2843
Wheat Ridge Senior/Community Center.. 303-205-7500

SERVICES FOR PEOPLE WHO ARE DISABLED
Rocky Mountain Americans with Disabilities Act (RMADA) Center 1-800-949-4232
Atlantis/ADAPT.. 303-733-9324
Center for People with Disabilities 303-790-1390
Client Assistance Program (CAP) 303-722-0300
Colorado Cross Disabilities Coalition.. 303-839-1775
Denver Commission on the Disabled 720-913-8480
Easter Seals Day Program 303-233-1666
Legal Center for People with Disabilities 303-722-0300

TELEPHONE REASSURANCE
Quick Call 303-457-1294
ResponseLINK 303-805-5979
Tel-A-Sure (Seniors' Resource Center).. 303-238-8151

TRANSPORTATION
Adams County:
A-Lift/Seniors' Resource Center 303-235-6972
Special Transit (Brighton and Tri-Valley Area) 303-447-9636
Town of Bennett 303-644-3249

Arapahoe County:
First Ride... 720-540-5566
Littleton City Government – Omnibus/Shopping Cart.......................... 303-795-3700
Special Transit (Tri Valley Area).. 303-447-9636

City and County of Broomfield:
Broomfield Senior Center Easy Ride (Broomfield only)....................... 303-464-5534

City and County of Denver:
First Ride 720-540-5566

Clear Creek County:
Volunteers of America – Senior Transportation Program 303-567-2382

Douglas County:
Douglas County Department of Human Services 303-688-4825

Gilpin County:
Volunteers of America:
(Gilpin County Senior Transportation Program................................. 303-582-5444

10

Jefferson County:
Lakewood City Government/Lakewood Rides 303-987-4826
Seniors' Resource Center 303-235-6972
Seniors' Resource Center/Evergreen 303-674-2843

Metro Area:
American Red Cross 303-235-6972
LogistiCare (Medicaid eligible only)..1-800-390-3182
Regional Transportation District 303-299-2960
  Access-a-Cab 303-244-1388
  Access-a-Ride 303-292-6560
  Senior Ride...303-299-6503
  Telephone Information Center...303-299-6000

11

Chapter 31

Aging in Place: Maintaining Your Independence at Home

Michele M. Lawonn, J.D., P.T.
Medical-Legal Advocates, L.L.C.

SYNOPSIS

"Aging in place" is a rapidly expanding movement with emphasis on creating a safe and workable alternative to the traditional model of out-of-the-home living and care for aging adults. This model utilizes all available financial resources of the aging adult and all available community resources to create a safe environment for the individual to maintain his or her independence in the least restrictive environment possible. The number one choice of aging adults is to "stay put" and to continue living in their own home.

This chapter discusses the "aging in place" model, universal design of homes, and suggestions to assist Denver metro area aging adults to maintain living independently in their homes. Aging adults in other communities can use this model to explore resources available in their communities.

31-1. Demographics

The State of Colorado anticipates a 20 percent increase in its total population, growing from 4.7 million to over 5.6 million in the decade of 2005 to 2015, according to the most recent Colorado Governor's White House Conference on Aging Report ("Governor's Report"). However, during this same decade, the aging adult population, comprised of people 60+ years of age, will increase 49 percent, from 651,000 to 970,000.

The Denver metro area presently has 46.7 percent of the state's senior population and will experience higher growth in this age group than the entire rest of the state. Overall, the Denver region has a lower concentration of older adults than the nation as a whole, at 12 percent versus 16 percent. More than one in four peole in Denver will be 60 years of age or older by 2035.

Additionally, Colorado ranks fifth in the U.S. in the number of baby boomers (those born between 1946 and 1964) as a percentage of the state's total population. Colorado ranks fourth in the U.S. out of states with the fastest growing senior populations. In 2011, the first baby boomers turned 65, qualifying them for Medicare and full-benefit Social Security Retirement Income. The Governor's Report states that Colorado will not realize the full impact of its aging baby boomers for another 15 or 20 years. Currently, 66 percent of Colorado's total senior population is between the ages of 60 and 74. Additionally, there are over 500 centenarians alive in Colorado.

Eight counties comprise the Denver Regional Council of Governments (DRCOG) Denver region: Adams, Arapahoe, Broomfield, Clear Creek, Denver, Douglas, Gilpin, and Jefferson. Adults aged 60 to 74 comprise 66 percent of the DRCOG Denver region's population. In 2000, there were 261,286 adults 60+ years old in this region. By 2010, this age group had a 48 percent increase in population, to 386,373. The 60+ age group is projected to increase 4 percent per year from 2004 to 2020 and double in number to 575,175 by 2020 due to the aging of the baby boomer population.

The DRCOG Denver region statistics include the fact that older women are three times more likely to live alone than older men. Fifty percent of the older adults living alone are ages 75 and older. Also, 77.4 percent of all groups of older adults live in owner-occupied units, with 80 percent of the 60- to 74-year age group, 74.4 percent of the 75- to 84-year age group, and 56.5 percent of the 85+ age group living in their own independent living environments.

As the demographics change, so, too, will the demands of our aging population to challenge the paradigm and the demand for home-based care and aging in place, rather than receiving care and living outside an aging adult's home, such as in an assisted living facility or nursing home.

31-2. Aging in Place

"Aging in place" is defined by the National Aging in Place Council as the ability to continue to live in the familiar environment of one's home in a safe, independent, and comfortable manner, regardless of age, income, or ability level. To accomplish this goal, at a minimum, an aging adult's home must have easy access in and out of the primary entrance; be free of clutter; and have safe, non-slip flooring surfaces, wide hallways, good lighting, easy access to bathroom and sleeping areas, and stable furniture. The very best time and way to accomplish this goal is to do so before there is a crisis and a need for barrier-free and easily accessible living.

Aging adults are encouraged to obtain universal design in any new home and to implement these modifications in any existing home. A good aging in place design checklist for applicability for new home and remodel construction can be found at www.toolbase.org/ Home-Building-Topics/Universal-Design/aging-in-place-checklists. Also, many good checklists are found on the AARP website. See "Resources" in section 31-8.

31-3. Creating a Safe Environment

Clutter, Lighting, and Rugs

Pick it up and store it away, throw it away, or recycle it — but get rid of it now! Clutter, be it magazines, newspapers, paper, clothing, boxes, too much furniture, hobby paraphernalia, or just plain "stuff," presents a very unsafe home environment ripe for causing medical conditions or falls that may result in serious physical injuries or even death. You need to have adequate maneuverability in all your rooms to access them safely, without risk for fall.

Throw rugs of any size, any style, and in any room are of significant concern for causing falls and injuries. The best advice is to remove them all. Always keep your bath rug off the floor until needed during bathing. If you just cannot bring yourself to get rid of the rugs, at least take the very basic step of securing the edges with two-sided tape. Carpeting should be in good condition and preferably pile carpeting having a thickness of one-half inch or less. If your carpeting has elevated ridges in it, get it restretched so it lays flat.

I met an octogenarian friend for dinner and found the following safety concerns in her home that are just ripe to cause her to fall: shag carpeting on the step from the garage to the house, topped with a second unsecured shag scatter rug; loose throw rugs placed on top of the carpet inside the entry room; no hand railing for the stairs; and very dim lighting immediately inside the house.

As a friend of an aging family member or adult, it is your responsibility to express your concerns and assist the aging adult to rectify these safety issues. Take a very gentle approach in expressing any concerns. Perhaps the aging adult is not objective enough to see these concerns and will appreciate your assistance. Maybe he or she will need time to think about these concerns. Or perhaps he or she will be unwilling to address any of these safety concerns, because "my house has been this way for 40 years."

Faster than the blink of an eye, an aging adult can catch his or her toes, cane, walker, or crutches on something, lose his or her balance, fall, and sustain an injury of some magnitude. Falls often also occur because of inadequate lighting, such as when the aging adult gets up at night and does not turn on a light.

More often than not, injuries such as head injuries and hip, arm, or back fractures are very serious. If the aging adult is you, this sort of fall accident and subsequent injuries may, unfortunately, cause you never to be able to return to living in your home. Do not take this chance: the odds are against you. Maintaining your safety and health is important. All of the rooms in your home must have good lighting and safe, non-slip flooring, and be uncluttered with furniture and "stuff."

Stairs

How can you get into and out of your home? Where would you live if you could not get into your home because of stairs and structural barriers, or if you could get inside your home, but then could not access the bathroom or bedroom because of stairs? Universal design recommends that your exterior entrance be barrier free and that you get rid of any stairs, both outside and inside your home. This may mean exploring the option of modifying your home to make it accessible or moving to a different home. While your health is good and stable, explore all of your living options.

Due to economic conditions, now is not the best time to sell your home anywhere in America, including in the Denver metro area. However, anyone who is over 60 years old ought to live in a ranch-style, single-level home with a step-free access. This is especially important for someone who already has had a stroke or a brain injury, or who has medical conditions such as diabetes, heart or lung disease, or severe arthritis. In an instant, you can sustain an injury or exacerbate an existing medical condition, which prevents you from living in your multi-level home. What are your options if you are unable to sell your home and need a different home? Explore them before the need arises, so you can make a good decision without the additional stress of having the necessity to act.

When you either start to modify your home or look for a new one, first examine the entrance. Do you need a ramp? Is there adequate room for one? Can the surface be protected from adverse weather? The majority of folks go in through their attached garage entrance, as it usually affords the fewest number of stairs.

If you need to install a ramp, the recommended ramp incline is a 12:1 ratio. What this means is for every inch of height, the ramp must be 12 inches in length. This keeps the incline safe and manageable for anyone propelling a wheelchair, pushing someone in a wheelchair, or walking up the ramp using an assistive device such as a walker or cane. If there is inadequate room for a permanent ramp, explore whether there is adequate room for a portable ramp, which tend to be lightweight, durable, and can be purchased at many medical supply or specialty stores.

Steps into a home usually do not have hand railings, as most city building codes only require a railing if you have four or more steps. However, do some good pre-planning and have stair railings installed on all your stairs, whether they are inside or outside stairs, preferably on both sides. AARP's website has a link to "certified aging in place" (CAPS) professionals who are trained in common remodeling projects and other home modifications that can help people live independently in their own homes.

Once you are inside your home, assess your other stair issues. Do you have a multi-level home? Are your bathrooms only on different levels, and if so, how will you access them? Do you need to remodel your home to add a main floor bathroom or master bedroom suite? Are there any steps to other rooms or areas? If the need arose, are your stairways designed to accommodate a "stair glider" or could you have an elevator installed? Plan your future need for an elevator by having closets built stacked on top of each other; later, they can be used as the elevator shaft.

A stair glider is an adaptive apparatus that has a railing installed on the stairs or wall with a seat attached to it and is electrically powered up and down by the person sitting on it or walking on the stairs next to him or her. If your home has a continuous stairway, the approximate cost of a new stair glider with a 300-pound weight capacity installed is $3,000. However, the price for the stair glider increases with increased load capacity, with a maximum of 500 pounds for most manufacturers.

If you have a flight of stairs with a platform halfway, or have two sets of stairs such as in a tri-level or bi-level, you may need to purchase two or more separate stair gliders to accomplish transit up or down these stairs. This situation requires a potentially dangerous transfer between the stair glider seats of each section. The recommended stair width if you are building a new home is four feet, which allows adequate space on the stairs for both the stair glider lift and people walking on the stairs. There are numerous websites for stair gliders.

Hallways and Doors

The minimum recommended hallway width is 36 inches. However, a width of 42 inches or more is optimal. Entrance doorways should be 36 inches to allow for 32 inches of clear width for ingress and egress. Bathroom doorways often are too narrow, especially in older homes. Homes built prior to the 1970s tend to have a standard width of 24 inches for bathroom doors. Most bathroom doorways now tend to be at least 28 inches, which is still too narrow to allow someone to walk in easily using a regular-width walker or crutches or to propel a wheelchair.

You need to be able to access and enter your bathroom easily and safely. Examine all your bathroom doorways to determine if the width can be increased, preferably to at least 36 inches to allow for 32 inches of clear width for passage of most wheelchairs and walkers. If it does not have this clearance, then widen the door as much as possible. Explore your options for all your doors. These may include installing a pocket door, which is a sliding door that fits entirely inside the wall, rather than a hinged door, or changing regular door hinges to hinges that allow for door setback. This will allow for increased inside space to maneuver and yields a wider door clearance.

Bathroom

Here's where the costly fun really begins. It goes without saying how important this room is to everyone's health and well being. Yet, the majority of homes have excessively small and inadequately designed bathrooms with narrow doorways. Many homes have no bathroom on the main living floor or none with a tub or shower. You need at least one fully accessible bathroom on the main floor that, preferably, also has either a shower or tub-shower combination for bathing.

After you have assessed your doorways, next assess your toilet setup. Consider installing an ADA-recommended toilet with 17 or more inches of floor-to-bowl height. Such a toilet may be high enough for most people without the need to purchase an elevated toilet seat for it. Then assess the clearance for installing grab bars on the walls. Frequently, there is inadequate space alongside the toilet because it is located between a sink vanity and bathtub or because you are renting your home. Both situations prevent the installation of grab bars. An excellent option is to purchase a "toilet safety frame" that easily installs on and removes from the toilet. This adaptive equipment allows for grab bars on one or both sides of the toilet and can be purchased from most medical supply companies.

The bathroom on the main living area needs to have a shower or tub-shower combination for bathing. In a new or remodel construction, it is important to brace the walls around the tub, shower, and toilet to prepare for the future installation of grab bars that can support 250 to 300 pounds. All towel bars should be replaced with securely anchored grab bars. Frequently, an aging adult will lose her or his balance in the bathroom and grab the towel bar for support, which promptly pulls out of the wall, thus not preventing the fall. Existing tub-shower combinations or showers can easily be adapted for safe use by the installation of a handheld showerhead, grab bars, and a portable bath bench. Bathrooms need to have a nightlight, non-slip flooring, and lever-style door handles.

In addition to the traditional medical supply stores, many "big box" stores are rising to the demand of baby boomers to carry adaptive bathroom equipment. Much of this adaptive equipment also may be purchased from online vendors. There are numerous options for bathroom and adaptive equipment that meets the specific needs of the aging adult and has an aesthetically attractive design. However, the best way to explore all options for this equipment is to work with rehabilitation professionals such as physical and occupational therapists.

Bedroom

When you purchase a new or existing home, always get one that has a main-floor master bedroom suite (*i.e.*, bedroom and full bathroom). The bedroom must have adequate room for you to maneuver around the bed and other furniture, should contain no clutter (including electrical cords on the floor and throw rugs), and should have safe flooring surfaces and good lighting. Your bedside lamp should be close to the bed so you easily can turn it on without falling out of bed. Nightlights and touch lights next to the bed are recommended. Always have an easy-to-reach telephone by your bed.

Assess your bed height for ease of getting on and off the bed. A good height for most people is approximately 22 inches. Thicker pillow-top mattress sets can be great if your bed height is too low, or a curse if you are short. If your mattress is too tall, you may need to place it directly on the floor to shorten its height. Step stools are not recommended, as it is just too easy to fall while using them.

If the bed is too short, placing blocks under the legs easily raises it. Many stores carry these pre-made blocks, usually four to six inches high. A "bed cane," which is a grab bar attached to a piece of plywood that slides between the mattress and box spring, can assist an aging adult in getting into and out of bed. These devices are available at most medical supply stores or online.

Finally, assess your clothing storage. Can you easily reach the clothing and shoes in your closet and dresser drawers? Does your closet need to be redesigned with lower clothing rods for easier reach? Is the clothing you most frequently use placed in the most easily accessible drawers or storage areas? Do you need to get rid of your unused clothing clutter? If you have a short reach or have difficulty bending, consider purchasing adaptive equipment such as a reacher.

Kitchen

Kitchens need to be "user friendly" and reflect the adaptations for any limitations, such as bending and lifting, you might have. Frequently used items need to be stored in easily reached cabinets, drawers, and shelves. The microwave should be placed at a comfortable height and a safe, reachable distance from the table or countertop edge. Does your kitchen have adequate usable counterspace next to the refrigerator? Again, the clutter issue arises: Can you store countertop items that are not frequently used? Do you have a side-by-side refrigerator?

If you use an assistive device such as a walker, does it have a tray so you can transport items such as food and dishes? Does your kitchen have a usable, seated workspace for you at the kitchen table or countertops? Do you have safe chairs to use that do not have rolling casters? Did you remove all throw rugs? Do you have a safe, non-slip flooring surface? If you have lifting concerns or tire easily, do you have a cart to transport food and other items around your kitchen?

Laundry Room

Many homes have a washer and dryer located in the basement. Safe independent living requires that these be located near the bedrooms or on the main floor of your home. A good option is to purchase a stackable washer and dryer, which can be placed in an existing closet. Front-loading machines are preferred because they are easy to use for anyone with or without compromised mobility and they are energy efficient. Many aging adults admit to being unable to carry their laundry down the stairs. To accomplish this task, many throw their laundry down the stairs to the basement, walk down the steps, and then pick it up and carry it to the washer. This option is fraught with obvious peril and danger. Bottom line: do not do this!

The Safety of Seniors Handyman Program

Volunteers of America has a "Safety of Seniors Handyman Program," which provides life enhancement services for limited income senior homeowners aged 60 and older who reside in Adams, Arapahoe, Denver, Jefferson, and Larimer counties. The Denver metro program can be reached at (303) 297-0408 ((970) 473-9630 for Larimer county).

This program's goal is to help seniors live safely and independently in their own homes. Skilled volunteer handymen and women can perform minor home repairs and safety modifications, conduct home safety assessments, and provide fall and fire prevention education. The labor cost is free and the charge for materials is income dependent.

The handyman program focuses on reducing falls and preventing fires. It includes, but is not limited to, providing installation of bathroom grab bars, handheld showerheads, non-slip surfaces in the tub or shower, stairway hand rails, carbon monoxide and smoke detectors, and plug-in night lights. Minor electrical and plumbing repairs; replacement of furnace filters, thermostats, light bulbs, and batteries in smoke detectors; and conducting home safety assessments are also services provided.

31-4. Nutrition

Statistics show that 85 percent of aging adults have some nutritional concerns. The options for meals, if you do not live in a retirement or other community that provides meal service, are to buy your groceries and cook, to eat out, or to sign up for Meals on Wheels through Volunteers of America. Frequently, use of paid home care assistance for grocery shopping and/or meal preparation is an excellent choice for the aging adult.

Grocery Shopping

For most aging adults who are unable to shop themselves, the optimal manner to buy groceries is to have a friend, family member, or a paid caregiver shop for them. If this is not a viable option for you, the next best option is to order your groceries from a local grocery store. Six local grocery store organizations were surveyed for this chapter.

King Soopers

King Soopers has the only program for grocery ordering and delivery service in the Denver metro area. Delivery is also offered in Castle Rock, Monument, Colorado Springs, Parker, Steamboat Springs, Fort Collins, Greeley, Loveland, Longmont, Boulder, Louisville, and Pueblo. Groceries can be ordered either by telephone at (303) 778-5464 ((303) 778-KING) Monday through Friday (7:00 a.m. to 7:00 p.m.) or 24 hours a day on the Internet at www.kingsoopers.com by clicking on the "Home Shop" button.

The delivery charge is $10.95, with a required minimum order of $50, if you choose a regular two-hour delivery window. An additional $5.00 charge applies if you choose a priority delivery window. Delivery is provided seven days per week, and the person must choose a two-hour delivery window of 10:00 a.m. to 12:00 p.m., 12:00 p.m. to 2:00 p.m., 4:00 p.m. to 6:00 p.m., or 6:00 p.m. to 8:00 p.m. The call center is open Saturday and Sunday only for purposes of handling delivery issues. A limited number of King Soopers stores make these deliveries, so your delivery might come from a store not located in your neighborhood.

Safeway

Safeway does not offer grocery delivery in Colorado.

Albertsons

Grocery delivery seems to vary store by store, with some stores doing limited grocery delivery. Talk to the store manager to find out if the store in your area delivers.

Sunflower Farmers Market

Grocery delivery seems to vary store by store, with some stores doing limited grocery delivery. Talk to the store manager to find out if the store in your area delivers.

Vitamin Cottage Natural Grocers

These stores do not offer grocery delivery. However, various supplements and health care products can be ordered online at www.vitamincottage.com, with delivery through UPS.

Whole Foods

These stores do not offer grocery delivery or online ordering of products.

Meals on Wheels

The Volunteers of America Meals on Wheels Program has operated since 1973 and serves adults aged 60 years and older in Adams, Arapahoe, Clear Creek, Denver, Douglas, Gilpin, Jefferson, and Larimer counties. Eligibility requirements for the program are being homebound and at least 60 years of age. The participant's spouse or disabled household dependents can determine their eligibility for meals by calling the Meals on Wheels program at (303) 294-0111 ((970) 472-9630 or larimer@voacolorado.org for Larimer County).

Participants' meals are free of charge, with a current suggested contribution of $2.50 per meal. However, no aging adult is denied meal service due to an inability to contribute. Additionally, Meals on Wheels provides nutrition education and assistance to help homebound, aging adults access other available services.

This program also has "Dining Center Services" in the eight counties it serves and operates 28 dining centers that serve hot meals in the Denver metro area, three in mountain communities, and 12 in Larimer county. The suggested contribution per meal also is $2.50. Participants in this program must be 60 years of age or older, and may include an eligible participant's spouse and residents who live in the facility where a dining center is located.

Volunteers of America also offers the "Market Meal Program" for homebound seniors who do not require daily home delivered meals. The baskets are available for pickup monthly from the Michael J. Kern Meals on Wheels Kitchen at 2620 Larimer St. in Denver.

They include 10 frozen meals and may include non-perishable foods, fresh produce, low-fat dairy products, and whole grain breads.

31-5. Emergency Response Systems

Any aging adult who lives alone is strongly encouraged to have an emergency response system and an emergency evacuation plan in place. At a minimum, an aging adult, especially someone who is mobility challenged, always needs to carry either a cordless phone or a cell phone and have "911" programmed into the phone. Also needed are working smoke and carbon monoxide detectors, a kitchen fire extinguisher, and a plan for evacuating the home, should the need arise. Additionally, you must plan for the possibility of power and/or heat outage, including having battery powered lights or lanterns in each room and hallways.

A highly recommended option is to obtain a 24-hour, corporate emergency response system. These systems require the aging adult to wear either a waterproof wristband or necklace that contains an alert mechanism, which can be easily located and used in an emergency situation such as a fall.

These systems also require installation of a box that plugs into a telephone line. There are numerous companies who provide this and additional services such as medication reminders. The companies researched for this chapter had advertisements in the published copy of the South Metro Denver *Seniors Blue Book*. (*See* www.seniorsresource guide.com.) Listings vary between the published guide, which has a North and South Metro Denver directory, and those listed on the website.

All companies had an initial installation and activation fee of $50 to $120 and a monthly charge of $25 to $50. Most companies operate on a month-to-month basis and do not require a contract. Some had *Senior Blue Book* installation and activation discounts. AARP members get special pricing on these emergency response systems through ADT by calling (800) 209-7599.

The companies researched for this chapter, but *not* endorsed as to quality of service, equipment, and products, include:

Gold Eagle Systems
www.goldeaglesystems.com
(888) 670-2227
(303) 770-2227

Personal Alert Systems
www.personalalert.com
(800) 728-0263
(303) 799-0767

American Medical Alert Company
www.amac.com
(800) 286-2622

Philips Lifeline
www.lifelinesys.com
(800) 380-3111

Prior to choosing an emergency response company, check out the products, service, and company in the same manner as you choose any service provider: carefully and after being fully informed.

31-6. Home Care

Home health care benefits under Medicare Plans A and B, including eligibility requirements, extensively are discussed in Chapter 2, "Medicare," and Chapter 22, "Hospital Discharge Planning." Skilled services through a home health agency may, in many cases, be enough in-home care to facilitate the aging adult to improve, transition to a higher functional level, and regain his or her independence. However, if it is not, unskilled home care may be needed. An aging adult who has no unpaid source of care from family and friends may have to rely solely on paid home care. This can be obtained through many agencies and increases the cost of independent living.

The *Seniors Blue Book*, available at www.seniorsresourceguide.com, has an extensive list of both skilled home health care and unskilled home care providers. The listings vary between the published guides and those listed on the website. Just as there are numerous home care providers who can provide unskilled care such as companion care, respite care, light cleaning, cooking, transportation to medical appointments, bathing, dressing, assistance with toileting, and doing laundry, so, too, do the hourly rates and services provided vary.

Home care rates average around $25 per hour. Most companies charge the lowest rate for basic companion care while doing no other work, such as light cleaning. Hourly rates tend to be lower for a longer shift; an overnight, 24-hour shift can be $250 to $300. If the aging adult needs round-the-clock care from an in-home care provider, the monthly cost can easily run $7,500 to $10,000. In comparison, the average monthly cost of an assisted living facility is between $3,000 and $4,300 and a skilled nursing facility is $6,900.

Most companies require a three-hour minimum commitment and have various cancellation policies. Some require a refundable deposit similar to a retainer prior to starting services. The majority of home care companies provide workers who are their employees, with all the benefits that go with being an employee, such as workers' compensation and liability insurance. However, some companies act only as a referral service and send "independent contractors" to work with you.

A word of caution if you hire an independent contractor and that person is injured while working for you: *you may be financially responsible for any workers' compensation claims.* This means you will have to pay *all* of the injured person's medical bills, potentially his or her lost wages, and any other costs of the claim. Most liability coverage on a person's home will be inadequate to cover a workers' compensation claim, so be very careful in these hirings. It may be well worth the extra $4 to $5 per hour to hire someone who is fully bonded, insured, and employed by a company.

Finally, many home care companies will bill your long-term care insurance for you or accept Medicaid home and community-based services (HCBS) for your home care services. However, you are ultimately responsible for these costs if you pay privately and not through HCBS.

31-7. Funding Your Home Care Needs

The cost of maintaining independent living in your own home can become very expensive depending on your care requirements. The optimal time to explore your options is in advance of these needs. Long-term care insurance is the very best option for future funding of unskilled home care services. However, this insurance only can be purchased while you are healthy and eligible for this insurance. See Chapter 7, "Long-Term Care Insurance," for more on this option.

Another option for funding your home care is to explore a reverse mortgage on your home. See Chapter 20, "Reverse Mortgages," for more information. Talk to an elder law attorney prior to finalizing the reverse mortgage option, if you think you may ever need to apply for Medicaid to fund your unskilled home care and any future skilled nursing care. Medicaid will fund HCBS to help you stay living as independently as possible in your own home. See Chapter 4, "Medicaid," for more information. However, pulling cash out from your home may adversely affect your Medicaid eligibility. Veterans may be eligible for home care assistance and should explore this possibility. For further information, see Chapter 6, "Veterans' Benefits."

Also see the National Council on Aging publications, "Use Your Home to Stay at Home: A Planning Guide for Older Consumers" and "Use Your Home to Stay at Home: A Guide for Homeowners Who Need Help Now," which can be found at www.naipc.org by clicking the "Practical Advice" button, followed by the "Consumer Advice Booklets" button.

Finally, there might be some community resources, such as faith-based and charitable organizations, that can provide assistance.

31-8. Resources

National Aging in Place Council
1400 16th St. NW, Ste. 420
Washington, D.C. 20036
(202) 939-1770
www.ageinplace.org

This organization has great information. Go to the link on their website titled "Practical Advice," then "Consumer Advice Booklets," which connects you to the consumer booklets entitled "Use Your Home to Stay at Home: A Planning Guide for Older Consumers" and "Use Your Home to Stay at Home: A Guide to Homeowners Who Need Help Now." There are numerous other helpful articles on this website under the "Practical Advice" link.

AARP

    601 E St. NW
    Washington, D.C. 20049
    (888) 687-2277
    www.aarp.org

    Go to the AARP website and click on "Home & Garden," then "Housing," "Home Improvement," or "Livable Communities." You also can search "universal design" for housing information. This website has numerous excellent articles on universal design and aging in place, including checklists for bathrooms, bedrooms, kitchens, entrances, lighting, stairways, and hallways. Suggestions include:

    "Universal Design Can Help People Age in Their Homes"
    www.aarp.org/home-garden/livable-communities/info-04-2011/universal-design-helps-people-age-in-their-homes.html

    "What is Universal Design?"
    www.aarp.org/home-garden/home-improvement/info-09-2009/what_is_universal_design.html

    "7 Steps to Hiring a Contractor"
    www.aarp.org/home-garden/home-improvement/info-11-2008/7_steps_to_hiring_a_contractor.html

    Checklists for rooms and areas in the home, including bathroom, bedroom, kitchen, and hallways include:

    www.aarp.org/home-garden/livable-communities/info-07-2011/make-your-home-a-safe-home.html

    Booklets available from AARP under Housing and Mobility Publications:
    www.aarp.org/home-garden/livable-communities/info-05-2010/ho_order_form.html

    "The AARP Home Fit Guide"
    "Your Home and Community: Are They Ready for You?"
    "Taking Steps to Prevent Falling Head Over Heels"

Denver Regional Council of Governments (DRCOG)

    1290 Broadway, Ste. 700
    Denver, CO 80203
    (303) 455-1000
    www.drcog.org

The link to "Area Agency on Aging" has good information on aging in our community, especially in the "2011-2015 Area Plan on Aging" and "Network of Care." This website also has an excellent list of links to other websites of interest to aging adults.

Volunteers of America (VOA) Meals on Wheels Program
> 2660 Larimer St.
> Denver, CO 80205
> (303) 297-0408
> www.voacolorado.org/Services/We-Feed

The Safety of Seniors Handyman Program through VOA Colorado
> Denver metro: (303) 297-0408
> www.voacolorado.org/Services/We-Support/Handyman-Denver-Metro
>
> Larimer county: (970) 472-9630
> www.voacolorado.org/Volunteers-of-America-Northern-Colorado/
> Northern-Colorado-Services/Handyman-Program

Chapter 32

Lifelong Learning and the Aging Brain

Zane Robertson
Active Minds

SYNOPSIS

32-1. Introduction

The human brain is the largest muscle in the human body. At roughly three pounds, it is also easily the most impressive. The source of the Mona Lisa, the atomic bomb, and rap music, the workings of the human brain have both mystified and inspired us since the beginning of time. While its functioning is still a mystery on many levels, we have learned more about how the human brain works in the past five to ten years than in any other period of history. Advances in brain imagery technology have allowed us to "peer inside" and observe neural circuitry in ways previously only imagined.

As our understanding of the brain has increased, many old beliefs have fallen by the wayside. A new model of the brain is emerging — one that embraces self-determination, flexibility, growth, and optimism. It is a whole new way of looking at how our brain works and what the future holds for us as we age. And it is filled with amazing hope.

32-2. Brain Basics

Let's begin with some basics regarding the brain. It might be helpful to define a few key terms:

▶ **Neurons** — These are your "brain cells." They function electrochemically to relay signals throughout your brain.

▶ **Synapse** — This is the gap between neurons. Synaptic firing represents one brain cell communicating with another one.

▶ **Brain regions** — These are the areas of the brain that we typically associate with certain types of cognitive functioning. Examples include the auditory cortex, the visual cortex, and the frontal lobe.

▶ **Hemispheres** — The brain is divided into left and right hemispheres, and different brain regions are located in different hemispheres.

32-3. The Old Paradigm

Prior to the 1990s, the conventional model of the brain can reasonably be summarized as follows:

▶ **The brain is fixed and finite.** You are born with a finite number of brain cells with fixed pathways and you cannot grow your brain at a cellular level.

▶ **Brain regions are dedicated to specific functions.** Certain parts of the brain have certain functions that can only be processed in that region. For example, visual signals must always be processed by only the visual cortex.

▶ **Once mature, the brain declines steadily.** Brain functioning peaks sometime in early adulthood, then begins a slow, inexorable decline.

This was the model of the brain that scientists firmly believed for decades, if not centuries. One implication of this paradigm was to focus research efforts on medical or surgical solutions for treating brain-related afflictions. Unfortunately, this focus neglected many potential avenues that have subsequently shown promise.

32-4. The New Paradigm

With the advent of technologies such as MRIs and CAT scans, scientists began to explore new realms of brain research and revise old theories about how the brain works. While still evolving, a new paradigm has emerged. Key components of the new understanding of the brain include:

▶ **The brain grows new neurons.** The old notion that growing new brain cells was impossible has been proven wrong. In a landmark study in 1998, scientists proved conclusively that the human brain grows new brain cells. Even 70-year-old (and older) brains produce new neurons and new neural pathways. Important factors in brain cell growth are exercise and mental stimulation.

▶ **Brain regions are flexible.** Studies have demonstrated that while regions do tend to specialize in dedicated ways, this is *not* absolute. The human brain is capable of rewiring and reallocating its "real estate" in ways that the old paradigm believed were impossible.

▶ **As the brain ages, functionality may decline, maintain, or even improve.** While it is true that processing speed generally slows with age, one-third of older brains in one study had functioning characteristics that closely resembled those of younger brains. Furthermore, certain types of functioning (integrated thinking, flexible problem solving) appear to improve with age.

▶ **We can have an impact on how our brain ages.** Perhaps the most profound conclusion in recent years is the notion that there are things we can do to maintain our brain and potentially protect it from certain types of cognitive decline.

32-5. The Older Brain

As our understanding of the brain has increased, it has been clear that the older brain has been underestimated on a number of dimensions.

Cognitive Processing

▶ **Bilateral (or multi-region) activation.** Older brains frequently use multiple parts of the brain to perform tasks that younger brains accomplish with a single region. This may be a way of compensating for lost processing speed, but it may also be a superior approach for certain types of tasks that require more integrated or flexible thinking.

▶ **Expert knowledge.** Knowledge that has been accumulated over 10 years or more appears to be far more resistant to the effects of aging than previously thought.

▶ **Managing information.** The ability to manage information and extract meaning generally increases with age.

▶ **Focus and attention.** The ability of the brain to focus on a task without getting distracted by other input increases with age.

▶ **Vocabulary.** Verbal abilities, including vocabulary and facility with synonyms and antonyms, increase with age.

Emotional Maturity

Studies have shown that, *on average*, older adults exhibit:

▶ **Less:** Impulsiveness, fear, impatience, anger, frustration, irritability, and hatred.

▶ **More:** Empathy, comfort with ambiguity, sense of peace, and ability to judge character.

Scientists are able to measure the frequency of these emotions in older adults by using brain imaging technology along with the knowledge of where in the brain certain types of emotions are located.

32-6. Neuroplasticity

One of the key shifts in our understanding of the brain has been the change from the old paradigm view that the brain is fixed and finite to the new paradigm understanding that we can rewire our brain in a wide variety of ways. The seminal study in this area was done by renowned neuroscientist Michael Merzenich in 1993 at the University of California at San Francisco. Dr. Merzenich designed an experiment in which a group of monkeys were exposed to two types of stimuli: (1) auditory (listening), and (2) somatosensory (touch). Half the monkeys were trained (through rewards) to pay attention to changes in the auditory signals, while the other half were trained to pay attention to changes in the somatosensory signals. After six weeks, the brain region dedicated to the stimuli that was being rewarded was two to three times larger than that same region for the monkeys that were not paying attention to that stimulus. This clearly established that *our very thoughts affect the physical structure of our brain.*

This ability of the brain to rewire itself is called *neuroplasticity* or *cortical remapping.* Scientists have discovered evidence of neuroplasticity in a wide variety of situations, including:

▶ Blind individuals have reallocated the visual brain regions to touch and hearing, resulting in the ability to read Braille (a feat beyond most sighted people) and make sense of complex auditory signals that most sighted people cannot.

▶ Deaf individuals have reallocated the auditory cortex to visual processing and are frequently reported to have superior peripheral vision than hearing individuals.

▶ Concert violinists have more space in their brains dedicated to controlling the fingers used to play the violin.

▶ Stroke victims have been successfully treated using a form of physical therapy that forces the brain to rebuild damaged circuitry.

▶ Psychiatric diseases such as depression and obsessive compulsive disorder have been successfully treated using techniques that encourage the brain to construct alternative synaptic pathways.

The implications of neuroplasticity are vast and are just beginning to be understood. Some developments to watch include:

▶ **Alternative brain inputs.** A new frontier is developing in which scientists may be able to artificially supply the brain with missing inputs. The best example of this is a device known as a cochlear implant. Cochlear implants allow deaf individuals to potentially "hear" by translating sound waves into electrical signals that the brain can learn to interpret in a way that substitutes for actual hearing.

▶ **Alternative brain outputs.** Similarly, computer chips have been successfully implanted in the brains of physically handicapped individuals which, through training (read: neuroplastic brain rewiring), can then be used to control external devices such as a computer, TV, or a robotic arm.

▶ **Emotional transformations.** The potential for us to rewire our brain in ways that positively affect our emotional well-being or overall happiness is an area of research that is just beginning, but seems to hold considerable promise.

Bottom Line: *The aging brain is not necessarily a fading brain.* As Dr. Merzenich stated, "Under optimal environmental conditions, almost every physical aspect of the brain can recover from age-related losses."

32-7. Lifelong Learning and Healthy Aging

Against this backdrop of new understanding of the human brain, the role of lifelong learning takes on new importance. Indeed, for a variety of reasons, most experts would agree that *lifelong learning is a key part of healthy aging.*

If one were to attempt to establish the four cornerstones of healthy aging, they would most likely be:

▶ Nutrition;

▶ Exercise;

▶ Social interaction; and

▶ Lifelong learning/purpose/meaning.

A number of recent studies have shown a positive correlation between pursuing mental stimulation and brain health. These show up in a number of areas, including:

▶ Global cognition;

▶ Working memory;

▶ Perceptual speed;

▶ Likelihood of Alzheimer's disease;

▶ Likelihood of dementia;

▶ Psychological/emotional health; and

▶ Physical health/mortality rates.

One study found a 33 percent lower likelihood of Alzheimer's disease among those who engaged in as little as one additional cognitive activity per week.

"Enriched environments" (more cognitive stimulation) are associated with a 5 to 9 percent increase in brain size and 25 percent more neuron branches. Many scientists believe that this represents a "cognitive reserve" that better prepares an aging brain for the potential challenges it may face as it grows older.

32-8. What Brain Exercise Is Best?

If your goal is to improve your brain health, the key element in selecting your form of brain exercise is *newness*. That which is new stretches your brain. Stretching your brain makes it stronger. The brain has a chemical called acetylcholine that is increased by exposure to new challenges. Acetylcholine increases our ability to pay attention, which results in the cognitive improvements we want to encourage.

Recommended activities include:

▶ Attending lectures and seminars;

▶ Doing crossword puzzles;

▶ Participating in discussion groups;

▶ Reading a book or the newspaper;

▶ Learning a foreign language;

▶ Playing a musical instrument;

▶ Learning to dance the tango; and

▶ Traveling.

Activities that have proven not to be particularly helpful for the brain include bowling, babysitting, golfing, and watching TV.

An important component to consider is the level of social interaction. While solitary activities are beneficial, social activities are even more so. Declining social interaction predicts declining cognitive function and higher mortality rates. A recent study found that chronic loneliness is associated with a twofold increase in the likelihood of developing dementia.

Recently, a whole host of software programs have hit the market designed to provide the equivalent of a gym workout for your brain. Feel free to give these a try. Many individuals have reported noticeable changes working with these programs. Unless, however, you find these programs to be highly entertaining (most are not), it probably makes sense to also seek activities that you really enjoy and can do with other people. Your best bet is to develop a variety of interests that stimulate your brain in different, enjoyable ways.

Bottom Line: Find activities that are new, challenging, and fun. You and your brain will thrive.

32-9. Resources

Below are a variety of resources for further information or programs to stimulate your brain.

Organizations

Active Minds

Courses, lectures, and seminars on a wide variety of topics.
(303) 320-7652
info@ActiveMinds.com
www.ActiveMinds.com

Alzheimer's Disease Education and Referral Center

Information and programs relating to Alzheimer's disease.
(800) 438-4380
www.nia.nih.gov/alzheimers

Colorado Academy for Lifelong Learning

Courses on a wide variety of topics.
(303) 770-0786
info@AcademyLL.org
www.academyLL.org

Osher Lifelong Learning Institute University of Denver

Courses on a wide variety of topics.
(303) 871-3090
www.universitycollege.du.edu/learning/viva/index.cfm

Internet Resources

The Healthy Brain Program: www.healthybrain.org
Society for Neuroscience: www.sfn.org

Books for Further Reading

Begley, Sharon. *Train Your Mind, Change Your Brain: How a New Science Reveals Our Extraordinary Potential to Transform Ourselves* (Ballantine Books, 2007).
Doidge, Norman, M.D. *The Brain That Changes Itself* (Penguin, 2007).

Chapter 33

Facebook: The Good, the Bad, and the Ugly

Michael Benidt
Sheryl Kay
Golden Compass, Inc.

SYNOPSIS

The world around us just won't slow down. Consider how quickly people in the U.S. have embraced online social networking:

> Two-thirds of adult internet users (65%) now say they use a social networking site like MySpace, Facebook or LinkedIn, up from 61% one year ago. That's more than double the percentage that reported social networking site usage in 2008 (29%).

Those statistics are from an August 2011 study done by Mary Madden and Kathryn Zickuhr of the PEW Internet and American Life Project. Dig a little deeper into their report and you'll find that 33 percent of adults over the age of 65 are using online social networking. One in three! But, as they say, "Wait, there's more!"

Just a few months earlier, the PEW Project reported in *Generations 2010*:

> While the youngest generations are still significantly more likely to use social network sites, the **fastest growth has come from internet users 74 and older**: social network site usage for this oldest cohort has quadrupled since 2008, from 4% to 16%.

If you're reading this and your mouth is hanging open in amazement, you're certainly not alone. On the other hand, if you're reading this and saying, "Well sure, my friends and I are all on Facebook. What's the big deal?" — Well, you're not alone, either.

33-1. Boosters and Detractors

When it comes to social networking sites like Facebook, Twitter, LinkedIn, and YouTube, people tend to fall into two groups — they either love them or they hate them. The boosters are everywhere, loudly promising social bliss and business success. The detractors are also out in force, warning you to never do anything online for fear of identity theft, computer viruses, and financial calamity.

We've noticed that very few people fall somewhere in the middle. Yes, there are good things about Facebook and other social networking sites. And, certainly, there are also some very bad things about Facebook and the others. Finally, and, unfortunately, there are even some truly ugly things going on.

So, with apologies to Clint Eastwood (who does have a Facebook page, by the way), we'd like to visit the good, the bad, and the ugly of the social network. In this case, we'll be writing mostly about Facebook, but Twitter, YouTube, and LinkedIn all suffer from the same split personalities.

If you've never stepped foot in any of these sites, read on. If you've just recently joined and are learning the ropes, read on. And, even if you're a veteran of the social media sites, read on. We'll bet you will all learn something.

33-2. The Good

Family and Friendly

The first thing most of us think about when we think about the good things in Facebook is family. Websites like Facebook allow us to connect, update, and chat easily with our family, both those who are across the room from us and those who are a continent away.

Grandparents are surely swelling the ranks of Facebook members because it's the perfect way to stay close to their grandchildren, nieces, nephews, and even their own children.

In fact, there are now so many older people on Facebook that a few in the younger generation are moving on, fleeing what they see as too many parental authority figures. "Oh no, my mom's on Facebook!"

Still, most are staying, and yes, your relatives are on Facebook. And so are your friends.

Facebook makes it easier and easier to find and be found by those long-lost friends and distant relatives. Almost everyone has a story about someone who used to be near and dear to them, and how they accidentally ran into them online and renewed an old friendship (or love affair!).

In fact, there's even a Facebook page for Page School in Minneapolis, Minnesota — where I went to elementary school many, many years ago. It was torn down in the late 1970s, but because of Facebook, I can now look forward to finding a few of my old grade school chums (and girlfriends!).

It's hard to argue with how good it feels to re-connect with old friends and lost relatives (except those you wish had remained lost!).

Better Social Citizens

One of the worries about computers and the internet has always been that computer addicts might squirrel themselves away in their basements and never come out into the real world. However, when it comes to social networking sites like Facebook, LinkedIn, and Twitter, studies are showing quite the opposite to be true.

Early this year, the Pew Internet & American Life Project released a report that suggests that those involved in online social networking are actually MORE involved in their communities, not LESS. The report, "The Social Side of the Internet," said:

> It becomes clear as people are asked about their activities that their use of the internet is having a wide-ranging impact on their engagement with civic, social, and religious groups.

But, wait, there's still more! Not only are those on Facebook and Twitter more likely to be involved in real-world groups and organizations, they also feel more of a sense of accomplishment in those same groups:

> Perhaps reflecting their higher levels of participation, internet users are also more likely than non-users to say that, in the past 12 months, they have felt really proud of a group they are active in because of something it accomplished or a positive difference it made (62% v. 47%) and that they have accomplished something as part of a group that they could not have accomplished themselves (48% v. 35%).

These are remarkable conclusions – again challenging our pre-conceived notions about just how these modern tools are affecting our lives. And, that's a good thing.

The Business of Business

We will certainly not be able to cover all the good things about Facebook in this article, but we can't leave without mentioning Facebook and social media's effect on businesses, both big and small.

Facebook makes it easier for those in business, whether they are carpet cleaners, musicians, or international oil companies, to connect to their customers, facilitate customer service, and keep their raving fans.

These tools also make it easier for the customer to jump on their Twitter or Facebook high-horse and tweak Comcast or Netflix in front of thousands of onlookers. Believe me, Comcast and Netflix do respond — and quickly!

Beyond business, Facebook also makes it easier for churches, sports leagues, fundraising groups, book clubs, neighborhood associations, and political parties to gain members, keep members, and communicate with those they already have.

And, certainly, recent world events have shown us just how powerful Facebook and Twitter can be on the international political scene.

33-3. The Bad

Too Good to Be True

If you've heard it once you've heard it a thousand times, "If it sounds too good to be true, it is."

Most of us let television ads like, "Look 20 Years Younger in Just Two Weeks" roll right off our backs. However, a similar pitch on Facebook, such as, "Make thousands of dollars from the comfort of your home!" often has a newer and more believable feel to it. Repeat after me, "If it sounds too good. . . ."

Let's take it one step further. What if a friend posts this to your wall on Facebook, "I just got a free iPad and you can too!" What should you do? Repeat after me. "If it sounds too good. . . ."

Good for you, you're catching on — and that's not bad.

Too Bad to Be Ignored

Tons of Facebook members (and Twitter and LinkedIn) have their computers hacked every week, and then send out malicious messages to you without their knowledge. In these cases, your friends are not the culprits. They've been hacked.

This happened just a few months ago to a musician friend of ours. He would never send us something nasty. Would he? The thing is, he didn't do it on purpose — he got it from Facebook.

By now, we're all pretty savvy when it comes to email spam. We know our bank is not really asking us to verify our account and we know that Susie Que doesn't really want to date us.

But, on Facebook, sometimes it's our trusted friends who send these messages. In my case, because my friend has a band, I just figured his link would connect me to one of his song videos, or maybe an upcoming concert. But I was wrong.

When I clicked the link, my computer went nuts and warned me that cyber bots from evil lands were trying to take it over.

Our friend, of course, was mortified. But, it's more than that. For him, trust is his band's most precious asset. Just think about the kind of person who follows his Facebook Fan Page:

> The thing of it is, Michael, many of my Facebook friends are important music business contacts, and that business is built on trust. Anything that damages it could endanger my livelihood.

While you might think this sort of thing is just a pain in the rear end, it's not. It's a real threat to you, your family, and your business.

And that, my friends, is very bad.

Paging Ms. Billboard

Earlier we mentioned that my grade school in Minneapolis has a Facebook page. While it's been fun to see other former students post pictures and share memories on the school's Facebook page, it hasn't been fun to see the spammers do their work on it.

One aggressive marketer boasted about her weight loss miracle. She scrawled it on the Group's wall, "How I Lost 5 Stone 4 Pounds In 15 Weeks?" (I guess she wasn't sure).

These kinds of nitwits usually have very few, if any, friends, and sometimes even have fictitious names like Melba Toast or Picken Berries. (Don't you love it?) The sad fact is that even though they pollute the entire Facebook experience, Facebook almost never kicks them out.

You can do a Google search that will show the literally millions of postings for "How I lost 5 Stone 4 Pounds in 15 Weeks?" by thousands of these dingbats, on Facebook alone. It is that pervasive.

Real businesses do not use school alumni pages to pitch their products. But, the explosive growth of these lowlife "billboarders" is making it more and more difficult every day for the good guys.

And, that's bad.

33-4. The Ugly

The Friend of My Friend Is Ugly

Now, we're not suggesting your friends are ugly. However, we do want to make you aware that some of your friend's friends are questionable, at best.

Perhaps you've done a good job of connecting on Facebook to only those you know, respect, and admire — and of course, your relatives, too. Believe me, though, not everyone is as careful as you are. In fact, for one reason or another, some folks on Facebook will become friends with just about anyone who asks them. They say, "why not?"

Yes, just like in real life, lots of people could care less who they are hooking up with. For instance, why would anyone become friends with Katz Pajamas? When you become friends with Katz, you also become friends of friends with anyone he's hooked up with. And, Katz, you see, is also friends with Sally Salacious and Yused Carguy.

When Katz wanted to connect to me, I wrote to a bunch of his friends and they had no idea who Katz Pajamas was. And, most of them didn't really much care. You see, they have thousands of "friends" and they just automatically approve anyone who asks.

That's certainly warm and fuzzy, but just not very smart.

Think about it. If Sally and Yused can easily become a friend of your friend (Katz, like many others, has little discretion), then so can the bad guys. And yes, Virginia, there are bad guys. And, some of them are very bad indeed, as you will see in the section below.

Yes, your friends are all wonderful folks, but what about their friends? Can they see the photos and private information that you post? Usually, unless you've been very careful — the answer is "yes."

Which is why you need to go to your Facebook privacy settings and un-check those boxes that say "Allow Friends of Friends." And, while you're at it, you might want to make sure your granddaughter does the same with her "Friends of Friends."

And, it's a good idea to become more wary of those folks who have jillions of "friends" on Facebook. What we found out is that folks like that just don't care. But you certainly want to.

Otherwise, it could get ugly.

It's No Mystery

Recently, Mike Melanson of ReadWriteWeb complained, "Facebook Friendship Pages are the ultimate tool for stalkers, nosey friends and jealous significant others." The word you want to pay attention to here is "stalkers."

Just ask best-selling mystery writer, Michael Connelly. He knows what the criminals and the stalkers are up to these days. In Mr. Connelly's mystery, *The Scarecrow*, the bad guy finds out about his young prey by visiting her social networking sites, even her LinkedIn page. He learns her dog's name, her favorite band, and the name of her favorite pizza hangout. He muses on the naïveté of his victims: "They believed they could bare their souls on the Internet, post photos and information at will, and not expect any consequences." We won't tell you what happens or what other dangers lurk in this masterful mystery. But we will tell you that: "He was circling her and she didn't even know it."

Are you and your family at risk when you post information to social networking sites? Well, have you ever posted about your upcoming vacation to France? Burglars would love to know about that.

Our guess is you'll head right to your privacy settings, no matter what social network you're using. You'll find that they make their privacy settings difficult to find, and even harder to navigate and understand. But, keep at it. It's worth it to protect you and your family.

Otherwise, it could get really ugly.

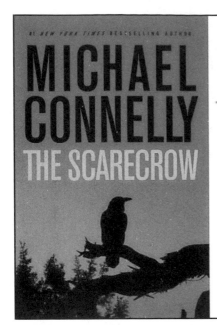

MySpace page a few years earlier but had not deleted it. He also found a professional profile on LinkedIn and that led to the motherlode—a blog page called www.CityofAngela.com in which she kept an ongoing diary of her life and work in Los Angeles.

The latest entry in the blog brimmed with Cook's excitement over being assigned to the police and crime beat, and being trained for the position by the veteran Jack McEvoy.

It was always amazing to Carver how trusting or naive young people were. They didn't believe that anybody could connect the dots. They believed that they could bare their souls on the Internet, post photos and information at will, and not expect any consequences. From her blog he was able to glean all the information he needed about Angela Cook. Her hometown, her college sorority, even her dog's name. He knew Death Cab for Cutie was her favorite band and pizza at a place called Mozza was her favorite food. In between the meaningless data, he learned her birthday and that she only had to walk two blocks from her apartment to get her favorite pizza at her favorite restaurant. He was circling her and she didn't even know it. But each time around he got closer.

33-5. So, What's a Facebooker to Do?

Clearly, this is not a step-by-step "how-to" article on social networking. Facebook, Twitter, and LinkedIn change their formats, rules, and settings so often that attempting that would be futile in this format for the *Senior Law Handbook*. But, we hope it does make you aware that Facebook and the other social sites are neither all good nor all bad.

We do, however, have 5 suggestions that you might consider right away:

1) **Don't believe it if it's too good to be true** — Increasingly, all social networks are being manipulated by individuals and companies (big and small) who want to sell you something. Some of these are legitimate, some are not. The number one warning has always been "If it sounds too good to be true, it is." Don't fall for it.

2) **Keep a small circle of connections** — Because it's easy to make scams sound reasonable, and because it's often your "friends" who carry these messages, be very careful who you connect with on these sites. Don't connect with people you don't know and trust. (Oxford's Robin Dunbar says that most of us can't handle the thousands of "friends" we could have on Facebook. He suggests that throughout history, computers or not, we all max out at somewhere around 150 friends and acquaintances).

3) **Protect your information** — Most people are still unaware that unless they are proactive their private and personal postings on Facebook (and elsewhere) can be seen by everyone.

4) **Don't give out your User Name and Password for your address book** — Every social networking site suggests (often) that you should just upload your Outlook, Gmail, or Yahoo contact list to them. In order to do this, you have to give them your User Name and Password. Don't do it!

5) **Have fun** — yes, we certainly caution you to be watchful. But when an old friend pops up out of the blue, when someone writes a nice note about your photo, or when you can impress your grandniece with your social media savvy — those are good moments. Enjoy them.

If you find social networking daunting, seek out someone you trust to help you. But, be careful. There are scads of people claiming to be social networking experts. Find out first if they're only a "booster" or only a "detractor." Either way, be careful. Test out their claims and their credentials. Usually, someone in your family or group of friends will know someone who will often know just as much (or more) than the so-called "experts."

33-6. Resources

We have quoted several times from reports and studies done by the PEW Internet and American Life Project — www.pewinternet.org. There's a reason for that. When it comes to Internet use, they are the gold standard. This non-profit and non-partisan center is one of seven branches of the Pew Research Center. They study the impact of the Internet on virtually every area of our family, community, business, and daily life. You can do keyword searches to easily find the studies we've quoted from.

The Wall Street Journal produced a series of exceptional investigative reports in 13 parts called "What They Know." This series covers many areas of safety and privacy on the Internet, and is a must-read if you want to be aware of privacy and safety on the Internet: http://online.wsj.com/public/page/what-they-know-digital-privacy.html.

You can read more about Oxford professor Robin Dunbar's theoretical limit to social relationships in Malcolm Gladwell, *The Tipping Point – How Little Things Make a Big Difference* 177-81, 185-86 (New York: Little, Brown and Company, 2000).

Mike Melanson, "Facebook Friendship Pages are Just Plain Creepy," *available at* www.readwriteweb.com. Do a keyword search for that article.

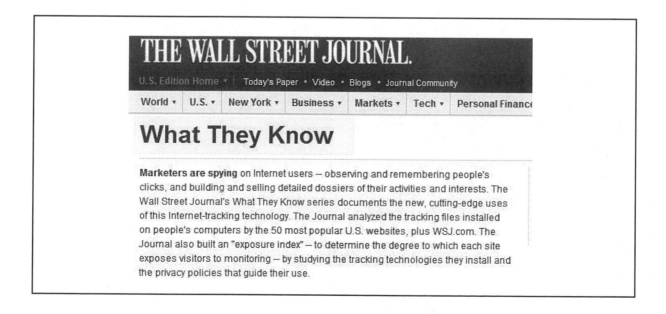

445

Appendices

Appendix A.
Glossary

Accreditation. A process undertaken by private organizations by which a hospice is determined to be following all the rules and regulations governing hospice care. (Compare with *Medicare Certification*.) *See* Chapter 27, "Hospice and Palliative Care: Options for Care at the End of Life."

Adult. A person over the age of 18 years. *See* Chapter 23, "Powers of Attorney;" and Chapter 24, "Medical Advance Directives."

Advance Directives. Written instructions that state, in advance, how you want to be medically treated if you cannot speak or decide for yourself. *See* Chapter 24, "Medical Advance Directives."

Affidavit. A statement sworn to, under oath, before a notary public or clerk of the court. It verifies that every fact stated is true and correct to the best of the affiant's (signer's) knowledge, information, and belief. *See* Chapter 14, "Grandparent Custody and Visitation Issues."

Agent/Attorney-in-Fact. The person whom you designate to act and make decisions for you under a power of attorney. *See* Chapter 23, "Powers of Attorney;" and Chapter 24, "Medical Advance Directives."

Alimony. Now called maintenance or spousal support. Financial support provided by one spouse to the other spouse after divorce or legal separation. *See* Chapter 13, "Family Relationships."

Allocation of Parental Responsibilities. Formerly "custody." It is the right of an adult to make decisions for a child, including the right to decide where the child lives, where he or she goes to school, and who the child's medical or mental health care providers will be. *See* Chapter 14, "Grandparent Custody and Visitation Issues."

Approved Charge. The amount Medicare approves as the value of services received. It is not always what the provider charges. *See* Chapter 2, "Medicare."

Asset. An item of real or personal property owned by an individual or by an entity, such as a trust. *See* Chapter 15, "Estate Planning: Wills, Trusts, and Your Property."

Assignment. A method of payment under Medicare Part B, in which the physician or supplier agrees not to charge the patient more than the Medicare-approved charge. The doctor sends the completed Medicare claim form to Medicare. Medicare then pays the doctor 80 percent of the approved charge after deductibles have been met. *See* Chapter 2, "Medicare."

At-Risk Adult. An individual 18 years or older who is susceptible to mistreatment or self-neglect because the individual is unable to perform or obtain services necessary for the individual's health, safety, or welfare, or lacks sufficient understanding or capacity to make or communicate responsible decisions concerning the individual's person or affairs. *See* Chapter 12, "Protecting Yourself From Crime."

Attending Physician. The doctor who at a given time is most responsible for your care. *See* Chapter 27, "Hospice and Palliative Care: Options for Care at the End of Life."

Attorney in Fact. The person who acts as an agent for another person, called the principal, who created a Power of Attorney. *See* Chapter 15, "Estate Planning: Wills, Trusts, and Your Property."

Bargain and Sale Deed. A type of deed that transfers whatever title or interest you may have at the time of the transfer or later acquire, but does not guarantee the title is good. *See* Chapter 15, "Estate Planning: Wills, Trusts, and Your Property."

Beneficiary. Anyone named to receive money or property, such as from a will, a trust, a life insurance policy, or a retirement account. *See* Chapter 15, "Estate Planning: Wills, Trusts, and Your Property."

Bereavement Care. A service provided as part of the hospice care program at no charge to family members for 13 months after the patient has died. This can involve grief support groups, occasional phone or mail contact, education classes, or individual counseling. *See* Chapter 27, "Hospice and Palliative Care: Options for Care at the End of Life."

Best Interests of the Child. The right of the child and the responsibility of the court to make sure that a child's physical and emotional needs come first when decisions are made that affect the child's life and future. *See* Chapter 14, "Grandparent Custody and Visitation Issues."

Capacity. The ability to make and communicate responsible decisions. *See* Chapter 23, "Powers of Attorney."

Capital Gains Tax. A tax on the amount that is the difference between the original price of property and the selling price (assuming you sold it for more than you paid). *See* Chapter 15, "Estate Planning: Wills, Trusts, and Your Property."

Charitable Bequest. A provision in a donor's will that designates a charity as a beneficiary. *See* Chapter 18, "Philanthropy and Planned Giving."

Charitable Gift Annuity. A gift of securities or cash transferred to the charity of the donor's choice in exchange for a contractual life income paid at least annually to the donor or donors. *See* Chapter 18, "Philanthropy and Planned Giving."

Charitable Lead Trust. A trust that pays income to a designated charity first, then returns the remaining assets to the donor or to other beneficiaries designated by the donor. *See* Chapter 18, "Philanthropy and Planned Giving."

Charitable Remainder Trust. An irrevocable planned gift in which a donor reserves the right to receive payment from the trust, or can provide for payment to other beneficiaries. When the trust is dissolved, the remaining principal is distributed to the charity or charities specified by the donor. *See* Chapter 18, "Philanthropy and Planned Giving."

Charitable Remainder Unitrust. A charitable trust that pays its beneficiaries a fixed percentage of the net fair market value of the principal, as revalued annually, with the remainder of the trust assets to be provided to one or more charities upon the death of the life income beneficiaries or after a set amount of time. *See* Chapter 18, "Philanthropy and Planned Giving."

Child Custody Case. Under the Colorado grandparent visitation statute, any case where a court has become involved in a child's life, including cases where parents are divorced or legally separated or where, if parents have never married, a court has made a decision concerning the allocation of parental responsibilities. *See* Chapter 14, "Grandparent Custody and Visitation Issues."

Chronic Illness. An illness that cannot be completely cured and persists over time, likely getting gradually worse, but is not considered "terminal" or "end stage." *See* Chapter 27, "Hospice and Palliative Care: Options for Care at the End of Life."

Clear and Convincing Evidence. Evidence that is unmistakable and free from serious doubt. *See* Chapter 14, "Grandparent Custody and Visitation Issues."

Coinsurance. The portion of the bill that the beneficiary is required to pay, even after the deductible is met. For example, Medicare pays 80 percent of the Medicare-approved rate for a doctor's visit and the beneficiary is responsible for the other 20 percent coinsurance. *See* Chapter 2, "Medicare," and Chapter 3, "Health Insurance Beyond Medicare."

Colorado Property Tax/Rent/Heat Rebate Program. A Colorado state income tax program that gives income tax money back to low-income senior citizens and persons with disabilities. *See* Chapter 5, "Government Programs and Financial Assistance."

Comfort Care. Care focused on comfort and relief of suffering rather than cure. It is often used to mean hospice care or palliative care but may indicate pain relief only, without emotional, practical, and spiritual support. *See* Chapter 27, "Hospice and Palliative Care: Options for Care at the End of Life."

Conservation Easement. A voluntary, legally binding agreement that limits certain uses and/or prevents development from taking place on a property now and in the future. *See* Chapter 16, "Estate and Succession Planning for Farmers and Ranchers."

Conservator. A person at least twenty-one years of age, resident or non-resident, who is appointed by a court to manage the estate of a protected person. The term includes a limited conservator. *See* Chapter 12, "Protecting Yourself From Crime;" Chapter 23, "Powers of Attorney;" and Chapter 15, "Estate Planning: Wills, Trusts, and Your Property."

Conservatorship. A legal proceeding giving a person, the conservator, power to manage the property and finances of a minor or protected person. *See* Chapter 15, "Estate Planning: Wills, Trusts, and Your Property."

Consideration. What was given or paid in return for property. *See* Chapter 15, "Estate Planning: Wills, Trusts, and Your Property."

Constructive Delivery. Delivery in which the person receiving a gift is given the means of receiving a gift; for example, the person receives the keys to a safety deposit box or to a car. *See* Chapter 15, "Estate Planning: Wills, Trusts, and Your Property."

Convenience Account. An account that allows another person to sign on your account. This does not allow another person any right to the funds in the account. *See* Chapter 15, "Estate Planning: Wills, Trusts, and Your Property."

Corporation. A business organization chartered by a state and given many legal rights as an entity separate from its owners. *See* Chapter 16, "Estate and Succession Planning for Farmers and Ranchers."

Countable Resources. In order to be eligible for most public benefit programs, including Supplemental Security Income (SSI), an applicant's assets must be below a certain level. Only certain kinds of resources are included in determining eligibility. Assets that are taken into account are called countable resources. *See* Chapter 1, "Social Security Benefits;" and Chapter 5, "Government Programs and Financial Assistance."

CPR Directives/DNR Orders. Orders signed by a doctor directing that in the event that your breathing or heart stops, you should not be resuscitated by medical professionals. *See* Chapter 24, "Medical Advance Directives."

Culture Change. Culture change is about creating a home inside a nursing home that gives a resident-centered approach to providing care. Assisted living residences and nursing homes that are part of the culture change movement have abandoned an institutional approach to providing health care and have adopted a philosophy that treats the resident with dignity, respects their right to make decisions about their care, and provides individualized care. *See* Chapter 21, "Assisted Living and Nursing Home Issues."

Curative Care. Medical care that is focused on curing disease. *See* Chapter 27, "Hospice and Palliative Care: Options for Care at the End of Life."

Declaration as to Medical or Surgical Treatment. The legal name in Colorado for an advance directive, concerning your preferences regarding allowing, withdrawing, or withholding life-sustaining treatment and nutrition and hydration in the event you are declared to be terminally ill or in a persistent vegetative state. Also commonly known as a living will. *See* Chapter 24, "Medical Advance Directives."

Decree of Dissolution of Marriage. A court order dissolving a marriage; a divorce decree. *See* Chapter 14, "Grandparent Custody and Visitation Issues."

Decree of Invalidity. A court order declaring a marriage annulled, as though it never happened. *See* Chapter 14, "Grandparent Custody and Visitation Issues."

Deductible. Amount of the medical bill you must pay before Medicare begins coverage. *See* Chapter 2, "Medicare."

Deed. A document used to transfer your interest in real property. *See* Chapter 15, "Estate Planning: Wills, Trusts, and Your Property."

Deeming. Counting one person's income or resources as if it is available to another person, regardless of whether it actually is. *See* Chapter 1, "Social Security Benefits."

Deferred Charitable Gift Annuity. The current transfer of cash or marketable securities to a charity in exchange for the payment of an annuity starting at a future date. *See* Chapter 18, "Philanthropy and Planned Giving."

Direct Deposit. An arrangement for automatically depositing public benefits in the recipient's bank account. *See* Chapter 5, "Government Programs and Financial Assistance."

Disposition of Last Remains Directive. A written statement, signed by you, indicating what you wish done with your last remains at the time of your death. *See* Chapter 24, "Medical Advance Directives."

Dissolution of Marriage. Divorce. A legal action seeking a divorce decree. *See* Chapter 13, "Family Relationships."

Donor. The person who makes a gift. *See* Chapter 15, "Estate Planning: Wills, Trusts, and Your Property."

Due Care. The care a reasonable person would exercise under the circumstances. *See* Chapter 23, "Powers of Attorney."

Durable Power of Attorney. A power of attorney that is valid even if the principal becomes incapacitated or unable to manage his or her affairs. *See* Chapter 23, "Powers of Attorney;" and Chapter 15, "Estate Planning: Wills, Trusts, and Your Property."

Employer Group Health Plan (EGHP). Health insurance coverage provided through an employer group to workers and/or retirees. *See* Chapter 3, "Health Insurance Beyond Medicare."

End-Stage Illness. An illness that has progressed to the point that curative treatment is not effective and death is likely within months or weeks. *See* Chapter 27, "Hospice and Palliative Care: Options for Care at the End of Life."

Estate. All personal, financial, insurance, and real property owned by the individual. *See* Chapter 15, "Estate Planning: Wills, Trusts, and Your Property."

Estate Recovery. A method by which the state seeks to recover the costs of medical care provided to Medicaid recipients age 55 or older and to all institutionalized individuals, through imposition of a lien on real property, which is acted upon after the person dies and from assets in the probate estate. *See* Chapter 4, "Medicaid."

Exempt Resources. Assets that are not counted in determining eligibility for public benefits. *See* Chapter 5, "Government Programs and Financial Assistance;" and Chapter 9, "Employment Discrimination."

Finance Charge. The total dollar amount of interest you pay for buying a product or service on credit. *See* Chapter 11, "Arm Yourself with Consumer Protection Information."

Financial Exploitation. The illegal or unauthorized use of an individual's funds, property, or resources for profit or advantage. *See* Chapter 12, "Protecting Yourself From Crime;" and Chapter 23, "Powers of Attorney."

Financial Power of Attorney. Also known as a General Power of Attorney or General Power of Attorney for Property. A document whereby the principal gives legal authority, in writing, to another person to handle all (or some) of the financial affairs for the person creating the power of attorney. Such a power may also be durable. *See* Chapter 23, "Powers of Attorney."

Fixed Income Charitable Annuity Trust. A charitable annuity trust in which the annual income to the beneficiary or beneficiaries never changes. Upon the death of the beneficiary or beneficiaries, or after a set amount of time, the remaining trust assets are transferred to one or more charities. *See* Chapter 18, "Philanthropy and Planned Giving."

Food Stamps. Coupons that can be used to buy food items, now provided in the form of an electronic Quest Card. *See* Chapter 1, "Social Security Benefits."

Fully-Funded Living Trust. All of the settlor's assets are placed in a living trust. *See* Chapter 15, "Estate Planning: Wills, Trusts, and Your Property."

General Power of Attorney. The principal gives legal authority, in writing, to another person to handle all the financial affairs for the person creating the power of attorney. Such a power of attorney may also be durable. *See* Chapter 15, "Estate Planning: Wills, Trusts, and Your Property."

General Warranty Deed. A type of deed that tells the person to whom the property is being sold or transferred that you guarantee the title except for any conditions specifically listed in the deed, and make other guarantees about the property. *See* Chapter 15, "Estate Planning: Wills, Trusts, and Your Property."

Gift. A voluntary transfer of real or personal property for nothing in return. *See* Chapter 15, "Estate Planning: Wills, Trusts, and Your Property."

Gifts of Appreciated Stock. Donation of securities held long-term (more than one year) to a charitable organization. *See* Chapter 18, "Philanthropy and Planned Giving."

Grief Counseling. A special kind of emotional/psychological counseling that helps persons cope with the effects of normal or, in some cases, abnormal grief. *See* Chapter 27, "Hospice and Palliative Care: Options for Care at the End of Life."

Guardian. An individual at least 21 years of age, resident or non-resident, who has qualified as a guardian of a minor or incapacitated person pursuant to appointment by a parent or by the court. The term includes a limited, emergency, and temporary substitute guardian but not a guardian *ad litem*. *See* Chapter 12, "Protecting Yourself From Crime;" Chapter 23, "Powers of Attorney;" and Chapter 24, "Medical Advance Directives."

Guardianship. A legal proceeding giving a person, the guardian, the power to provide for the care and custody of a minor or an incapacitated person. *See* Chapter 13, "Family Relationships;" and Chapter 23, "Powers of Attorney."

Health Maintenance Organization (HMO). An insurance that limits enrollees to a network of physicians and other health professionals who in turn provide a full range of medical care and treatment for a set monthly fee. *See* Chapter 3, "Health Insurance Beyond Medicare."

Heirs. People who, because of their relationship to the decedent, are entitled to the decedent's property if the decedent dies without a will. *See* Chapter 15, "Estate Planning: Wills, Trusts, and Your Property."

HIPAA (Health Insurance Portability and Accountability Act of 1996). A privacy rule that establishes federally protected rights under which an individual can control the uses and disclosure of protected health information. *See* Chapter 23, "Powers of Attorney."

HIPAA Authorization. A written directive authorizing your personal representative (the HIPAA term for an agent) to discuss your medical records, conditions, and medical treatment with your medical professionals. *See* Chapter 23, "Powers of Attorney."

Home and Community Based Services (HCBS). Services paid for by Medicaid that are provided in an individual's home or in a Medicaid certified Alternative Care Facility. HCBS includes personal care, as well as traditional Medicaid (medical) services. *See* Chapter 4, "Medicaid."

Hospice. Care provided for the terminally ill that emphasizes comfort rather than aggressive treatment. *See* Chapter 2, "Medicare."

Hospice Agency. A health care organization or company that provides hospice care to patients and families. *See* Chapter 27, "Hospice and Palliative Care: Options for Care at the End of Life."

Hospice Care. An approach to care for persons with terminal illness and their families, involving a team of professionals — doctor, nurse, nurse's aide, social worker, chaplain — that focuses on quality of life and relief of pain and suffering. *See* Chapter 27, "Hospice and Palliative Care: Options for Care at the End of Life."

Hospice Enrollment. The process of signing up to receive hospice care. *See* Chapter 27, "Hospice and Palliative Care: Options for Care at the End of Life."

Hospice Evaluation. A physical examination by a hospice doctor to determine if you are eligible for hospice; that is, that your illness is "terminal" and that your life expectancy is six months or less, and that you are willing to forego curative treatment. *See* Chapter 27, "Hospice and Palliative Care: Options for Care at the End of Life."

Hospice Medical Director. A doctor specially trained in hospice or palliative care who supervises the care of patients for a hospice agency. *See* Chapter 27, "Hospice and Palliative Care: Options for Care at the End of Life."

Hospice Residence. A specially designed or adapted facility for hospice patients only. Most hospice residences are designed to feel more like home than a health care facility. *See* Chapter 27, "Hospice and Palliative Care: Options for Care at the End of Life."

Hospitalist. A doctor who is employed by a hospital and supervises the care of patients while they are in the hospital. *See* Chapter 27, "Hospice and Palliative Care: Options for Care at the End of Life."

In Forma Pauperis. A procedure to request that the filing fee be waived because you cannot afford to pay it. *See* Chapter 13, "Family Relationships."

Incapacity. The inability to make or communicate responsible decisions. *See* Chapter 23, "Powers of Attorney."

Injunction. A court order directing the people named within the order to refrain from doing certain specified acts or to do a particular act. *See* Chapter 12, "Protecting Yourself From Crime."

Installment Sale. The sale of a property where at least one payment is received after the tax year in which the sale occurs. *See* Chapter 16, "Estate and Succession Planning for Farmers and Ranchers."

Intervene. The process of joining in a legal proceeding, as a party. *See* Chapter 14, "Grandparent Custody and Visitation Issues."

Intestate Succession. A process in which Colorado law decides how your property will be distributed if the property is not disposed of through your will. *See* Chapter 15, "Estate Planning: Wills, Trusts, and Your Property."

Irrevocable Trust. A trust which cannot be changed after it is signed. *See* Chapter 15, "Estate Planning: Wills, Trusts, and Your Property."

Joint Tenancy. A type of ownership in which you own property with another person with a right of survivorship, which gives each owner the right to receive the property at the death of the co-owner. *See* Chapter 15, "Estate Planning: Wills, Trusts, and Your Property."

Legal Separation. A court order that divides property and debts and provides for maintenance when appropriate. It does not free spouses to remarry. *See* Chapter 13, "Family Relationships."

Life Estate. A type of ownership that protects a person's right to live on property and receive any income generated by the property during that person's lifetime. After the person's death, the property passes to another. *See* Chapter 15, "Estate Planning: Wills, Trusts, and Your Property."

Life Expectancy. The period of time a person is expected to live. *See* Chapter 27, "Hospice and Palliative Care: Options for Care at the End of Life."

Life-Sustaining Procedures. Medications, surgeries, or other medical therapies which would lengthen your remaining lifetime, but not reverse your medical condition. Under Colorado law, this does not include provision of nutrition and hydration. *See* Chapter 24, "Medical Advance Directives."

Lifetime Reserve Days. Sixty extra days you may use for hospitalization. You share daily costs with Medicare. These days can be used only after you have stayed more than 90 days in a hospital and can be used only once. This benefit is *not* renewable. *See* Chapter 2, "Medicare."

Limited Liability Company (LLC). A business structure allowed by state statute that provides limited liability to its owners. *See* Chapter 16, "Estate and Succession Planning for Farmers and Ranchers."

Limited Power of Attorney. Also known as a Special Power of Attorney. It gives legal authority to perform a specific act or acts on behalf of another person (for example, the power to cash checks). Such a power of attorney may also be durable. *See* Chapter 23, "Powers of Attorney;" and Chapter 15, "Estate Planning: Wills, Trusts, and Your Property."

Living Trust. A type of trust in which one party, the settlor, during his or her lifetime, creates a trust for himself or herself and/or for others. Property may be transferred to the trust during the lifetime of the settlor of the trust or after his or her death. Once property is transferred to the trust, it is under the control of a trustee and distributed according to the terms of the trust. *See* Chapter 15, "Estate Planning: Wills, Trusts, and Your Property."

Low-Income Energy Assistance Program (LEAP). A program that helps low-income persons pay winter heating bills. *See* Chapter 5, "Government Programs and Financial Assistance."

Maintenance. Also called alimony or spousal support. Financial support provided by one spouse to the other spouse after divorce or legal separation. *See* Chapter 13, "Family Relationships."

Marital Agreement. An agreement, in writing, between two people before or during marriage on what rights each of them will keep over certain property if a divorce or death occurs. *See* Chapter 13, "Family Relationships."

Medicaid. A joint federal/state program that pays some health care costs for qualifying individuals with low incomes and assets. It will cover some expenses that Medicare does not (for example, outpatient prescriptions). *See* Chapter 1, "Social Security Benefits;" Chapter 5, "Government Programs and Financial Assistance;" and Chapter 4, "Medicaid."

Medical Power of Attorney. Also known as a Power of Attorney for Health Care. A legal document appointing an agent to make medical decisions for you in the event you are unable to make your own medical decisions. Such a power may also be durable. *See* Chapter 23, "Powers of Attorney;" and Chapter 24, "Medical Advance Directives."

Medicare. A health insurance program for recipients of Social Security and some other federal programs. *See* Chapter 1, "Social Security Benefits;" Chapter 5, "Government Programs and Financial Assistance;" and Chapter 2, "Medicare."

Medicare Certification. A process by which state Health Department or Medicare officials determine a hospice is following all the rules and regulations governing hospice care. *See* Chapter 27, "Hospice and Palliative Care: Options for Care at the End of Life."

Medicare Hospice Benefit. A Medicare Part A benefit available to all Medicare enrollees, which covers all the costs of hospice care — the services of the care team, medications, equipment, supplies, etc. — related to the terminal illness. *See* Chapter 27, "Hospice and Palliative Care: Options for Care at the End of Life."

Medicare Hospital Insurance (also called Medicare Part A). Insurance that covers a necessary hospital stay, skilled nursing care in a nursing facility, and other home health services. *See* Chapter 2, "Medicare."

Medicare Medical Insurance (also called Medicare Part B). Insurance that covers doctors' and outpatient services, medical supplies, ambulance, and other services. *See* Chapter 2, "Medicare."

Medigap Insurance. Private insurance that supplements Medicare, providing coverage for benefits that Medicare does not provide. See Chapter 3, "Health Insurance Beyond Medicare," for a detailed explanation of Medigap coverage. *See also* Chapter 2, "Medicare."

Miller Income Trusts. If an individual has monthly income in excess of $2,067 in 2012 but less than the average private pay rate for nursing home care in the geographic region in which he or she resides, that individual may qualify for Medicaid benefits for long-term nursing home care or Home and Community Based Services (HCBS) by means of a trust. *See* Chapter 4, "Medicaid."

Multiple Signature. A bank account that requires more than one signature on a check. *See* Chapter 15, "Estate Planning: Wills, Trusts, and Your Property."

Need Standard or Standard of Need. In order for a person to be eligible for some public benefits, such as Supplemental Security Income (SSI) or Old Age Pension (OAP), an applicant's income must fall below a level called the need standard. *See* Chapter 1, "Social Security Benefits;" and Chapter 5, "Government Programs and Financial Assistance."

No-Fault Divorce. A divorce granted to a couple based on their inability to get along with each another. *See* Chapter 13, "Family Relationships."

Non-Assigned Claims. A method of payment under Medicare Part B. The doctor sends Medicare a completed claim form, but you are responsible for paying the doctor the full billed amount. Medicare will send you 80 percent of the approved charge if all of your yearly deductible is paid. *See* Chapter 2, "Medicare."

Office of the Public Administrator. A person appointed by the Chief Judge in each judicial district in Colorado who is authorized to deal with the last remains and estate of a deceased individual in the event there is no appropriate family member or other interested individual to serve in this capacity. *See* Chapter 24, "Medical Advance Directives."

Old Age Pension. A state program that provides a minimum income to low-income Coloradoans over 60. *See* Chapter 5, "Government Programs and Financial Assistance."

Older Americans Act. A federal program, initially passed in 1965, to encourage the development of comprehensive planning and to coordinate the provision of services for the elderly. *See* Chapter 21, "Assisted Living and Nursing Home Issues."

Organ/Tissue Donor Card. A document, signed by you, which declares your intentions as to whether or not to donate your organs and tissue. *See* Chapter 24, "Medical Advance Directives."

Overpayment. A public benefit payment higher than a recipient was entitled to; not necessarily the fault of the recipient. *See* Chapter 5, "Government Programs and Financial Assistance."

PACE. Program of All Inclusive Care for the Elderly that provides comprehensive health care and supportive services for frail individuals over the age of 65. This is Secondary Insurance coverage, which is accessed only after the primary insurance benefits are exhausted. *See* Chapter 4, "Medicaid."

Palliative Care. Care focused on comfort and relief of suffering rather than cure. Differs from hospice care in that it can be offered along with curative care and is not limited to terminal illnesses. *See* Chapter 27, "Hospice and Palliative Care: Options for Care at the End of Life."

Partnership. The collaboration of two or more owners to conduct a business for profit. *See* Chapter 16, "Estate and Succession Planning for Farmers and Ranchers."

Payable on Death Account (POD Account or a Trustee Account). A bank account that, upon the account holder's death, distributes money to the person or people named by the account holder. *See* Chapter 15, "Estate Planning: Wills, Trusts, and Your Property."

Payee(s). The person(s) named to receive the money from a POD account after the account holder's death. *See* Chapter 15, "Estate Planning: Wills, Trusts, and Your Property."

Personal Property. Property other than real property, such as stocks, bonds, bank accounts, cars, boats, clothing, and personal items. *See* Chapter 15, "Estate Planning: Wills, Trusts, and Your Property."

Personal Representative. The person who handles your affairs after your death. This person is either nominated by you in your will or is chosen by a court if you die without a will. *See* Chapter 15, "Estate Planning: Wills, Trusts, and Your Property."

Planned Gift. A charitable giving method that allows donors to express their personal values by integrating charitable, family, and financial goals. *See* Chapter 18, "Philanthropy and Planned Giving."

Pour-Over Will. A will that provides that all property administered in probate is distributed to a living trust. *See* Chapter 15, "Estate Planning: Wills, Trusts, and Your Property."

Power of Attorney. A written instrument by which one person, called the principal, appoints another as his or her agent or attorney in fact, and gives the agent the authority to perform certain specified acts or kinds of acts on behalf of the principal. *See* Chapter 12, "Protecting Yourself From Crime;" and Chapter 23, "Powers of Attorney."

Pre-Hospice Program. A program offered by a hospice agency that offers palliative care to patients without requiring a hospice enrollment. *See* Chapter 27, "Hospice and Palliative Care: Options for Care at the End of Life."

Presumption. A rule of evidence that states that, from the beginning, something is presumed by the law to be true. The person attacking the presumption has the burden of going forward with evidence to overcome it. *See* Chapter 14, "Grandparent Custody and Visitation Issues."

Pro Se *Divorce*. A do-it-yourself divorce where you do the work without hiring an attorney. *See* Chapter 13, "Family Relationships."

Probate. The legal process by which your property is collected and distributed according to your will or by intestate succession. *See* Chapter 15, "Estate Planning: Wills, Trusts, and Your Property."

Protected Person. A person subject to a conservatorship. *See* Chapter 23, "Powers of Attorney."

Prudent Man Rule. An agent must exercise the care a reasonable person would exercise under the circumstances and manage the principal's funds not as if they were the funds of the agent, but with the care needed for managing funds of another. *See* Chapter 23, "Powers of Attorney."

Quit Claim Deed. A type of deed that only transfers whatever title you may have at the time of the transfer; no representation is made about the validity of the title. *See* Chapter 15, "Estate Planning: Wills, Trusts, and Your Property."

Real Property. Land and buildings or structures placed on land, such as houses, commercial buildings, and agricultural buildings. *See* Chapter 15, "Estate Planning: Wills, Trusts, and Your Property."

Recertification. After two 90-day periods following enrollment, and then after each subsequent 60-day periods, the process by which a hospice patient is evaluated and considered to qualify for continued hospice care. *See* Chapter 27, "Hospice and Palliative Care: Options for Care at the End of Life."

Remainderman's Interest. A type of ownership interest in which your rights arise after someone else's rights end (see "Life Estate" section of Chapter 15). *See* Chapter 15, "Estate Planning: Wills, Trusts, and Your Property."

Representative Payee. A person chosen by the Social Security Administration to receive and manage the recipient's Social Security or Supplemental Security Income benefits for a recipient who cannot manage his or her own money. *See* Chapter 5, "Government Programs and Financial Assistance;" Chapter 12, "Protecting Yourself From Crime;" and Chapter 15, "Estate Planning: Wills, Trusts, and Your Property."

Request for Reconsideration. The first step in an appeal of a decision by the Social Security Administration. *See* Chapter 5, "Government Programs and Financial Assistance."

Respite Care. Services provided on a short-term basis to a dependent individual whose usual caregiver is temporarily unavailable or in need of a break. *See* Chapter 21, "Assisted Living and Nursing Home Issues," and Chapter 27, "Hospice and Palliative Care: Options for Care at the End of Life."

Restraining Order. An injunction directing the person named within the order to refrain from doing certain specified acts. *See* Chapter 12, "Protecting Yourself From Crime," and Chapter 13, "Family Relationships."

Retained Life Estate. Donation of a personal residence, farm, or vacation home to charity while retaining the right to live on and use the property for life, or for a fixed number of years. *See* Chapter 18, "Philanthropy and Planned Giving."

Retirement Plan Gifts. Designation of a charity as a beneficiary of an individual retirement account (IRA), 401(k), or other qualified retirement plan. *See* Chapter 18, "Philanthropy and Planned Giving."

Revocable Trust. A trust that can be amended or changed by the settlor of the trust, which is similar or often the same as a living trust. *See* Chapter 15, "Estate Planning: Wills, Trusts, and Your Property."

Revoke. To disenroll from hospice care. *See* Chapter 27, "Hospice and Palliative Care: Options for Care at the End of Life."

Right of Survivorship. The right a person has to receive property when a co-owner dies. *See* Chapter 15, "Estate Planning: Wills, Trusts, and Your Property."

Room and Board. Costs charged by a nursing facility, assisted living residence, or hospice residence for the room and meals provided to a patient resident. *See* Chapter 27, "Hospice and Palliative Care: Options for Care at the End of Life."

Secondary Insurance. Insurance coverage that is accessed only after the primary insurance benefits are exhausted. Usually refers to employer group health plans. *See* Chapter 3, "Health Insurance Beyond Medicare."

Secured ALR. Secured or locked assisted living residence. *See* Chapter 21, "Assisted Living and Nursing Home Issues."

Settlor. The creator of a trust. Settlors often put money or property into a trust. *See* Chapter 15, "Estate Planning: Wills, Trusts, and Your Property."

Skilled Nursing. The need for daily inpatient skilled care or rehabilitation. It does not include "custodial care," which is care that could be given by someone without medical training, such as help with dressing or eating. *See* Chapter 3, "Health Insurance Beyond Medicare."

Social Security Administration. The federal agency that administers Social Security, Supplemental Security Income, and many aspects of Medicare. *See* Chapter 1, "Social Security Benefits."

Social Security Disability Insurance Benefits (SSDIB). Disability benefits based on a worker's earnings history. *See* Chapter 1, "Social Security Benefits."

Sole Ownership. A type of ownership in which you own property solely in your name, giving you all rights to that property. *See* Chapter 15, "Estate Planning: Wills, Trusts, and Your Property."

Special Power of Attorney. Also called a "Limited Power of Attorney." It gives legal authority to perform a specific act for another person (see Chapter 24, "Medical Advance Directives"). *See also* Chapter 15, "Estate Planning: Wills, Trusts, and Your Property."

Special Warranty Deed. A deed usually used in fulfillment of a land sale contract and similar to a general warranty deed. *See* Chapter 15, "Estate Planning: Wills, Trusts, and Your Property."

Spells of Illness. Benefit periods beginning with the first day you enter the hospital after your Medicare goes into effect. These benefit periods end when you have been out of a hospital or skilled nursing facility for 60 days. *See* Chapter 2, "Medicare."

Springing Power of Attorney. A power of attorney that becomes effective on the happening of some later event, such as a declaration by a physician that the principal is incapacitated. *See* Chapter 23, "Powers of Attorney."

Standing Power of Attorney. A power of attorney that is effective immediately and is not contingent upon the happening of a later event. *See* Chapter 23, "Powers of Attorney."

Supplemental Security Income (SSI). Federal income maintenance program for elderly and disabled persons with low income and resources. *See* Chapter 1, "Social Security Benefits."

Symbolic Delivery. A way to deliver a very large gift by giving something that represents the gift. *See* Chapter 15, "Estate Planning: Wills, Trusts, and Your Property."

Temporary Power of Attorney. A notarized form giving you authority to make health care and other decisions for minor children for up to nine months. *See* Chapter 13, "Family Relationships."

Tenancy in Common. A type of ownership in which you own a percentage of the property with another person. If one owner dies, the property does not automatically transfer to the co-owner(s). *See* Chapter 15, "Estate Planning: Wills, Trusts, and Your Property."

Terminal Condition. An incurable or irreversible condition for which the administration of life-sustaining procedures will serve only to postpone the moment of death. *See* Chapter 24, "Medical Advance Directives," and Chapter 27, "Hospice and Palliative Care: Options for Care at the End of Life."

Testamentary Trust. A type of trust that is set up in your will. It only takes effect after your death. *See* Chapter 15, "Estate Planning: Wills, Trusts, and Your Property."

Trust. An arrangement in which one person, the trustee, holds property for the benefit and use of another, the beneficiary. *See* Chapter 15, "Estate Planning: Wills, Trusts, and Your Property."

Trustee. The person who manages and distributes the property held in a trust. *See* Chapter 15, "Estate Planning: Wills, Trusts, and Your Property."

Waiver. A request to be excused from repaying an overpayment. *See* Chapter 5, "Government Programs and Financial Assistance."

Ward. A person found by a court to be an "incapacitated person" and subject to a guardianship. *See* Chapter 23, "Powers of Attorney."

Will. A signed, written legal document that describes how you want your estate to be distributed after you die. *See* Chapter 15, "Estate Planning: Wills, Trusts, and Your Property."

Work Quarters. In order to be eligible for Social Security benefits, wage earners must have worked for a minimum number of "work quarters." *See* Chapter 1, "Social Security Benefits."

Appendix B.
Legal Resources*

As noted in the Preface to this *Senior Law Handbook*, this Handbook is for informational purposes only. In addition to the resources listed at the end of many of the chapters of the *Senior Law Handbook*, there are others that you may contact to seek legal representation or advice. Some of these are listed here.

Colorado Legal Services

Provides legal representation and advice in civil legal matters such as housing, public benefits, welfare, social security, mental health, and elder law. Also provides a list of self-help resources on civil legal topics. You must apply for representation.

(303) 837-1313
www.coloradolegalservices.org

The Legal Center for People with Disabilities and Older People

Promotes and protects the rights of people with disabilities and older people in Colorado. Provides representation in issues of fair housing, access to state or federally-funded services, and addresses complaints of residents in nursing homes. There is a sliding scale based on income.

(800) 288-1376
(303) 722-0300
www.thelegalcenter.org

The Guardianship Alliance

Provides information and instruction about guardianships of adults in Colorado.

(303) 228-5382
www.guardianshipallianceofcolorado.org

Denver Bar Association: Public Legal Education

The Public Legal Education website contains lists of brochures and clinics in Denver.

www.denbar.org/index.cfm/ID/1102/dba/Public-Interest

Sponsors of the *Senior Law Handbook*

Many of the sponsors of the Senior Law Handbook *are lawyers who may be able to provide representation or information. Each lawyer has their own fee schedule and availability, so please call to inquire. Contact information is listed in Appendix D, "2012 Senior Law Day Sponsors."*

Pro Bono Programs

Alpine Legal Services

Serves Garfield, Pitkin, and western Eagle counties

(970) 920-2828 (Aspen office)
(970) 945-8858 (Glenwood Springs office)
www.alpinelegalservices.com

Boulder County Legal Services

Serves Boulder county

315 W. South Boulder Rd., Ste. 205
Louisville, CO 80027
(303) 449-7575

Delta Montrose Free Legal Services

Serves Delta county

1200 N. Grand Ave.
Montrose CO 81401
(970) 249-9658

Heart of the Rockies Bar Association *Pro Bono* Program

Serves Chaffee county

1604 H St., Ste. 200
Salida, CO 81201
(719) 539-4251

Larimer County Legal Aid through Colorado Legal Services

Serves Larimer, Logan, Phillips, and Sedgwick counties

211 W. Magnolia
Ft. Collins, CO 80521
(970) 493-2891

La Junta CLS Office

Serves Baca, Bent, Cheyenne, Crowley, Huerfano, Kiowa, Kit Carson, Las Animas, Otero, and Prowers counties

207 1/2 Colorado Ave.
La Junta, CO 81050
(888) 805-5152

Mesa County — CLS, Grand Junction Office
Serves Mesa county

200 N. 6th St., Ste. 230
Grand Junction, CO 81501
(970) 243-7817

Metro Volunteer Lawyers
Serves Adams, Arapahoe, Broomfield, Denver, Douglas, Elbert, and Jefferson counties

1905 Sherman St., Ste. 400
Denver, CO 80203
(303) 837-1313

Northeast Colorado Legal Services
Serves Kit Carson, Logan, Morgan, Phillips, Sedgwick, Washington, and Yuma counties

350 Hagen St.
NJC Technical Bldg.
Sterling, CO 80751
(970) 265-4391

Northwest CO Legal Services
A branch of Colorado Legal Services
Serves Pitkin and Summit counties

602 Galena St.
Frisco, CO 80443
(800) 521-6968

Northwest CO Legal Services
A branch of Colorado Legal Services
Serves Eagle and Lake counties

505 Harrison Ave.
Leadville, CO 80461
(800) 521-6968

Northwest CO Legal Services
A branch of Colorado Legal Services
Serves Routt, Grand, Jackson, Moffat, and Rio Blanco counties

150 W. Jackson, #2A
Hayden, CO 81639
(800) 521-6968

Pikes Peak Pro Bono Project
Serves El Paso and Teller counties

P.O. Box 429
Colorado Springs, CO 80901-0429
(719) 473-9216

Pueblo County Pro Bono Project
Serves Pueblo County

1000 W. 6th St.
Pueblo, CO 81003
(719) 545-6708

San Luis Valley Bar Association Pro Bono Project
Serves Alamosa, Conejos, Costilla, Mineral, Rio Grande, and Saguache counties

603 Main St.
Alamosa, CO 81101
(719) 589-4993

Southern Colorado Bar Association Pro Bono Project
Serves Las Animas and Huerfano counties

314 Main St.
Trinidad, CO 81082
(719) 846-3334

Southwest Bar Volunteer Legal Aid
Serves Archuleta, La Plata, San Juan, Dolores, Hinsdale, Montezuma, Ouray, and San Miguel counties

1474 Main Ave., Ste. 200
Durango, CO 81301
(888) 298-8483

Uncompahgre Volunteer Legal Aid
Serves Delta, Hinsdale, Montrose, Ouray, and San Miguel counties

300 N. Cascade Ave., #U2
Montrose, CO 81401
(970) 249-7202

Weld County Legal Services

Serves Weld and Washington counties

P.O. Box 1283
Greeley, CO 80632
(970) 351-7300, x4514

---

* CBA-CLE would like to offer special thanks to Kathleen Schoen of the Colorado Bar Association for her gracious compilation of this legal resource list.

Appendix C.
Nutrition and Healthy Aging

This appendix was compiled by Natural Grocers by Vitamin Cottage.

These are your golden years. They are years to celebrate your life and nourish your mind and body with the nutrients you need to thrive. No matter what your age, there are steps you can take to revitalize and protect your mind and body, giving yourself the gift of optimal health. Once you understand that, at every stage of life, the foundation for good health depends on supporting the body with an optimal amount of nutrients, you can build the foundation to sustain many more years of an active and vibrant life.

Prevalence of Nutrient Deficiencies in the Senior Population

It is important to take in adequate nutrition through whole, healthy food choices. But in today's world much of the nutrient value in our food has diminished due to depleted soils, heavy use of herbicides and pesticides, and the prevalence of overly processed foods. This makes it difficult for us to obtain all the nutrients we need from even the healthiest food choices. In addition, as we age, our bodies simply do not absorb and utilize nutrients as efficiently; therefore, it may become necessary to add dietary supplements to obtain optimal amounts of the nutrients the body needs to properly function.

From studies that have been conducted on the nutrient deficiencies most common to seniors, it has been found that protein, calcium, magnesium, vitamin B-6, vitamin B-12, vitamin D, and zinc are most frequently deficient. **Protein** supplies the body with what it needs to make every body structure, from bones and cartilage to enzymes and neurotransmitters. **Calcium** is necessary for maintaining strong bones and is also necessary for nerve cells in the brain to communicate. **Magnesium** is involved in more than 300 essential metabolic reactions, including the production of serotonin, a brain chemical that is involved in mood stability and reduces feelings of anxiety and depression. **Vitamin B-6** is necessary for the function of approximately 100 enzymes that act as catalysts in essential chemical reactions, including the production of serotonin. **Vitamin B-12** plays an important role in brain function and energy production. **Vitamin D** plays a role in regulating gene expression and supports the proper functioning of every organ, tissue, and system in the body. **Zinc** plays an important role in the structure of proteins and cell membranes.

Frail seniors (those requiring assistance to carry out daily activities) are, in addition to the above deficiencies, more likely to be deficient in the B vitamins, vitamin C, and all of the minerals. These nutrients are necessary for the body to carry out day-to-day functions such as energy production, production of neurotransmitters, and making bone tissue. Low-income seniors and those older than 85 years are at an even greater risk for all of these deficiencies.

The Importance of a Nutrient-Dense, Natural-Foods Diet

The health of the body depends directly on the quality of what we eat. It is important to understand that certain foods are pro-inflammatory, while others are anti-inflammatory. The modern Western diet is full of processed foods, sugar, fried foods, and corn-fed meat. These foods contain large amounts of pro-inflammatory nutrients, meaning that the consumption of them tends to promote inflammation in the body. Chronic, low-level inflammation is at the root of many chronic, degenerative diseases such as arthritis, heart disease, Alzheimer's disease, and cancer — diseases prevalent in Western society. The connection between diet and disease is significant and cannot be ignored.

Natural foods are foods that are as close to the way they occur in nature as possible. This means whole, unrefined foods such as vegetables; fruits; wild-caught fish; grass-fed meats; naturally raised poultry, eggs, dairy, nuts, and seeds; unrefined oils; legumes; and whole grains. These foods contain nutrients that are anti-inflammatory. Ideally, these foods should come from organically fed animals and organically grown plants. A natural foods diet minimizes processed and refined foods — particularly sugar, high-fructose corn syrup, trans fats, and white flour — that are often found in bags, boxes, and cans, and, as mentioned earlier, promote inflammation.

Your Specific Diet

When planning your meals, start with a quality protein, then add two to three servings of vegetables and/or fruit, and, finally, make sure to use a healthy fat when cooking. It is ideal to center meals on fresh ingredients; however, we know that this is not always possible. We therefore have included some ideas for increasing the nutrient density of convenience foods.

Tips and Ideas for Increasing the Nutrient Density of Meals

- ▶ Turn a can of soup into a hearty meal by doing the following:
  - ○ Before heating, stir in a serving of fresh or frozen broccoli, spinach, green beans, diced tomato, red pepper, or any other vegetable of your choice. Canned beans, like black beans or navy beans, add protein, nutrients, and fiber.
  - ○ Add more protein by adding a couple of slices of diced nitrate-free sandwich meat, or add protein and calcium by melting cheese on top.
- ▶ Slice fresh cucumber; red, yellow, or green peppers; avocado; tomato; celery; carrots; or apples and serve with a natural nut butter or hummus.
- ▶ Try sardines or salmon on whole-grain crackers with sliced fresh avocado, cucumber, tomato, or alfalfa sprouts.
- ▶ Add canned fish (sardines, salmon, or tuna) to salads.
- ▶ Mix canned tuna or salmon with a little chopped celery and onion, and either a spoonful of mayonnaise or olive oil and lemon juice to make an easy and healthy salad.

▶ Make a sandwich using a lettuce leaf wrapped around nitrate-free turkey or ham, sliced cheese, sliced cucumber, and grated carrot.

▶ Dip banana slices in yogurt or natural peanut butter.

▶ Make a simple fruit salad by cutting up your favorite fruit of the season, thaw some frozen blueberries, and, if you wish, top with yogurt.

▶ Toss melon balls with shredded coconut.

▶ Add fresh fruit to cottage cheese.

▶ Try a traditional European dessert of fresh fruit with cheese slices.

▶ Thaw frozen berries and mash them into plain yogurt or eat them by themselves.

Dietary Supplements

▶ **Multiple Vitamin and Mineral Formula:** This is your insurance policy to guarantee your nutritional needs are met.

▶ **Vitamin D3:** Promotes bone and joint health, heart health, brain health, healthy immune function, and helps to maintain healthy glucose metabolism, supporting blood sugar stability, optimal energy, and a normal weight throughout one's lifetime. Current research suggests blood levels of 25-hydroxy vitamin D should be between 60 and 80 ng/ml.

▶ **Omega-3 Fish Oil (EPA and DHA):** Promotes optimal brain functioning and cardiovascular, bone, and joint health.

▶ **Glucosamine sulfate, Chondroitin, and MSM:** Promotes joint health.

▶ **Probiotics:** Supports immune and gastrointestinal systems.

▶ **Calcium and magnesium:** Promotes bone, muscle, gastrointestinal, nervous system, and brain health.

▶ **CoQ10:** Promotes cellular energy production; heart, brain, and muscle health; and supports the nervous system.

Appendix D.
2012 Senior Law Day
Sponsors

A very special thank you to the following businesses,
law firms, and individuals who, by their generous financial and
in-kind support, made Senior Law Day 2012 possible.

Platinum Sponsors

477

Jo Ann has been to over 100 countries, but chose to call our community home.

At Frasier Meadows, we believe everyone has unique stories to tell – like trying Haggis. And we'd like to hear yours. Come join our community and add your stories to those of the other vibrant residents here. Learn more at **frasiermeadows.org** or call **303-499-4888**.

FRASIER MEADOWS
RETIREMENT COMMUNITY

The Colorado Bar Foundation

Is Proud to Support the

Senior Law Handbook, 2012 Edition

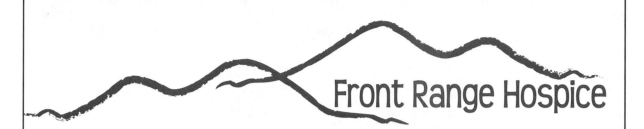

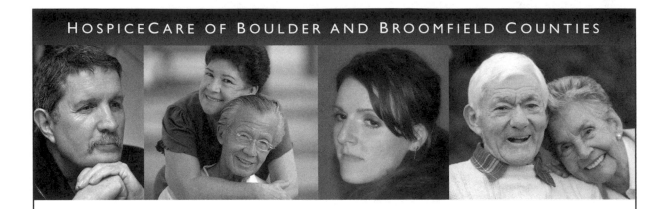

Proud Sponsor of the
2012 Senior Law Day

Gold Sponsors

EL PASO COUNTY BAR ASSOCIATION

THE TRUSTS AND ESTATES SECTION OF THE EL PASO COUNTY BAR ASSOCIATION IS HONORED TO BE A SPONSOR FOR THE 2012 SENIOR LAW DAY FOR SENIORS IN THE PIKES PEAK REGION, AS THEY HAVE FOR OVER TWENTY YEARS.

--- THE SECTION IS RESPONSIBLE FOR ORGANIZATION AND PRESENTATIONS AT THE SENIOR LAW DAY, AS WELL AS COMMUNITY SPONSORSHIP--

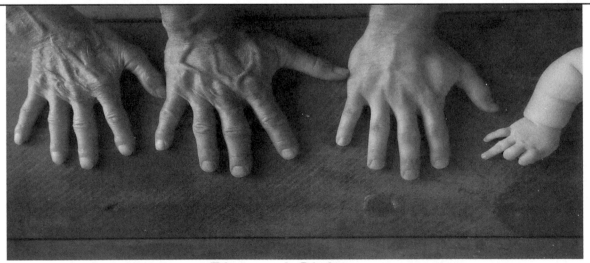

Planned Giving

Contact Annie Brunsell, Development Officer

at 970-495-4702

 MEDICAL CENTER OF THE ROCKIES *Foundation*   POUDRE VALLEY HEALTH SYSTEM *Foundation*

The Colorado Bar Association Elder Law Section is proud to support **the 14th Annual Senior Law Day**

The Colorado Bar Association

Trust & Estate Section

Is Proud to Support the 14th Annual Senior Law Day

Silver Sponsors

Aetna Medicare

Shirly Coloccia, Sales Representative
4833 Front St., Unit B PMB #418
Castle Rock, CO 80104-7901
(303) 660-2024
coloccias@aetna.com
www.aetna.com

AltaVita Memory Care Center

Carefully Designed Memory Care
800 South Fordham St.
Longmont, CO
(303) 300-3700
www.AltaVitaLiving.com

Onsite Medical Director, Dr. Nekoorad-Long,
Certified in Geriatric Psychiatry

The Boulder Estate Planning Council

Members practice as Chartered Life
Underwriters, Trust Officers, Attorneys at Law,
Certified Public Accountants,
Certified Financial Planner Practitioners,
and/or Chartered Financial Consultants

Please visit www.boulderestateplan.org

The Care Navigator

Pamela Wilson, President
P.O. Box 18349 • Golden, CO 80402
355 S. Teller St., Ste. 200 • Lakewood, CO 80226
(303) 205-7877
pamela@thecarenavigator.com
www.thecarenavigator.com

The Care Navigator helps caregivers and those
needing care by providing life management and
care coordination to reduce the overwhelming
work and worry of needing care or being a caregiver.

The Carillon at Boulder Creek Retirement Community

Live   Learn   Laugh
2525 Taft Dr.
Boulder, CO 80302
(720) 565-6844
www.TheCarillonAtBoulderCreek.com

A Vibrant Retirement Community in the
Heart of Boulder

Dietze & Davis, P.C.

Attorneys at Law

Celebrating 40 Years of Serving the West
2060 Broadway, Ste. 400
Boulder, CO 80302
(303) 447-1375
www.dietzedavis.com

Providing a Full Spectrum of Legal Services
to Boulder County Seniors

Ent Federal Credit Union

Ent Wealth Management
Paula Pollet, Vice President of
Wealth Management
7350 Campus Dr., Ste. 200
Colorado Springs, CO 80920
(719) 550-6414 / (800) 525-9623
ppollet@Ent.com
www.ent.com

Feldmann Nagel, LLC

Jenna Keller, Attorney
P.O. Box 775628
Steamboat Springs, CO 80477
(970) 879-8616
jkeller@feldmann-nagel.com
www.colo-lawyers.com

Feldmann Nagel LLC provides legal services for estate
planning, trusts, probate, conservatorship, guardianship,
guardian ad litem along with legal services for
farm/ranch, real estate, oil and gas, and family law.
Offices in Denver, Vail/Avon and Steamboat Springs

Golden West Communities

1055 Adams Cir.
Boulder, CO 80303
(303) 444-3967
www.gwboulder.org

Senior Living in Boulder

Haven Behavioral Senior Care

8451 Pearl St., Ste. 100
Thornton, CO 80229
(303) 288-7800
www.havenbehavioral.com

A Licensed Psychiatric Hospital Proudly
Serving Older Adults Throughout Colorado

InnovAge

Kay Volkema, Senior Marketing Specialist
8950 E. Lowry Blvd.
Denver, CO 80230
(888) 992-4464
kvolkema@myinnovage.org
www.myinnovage.org

InnovAge is a family of nonprofit organizations
serving as the comprehensive resource for
Colorado's aging population.

Law Offices of Sharon L. Svendsen, PC

824 Pine St.
Louisville, CO 80027
(303) 604-1762
Email: slsvend@hotmail.com
www.svendsenlaw.com

Estate Planning (Wills & Trusts) – Medicaid Planning –
Estate and Trust Administration –
Guardianships/Conservatorships –
Powers of Attorney/Medical Directives

Procter and Callahan, LLC

Attorneys at Law
155 E. Boardwalk Dr., Ste. 400
Fort Collins, CO 80525
(970) 266-9669
www.proctercallahanlaw.com

Purvis - Gray, LLP

Attorneys at Law
4410 Arapahoe Ave., Ste. 200
Boulder, CO 80303
(303) 442-3366
www.purvisgray.net

Experts in Personal Injury Law

Society of Financial Service Professionals

Rocky Mountain Chapter
Melissa Sugar, Sponsorship &
Public Relations Chair
3801 E. Florida Ave., Ste. 400
Denver, CO 80210
(303) 873-7579
melissa@sugar-law.com
www.financialpro.org

Bronze Sponsors

Alliance for Healthy Aging
Pam Peterson-Hohs, Treasurer/
    Board of Directors
P.O. Box 440512
Aurora, CO 80414
(720) 295-1242
pamph@thehlf.net
www.ahacares.com

Benson & Case, LLP
Mary Gaul, Marketing &
    Office Administrator
1660 S. Albion St., Ste. 1100
Denver, CO 80222
(303) 757-8300
mary@bensoncase.com
www.bensoncase.com

Brad Borncamp, CPA, LLC
1319 W. Baseline Rd., #201
Lafayette, CO 80026
(303) 530-4650
www.online-cpa.com
brad@online-cpa.com

Centura Health/Health Passport
Vicki Peterson, Data Analyst
11600 W. 2nd Pl.
Lakewood, CO 80228
(303) 629-4935
vickipeterson2@centura.org
www.myhealthpassport.org

**Colorado Fund for People with
    Disabilities**
Megan Brand, Executive Director
1355 S. Colorado Blvd., Ste. 120
Denver, CO 80222
(303) 476-6315
mbrand@cfpdtrust.org
www.cfpdtrust.org

Colorado Gerontological Society
Senior Answers and Services
Eileen Doherty, Executive Director
3006 E. Colfax Ave.
Denver, CO 80206
(303) 333-3482
doherty001@att.net
www.senioranswers.org

Colorado Mediation Center, LLC
Beth Brown Ornstein, JD
4450 Arapahoe Ave., Ste. 100
Boulder, CO 80303
(303) 415-2042
beth@mediationnow.com
www.coloradomediationcenter.com

Colorado Legal Services
Irma Stinnett
1905 Sherman St., Ste. 400
Denver, CO 80203
(303) 866-9305
istinnett@coloradolegalserv.org
www.coloradolegalservices.org

Comfort Keepers
4730 Walnut St., #212
Boulder, CO 80301
(303) 447-2008
www.comfortkeepers.com
boulderco@comfortkeepers.com

Compassion & Choices
Roseann Murray, Attorney/Board Member
1129 E. 17th Ave.
Denver, CO 80218
(303) 407-2050
rmurray@murraylawllc.com
www.compassionandchoicesofcolorado.org

Denver Triad Inc.
Rocky Williams, Chairman
1510 Dahlia St.
Denver, CO 80220-1231
(303) 393-0043
rockford.williams@gmail.com

Department of Veterans Affairs
Kevin Eherenman, VSR
P.O. Box 25126
Denver, CO 80225
(303) 914-5968
kevin.eherenman@va.gov
www.va.gov

Dignity Care LLC
1570 Lee Hill Dr., #7
Boulder, CO 80302
(303) 818-9006
www.dignitycare.com

DRCOG Area Agency on Aging
Nicole Hartog, Community Resource
    Program Manager
1290 Broadway, Ste. 700
Denver, CO 80203
(303) 480-6700
nhartog@drcog.org
www.DRCOG.org
www.DRCOGnetworkofcare.org

Elder Justice Colorado
Sharon Mohr, Executive Director
6200 S. Syracuse Way, Ste. 125
Greenwood Village, CO 80111
(720) 235-8713
sharonemohr@elderjusticecolorado.org
www.elderjusticecolorado.org

FirstBank of Colorado Springs
Dan Apricio, Vice President –
    Colorado Springs
817 Village Center Dr.
Colorado Springs, CO 80919
(719) 533-3703
daniel.apricio@efirstbank.com
www.efirstbank.com

Guardianship Alliance of Colorado
Sarah Solano, Lead Project Coordinator
801 Yosemite St.
Denver, CO 80230
(303) 228-5382
ssolano@guardianshipallianceof
    colorado.org
www.guardianshipallianceofcolorado.org

**Haven Behavioral Senior Care of
    North Denver**
Terry Lake, Director of
    Business Development
8451 Pearl St., Ste. 100
Thornton, CO 80229
(303) 288-7800
www.havenbehavioral.com

Homewatch CareGivers
Roger Rhodes, President
3333 S. Bannock, Ste. 740
Englewood, CO 80110
(720) 344-4700
rrhodes@hwcg.com
www.homewatchcaregivers.com

**Horan & McConaty Funeral Service &
    Cremation**
Dena Winters, Advance Planning
    Counselor
11150 E. Dartmouth Ave.
Denver, CO 80014
(303) 743-8804
dwinters@horancares.com
www.horancares.com

House Call Physicians
164 Primrose Ct.
Longmont, CO 80501
(303) 532-4171
www.hcphysicians.com

HUMANA MarketPOINT
Paula Noble, MSS
7400 E. Orchard Rd., Ste. 1000N
Greenwood Village, CO 80111
(303) 773-0300
pnoble@humana.com
www.humana.com

Kingsbery Baris Vogel Nuttall
CPAs and Advisors, PC
Brian C. Nuttall, CPA, J.D.
1401 Pearl Street Mall, Ste. 300
Boulder, CO 80302
(303) 444-2240
www.kingsberycpas.com
bcn@kingsberycpas.com

Kingsbery Johnson & Love, LLP
Eric V. Love, Managing Partner
2672 Northpark Dr., Ste. 100
Lafayette, CO 80026
(303) 443-4694
www.kingsberyjohnson.com
elove@kingsberyjohnson.com

Law Office of T.A. Taylor-Hunt, LLC
Colorado Center on Law and Policy
3773 Cherry Creek North Dr., Ste. 575
Denver, CO 80209
(303) 331-3400
tath@legalwellness.com
www.legalwellness.com

Life Quality Institute
Jennifer Ballentine, Executive Director
501 S. Cherry St., Ste. 700
Denver, CO 80246
(303) 398-6326
contact@lifequalityinstitute.org
www.lifequalityinstitute.org

MacKenzie Place Retirement Community
Diane Lozier, Marketing Representative
1605 Elm Creek View
Colorado Springs, CO 80907
(719) 633-8181
dlozier@leisurecare.com
www.mackenzieplace.com

MillBrook Homes
Janet Cornell, Administrator
5650 DTC Pkwy., Ste. 130
Greenwood Village, CO 80111
(303) 220-7989
millbrook5650jmc@live.com

Morning Star Elevator
Richard Markow, Owner/Manager
800 E. 64th Ave., Unit 6
Denver, CO 80229
(303) 623-7433
richard@mselevator.com
www.mselevator.com

**Office of the District Attorney,
    18th Judicial District**
John Skoglund, Director of
    Consumer Protection
6450 S. Revere Pkwy.
Centennial, CO 80111
(720) 874-8487
jskoglund@da18.state.co.us

**Pendleton, Friedberg, Wilson &
    Hennessey, P.C.**
Nancy R. Crow
1875 Laurence St., 10th Fl.
Denver, CO 80129
(303) 839-1204
ncrow@penberg.com
www.penberg.com

Pinon Management
Nancy Schwalm
12136 W. Bayaud Ave., Ste. 200
Lakewood, CO 80228
(303) 987-3088
nschwalm@pinonmgt.com
www.pinonmgt.com

Senior Advisory Network
Caroline VanVelkinburgh, Owner/Broker
6300 S. Syracuse Way, Ste. 150
Englewood, CO 80111
(303) 946-8821
caroline@turningpointerealty.com
www.turningpointerealty.com

Seniors' Resource Center
Mark Smiley, Director, Public Relations/
    Marketing
3227 Chase St.
Denver, CO 80212
(303) 235-6968
msmiley@srcaging.org

Special Needs Trust Network
Rita Blackwood
3773 Cherry Creek North Dr., Ste. 575
Denver, CO 80209
(303) 331-4420
rblackwood@sntnetwork.org
www.sntnetwork.org

Stan Garnett
Boulder County District Attorney
P.O. Box 471
Boulder, CO 80306
(303) 441-3700
www.bouldercounty.org/da

Stover & Spitz LLC
Attorneys at Law
Thomas L. Stover, Jennifer M. Spitz &
    David H. Brantz
636 Coffman St., Ste. 301
Longmont, CO 80501
(303) 682-0433
www.stoverlawcolorado.com

Thrivent Financial for Lutherans
Stephen Chase
9137 E. Mineral Cir., Ste. 100
Centennial, CO 80112
(303) 645-4181
stephen.chase@thrivent.com
www.thrivent.com

US Bank of Colorado Springs
Connie L. Gonser, Regional
    Administrative Assistant
6 S. Tejon St., Ste. 300
Colorado Springs, CO 80903
(719) 630-4350
connie.gonser@usbank.com
www.usbank.com

Vincent, Romeo & Rodriguez, LLC
Richard E. Romeo, Attorney at Law
1070 W. Century Dr., #200
Louisville, CO 80027
(303) 604-6030
rromeo@elderlawcolorado.com

Vi at Highlands Ranch
Sarah Harman, Community
    Relations Manager
2850 Classic Dr.
Highlands Ranch, CO 80126
(720) 348-7845
sharman@viliving.com
www.viliving.com/discoverhighlandsranch

Waddell & Reed
Benjamin E. Mossman, Financial Advisor
4582 S. Ulster St., Ste 103
Denver, CO 80237
(303) 770-5511
bmossman@wradvisors.com
www.waddell.com

YOUCAN TOOCAN
Martha Hansen, President
6460 E. Yale Ave., #E10
Denver, CO 80222
(303) 759-9525
martha@youcantoocan.com
www.youcantoocan.com

Legal Sponsors

Ambler & Keenan LLC
Nadine Bécerra-White, Marketing
   Coordinator
950 S. Cherry St., Ste. 1650
Denver, CO 80246
(303) 407-1542
nadine@ambler-keenan.com
www.ambler-keenan.com
Estate Planning, Probate & Elder Law

Andersohn Law Office, PC
Nathan L. Andersohn, Attorney
11971 Quay St.
Broomfield, CO 80020
(303) 650-6414
nandersohnlaw@yahoo.com
Probate Administration and Litigation

Baer Law Firm, LLC
John Paul Baer, Pharmacist • Attorney
25521 E. Smokey Hill Rd., Ste. 120
Aurora, CO 80016
(720) 222-1276
john@baerlaw.com
www.baerlaw.com
Elder and Pharmacy Law

Barbara Cashman, LLC
Barb Cashman, Attorney/Mediator
3600 S. Yosemite, Ste. 600
Denver, CO 80237
(303) 226-5466
barb@denverelderlaw.org
www.denverelderlaw.org
Estate | Elder Law | Mediation

Bell Law Firm
Sean Bell, Attorney
4450 Arapahoe Ave., Ste. 100
Boulder, CO 80303
(303) 415-2540
bellcoloradolaw@gmail.com
www.BellElderLaw.com

Boland Law and Mediation, LLC
Kate Boland, Attorney at Law
1525 Josephine St.
Denver, CO 80206
(303) 562-5973
kate.boland@bolandlawandmediation.com
www.bolandlawandmediation.com
Estate Planning and Probate

Branaugh Law Office PC
Preston Branaugh, Attorney
13949 W. Colfax Ave., Ste. 107
Lakewood, CO 80401
(303) 893-4122
preston@branaughpc.com
www.branaughpc.com
Estate Planning & Probate

Brandon Fields, P.C.
Brandon Fields
2595 Canyon Blvd.
Boulder, CO 80302
(303) 449-5602
brandon@elderlawboulder.com
www.elderlawboulder.com
Elder Law

Brown & Brown, P.C.
Clara Brown Shaffer, Partner
1250 E. Sherwood Dr.
Grand Junction, CO 81501
(970) 243-8250
clara@brownandbrownpc.com
www.brownandbrownpc.com
Estate, Trust & Tax Planning

Bryan Cave HRO
Letitia Maxfield, Attorney
1700 Lincoln St., Ste. 4100
Denver, CO 80203
(303) 866-0292
letty.maxfield@bryancave.com
www.bryancave.com
Estate Planning & Probate

Casey Williams
Glatstein & O'Brien LLC
2696 S. Colorado Blvd., Ste. 350
Denver, CO 80222
(303) 757-4342
Estate Planning, Elder Law & Probate

The Law Office of C. Jan Lord, LLC
Jan Lord, Attorney
1201 Lake Ave., Ste. A
Berthoud, CO 80513
(970) 532-4183
cjl@cjlordlaw.com
Elder Law, Estate Planning &
    Medicaid/VA Planning

Law Office of Claire E. Dineen
Claire E. Dineen
1444 Blake St.
Denver, CO 80202
(303) 567-7950
claire@dineenlaw.com
www.dineenlaw.com
Elder Law & Estate Planning

Dennis E. Valentine Law Firm
Dennis E. Valentine, Attorney
1776 S. Jackson St., Ste. 1107
Denver, CO 80210
(303) 758-5200
devalentine@earthlink.net
www.devalentine.com
Estate Planning & Probate

The Ebisch Law Firm
Jane Ebisch
12600 W. Colfax Ave., Ste. C-400
Lakewood, CO 80215
(303) 233-1232
jebisch@ebischlaw.com
www.ebischlaw.com
Probate Litigation & Elder Law

Front Range Fiduciary Services, LLC
Frank R. Baysore, President
12527 E. Amherst Cir.
Aurora, CO 80014
(303) 751-7579
fbaysore@comcast.net
www.frontrangefiduciaryservices.com
Conservatorship, Powers of Attorney &
    Estate Administration

The Germany Law Firm PC
Susie Germany, Attorney
685 Briggs St.
Erie, CO 80516
600 17th St., Ste. 2800S
Denver, CO 80202
(303) 454-3711
susie@coelderlaw.net
www.coelderlaw.net
Probate & Estate Planning

Glatstein & O'Brien LLP
Carl Glatstein, Partner
2696 S. Colorado Blvd., Ste. 350
Denver, CO 80222
(303) 757-4342
carl@denverprobatelaw.com
www.denverprobatelaw.com
Elder Law & Probate

Hanna M. Warren
Hanna M. Warren, Attorney
3755 S. Broadway
Englewood, CO 80113
(303) 762-1525
warren2017@aol.com
Probate & Estate Planning

Henning & Associates, P.C.
Marilyn Henning, President
3515 S. Tamarac Dr., Ste. 200
Denver, CO 80237
(303) 757-5000
dmjayhawk@aol.com
Estate Planning

Horen, Lockwood & Masters, LLP
Robert P. Horen, Partner
9559 S. Kingston Ct.
Englewood, CO 80112
(303) 436-9121
RPH@H-L-Mlaw.com
www.H-L-Mlaw.com
Probate & Estate Planning

Investment Trust Company
Marcy Carroll, Senior Vice President
3200 Cherry Creek South Dr., Ste. 730
Denver, CO 80209
(303) 778-6800
mlc@investmenttrust.com
www.investmenttrust.com
Investment Management &
    Trust/Estate Administration

James Black, Esq.
James Black, Attorney
2519 S. Clayton St.
Denver, CO 80210-6114
(303) 832-9600
jb@jamesblack.org
Guardianships, Conservatorships &
    Probate

Law Office of Jennifer S. Gormley, P.C.
Jennifer S. Gormley, Attorney
6060 Greenwood Plaza Blvd., Ste. 300
Greenwood Village, CO 80111
(303) 783-9600
www.elderlawsource.com
Elder Law, Estate Planning,
    Probate & Litigation

Law Offices of John J. Campbell, P.C.
John Campbell, President
4155 E. Jewell Ave., Ste. 500
Denver, CO 80222
(303) 290-7497
jcampbell@jjcelderlaw.com
Elder Law & Estate Planning

Joseph G. Hodges, Jr.
Joseph G. Hodges, Attorney
3955 E. Exposition Ave., Ste. 300
Denver, CO 80209
(303) 377-0070
jghodges@jghlaw.com
www.jghlaw.com
Probate & Estate Planning

Lawrence P. Hartlaub, Attorney at Law
Larry Hartlaub, Attorney
6464 S. Quebec St., Ste. 490
Centennial, CO 80111
(720) 488-2771
larryhartlaub@gmail.com
www.hartlaublaw.com
Estate Planning, Probate & Trusts

Medical – Legal Advocates LLC
Michele M. Lawonn
P.O. Box 371073
Denver, CO 80237
(303) 751-7012

Moye White LLP
Lorni Sharrow, Attorney
1400 16th St., 6th Fl.
Denver, CO 80202
(303) 292-2900
lorni.sharrow@moyewhite.com
www.moyewhite.com
Estate Planning, Administration &
    Litigation

Olsen & Traeger, LLP
M. Kent Olsen, Partner – Attorney
650 S. Cherry St., Ste. 850
Denver, CO 80246
(303) 329-4670
mkolsen@olsentraeger.com
www.olsentraeger.com
Probate & Estate Planning

Pelegrin & Radeff, P.C.
Virginia Frazer-Abel, Attorney
165 S. Union Blvd., Ste. 450
Lakewood, CO 80228
(303) 985-8787
home@pelegrinradeff.com
www.pelegrinradeff.com
Elder Law, Probate & Estate Planning

Law Office of Rebecca L. Shandrick
Rebecca L. Shandrick, Attorney
950 S. Cherry St., Ste. 912
Denver, CO 80246
(303) 292-1327
rshandrick@elderlawdenver.com
www.elderlawdenver.com
Elder Law

**RightPath Investments & Financial
   Planning, Inc.**
Steven R. Smith, Principal
P.O. Box 208
Frisco, CO 80443
(970) 668-5525
steve@rightpathinvestments.com
www.rightpathinvestments.com
Investments & Financial Planning

Rumler Tarbox Lyden Law Corporation PC
Cyndi L. Lyden, Esq.
1777 S. Harrison St., Ste. 1250
Denver, CO 80210
(303) 333-7733
cllyden@rumlerlaw.com
www.rumlerlaw.com
Conservatorships, Guardianships &
   Trust Litigation

Strandberg Law Office, P.C.
Steve Strandberg, Attorney
13072 Logan St.
Thornton, CO 80241
(303) 946-2363
strandberglaw@comcast.net
www.strandberglaw.com
Wills, Elder & Probate

Tamra K. Waltemath, P.C.
Tamra Waltmath, President
3843 W. 73rd Ave.
Westminster, CO 80030
(303) 657-0360
tamra@waltemathlawoffice.com
www.waltemathlawoffice.com
Probate & Estate Planning

Vincent, Romeo & Rodriguez, LLC
Richard Vincent, Elder Law Attorney
5460 S. Quebec St., Ste. 220
Englewood, CO 80111
(303) 770-0673
rvincent@elderlawcolorado.com
www.elderlawcolorado.com
Elder & Disability Law

Law Office of W. Dirk Costin
Dirk Costin, Attorney
1720 S. Bellaire St., Ste. 310
Denver, CO 80222
(303) 639-4999
dirkcostin@earthlink.net
Estate Planning & Probate

Wade Ash Woods Hill & Farley, P.C.
360 S. Monroe St., Ste. 400
Denver, CO 80209
(303) 322-8943
www.wadeash.com
Estate Planning, Estate Administration &
   Estate Litigation

Wolfe, Van Ackern & Cuypers LLP
Cheryl Lee Van Ackern, Partner
1008 Centre Ave.
Fort Collins, CO 80526
(970) 493-8787
clvanackern@wvc-law.com
Estate Planning & Administration

The Zapor Law Office, P.C.
Rose Mary Zapor, Owner
7475 W. 5th Ave., Ste. 107
Lakewood, CO 80226
(303) 866-0990
rose@zaporelderlaw.com
www.zaporelderlaw.com
Guardians/Conservators,
   Medicaid & Veterans

Notes

Notes

Notes

DATE DUE			